Online Competitive Intelligence

Increase Your Profits Using Cyber-Intelligence

©1999 By Facts on Demand Press
PO Box 27869
Tempe, AZ 85285-7869
(800) 929-3811
www.brbpub.com

Online Competitive Intelligence

Increase Your Profits Using Cyber-Intelligence

©1999 By Facts on Demand Press
PO Box 27869
Tempe, AZ 85285-7869
(800) 929-3811

ISBN 1-88915006-1
Cover Design by Robin Fox & Associates
Edited by Michael L. Sankey, James R. Flowers Jr., and Peter J. Weber

Cataloging-in-Publication Data

658.4 **Burwell, Helen P.**
BUR Online competitive intelligence : increase your profits
using cyber-intelligence / Helen P. Burwell
– 1st ed.

480 p. ; 7 x 10 in. – (Online ease)

Includes bibliographical references and index.

ISBN: 1-889150-08-8

1. Business Intelligence. 2. Business Intelligence —
Computer network resources. 3. Internet (Computer
network). 4. Web sites. I. Title

HD38.7.B87 1999   658.4'7'0285
                                   QBI98-1550

Acknowledgements

Thanks to my husband, Ed Burwell, for his patience, and understanding during the year in which this book has been "under construction."

Thanks also to my understanding publisher and to those who offered suggestions along the way. Their assistance was invaluable.

Finally, thanks and applause to those generous colleagues who help each other constantly by sharing tips, suggestions, and URLs for further exploration of the wonders of cyberspace, via AIIP_L, BUSLIB, and other Internet lists where this author participates.

Before You Start . . .

▬▬ Why Another Competitive Intelligence Book?

In recent years, the corporate world and the broader business community have increasingly acknowledged the value of using information to obtain a competitive advantage in business situations. Some companies have created special departments or units charged with this mission. These units work independently or assist other parts of the organization by gathering data, information, and knowledge regarding the company's competitors, the industries in which they compete, and industries that affect their own.

Job titles like Chief Information Officer or Director, Business Intelligence Unit now appear in corporate telephone directories. Membership rosters of organizations like the Society for Competitor Intelligence Professionals (SCIP) have grown rapidly. Books on CI strategy are available in the business books section at most large bookstores.

At the same time, the *New York Times* recently reported the following:

> A survey of about 50 large corporations by Fuld & Company, a consulting firm based in Cambridge, Mass., found that 20 percent of responding companies had shut down their corporate intelligence departments at a time when membership in a trade group, the Society of Competitive Intelligence Professionals, is reported to be growing by 25 percent a year.[1]

The article referenced above goes on to speculate about possible reasons for the demise of those CI departments. The fact remains, though, that with or without an official CI department, the company still needs business intelligence to succeed and move ahead! If there is no organized CI department, then the various departments within the company must call on their librarians for assistance or fend for themselves.

Attendees at seminars I've led have indicated the need to become experts on information sources — from researching privately-held companies to learning more about doing business around the world to identifying trends and locating industry forecasts. Some companies have sent a half dozen analysts to class, while others have requested special sessions tailored to the needs of their organization. There appears to be a real hunger among these people for tools that will help them to find the answers they seek.

---

[1] *The New York Times*, April 25, 1999; Page 4, Column 1 c. 1999 *New York Times* Company.

For some, searching online is something quite new, while for others the quest is for new or better sources of data that has eluded them. Some bemoan the fact that they can't find reference tools that describe and source required information from the perspective of the various departments within the organization. While Research and Development may be interested in a competitor's potential new products, Human Resources may be interested in a competitor's benefits package or executive's salaries. Meanwhile, the Sales and Marketing Department wants to know how other companies are attempting to gain market share through advertising or other promotions.

In meeting with many potential users of the information in this book, we have learned that their needs are at different levels, depending upon the nature of their work, their computer skills, and by the project immediately at hand. For that reason, the book addresses the topic of online information by presenting material that can be used by beginners (Parts I-III) and advanced searchers. The latter group may wish to start with Part IV. The book is organized as follows:

- An overview of CI in general, with some guidance in addressing CI research conceptually, to put the reader in tune with the thought processes necessary when selecting sources for searching online.

- An analysis of key information sources intended to explain how to use them to best advantage.

- An Industry Checklist and several different Company Checklists that help the searcher to gather all of the relevant data that should be included when compiling reports for different CI applications.

- A collection of more than 1500 bookmarks can be used by those who wish to search the Internet, going farther and wider than the resources mentioned above. These are also available at the *Online Competitive Intelligence* page on the Burwell Enterprises web site (www.burwellinc.com).

- A group of appendices and resources keyed to subject matter contained in the various chapters in Parts I-III. This is a selective list, which describes a few good sources for each topic, and explains where the source can be obtained or reached. Both commercial and Internet sources are mentioned here.

The reader may note that certain web sites are discussed in more than one chapter or section. Generally, these sites combine various types of intelligence or the data they provide may be used for several different purposes. The author has no connection with any of the vendors or sites mentioned in this book, other than that of Burwell Enterprises at www.burwellinc.com.

Whether the reader is strictly an Internet searcher, uses only commercial sources, or works with a combination of the two, he or she must be confident that information used to make the company's crucial business decisions is timely, accurate, and suited to the purpose for which it will be used. The tools necessary for such a task can be found between the covers of *Online Competitive Intelligence*!

Contents

Chapter 15 - Organizing CI Research 191

Chapter 16 – Industry Studies, Revisited –
The 'Do-It-Yourself' Approach 209

Part I

An Introduction to Competitive Intelligence

Chapter 1

What Is Competitive Intelligence, Anyway?

▬▬ It's Not What You Call It, It's How You Use It That Counts

Competitive intelligence. Competitor intelligence. Business intelligence. These terms describe one of the hottest areas in business-related information research. The concepts may be related, but each of these terms has a different connotation:

Competitive Intelligence: the use of publicly available information on competition and competitors to help your company gain an advantage, through strategic decision-making, in a line of business in which it competes.

Competitor Intelligence: information about another specific company, or group of companies, including such critical factors as financial performance, productivity, market position and strategies.

Business Intelligence: this is broader than Competitive Intelligenceand encompasses information that is not necessarily "competitive" in nature.

No matter what you choose to call it, the important thing to remember is that the use of such information has become a strategic necessity in today's competitive business environment. Some authorities have stated that ninety percent of the information needed in a company's CI program is available from publicly available sources, and that the other ten percent can be deduced.[2]

Gathering and applying competitive intelligence not only results in a more successful and profitable company, but it may be crucial to its survival.

---

[2] Combs, Richard E. and Moorhead, John D., *The Competitive Intelligence Handbook,* Metuchen, NJ & London, Scarecrow Press, 1992, p.13.

Why CI?

The rationale for gathering and using competitive intelligence might be "What's in it for me or my company?"

Use CI to Predict a Competitor's Next Moves

Knowing what a competitor is up to allows you to respond more quickly to that competitor's plans. The right response could mean greater market share, which translates into greater revenue.

The Difference Between Two Millionaires

To illustrate the benefit of predicting a competitor's moves, here is the story of two millionaires. And, it is true.

Both of our millionaires are self made. They're about the same age. In truth, they grew up very near to each other in Phoenix, Arizona. One made his fortune in a single industry. Starting with a one-room workshop, over a span of 13 years, he turned it into a 40,000 square foot furniture factory – all his own. The other, whose high school interest was in cameras and electronics, progressed his way up the ladder of success by going from company to company in Silicon Valley, in sales then development and marketing, and finally drawing his big hand in computer microprocessors. In fact, both our millionaires drew big hands – well beyond $50 million each.

Both own large acreage in Colorado and multiple homes in Arizona. By the time both men reached 47 years of age, they were virtually retired. Both rode the wave crest to success in their respective industries.

There is one major difference between our two men. The millionaire with the furniture factory had his success in one industry – manufacturing waterbed frames and alternative furniture. In part, he succeeded due to his perseverance and weak competition. He didn't have to do much competitive intelligence – what's to be concerned about when your competitors are found hanging out at rock concerts and neglect to follow good common work-sense?

Our computer industry millionaire, however, did have to use competitive intelligence. In his fast-paced competitive industry, when it came decision making time, he had to have inside information about the competition – what Apple was planning, and who the companies in Singapore were selling to, and who had factories in what country, and how many salespeople the competition had out there – and all sorts of precious tidbits of information that helped him make informed – and correct – decisions. Winning decisions.

Let's turn the clock ahead quickly. How are our two multi-millionaires doing? After selling off his factory, the furniture millionaire decided to help his son launch a racing bicycle manufacturing business. But, they neglected to investigate what they were getting into – and promptly ran amuck. Costs far out-stripped returns. The people they chose to assist them in the venture – largely friends from the former venture - couldn't and didn't perform. Next, he tried a return to furniture manufacturing, but the products didn't catch on.

Meanwhile, millionaire number two resigned from his seven figure job with the microprocessor mega-manufacturer (Did his own in-house competitive intelligence warn him to "get out now?"). Because so much of his experience involved competitive intelligence, he now consults mutual fund companies, advising them on the plusses and minuses of the electronics and computer firms the fund managers might invest in. His wealth continues to accumulate.

One rode the wave of the waterbed craze and thought he would be successful in any business. He failed twice. The other was in a competitive field where he had to use competitive intelligence. He continues to succeed at whatever business venture he chooses to engage in today.

Whether you are riding the wave of success or not, business intelligence and its application are something you need to know, now and forever.

Use CI to Turn a Weakness Into an Advantage

One mark of the successful competitor in the business world is the ability to triumph over adversity. All companies are faced with difficult decisions, from time to time. It's how they are handled that makes the difference! Here's an example:

From Fire Sale to Cyber-Sale

Because of tight money and a mild winter, Acme Manufacturing was stuck with a warehouse containing a million dollars worth of expensive ski wear that had not sold. Acme hired a consultant to devise a way to sell the merchandise without holding a "fire sale."

The consultant, Jane, began to research the problem. As part of her online research, she found several useful pieces of information:

♦ Omega Inc., a much larger competitor, was planning a major advertising campaign for next season. They would introduce a new line of mid-range priced ski wear aimed at the teenage market, and planned to spend "big money" on a major advertising campaign.

♦ Several e-commerce sites on the Web focused on selling sporting goods.

For a reasonable fee, it would be possible to establish a web page to tout the high quality and good looks of Acme's ski clothes, complete with graphics showing the product line. The e-commerce site owners would process orders. By eliminating the "middleman" (i.e. retailer), it would be possible to sell the goods at a reduced price using the Internet, and avoid taking a loss on the merchandise.

When Acme was presented with this news, they quickly decided to jump into e-commerce. Instead of losing money, they were able to turn the situation around.

This near disaster taught them several things:

♦ Given her valuable advice, paying Jane $2000 to be their consultant was clearly worth it.

♦ They could be successful in a new marketplace — the Internet.

♦ They could learn what competitors were planning, and get into the new marketplace well ahead of Omega Inc and others in the industry.

After expenses for their consultant and paying costs incurred using the e-commerce service on the Web, Acme still realized a profit. At the same time, they learned a valuable lesson!

Use CI to Become Aware of Change as it Happens, Before It's Too Late to Act

Librarians call it Current Awareness, others may call it an alert service. Whatever you call it, the ongoing monitoring of events in an industry, of preferences in the marketplace or of staffing changes that could take a company in new directions is crucial if your company is to be a leader rather than an a "also ran." What follows is the story of one company that successfully used CI to stay on top of change.

Managing Potential Problems Proactively

MegaCorp, a large multinational corporation, was planning some major changes which would impact employees across the world. Several departments in the company were interested in how these changes would be covered and presented by the media, as well as how the changes would be perceived by the employees and stockholders.

Early in the game, special monitoring was undertaken to detect and measure the reactions of these groups, as the various announcements were made over a period of a few months. Bob was assigned to coordinate this activity.

MegaCorp needed to monitor the media in a dozen different countries in addition to the US, so Bob arranged for automatic alerting services with LEXIS-NEXIS and set up Custom Clips on Dow Jones Interactive.

As a precaution, MegaCorp also decided to monitor broadcast news in case enterprising radio and TV personnel got the story and decided to interview employees. To that end, they signed contracts with the Video Monitoring Service and Financial Times for coverage within and outside of the US (see Chapter 6 for more detail on these services).

To put an ear to what employees and stockholders were saying, they used a free Internet service, Company Sleuth (<u>www.companysleuth.com</u>). This service monitored the major Internet message boards on a daily basis, providing a running commentary on what was being talked about in cyberspace by employees, stockholders and other interested parties. Each day, Bob received an e-mail that told him which message boards contained new discussions regarding MegaCorp. He read the messages and identified areas that seemed to be causing concern.

As a result of the intelligence turned up during the monitoring, several beneficial results were achieved:

◆ The Human Resources Department learned what employees were thinking. Several detailed articles were published in employee newsletters, expounding upon the data that had been included in "official" announcements, and defusing what could have been a negative situation regarding employee morale.

◆ The Public Relations Department developed a series of press releases stating that the facts of the situation. These were designed to anticipate queries by the media, and to avoid misinterpretation or publication of only "half of the story."

◆ Investor Relations used the input from the message boards as a "heads up." They added explanatory documents to the company web site. In addition, they were able to better prepare their officers to respond to shareholder questions from the floor at the next annual meeting.

Use CI to Gain Competitive Advantage

Uncovering what the competition is planning provides an opportunity for action — either defensively or offensively, such as actions designed to gain or retain competitive advantage or market share. The story that follows illustrates the concept of CI being used to gain competitive advantage.

Beating the Competition to Market

Alpha Company discovered that Beta, Inc, a small start-up company, had apparently begun clinical trials of a new drug. Alpha company had invested significant money and personnel in the development of a similar drug, believing that they had a unique product in mind. Alpha Company also discovered that Beta, Inc's CEO was Mr. X, who was formerly employed by a large international pharmaceutical company. They were very concerned about possible ramifications of this connection, as well as some other "coincidental" facts that had turned up regarding connections between Beta, Inc and large drug companies.

Alpha Company's researchers undertook a RUSH online research project to determine (1) where Beta, Inc's clinical trials were underway, (2) what stage the clinical trials had reached, and (3) whether any connection could be established between the small start-up company and one of the large international companies. They were also interested in collecting more information about some of the other people whose names began to appear as the research progressed.

The searchers combed the Internet and several specialized commercial databases, and quickly learned where the clinical trials were taking place as well as the stage that had been reached. Scholarly articles from the commercial sources provided solid scientific information. On the Internet, they identified several web sites that track clinical trials, as well as homepages for many pharmaceutical companies, both large and small. Data found here was useful to telephone researchers who conducted interviews with key personnel at several companies.

Additional information regarding Beta, Inc's activities was located at the web site of the Food & Drug Administration, where calendars provided information regarding the subject matter of meetings, attendees' names, etc. Alpha also established a connection between Beta, Inc and a former FDA employee who apparently was a Beta lobbyist.

By putting together the information retrieved online, and then combining it with the results of telephone interviews and other research, Alpha Company was able to determine what Beta, Inc was "up to."

Alpha Company speeded up its own efforts to complete trials, obtain the necessary FDA approvals and bring the product to market long before Beta, Inc was able to do so, thus gaining a crucial competitive advantage.

Because of the nearly instant availability of information, and the broad range of resources available in electronic format, Alpha Company was a winner in this battle in the "drug wars."

Alpha Company's cost to conduct the competitive intelligence project was $10,000. The estimated profit returned from their new product was in excess of $1,000,000.

Who Gathers Competitive Intelligence?

Now that we've discussed the uses for CI and reviewed some examples of these uses in action, it's important to discuss who gathers competitive intelligence information.

Some searchers for competitive intelligence may not think of the information in those terms. The company may not have given the name CI to what these people do, even though they spend a great deal of time doing it.

In-House Specialists & End Users

Gathering information may be assumed to be "part of the job." Some people identify a question or need, and set about gathering the information to find answers. Others may be asked by someone else to research a question or problem that involves information about competitor companies or about an industry. The "real jobs" held by these people may include these:

♦ **Key player** in a small company or in a start-up company who is charged with certain responsibilities for helping the company to grow.

♦ **Professional librarian**, responsible for supporting the information research needs of various people or departments in the company. (Librarians call this the Reference function, when describing their work.)

♦ **Executive** engaged in sales, marketing, research and development, human resources, planning or other areas, who needs certain information to fulfill responsibilities that are part of the job description.

- **Sales person** competing with dozens or hundreds of others, sometimes working for the same organization, to compile lists of potential buyers for their products or services.

- **Entrepreneur** starting a new business, trying to create business and marketing plans.

- **Independent information professional**, sometimes known as an information broker, who is hired by-the-project or on a contract basis to gather information required for use in-house by the client.

CI Practitioners – A New Breed

More and more these days, we see job descriptions or meet people who describe their position at work as involved *chiefly* in the area of competitive intelligence. CI practitioners help businesses gather and analyze data to create information, which is combined with what is already known, to create the *knowledge base*. Words like "interpret," "deduce," or "intuition," are sometimes mentioned in the context of their work, since the knowledge base involves human interaction, and taking advantage of what is already known by those within the organization. The knowledge base is used when studying companies or industries or making various decisions that are crucial to a company's growth or survival.

CI professionals come from varied backgrounds, most frequently building upon experience in some area of the business arena, or from working in information research. In general, they fit one of these profiles:

- Their background and education is in business or a business-related field. Experience in one or more areas of a company's activity such as sales and marketing, research and development, planning, or other areas, has led to an assignment working in CI.

- They have a degree in library or information science and have worked in the company's library or information center, fielding research questions from others in the company. They are now part of the company's CI team, or they receive research requests from that group.

- They are a manager, with an understanding of the "big picture" of the company's information needs and challenges, who is expected to have, or to gather, the knowledge required for making decisions that are in the company's best interests.

Additionally, some CI practitioners have experience working for the government, often in some intelligence-related capacity.

CI Teams Come in All Sizes

In the past ten years, more and more large companies have staffed teams or groups that support other departments in the organization, providing the research and analysis needed by the decision-makers. But just as often, smaller businesses have recognized that they, too, cannot thrive and grow unless they use information to their advantage.

Business magazines are full of articles about small companies that grew into large ones, because they figured out how to do something better or faster than their competition. This "figuring out" took an awareness of what was happening, of what was needed, and of how other companies were handling the issue.

CI activity in your company may be the responsibility of a CI group, or the task may be in the hands of a nucleus of research-oriented people within your department. Likewise, the CI "department" may be a "one person band," (translate that to mean *YOU*). What is important is that within your company, the right information must reach the right people at the right time. In the case of factual information, you probably have a deadline. In the case of trends or consumer behavior, or new competitors, however, this means as early as possible.

Why CI is Important as We Enter the 21st Century

While the development of computers revolutionized life on Earth, events occur just as they have for hundreds of years: wars are won and lost, treaties are made and broken, styles in clothing come and go, new modes of transportation take us further, faster. Yet each of these things has been influenced by new technology. The forward movement that we've made in the Twentieth Century is indicative of the speed with which we are likely to move in the Twenty-First. For a business to prosper, it will be necessary to be able to look ahead and to anticipate change.

Competition for Foreign Markets – The Global Challenge

In spite of the daily ups and downs of the financial markets, ethnic wars, sanctions, taxes and politics, new markets have opened and are expanding in many parts of the world. The company that gets there first or best meets the demands of the market, stands to profit.

The Changing Face of Business

Changes in the business environment make competitive intelligence more important than ever. Treaties like the North American Free Trade Agreement (NAFTA), the emergence of the European Union and similar bilateral treaties have lowered or eliminated trade barriers between countries. Your competition is no longer down the street — it may be halfway around the world.

You can identify competitors by analyzing the growing amount of company information online. One "quick and dirty" way to do this is to search for companies which have the same Standard Industrial Classification (SIC) code as your company.

Narrowing your search further might limit results to companies with sales over a certain dollar figure or to those that have more than a certain number of employees. Many free web sites provide SIC code searching, but to limit further, a commercial file like *Dun's Market Identifiers* would be a good choice. This database can be found on the DIALOG service in File 516, among other places.

Hoover's at <u>www.hoovers.com</u> **provides a list of competitors in its company records. Hoover's is a good start, but you should also look further.**

Identifying a company's competitors is a much more complex undertaking than merely generating a list by classification code. The challenge comes in finding more and more details about companies so that you can identify your company's *true* competitors. That is one of the reasons for this book – to assist in that identification!

Finding Leads Outside of the US

But how could a company in middle-America, for example, find leads in places like Eastern Europe?

The Traditional Approach

A few years ago, you might have contacted a local or regional "incubator" or similar organization. Organizations like the US Department of Commerce offer various programs designed to assist businesses interested in importing or exporting goods and services.

Another option was to join a trade mission to a particular country or region. This approach, however, costs time and money, and you might have found yourself competing with other members of the trade mission for contacts in the target country.

In the past, you might have hired a consultant. This also costs money, and finding a consultant with good contacts and knowledge of your company's industry presented a challenge.

Perhaps you searched the *Journal of Commerce* or a comparable publication. To get timely leads, you needed a subscription to the publication or access to an online service like DIALOG, which again costs money and required specific searching skills.

The Y2K Approach

These strategies still are useful, but today, as we approach the new millenium, you have a powerful new tool in cyberspace, which provides additional, less costly possibilities. You can meet, greet and learn using the Internet. The World Wide Web is rife with trade-related sites, and listservs, which are electronic mailing lists or discussion groups that usually require a subscription or registration. Those who wish may participate actively. However, many subscribers prefer to "lurk," which means reading selectively and ignoring items of no interest, rather than frequently contributing to the discussion. This provides an excellent way to keep up with what's being said by others, without becoming entangled in lengthy discussions. For more information on this topic, see "Usenets/Listservs" in the Bookmarks & Favorites section of Part IV.

You can search your industry's trade publications using electronic sources. The full text of thousands of newspapers and magazines can be searched in seconds using some of the major commercial database services, see Comparing the "Big Three" Online Services Section in Chapter 3 - Is Everything Really on the Internet?

The Purpose of this Book

Increased awareness of the need for actionable business intelligence has been fed by a continuous flow of books and articles on the subject. There are books of success stories detailing the results achieved by CI task forces formed at major US corporations, as well as "how to" books which address all aspects of competitive intelligence work, including telephoning, interviews, manual research techniques, or online searching.

In addition, specialized works can be found on individual topics like market research or benchmarking. This book is intended as a specialized resource for CI practitioners and others who search for business intelligence. You, the reader, may use it in one of these ways:

♦ To learn about the information tools that are available, if you don't keep up with this topic regularly or if you are new to electronic information research.

♦ To add to your existing list of sources for intelligence gathering. Nobody knows *every* good online vendor or Internet site regarding a topic. New products or sources come along every week.

♦ To learn how to use familiar tools differently or better, or from another vendor, or for a lower price.

Learning More About CI – Join the Pros

One of the most significant events in the evolution of business intelligence gathering was the founding of *The Society of Competitor Intelligence Professionals (SCIP)*, in 1986. Since that time the organization has grown to more than 6000 members in 44 countries, with an annual membership increase of forty percent. As described on the SCIP web site, www.scip.org, this organization provides its members with networking, educational opportunities, and a Code of Ethics that is taken very seriously by the membership. Annual conferences in the US and in Europe provide additional opportunities for members to expand their knowledge and understanding of the field.

Many SCIP members have backgrounds in market research, government intelligence, or science and technology. The FAQ (Frequently Asked Questions) page at the SCIP site makes clear the fact that CI is not industrial espionage, digging through trash bins, or warfare. It is an ethical business practice carried out by those who are smart enough to learn what information to go after, and how to do so.

Greater Awareness of CI's Importance

If something is a "hot topic" it generates a volume of written material. By that measure, CI is definitely hot. A recent search of magazine and journals in a single business-oriented database located dozens of recent mainstream and scholarly articles about CI.

The authors of these articles are not just CI practitioners "preaching to the choir." Publications such as *American Salesman*, *Employment Relations Today* and *Management Services* have published articles on CI, making it clear that interest in CI is corporate-wide.

A representative list of books and articles may be found in Part IV of this book in Appendix E. These will provide further information on the practice of competitive intelligence for those new to the field.

Chapter 2

Basic Tools & Strategies for Online CI

Key Online Tools of CI Professionals

One great way to keep up with trends or events that will impact your company is through searching online using commercial databases or the Internet. Thanks to developments in technology, here is a much greater awareness of online databases in the business community these days. The popularity of the Internet, coupled with the increased use of personal computers, means that databases are no longer mysterious programs used by computer "geeks," but a basic tool used by many of us to manage all kinds of information for business or personal purposes.

The Changing Face of Business is Changing the Tools We Use

As recently as two or three years ago, online research sources were divided into two categories:

Internet sources...

...reached via File Transfer Protocol (FTP), Telnet, or the World Wide Web.

Commercial sources...

...accessed via modem using communication software.

With improved technology and increased awareness of the Internet as an information source, the demarcation line between the two has become practically non-existent. We have more choices. Now the players look more like this:

♦ **Major commercial online services,** such as DIALOG, Dow Jones Interactive, and LEXIS-NEXIS, who have mounted increasingly sophisticated web sites on the Internet to take advantage of improved technology and potential new desktop clients. Using the World Wide Web, they provide features not previously available, such as graphics capability or PDF files. At the same time, they must continue to address the needs of a large client base that resists entirely to the Internet until that platform can offer popular functions provided in dial-up mode. As a result, some vendors continue to offer both Internet and dial-up service.

♦ **New commercial vendors,** such as Northern Light and Infonautics Corporation, who recognize the Internet's potential. These companies took advantage of Internet technology to give the old-timers a run for their money - or for ours. They offer some of the same database files available on the major services in addition to files that the major vendors might not consider cost-effective. Some of these sites offer credit card access for pay-as-you-go customers or deposit accounts where users charge against a previously deposited amount. However, their search engines may be less sophisticated and they may not offer the level of support that the major commercial online services provide.

♦ **Database producers** have created their own web-based commercial services that compete with major vendors. Some, such as Reuters, remove their files from other vendors' systems as license agreements expire. Others, like Information Access Company, have commercial services of their own, but also allow their files to remain available through major vendors. This new competition has resulted in benefits like pay-as-you-go pricing at some sites, along with faster availability of new information and graphics.

In other cases, however, some searchers can no longer afford to search favorite databases, because they cannot justify the substantial subscription cost charged by the database producer. Removal of files from the major services means that you lose some of the cross-file searching ability that the big vendors formerly touted. For example, you can no longer search Reuters files and other favorite business or news files simultaneously on DIALOG or LEXIS-NEXIS, eliminate any duplicates, and pay one vendor for the documents retrieved from different producers' databases.

♦ **Internet sites** intended to inform, educate, or entertain. Some contain searchable databases and provide copies of documents. These sites have been created by trade associations, industry groups, academic institutions, individual companies, the media, and others. Many of them are crowded with advertisements that offset the cost of providing the searcher with "free" information. Although FTP and telnet still exist, these resources are used less frequently than in the past.

Greater awareness of the existence of online information, coupled with increased options for accessing it, makes it easier to justify using online research as part of your CI activity. However, because of a popular misconception, some people find it difficult to warrant subscriptions to commercial services.

It's *Not* All On the Internet, Free

You've probably heard someone in your company say that, "Everything is on the Internet, and it's free." While it is true that we can access a great deal of valuable data there, the Internet is fraught with peril for the unwary.

There are some very positive things about the Internet. It presents us with opportunities for researching new and different bodies of information, such as the archives of discussion groups where people with common interests express opinions or share ideas. It also provides us with access to some materials that were previously available in electronic format or only through subscription-based online services. In addition, we now have more rapid access to a large body of government information that was formerly out-of-date by the time it appeared in print.

Since it is not managed or regulated by any central body, you may find information on the Internet that is out-of-date, incomplete, thoroughly biased, or just plain inaccurate. It is important to understand this (or to get the Boss to understand), and to consider a combination of commercial and Internet sources for gathering business intelligence.

The *New York Times* recently published a lengthy article in *Circuits*, one of the newspaper's weekly supplements. Entitled "Whales in the Minnesota River? Only on the Web, Where Skepticism Is a Required Navigational Aid,"[3] the article provides a lengthy discussion of the issue as to whether to trust what you find on the Internet. Special sidebars mention web sites that tell you what to look for when seeking reliable information on the Web, and how to separate good data from bad. Subsequent chapters in this book also address this topic. You will learn how to decide when to choose the Internet, and when to go to commercial sources for business intelligence.

Be cautious in choosing sources if anonymity is important. The host at that "free" site can track the identity of computers that search the site, and which pages are searched. Someone might deduce information about your product development activity by seeing what patents or other types of files you've searched using their site.

Using Free Sources May Involve Tradeoffs — Let's Examine Them

With free sites there are often tradeoffs. The search engines on these sites may not be as powerful as those used by commercial vendors, so getting the desired information without spending money could mean spending extra time searching, switching databases, or reviewing lengthy search results.

The *Thomas Register of American Manufacturers* web site is a case in point. When using the free Thomas Register site at <u>www.thomasregister.com/index.html</u>, you can't sort companies by state - you must browse what may be a lengthy list. As an alternative you might go to the *Thomas Regional Directory*, at

---

[3] "Whales in the Minnesota River? Only on the Web, Where Skepticism Is a Required Navigational Aid" *New York Times*, March 4, 1999. Page D1.

www.thomasregional.com/newtrd/c_home.html, which offers searching in 19 US regions, or the *Thomas Register Europe* Home Page at www.tipcoeurope.com. At these sites, you must choose a region and search individually. Registration is required to use both sites, but there is no cost involved.

The Web version of the Thomas Register does **not** include the entire database. The full database is found *only* in the commercial versions of the product. If you are willing to pay for the information, the commercial version of Thomas Register can be searched as File 535 on the DIALOG service, available at www.dialog.com. In addition, a CD-ROM version of the product is available for purchase from the Thomas Register web site.

Using these commercial products, you can search more widely, sort the results, and limit results by company size, geography, etc. You also have flexibility regarding which pieces of data will be included in the records that you download or print.

Dun & Bradstreet's database products present similar options or problems, depending upon your point of view. There are both free and fee-based Dun & Bradstreet files available, and records contain varying amounts of information. The trick with Dun & Bradstreet is to figure out which of the many reports, available on web sites or from commercial sources, will provide the information you need, at the best price.

Are CD-ROM Products the Answer for You?

Many popular databases are available in CD-ROM format. Where multiple users are involved, these products may be loaded on local area networks and made available at the desktop. CD-ROM works well in some environments, but not so well in others. Consider these points:

- For heavy use, CD-ROMs may be extremely cost-effective.

- The CD may have a user-friendly interface.

- CD-ROM search engines are often comparable in power to those used by online versions of the database.

But, there are tradeoffs, as you will see below:

- CDs are purchased for a flat fee, which is sometimes substantial. For only occasional use, this may not be a wise choice.

- The purchase price may or may not include periodic shipments of updates.

- CDs are only as current as of the cutoff date indicated by the publisher. You may still have to go online to update search results.

Searchers using CDs aren't pressured to search quickly because "the meter is running," and the interfaces are usually quite straightforward. Where current information is required, some of these products can be used in conjunction with online versions of the same database. Names of some of the major vendors in this area are shown below:

Subject Matter	Vendor Name
80+ Assorted Databases	DIALOG OnDisc
Financial/Securities	Disclosure
Business, Medical, Scientific	SilverPlatter
Associations, Companies, Computer Products	The Gale Group
Companies	Thomas Register

To sum up, the commercial versions of online databases provide greater power and flexibility in searching and sorting, but may be more expensive, since CDs and online subscriptions cost money. The database producer may make some, but generally not all, of the information available on the Internet for free. Two old adages apply here — "Time is money," and "You get what you pay for."

Check vendor documentation in advance to determine which database files cover your topic, and to what depth. No database contains *everything*, so it's often necessary to consult several Internet sites or commercial databases before getting a "hit" on your topic. Consider using services that allow you to search several files simultaneously.

Develop Online Search Strategies to Get the Job Done

A successful online search doesn't just happen. Thinking the project through in advance will help assure the best possible results.

The Value of Careful Preparation

The purpose of the needed information defines the search. The approach to finding answers will differ, therefore, depending upon the requestor's type of work and how they intend to use the information. If you do your own research, or work with the person making the request, you are probably familiar with the subject matter, related publications in the field, and the names of key players in your industry.

If you are doing online research for someone else, ask the person making the request for any additional background information, titles of important publications on the topic, and what exactly will satisfy their need. This information will be useful in determining how and where to search. It's a waste of time and money to gather reams of statistics and dozens of articles if what was needed could be found in a recent issue of a trade publication that the requestor could have mentioned.

If you are the requestor, you can improve the quality and turnaround time for a request by providing accurate information and possibly briefing the searcher on what you *really* need, or

how the data will be used. Good preparation before going online will save your company time and money during the search process.

Strategy Depends Upon the Question At Hand

One factor in deciding whether to search free or fee-based services is the desired outcome. If you are attempting to answer a question of fact, the answer may be readily available from a particular source or type of source. (The various types of sources are covered in more detail later in this book.) Having zeroed-in on the type of source to search, the next step is to find that source online on one of the commercial services or in free sources such as government files and Internet sites.

Here are some examples of the types of projects that you can expect:

━━━ The Compilation Project – "Get Me A List of Companies That..."

List building questions often require using one or more directories in electronic format. Many of these are industry specific, but others may cover a wide range of businesses or industries.

Suppose that you need to create a list of manufacturers of PVC pipe within a particular geographic area. You're looking for basic information — company name, address, and contact information. One of the first places searchers go is to the Thomas Register of American Manufacturers. The Thomas Register site, www.thomasregister.com, is a good source for this type of information because it allows searching by company name, product/service, and/or brand name. The database is user-friendly and will let you search on common product names such as PVC without knowing that the full name for PVC is polyvinyl chloride. Searching on "PVC pipe" retrieves a number of hits, as seen in the following picture:

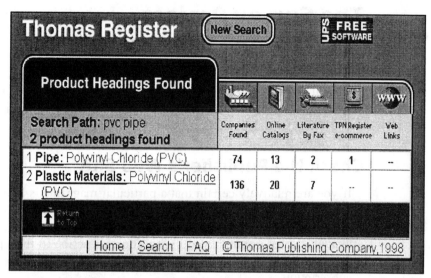

A view of the Thomas Register of American Manufacturers web site.

By clicking on one of the two product headings, you can access a hot-linked list of company names and addresses. Another click, and a company record is displayed, providing you with an individual company's name, address, and possibly a description of their business activity.

Is Your Mission Accomplished?

At this point you can print a group of company records. But is this a list or a pile of printouts? Using free sources on the Internet, you must click on a series of hotlinks, and display or print records one at a time. You might print out a pile of individual company descriptions, or create a list by cutting and pasting information into a list in word processing,

By contrast, performing this search in a commercial database would usually provide an answer in the form of a number indicating how many companies in the database contain your search terms, ((pvc or polyvinyl chloride) and pipe). If the number is too high, you could narrow the search results using other criteria such as geography or annual sales, to reduce the expense. The search in a commercial database will cost money, but you can refine the search result in advance, and can print out a list of possible companies, including all or part of each record retrieved.

Refer to Chapter 7 – Deeper Sources for some other excellent directories.

The Survey Project — "Get Me An Overview of XYZ"

Suppose you want to determine some of the trends in an industry over the past several years. This may mean you want an overview — something general, like a survey article in a trade publication. Either commercial or Internet sources may work well for this type of question.

Check the Publisher's Web Site

If you are relatively certain that a particular magazine is likely to have covered the matter you're researching, you might go directly to the Internet to locate the information you need, free of charge. Lots of magazines or newspapers are available to you online even if you don't subscribe to their print version. In other cases, print subscribers may receive a price break if the web site requires a subscription.

Popular business publications such as *BusinessWeek*, *Forbes*, *Fortune* and many others have built sizeable web sites, which often include links to other useful information sources. (Internet addresses for these and other important business information sources can be found in Bookmarks & Favorites section of Part IV) A search engine may allow you to access recent issues or search an archive by entering keywords, and to quickly locate one or more articles on your topic. The *Forbes* web site, at www.forbes.com, shown below, is a good example:

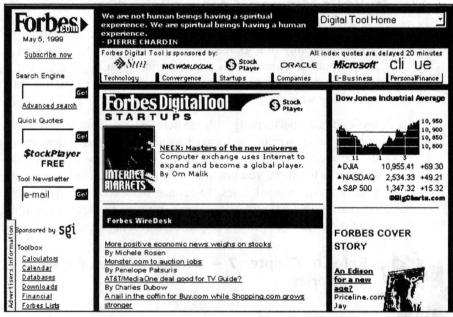

Business publications such as Forbes have created web sites that include a variety of useful tools in addition to articles from their current or recent issues.

While viewing the *Forbes* page, explore the links under the heading "Toolbox." Hiding behind these links are a wealth of tools and resources that are of tremendous use to any CI research effort.

To quickly locate business publications by industry or by topic, try the Michigan Electronic Library web site at http://mel.lib.mi.us/business/BU-IPair.html. This is an excellent site that contains hot-links to take you directly to the web site of the titles listed. Web addresses sometimes change. A site like this one is generally kept up-to-date, so it may be more reliable than bookmarks that you saved weeks or months ago.

Download Articles from Commercial Online Services

To determine where a magazine or journal is available in either commercial online services or on the World Wide Web, you might also consult one of two /useful print directories, which are included in the Appendix E of Part IV.

♦ *Fulltext Sources Online* is published by Information Today, which can be found at www.infotoday.com. *FSO* provides commercial database locations or web addresses for periodicals, newspapers, newswires, newsletters, and TV/radio transcripts. Special codes indicate publications where a fee is charged for online access to back issues and also where no archives are available.

♦ *Net.Journal Directory* is published by Hermograph Press, which has a web site at www.hermograph.htm. This is a catalog of full text periodicals archived on the World Wide Web. Included are consumer or trade magazines, scholarly journals and newsletters, business newspapers and trade journals. General newspapers are included in a special section. Article costs, availability of graphics, and coverage are included for each periodical.

A list of publications considered to be essential reading for those who keep up with online information sources is also found in the Appendix E of Part IV. These publications typically contain carefully researched reviews of important database files and web sites, news about developments in the field, research tips and hints for searching specific topics, and more.

The More Complex Project – "We Need Some Facts & Figures…"

An example of this type of question might be something like,

> "What is Company X's share of the widget market, and what were last years sales figures for their new electronic widget?"

Another variation on this theme might sound like this:

"We're considering the manufacture of electronic widgets, possibly expanding into new markets. We need to know who else manufactures these products, whether they market them in California, or Croatia, or China, and what the size of the world market for electronic widgets is now and will be in five years."

To answer this type of question, you need facts and figures. The results will most certainly impact an important decision that could determine the company's future. Although some useful information may appear in trade publications, there are also other types of sources that could be treasure troves of intelligence, containing the data that you need, or providing clues to their whereabouts. Here, briefly, are some possibilities that will be expanded upon later.

Statistical Data Compiled by Government Agencies

Government files containing reams of statistical data, spanning hundreds of subjects, are available from agencies such as the US Census Bureau, the US Bureau of Labor Statistics, and the US Department of Commerce, among others. These sources will supply the demographic data needed to determine whether there is a market for electronic widgets, and the size of that market. If you contemplate actually manufacturing those electronic widgets in a new area, you will be concerned with labor-related matters such as wage rates, etc. Some of this data can be downloaded and imported into spreadsheets or other software, for additional massaging or analysis.

Laws, Regulations, & Intellectual Property

Doing business in new markets means that the company may be subject to the laws and regulations promulgated by individual states or provinces in the US or Canada, or to entire legal codes for foreign countries. Much of this data is now available on the Internet at little or no cost. It is important, of course, to check for recent updates to any law or regulation, as your lawyer or company Legal Department will attest. Several university web sites offer both US and non-US laws in searchable electronic format. See "Legal Information" in the Bookmarks & Favorites section of Part IV.

Increasing availability of laws and regulations in electronic format does not mean that we should all begin doing our own legal work. *Always* consult your attorney when making important business decisions involving the law, especially when it comes to *interpreting* it.

Ownership of intellectual property such as patents, copyrights, or trademarks also must be considered before developing new products, or moving into new markets.

Public Records Information

A variety of public records may be used when researching new products or markets. You must decide the name under which to do business in the new jurisdiction, and may find that your first choice is in use, or reserved by a competitor. You may wish to research real estate records, particularly if considering buying property in the proposed new market area. (This also will help identify competitors' real property.) Ultimately, your Human Resources Department may use public records if hiring is undertaken.

Scientific & Technical Reports — An Underutilized Bonanza

Scientists and engineers often need specifications and standards, patents, and similar information that can now be located quickly and easily in electronic format. Examining specifications and standards early in the product development process may result in good choices that reduce or eliminate potential problems later on. Examining existing patents could result in a decision to license technology rather than invest in research and development. These types of decisions may have a dramatic impact on whether the company develops those electronic widgets and on whether they compete successfully with other products on the market.

Trusting Your Sources — If It Matters, Verify & Validate!

If your doctor suggests radical brain surgery for a pain in your foot, you may decide to seek a second opinion. The same holds true when making business decisions based on something you've read or heard.

Commercial database services are an excellent tool for verifying information because many vendors allow you to quickly search and retrieve articles from a number of sources simultaneously, with provisions for removing unnecessary duplicates. This makes it easier to compare and verify data.

Document the Source of the Information

Database files usually consist of individual records, each containing discreet fields of data. For each record retrieved by a search, the source, date, and other important information needed for credibility and accountability are presented up front. Usually the vendor's Customer Support telephone number is easily visible should additional questions arise.

If you were looking for market share data in the PC industry, the sample database record shown below would appear to be a "dream come true." It comes from Business & Industry, available as File 9 on DIALOG, at www.dialog.com. It also could have been retrieved directly from the database producer, Responsive Database Services, at www.rdsinc.com. Note that the article's title, the name of the publication, and the date of the issue containing the article are readily available. Within the article, the table's caption probably identifies the source or sources of the figures that are presented. You can go to those sources, if desired, to verify that the figures are correct.

01758204 (THIS IS THE FULL TEXT)

PC Market Share, By Vendor
(PC market share by vendor is tabulated for 4th qtr-1995
and 4th qtr- 1996; shipments for 4th qtr-1996 are 6.8 mil units, vs 7.7 mil in 4th qtr-1995)

Information Week, n 620 , p 37
March 03, 1997
Document Type: Journal ISSN: 8750-6874 (United States)
Language: English Record Type: Fulltext
Word Count: 53

TEXT:

	4Q 1996	4Q 1995
Compaq	14%	12%
Packard Bell	10%	16%
IBM	10%	8%
Dell	7%	5%
Gateway 2000	7%	5%

The title of the article cited above is indicative of the detailed data available online. This article could be printed immediately in full text without requiring a trip to the library.

Use Caution on the Internet

Internet sources vary greatly as to credibility and reliability. If you located the article regarding PC market share on a well-known publisher's web site, or found figures on a US government agency site, you might feel comfortable in using them. But what if you located them by doing a search using a popular search engine, and the information was found on something called "Joe's Home Page"? Who is Joe? How can you be sure he knows anything about the subject? Would you be comfortable citing Joe as a source if the Boss asks where the data came from?

Remember that quality control is often greater in commercial databases than in some types of "free" sources. A deal worth thousands or even millions of dollars to your company, may well justify the expense of using commercial databases to gather the information you need.

Chapter 3

Is Everything *Really* on the Internet?

Can You Trust What You Find?

Free vs. Fee Sources:
How to Choose Between Them

Why spend money when you can get information or documents for free? The answer harkens back to an old saying: "Don't look a gift horse in the mouth." Upon checking, you may determine that the "gift" may not be quite as good as you suspected!

It's important, therefore, to examine the differences between the types of online information sources, both free and fee-based, and to make informed choices. The information sources have evolved into four major categories:

♦ Commercial Online Services, reached via dial-up telephone connection.

♦ Commercial Databases on the Internet.

♦ Free sources on the Internet, sponsored by recognized, reputable sources.

♦ Free sources on the Internet, maintained by companies, individuals, or organizations with whom you may not necessarily be familiar.

Getting expert business intelligence from the Internet at no cost can be fraught with peril. Considering which sources to search in, which ones to trust and which approach will be most productive can be complicated. Consider these basic truths:

♦ It's possible to waste a lot of time on the Internet trying to find a free source for data that is readily available in a familiar commercial online source, if you are willing to pay for it.

♦ The Internet provides a wealth of valuable information not available from commercial services.

♦ By having a clear understanding of the possible pitfalls inherent in the use of Internet sources, you can combine the best of both worlds.

To make your decisions easier, ask yourself these questions when making choices about online sources:

Is there a "free" source that contains the same documents that are available from a fee-based source like a commercial online vendor?

Many publishers have now made current issues of their newspapers, magazines or journals available on their web sites, at no cost. Some publishers have even loaded searchable archives, as mentioned in Chapter 2 - Basic Tools & Strategies for Online CI. *Net.Journal,* mentioned earlier, can help you identify these archives.

Suppose that your company is planning to add to its Board of Directors. Perhaps the time has come to include someone who happens to be female among the candidates. You need to identify some qualified female candidates. You could, of course search a large file like the Dow Jones Publications Library, or one of the business publications on DIALOG or LEXIS-NEXIS. You would decide on appropriate search terms, and receive a list of articles. By scanning the titles, you might zero-in on one or more documents that you wished to purchase in full text.

You might, of course, have been told or remember that business magazines often publish lists whose names begin with words like *The Top 100....* By checking the *Fortune* web site, you would find references to a list ranking *The 50 Most Powerful Women.* (You might even have located that information because you looked at the Bookmarks & Favorites section of Part IV.) You could hot-link to the right document, and print it for free. This is the type of question that is handled well using free sites on the Internet, provided the site is one that you trust.

Can I depend that the free source will continue to be available at no charge?

With major publications like *Forbes, Fortune*, etc., you can probably assume that current material will be available free. It's part of the publisher's marketing plan to allow such access to recent issues, in hopes that you will become a subscriber or patronize their advertisers.

Certain other Internet sites that provide free reports, company profiles, or other material today, may announce next week that you must pay for the material that was formerly free. In these cases, the "introductory" period is over, even though the "introductory" part was not previously made clear. Other web sites provide a brief report at no charge, but the "good stuff" is available only to those with a subscription.

The worst case scenario here would be that you are under a time crunch, you need to locate some crucial information, and you plan to use that great Internet site that you found a couple of weeks ago. Lo and behold, the introductory period is indeed over, you've spent 15 minutes, and have nothing to show for it.

Or you use your favorite Internet search engine, locate a reference that sounds promising, but the pieces of data that you need are listed in the "For Members

Only" column on the site's homepage. Unless you have your credit card handy, and plan to sign up for a subscription, you may have to look elsewhere for the information. Meanwhile, the clock is ticking away.

Do I need one specific article? Or am I looking for everything that can be found on the subject?

Suppose you want to check all possible sources for references to your company. This would include searching many types of materials, such as newspapers and magazine articles, scientific or technical sources, trade publications, etc. You need to search widely and deeply in a reasonable amount of time.

This is not the time to rely on your favorite Internet search engine, and begin to wade through the 4,929 hits retrieved. For this type of search, you need to choose tools that will cover the greatest number of sources, for as far back as you choose to go (or as far as possible).

In this type of search, you may not rely on one commercial online service, either. None of them has everything. The vendors send out press releases every week, announcing that this or that book, journal, or tool has been added to their service. Sometimes these announcements brag about an "exclusive." To be as thorough as possible, you need to search across the offerings of several vendors. If you don't have the subscriptions to do this, consider outsourcing the project to an information broker.

By considering these questions, you can make some decisions about handling choices when it comes to searching in cyberspace instead of in the stacks at the library. In general, you will probably conclude, as many professionals have, that it's wise to have a variety of tools at your disposal, if possible, and to think the question through before turning on the computer.

How to Ensure That You're Getting What You *Think* You're Getting

Your goal is to stay ahead of the competition, to learn what they are doing or planning and to keep abreast of developments, trends and forecasts in the industry. You want to access intelligence in both as timely and as comprehensive manner as possible. To be sure of what you are getting, it is helpful to understand the "nuts and bolts" of the types of available sources.

The table below outlines the issues that should be considered when comparing commercial sources with free ones.

Comparing Features:
Commercial Databases vs. Free Internet Sources

	Commercial Sources	Non-commercial Internet Sources
Standardized Language/Indexing **(Authority Control)**	Articles in the database using an official list of index terms. You can check the vocabulary list. If you search on the proper keyword, you will retrieve all relevant articles.	Documents not indexed; no controlled vocabulary. One document may refer to "car," while another mentions "automobile." You must enter synonyms to retrieve as many articles as possible.
Access To Full Text Databases	Full text services like the Dow Jones Library or LEXIS-NEXIS provide segment searching to limit searches to specific areas of documents, for greater precision.	These files are searched using a variety of search engines, which use different sets of "rules." In general, you must use the synonym approach and hope that the words you've chosen appear in the documents, causing the item, therefore, to be retrieved.
Quality Control	Articles come from published sources, with attribution. Source lists are generally available. The database producer can be contacted for questions regarding quality of information.	There is no supervision of data loaded on the Internet. Out-of-date material is rarely removed. Dates on documents retrieved by a search engine may refer to date loaded on the Internet, not date of the document itself. It is difficult, if not impossible, to contact the responsible party.
Consistency of Format	Format varies across databases, but records generally contain basic information such as title, author, publisher and date. The pattern is consistent for all records within one database.	Search engines retrieve documents from sites all over the Internet. No uniformity exists as to style. Likewise, no uniform set of standards is followed when loading documents to web sites.

	Commercial Sources	Non-commercial Internet Sources
Continuity/Timeliness	Updates are loaded on a regular schedule, which is published. Subscribers are given notice if a database is going to be removed or is not being updated.	Web sites come and go without notice. Sites frequently include the date the site was last updated, but this may apply to design, and not necessarily to content.
Objectivity	Most documents come from named sources. You can consider the source when you read a document or article. Commercial vendors don't usually have a political or social agenda.	Not all documents are attributed. You may not easily realize that the site you are viewing belongs to someone with a particular bias.
Accountability	The online vendor is accountable for the material retrieved using their service. You won't stumble onto objectionable material by accident.	You may innocently link from an innocuous site to something that offends you or which you would not consider appropriate for certain audiences.
Availability	Direct dial method generally means fast, reliable access. Using a commercial vendor's web site means that "Internet rules apply." **You usually pay for connect time as well as for documents.**	The volume of web traffic, type of phone line or slow-loading graphic files may affect retrieval time. Executing a search on a commercial vendor's web site often takes longer than using direct dial method, but **you don't pay for connect time.**
Navigation Between Files	Search across multiple files simultaneously or use "in and out" approach to move between databases.	Fast hot-link access to other sites of interest.

	Commercial Sources	Non-commercial Internet Sources
Interface	With dial-up access, data appears without photos, charts, graphs, etc. which may be the most important part of the document. Web-based commercial services may offer these features.	PDF and other graphic files are used frequently, allowing you to save or print documents as they originally appeared, **retaining graphic elements.**

If you plan to access both commercial and free sources, the next decision becomes whether to choose direct dial or web access to the commercial vendors of choice. There are tradeoffs to be made, no matter which approach you choose. The table below examines some of these items:

Comparing Access to Commercial Databases

	Direct Dial	Web Access
Navigating Between Services	Log off of a service, dial another phone number, log on to another service.	Enter URL of next service to search. Log on to that service without having to go offline.
Tracking/Audit Trails	Session logs may capture all keystrokes during online session, for easy retrospective analysis.	No session logs for documenting each keystroke, but other "save" functions are available.
Reliability of Access	Connection is less complex; fewer access interruptions encountered.	Internet connection may experience interruptions; often less reliable than direct-dial, depending upon type of connection.

	Direct Dial	**Web Access**
Interface	Proprietary software may be available. No hot links.	Generally more intuitive and easier to use. Some vendors offer both "easy" and "professional" searching options.
Search Efficiency	Searching can be done rapidly, using special command language.	Searches may take longer using Internet hot-link approach. Using "Command Mode" may be an option on vendor's web version of service.
Reliability of Connection	Generally quite stable.	Varies with type of connection. The modem/telephone line method can be unstable, depending upon location.

Major Vendors Are Migrating to the Internet & There May Be Tradeoffs

We're getting closer and closer to the point where we'll do all of our online searching using the Internet. Most of the major commercial online vendors have premiered web sites that combine their high-quality data with the functionality of the Internet.

If you are new to searching these commercial sources, you probably appreciate the fact that when using the Internet, you do not constantly have to worry about how much time you are spending online. You can click on the "Help" button to see searching hints, check the database documentation or browse the search results to select useful articles. There is no worrying about the cost of online time. When you're ready, you select and print or download the documents of your choice.

More experienced searchers grumble about the fact that, on the Internet, they must click on several links, and then wait for screens to appear, in order to do a search that formerly took only seconds in dial-up mode. These same people are pleased, however, when they can print an article in PDF format. Files generated in PDF format retain graphics such as colored fonts, pictures, charts, or drawings that are part of the original. Documents are literally an exact copy of originals. For display, they require Adobe software, which is available free.

Hail, Hail, The Gang's All Here...

With the fourth quarter 1998 announcement by LEXIS-NEXIS that their new LEXIS-NEXIS Universe was up and available, the three major commercial services for business research have all migrated to the Web, along with several of the vendors of popular specialized databases in the legal, science and technology areas.

In designing their web sites, LEXIS-NEXIS and Dow Jones have taken the approach common to the Internet, where the homepage for the service includes popular Internet features such as news and headlines, with links to the major subject areas covered on the service. This convenience, combined with the additional functionality inherent in web access, makes these sites great "jumping off places" for performing many types of CI research.

The DIALOG web site now contains links to news, connections for Lotus Notes users, and even a source for ordering office supplies. Also, the DIALOG site allows access to its sister service, DataStar, if you have a DataStar subscription.

Comparing the "Big Three" Commercial Online Services

For business intelligence, DIALOG, Dow Jones Interactive, and LEXIS-NEXIS are the US survivors among the large commercial online services that were created years ago as dial-up systems. Over the years, popular services such as DataTimes and Newsnet have folded. Other services such as DataStar and FT Profile are popular in other parts of the world. Since you may have decided to subscribe to a commercial service, and may have to choose between them, you may wish to compare them.

ACCESS

All of the "Big Three" services require subscriptions. With DIALOG and LEXIS-NEXIS, a monthly fee is assessed in addition to search-related expenses and per-document costs. Dow Jones Interactive charges a nominal annual fee, with a price break for subscribers to the *Wall Street Journal.*

INTERFACE

Of the three services, Dow Jones Interactive probably has the most intuitive interface. This is a good trait if you are not a highly experienced searcher. The LEXIS-NEXIS Universe site operates much like many other popular Internet sites, with links to broad categories which you can explore to narrow your search. DIALOG has released a new improved version of its web site. Recent press releases are featured, with hotlinks to database documentation, sister company online services, etc. DIALOG has provided easy access for beginnners, while providing a link to "command mode DIALOG" for longtime searchers.

CONTENT

DIALOG offers a variety of files; its science and technology offerings aren't available on LEXIS-NEXIS or Dow Jones Interactive. File 411, DIALINDEX, allows you to search across all 500+ databases simultaneously, or across any mixture of file numbers entered. This is a useful method for retrieving references to a competitor in business files, trade publications, and scientific files — all at the same time, if you choose to do so.

Dow Jones Interactive is focused on business-related files, and offers access to some databases not available on its competitors' services, such as its historic stock information files and the Multex reports. Its Web Center provides links to a number of other important Internet sites, providing a unique combination of "free" and "fee" sources, all within easy reach. Dow Jones Interactive is aggressively adding new resources to its collections.

LEXIS-NEXIS is noted for its legal databases, but competes well with the other two vendors when it comes to news, business, and specialty files.

Because each has unique offerings, however, many companies use all three services. The constant competition between these vendors promises to benefit your online research undertakings in the form of new interfaces, additional sources, and other improvements.

An Alternate Route to Key Business Databases

The boss or the budget may allow a subscription to Dow Jones Interactive because you'll get a price break if you're a *Wall Street Journal* subscriber, and the annual fee is nominal, anyway. You may be a bit reluctant to commit to the monthly subscription fees inherent in access to DIALOG or LEXIS-NEXIS, however.

The big news is that WinStar's **BRAINWave**, an Internet-based service, contains the LEXIS-NEXIS legal databases and many of the DIALOG files, where you can pay by credit card with no subscription fees. Some searchers will find this approach both attractive and sufficient for their commercial online source requirements. You may pay more for a search here, but you avoid those monthly subscription fees. There is an amazing amount of business intelligence searchable in BRAINWave's 200+ databases, and it is well worth a look, especially for searchers who lack either LEXIS-NEXIS or DIALOG, but who need those files occasionally.

Others may try BRAINWave at www.n2kbrainwave.com (see the image that follows), identify favorite files that are also on the subscription services, and decide that a subscription to one or another of the services is worthwhile because they have become high volume frequent searchers.

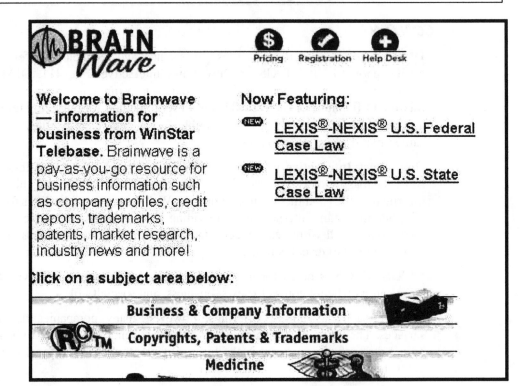

Don't Forget the "Techies"

Competitive intelligence includes much more than searching business databases. As a matter of fact, scientists and engineers were the earliest users of computers in their work. Business applications came years later, as use of computers became more common, technology improved and interfaces became more "user friendly."

Science and technology still rely heavily on computerized databases. STN, that cyberspace bastion of scientific knowledge, is found on the Web at http://info.cas.org/stn.html. STN also offers STN Easy through this site, allowing an easy interface for accessing what could otherwise be rather complex material. Access is also available by direct dial.

Other scientific or patent database services like Questel-Orbit, www.questel.orbit.com, or Derwent, at www.derwent.com, also are found on the Web. True web access is still a thing of the future for Questel-Orbit subscribers, but its subscription based QPAT service, www.qpat.com, allows you to search the full text of all US patents issued since 1974 and to retrieve 100%-secured images from IBM's patent image server. Although images from the IBM server are available free at http://patent.womplex.ibm.com, QPAT provides the images using a secure server.

Online services intended for desktop use may omit certain material, or even entire databases. Detailed online research in science and technology should only be performed by experienced searchers who have a good understanding of, or background in, the subject matter.

Chapter 4

Begin At the Beginning

Test Driving Your CI Vehicle

▬▬ Who Is Your Competition?

Having defined competitive intelligence and identified information sources available in electronic format, it's time to begin to apply this information to the task of gathering business intelligence. Start by knowing the competition. This is one of the keys to competing successfully in business, and it is not always as easy as some people might think.

Suppose that there are five major manufacturers of remote-controlled electronic gizmos in the country and your company is the one of the five. Your company's competitors are the other four companies on the list. Right?

Not necessarily! You may think that you know your competitors, but with some online sleuthing, you may find that your list of four companies gets longer. There could be new companies entering the industry, or other companies venturing into new markets that you thought your company had "sewed up."

Perhaps new products are being introduced that will make your company's gizmo as obsolete as buggy whips. How can you identify the competition and retain or increase your company's market share? Begin by creating a realistic list of competitors. They usually fall into three categories:

Direct Competitors

Identifying a company as a direct competitor depends upon how you describe what that company does. Are their products or services the same as those produced by your company? Are you competing in the same marketplace, either by geography or type of customer? Generally your company's direct competitors are those who sell the same products or services that you sell, to the same customers, perhaps in the same geographic area.

Indirect Competitors

Identifying indirect competitors takes a bit more thought. Those companies may offer products or services that are quite different from your own, but which can be used for the same purpose. If customers buy their goods instead of yours, your company loses revenue

Potential Competitors

A third group to consider is potential competitors. These are companies that might become direct competitors. They could, for example, be companies that are considering entering the same business arena that your company is in. The rumor mill may provide a tip-off in this situation. You also may identify other companies as potential competitors because if consumer trends change, their products will grab market share while yours become endangered species.

Practice Good Defense, CI Style

Once you begin to research competitor companies, questions arise: Should we believe what we read about that company? Are we finding information that helps us to deduce their plans or strategy? Have we searched in the right places? Have we found everything? Did we ask the right questions?

One good way to answer some of these questions is to research your own company first, using the company's name, key personnel, trade names, or products as search terms. This helps you to accomplish the following:

◆ **Identify sources for researching your competitors**. Search broadly and deeply, and see where information on your company is found. It's likely that the competition will be mentioned as well.

◆ **Determine what the competition knows about your company**. If this information is available on your company, it may be available on the competition's as well.

◆ **Validate the credibility of sources** by asking in-house sources to verify the information found on your own company.

How can you be sure that you've found everything? You can't. But, by thinking creatively, you'll find most of what is available. You may be surprised at what others can learn about your company. Here are some tips to use when performing defensive CI using online sources:

Can You Trust the Author?

Consider who is responsible for each article or document about your company. Did someone who specializes in your industry write the article? Look at several of this person's articles to get a feel for whether the writer's work seems fair and unbiased, whether it appears to be well researched and whether the author appears to have access to credible sources.

The next time you search for information on a competitor, take your conclusions into consideration. You may discount articles written by this person based on how he or she measured up when you read about your own organization. You may, on the other hand, decide that the writer is generally credible, and use articles by the writer as sources of information about your competition.

The Trap of Thinking Too Narrowly

Is your company frequently mentioned in certain publications outside your industry? It's possible that something triggers an article or reference within the trade press of another industry. If you produce raw material used in that industry or you purchase that industry's goods and services, your company may be discussed in that industry's trade publications.

Service industries often mention their clients, so you should consider whether those who think of you as a client may have bragged about it. Let's call your company MegaCorp. MegaCorp is mentioned in a public relations/advertising trade journal. It's easy to envision headlines like:

Gotham Advertising Wins the MegaCorp Telecommunications Account

This reference regarding your own company indicates that there may be similar references to your competition as well. There may be a discussion of the new direction your competition plans to take in its advertising and marketing program. The *Advertising Age* Web site at `http://ads.adage.com` has a searchable archive back to 1995. You must register, but there is no charge for searching. *Jack O'Dwyer's Newsletter* or *O'Dwyer's PR Services Report*, both available on LEXIS-NEXIS, are also good places to do this type of searching.

The name of the advertising agency that represents a particular company is an isolated fact, which may not seem significant to you. But it may mean a great deal to the folks in your company's marketing or public relations departments. They are familiar with the agencies, and can possibly predict the direction that a competitor's advertising is likely to take, based on the track record of the agency concerned.

Even if you aren't "mega" in size, check the advertising industry publications for columns that might contain regional news. If you are located in or near a large city, watch major newspapers for weekly columns covering the local public relations/advertising scene. In this way, you may pick up intelligence regarding which agencies work for which companies in your geographic region, changes in personnel, or other useful intelligence.

News and trade publications aren't the only good places to search. You might discover that your company is cited in conference proceedings, scientific or technical reports, and many other types of information sources that are discussed in detail in Chapter 7 - Deeper Sources.

Keep an Ear to the Rumor Mills

Did any references appear in Internet chat rooms or print media columns that contained words like "rumor"? We've all seen these. You may be a member of the "Where There's Smoke, There's Fire" school of thought, or you may not trust such rumors. A rumor may, however, be worth a few seconds of time spent searching for verification or corroboration. Here is an example where the rumor started on the Internet and was picked up in the press:

KRTBN KNIGHT-RIDDER TRIBUNE BUSINESS NEWS (DALLAS MORNING NEWS)
August 03, 1998   16:46
JOURNAL CODE: KDMN   LANGUAGE: English   RECORD TYPE: FULLTEXT

WORD COUNT: 1414

Aug. 3 - More than six weeks before Texas Instruments Inc announced plans to sell its memory chip operations, rumors about a potential deal were buzzing on the Yahoo! Finance message board on the Internet.

One late-night entry on May 4, from an anonymous participant who said he is "a manager for TI," reported that the Dallas-based company would be "very interested" in selling its Richardson memory plant to Micron Technology Inc., if the Idaho chipmaker could swing the financing.

Another contributor to the site, identified only as a 36-year-old man from Allen, said he heard Micron was bidding on the plant."

In the story referenced above, the rumors turned out to be true. The story was found using the DIALOG service.

If you don't have time to search the Internet message boards like Yahoo! Finance and Motley Fool yourself, consider using an Internet Monitoring Service such as Global Integrity, a division of Science Application International Corp and located on the Web at www.globalintegrity.com, **or consider other possibilities such as Company Sleuth, described in Chapter 11.**

Check What's Coming Out of the Horse's Mouth

Broadcast transcripts are now searchable on several major online services, including DIALOG, Dow Jones Interactive, and LEXIS-NEXIS. Search these for transcripts of interviews given by your CEO or other members of senior management. These people are well prepared for such interviews, so they are likely to quote numbers and other useful facts. Depending upon the questions asked, you may pick up an indication of where the company is going in the next five years, production numbers, or similar statements.

If it works on your company, it may work on competitors. Learn the names of the VIPs who act as company spokespersons, or just search using words like "mega corp and interview." You may fill in some of the blanks in the information you're gathering about that company, or at least validate information gathered from another source. The example below shows search results using the keywords "bill gates and interview."

Library	CustomClips	Company	Market Data

☐ 🗎 Interview: Microsoft founder Bill Gates discusses the antitrust lawsuit ...
NBC Nightly News, 05/18/1998, 372 words.
TOM BROKAW, anchor: Microsoft's founder, Bill Gates, took the lead in defending the actions of his company, which has made him the richest man in the world. ...

☐ 🗎 Interview: Bill Gates, Microsoft chairman, discusses the government's ...
CBS Evening News, 05/18/1998, 367 words.
DAN RATHER, anchor: Some historical perspective now on the government's antitrust suit against computer giant Microsoft. In similar suits this century, the ...

☐ 🗎 Interview: Bill Gates about the government's try to stop Microsoft's ...
NBC Nightly News, 05/05/1998, 544 words.
TOM BROKAW, anchor: It appears tonight that the showdown is near between state and federal governments and the computer software giant Microsoft ...

☐ 🗎 SOFTWARE INDUSTRY
Congressional Testimony by Federal Document Clearing House, 03/03/1998, 3998 words.
TESTIMONY OF JAMES BARKSDALE

The search shown above from Dow Jones Interactive, returned 14 hits, of which four were actual interviews of Bill Gates, while the rest were interviews of other people, generally connected with Gates and Microsoft. The search results also point out that Congressional testimony can be located, using Dow Jones Interactive, providing yet another source of commentary by company officials.

Call the person who handles public relations for your company to determine what interviews company VIPs have given, to which media outlets. If your search doesn't turn up these transcripts, re-think the search strategy.

Loose Lips Sink Ships

Perhaps management is considering closing a certain domestic plant and moving the operation to another location outside the country. They have a team preparing a "top secret" study on the subject. Suppose that your online search turns up a message on the Internet, or one of the "rumor columns" in a trade publication, mentioning that such a study is underway, or that the company is planning to close the plant. Company insiders generally know what would be, and has been, officially released. There may have been a slip-up or a leak. If you do find something along these lines, consider monitoring the same source for news on competitors. After all, they may make mistakes, too.

Taking the Next Step Toward Effective CI

After searching exhaustively for your company, analyze the information you found and note the places where you found it. Create a checklist for future use, including the following categories of sources to search. Within each category, note individual items.

As an example, suppose your company is in the apparel industry. The checklist might include the following among sources mentioning your company:

Publications

The *New York Times* (center of US fashion/apparel industry)

Other national/international newspapers that cover business news

Various company/industry directories

Local newspapers wherever you have a plant

Industry trade publications

Apparel Industry Magazine

Bobbin

Women's Wear Daily

Business oriented mass-market publications

The *Wall Street Journal*

Business Week, Forbes, Fortune

Businessworld (Philippines) (Perhaps you have factories there)

Indonesian Commercial Newsletter (If you do business there)

Trade publications for related industries that referenced "your" industry

Discount Store News

Fibre Organon

Footwear News

Textile World

Names and contact information for useful individuals or organizations.

Government agencies that regulate the industry

Other categories or sources where you expected your company to be mentioned, but they weren't. These should not be totally overlooked as potential information sources. Check them periodically or as a last resort when all else fails.

This process should get you thinking more creatively about other places to look for information on your competitors. However, we have just seen the "tip of the iceberg."

Part II

Choosing & Using Online Sources for Gathering CI Data

Chapter 5

The Key to Choosing Online Sources

Ask the Right Questions!

All Online Sources Are Not Created Equal

Searching for competitive information, whether in relation to companies or industries, is serious business. Missing an opportunity or making a bad decision can cost your company millions of dollars, or worse!

Whether considering subscribing to a commercial online service or treasure hunting on the World Wide Web, it's best to be an informed shopper. You cannot assume that a given source has all available information on the subject, is accurate and timely or that there isn't a better source out there. There might even be an alternate source that has more to offer at a lower cost.

In the commercial online environment, sales representatives are naturally going to present their product in a favorable light — it's their job. Your job, as a consumer, is to make informed buying decisions.

When it comes to searching the Internet, your task becomes more complex. With the exception of commercial vendors' sites, there is no salesperson trying to convince you to choose this or that site. Word of mouth, magazine articles, swapping bookmarks or following links on other web sites tend to be the common ways to identify useful or interesting material on the Internet. The problem is that that more and more material on the Internet is *not* free. In addition, there isn't always a responsible party to contact if questions arise regarding the information contained on the site.

Whether paying to use a source or searching it free, it is crucial to know *beforehand* what to expect from that source. Otherwise, you may waste money, or worse yet, get bad data that leads to the wrong business decision.

Choose the Online Services Closest to Your Needs

The time to sign up for commercial online services is *not* when you're under a deadline or when others are waiting for results. Examine your company's needs before visiting Web sites or telephoning online services for information. A few minutes spent getting this information down on paper will be well invested as you proceed. Start out by answering these broad questions, and then move on to the more specific items listed in the Twelve Guidelines, below.

Consider whether your company's online information needs are varied or focused.

Consider whether online resources will be used to search for many types of information or for only a few. When considering subscribing to commercial online services, you will find that there are both "boutiques" and "supermarkets" available. If there is a single department or a small group of key personnel making requests, it will be possible to zero in on an information boutique that covers the appropriate subject matter, while outputting the data in the desired format.

The table below includes a representative group of specialized subscription-based online services. Although they may offer a some general files, the majority of their offerings are in the subject areas listed. Further details about these services and many others may be obtained by contacting the vendors, using the information provided in the Vendors List at the back of this book.

Subject Matter	Vendor Name
Credit/Company Information	Dun & Bradstreet
	Experian
Financial / Securities	CDA Spectrum
	Disclosure
	Dow Jones Interactive
	Investext
	Multex
Legal	LEXIS
	Westlaw
Market Research	Profound
Medical	Ovid
Patents/Trademarks	Derwent
	Questel-Orbit
Public Records	CDB Infotek
	Information America
	Lexis Public Records
	Merlin Information Systems

If you are not the only searcher, however, and if several different departments will use online services for research, a supermarket may be the best choice. The list below includes some of the commercial online vendors whose services cover a variety of subject matter.

Description	Vendor Name
Multiple Subject Areas	DataStar
	DIALOG
	NEXIS
Science/Technology Subjects	STN

For those occasions when you need additional sources, services from these lists of these could be supplemented with pay-as-you-go services available on the Internet.

Who will use the data?

The sales team needs different types of material than the research and development department. Will the users be rocket scientists or someone who generally requires a fast overview on a topic that may come up in a meeting with a client? Essentially, the online source chosen should complement the end users, i.e. those who will ultimately use the information.

How frequently will you (or others in the company) search?

Ask, will the service be used frequently enough to justify the expense of set-up and/or subscription fees? If the source that meets your needs is high-priced and your need for it would only be occasional, you may want to consider a cheaper alternative — hire an independent researcher, (also known as an information broker). To locate an independent information researcher, search the *Burwell World Directory of Information Brokers* at www.burwellinc.com.

Is online access really the best choice for your needs?

Searching the Internet can be time-consuming. With some online services, per-minute communication charges are incurred. If receiving only monthly or quarterly updates is not a concern, you might wish to consider subscribing to certain databases in CD-ROM format.

12 Guidelines for Evaluating Online Sources

1. Examine the subject matter offered — you can't find what isn't there!

It is important to learn what subject matter is offered by a service before committing to a subscription. Some online services contain large numbers of databases covering a wide range of disciplines.

DIALOG at www.dialog.com, one of the services used most frequently by librarians and professional searchers, is good example. The nearly 500+ databases found on this service are grouped into topics like engineering, chemistry, business, cinema, company information and so on. In addition, the service provides full texts from many newspapers and an extensive group of market research reports on dozens of different products and services. One could call this type of service an "information supermarket," since it is geared toward a wide variety of users who require a wide range of subject matter when they search. Thus, if the needs of your company are "varied," DIALOG or a similar service would be the most likely to meet your needs.

By contrast, Dow Jones Interactive at www.djnr.com is more business oriented. News, stock quotes and other company/industry financial data are the core of the material offered, with a large library of online publications available as well. The Dow Jones Interactive *Web Center* offers what is described as "an intelligent collection of high-quality business and news sites" that have been reviewed by Dow Jones staffers.

If a company's searching needs are "focused" on business-related data, Dow Jones Interactive would be a good choice.

Some services, such as LEXIS-NEXIS are appropriate for both focused and varied needs. LEXIS-NEXIS is available in dial-up mode and on the Web as LEXIS-NEXIS Universe at www.lexisnexis.com. This service is offered as separate components (LEXIS or NEXIS) and as a package. The LEXIS portion is focused. It serves the legal market, covering extensive case law, statutes, regulations, and other legal matters. The NEXIS part of the product is varied, containing news, financial, medical and other more general sources.

2. Know the age of the available information

Keep your most frequent search questions in mind when choosing where you will search. Does the database file contain recent information only? Is historic data included? How far back does the information go, and how often is it updated? Do you need only the latest, or retrospective information or both? Also, be aware of any lag time that exists for databases that will be important in your research. The publisher may restrict publication of the most recent data for a fixed period of time in order to preserve its sale of print products.

3. Determine frequency of updates or reloads

If all you need is a little bit of information on the trends in the mousetrap industry, perhaps an article published three months ago will be good enough to give you an overview of what's happening in that sector of commerce.

But what if you *must* have the most current information possible on what analysts are saying about a competitor's company? Last month's newspaper would not suffice.

The frequency of update varies with type of, availability of, and demand for the information as well as other factors. Certain sources are updated annually, while others, like newswires and stock market quotes are available in real time or with only very brief time lags.

It is possible that the same database is available on multiple online services, with different lag times and different update or reload schedules. If very timely data is crucial to your choice of vendor or file, it is best to call each database vendor to determine current availability and make the search decision based on what you have learned. The list of vendor contact information in the Resource List Section of Part IV will prove helpful here. Database documentation usually indicates how often the file is updated. Many commercial vendors provide messages on the search screen before you perform a search.

Sometimes those "site last updated on…" messages aren't specific enough to tell you *what* was updated. It could have been the entire database, a portion of its content or even the background color of the homepage. If you can't determine when the database was last updated, a telephone call should produce answers.

On the whole, commercial sources tend to be updated more frequently than free sites. Why? Commercial sites have a responsibility to keep things up-to-date to meet the demands of paying customers. Free services are under no such obligation. To determine how frequently and/or regularly updates occur on an Internet site, try inquiring by e-mail, or use a commercial source because of the "comfort factor." Regardless of the service(s) you choose, be aware of the update frequency of the databases you use, and choose those that meet your requirements for timeliness.

4. Examine the format of the results

Most people expect to obtain full text documents when retrieving intelligence information from online sources. However, it's important to realize that certain older databases only contain abstracts or worse yet, merely citations that refer to other sources. Sometimes additional work is required to obtain the full text of older documents, which are often necessary to establish a historical perspective. A good abstract may be sufficient for your needs. More is not always better.

If time is not limited, and you have a large library at hand, you can simply take your list of citations to the library, locate back issues of publications containing the cited articles and head for the photocopy machine — keeping the copyright laws in mind, of course.

It's much smarter to know the database format in advance, download the data and spend time offline figuring out how to apply it, than to discover at the last minute that the service you're searching doesn't offer data in the format you require! Even worse is having your boss question why you didn't know how inadequate the source was to begin with.

The important thing to remember is that you don't need unplanned surprises or delays when competitive information is concerned. If you know what to expect in a file, you can plan accordingly. Ask, "Will the results be full text, abstracts, citations or a combination thereof?" and "Which would meet my needs?"

5. Consider both prepared & unformatted results

Is it smarter to pay money to download prepared (i.e. formatted) documents that are ready to use, or to download raw, unformatted data free from the source with the intention of cleaning it up later?

If the information is for your own use, you may not mind extraneous characters and lack of good formatting. If, however, you need to take copies of a competitor's 10-K report to an important meeting, obtaining a professional-looking report from a commercial vendor is probably your best option. In some cases a combination of both approaches will be most successful, depending upon the time and budget for a given project.

A financial professional recently described his online source requirements as follows:

♦ Companies must be searchable by criteria, such as SIC code.

♦ Data must be downloadable in tagged format.

Once information has been received, each "tagged" field is imported into a specific cell of a computer spreadsheet. Then, the data is exported from the spreadsheet into ASCII delimited format and loaded into his own database.

Essentially, he downloads information on dozens of companies at a time, and by following the above restrictions, he is able to build a database without re-keying a single word. The whole process takes only a few minutes, and does not require clerical assistance. Without establishing and adhering to these very specific format requirements, a lot more work would be involved.

By selecting a database source that offers an adaptable format, this man automates what could be a tedious process. He is free to spend the bulk of his time using his professional expertise, analyzing the data for use in his practice.

6. Determine the geographic coverage of the source

Is the information in the database worldwide in origin or country-specific? It's important to ask this question carefully. Some vendors provide a few sources from only a handful of countries and then claim they offer "worldwide coverage."

With some online vendors, geographic coverage is apparent from the name of the service. *Asia Pulse*, for example, is the joint venture of a number of Asia's major news and information providers, all experts in their own countries. *Asia Pulse* also covers one hundred categories of information. Specialized databases include these:

♦ Asia Markets

♦ Business in Asia

♦ Power Weekly Industry Report

♦ Automotive Weekly Industry Report

The important thing is to determine if the geographic areas of interest to your company are included in the product or service *before you subscribe.*

7. Ask about languages in which documents are available

While the search results of US online services are usually in English, it is important to know whether you can expect to find articles in other languages as well. If you work in a field where major contributions are made in other countries, you or your company may profit from valuable new developments sooner if you can read them in the language in which they were written, rather than waiting for translated versions to be published. Furthermore, translations can be problematic. Various nuances disappear in translation, or errors creep in because of multiple meanings for words. Several major commercial online sources offer documents in multiple languages.

The language issue is very evident on the Internet. One can easily locate foreign web sites. Sometimes they even appear in unfamiliar alphabets. Some of these sites are available in multiple languages. If available, English speakers should look for and click on the word `English` on the site to access an English language version. See Chapter 10 for a list of search engines available in languages other than English.

The AltaVista search engine offers translation for some of the documents retrieved from its system. If the word "Translate" appears in the search results, a simple click will bring up the English language version. However, the feature is not available for *all* non-English material, and you may encounter some unusual results when you read the translation.

8. Consider the interface

This is a very straightforward issue. The service's interface is either complex, requiring experience and/or training, or it is simple and user friendly.

Some high-powered database products require both training and extensive experience if one is to use them for maximum efficiency. Other services are easily and effectively searched using a simple menu interface. With easier systems, the searcher often picks a category of information from a list on the screen. Next, the program prompts the user for information and gives an example of how it should be entered. Then the searcher enters something brief like the name of a company or individual, hits the appropriate key and the search is underway.

Interfaces are evolving. Products that were originally offered only via direct dial-up connections are now available on the Web. However, technology has yet to allow the same level of functionality that is available in the direct dial-up versions. Nonetheless, vendors recognize that by offering their services on the Web they are able to expand their customer base. A beneficial "side effect" of increasing Web availability is that it is no longer necessary to learn "command languages," something often required for direct dial-up systems. In addition, World Wide Web versions allow for the use of graphics, sounds and other forms of multimedia offerings.

9. Shop for special features

any feature that saves time and labor usually saves money, either directly or indirectly. What follows are some examples of features to watch for when looking at a vendor's wares:

Useful Features Checklist

☑ Arrangement of data in tagged or ASCII delimited format for importing into another software program.

☑ The ability to generate a customized report that includes the database fields of your choice.

☑ Current awareness service (See Chapter 11 for more information).

☑ Software or documents in multiple languages (especially useful for international companies).

☑ The ability to choose to see selected portions of database records, and to be charged less than full price per record.

☑ Sub-account billing, which categorizes your online costs according to specified "clients." (This helps if you bill various accounts or departments for charges incurred.)

10. Consider all pricing options

Some vendors have a reputation for being "expensive." This is a relative determination. What one company dubs expensive may be considered necessary *at any cost* by another.

Also, acceptable payment methods vary. Some vendors require a credit card whereas others will invoice. Increasingly, vendors are adding secure servers to alleviate concerns about the use of credit cards on the Internet.

Several pricing options exist in today's market:

Subscriptions: Payment of a monthly or annual fee provides you with a password. Depending on the vendor, the subscription rate may include free access up to the equivalent of a certain dollar amount, at which point additional usage is billed at the published rates. A variation on this approach involves a subscription fee plus per-document costs. Dow Jones Interactive uses this approach.

Usage-Based Pricing: A flat monthly rate is agreed upon based on your company's previous or projected usage. This rate is renegotiated at the end of a specified period and then adjusted accordingly. LEXIS-NEXIS and the Dialog

Corporation both include this arrangement as one of their pricing options.

Deposit Accounts: Search charges are made against an amount previously paid to the vendor and kept on deposit until used. Deposit accounts reduce the need for frequent check writing. KnowX, the popular Internet public record service, uses this method for charging clients.

Enterprise Pricing: This refers to a pricing scheme that allows for use by large numbers of users within a single company. It may be combined with some of the other pricing options. Most of the major vendors offer some form of this convenient arrangement. It reduces paperwork for both customer and vendor, and usually means lower per-search costs. The customer controls access in-house by granting network "rights" to those who need access to the service.

Pay-As-You-Go: A few online vendors allow access to occasional users, who enter a credit card number before searching. With "Pay-As-You-Go" pricing, the credit card verification and charges apply only to the current usage session. Subsequent visits to the site will more than likely involve additional verification and charges. This payment arrangement is becoming more and more common as newspapers, for example, find that they can gain extra revenue by offering their archives for searching, at fees like $1.95 per article retrieved in full text. Some government entities, such as county tax assessors, have signed on with entrepreneurs who have mounted systems that charge for access to public records made available on the county's web site.

To learn more about pricing in the online industry, look at *BiblioData's Price Watcher* at <u>www.bibliodata.com</u>. Linda Cooper, a seasoned online searcher and price watcher, edits this publication. Other articles on the subject appear in publications such as *Database*, *Online*, and *Searcher*, which are included in Appendix E in Part IV, at the back of this book.

If you are part of a large company, talk with other online users in the company to see if you are paying for multiple subscriptions with the same vendor. Get together and negotiate a group rate that saves money for each department. Don't forget to include your offices in other countries.

11. Evaluate education & training opportunities offered by the vendor

With the possible exception of the simplest of menu-oriented interfaces described previously, most commercial online services require at least some orientation before use. While basic training is usually free, some vendors charge for advanced level instruction. The need for training is reduced for online services that are searched using the Internet.

Online vendors have moved away from printing extensive manuals, and often make such material available for download. This may range from a few pages to a 200+ page manual downloadable from the Internet! Adequate descriptions of database files, instructions for searching effectively, samples of output, and contact information for obtaining further assistance are a must.

Web technology allows commercial vendors to incorporate a great deal of useful, easy-to-locate help screens in strategic locations on web pages. Since usage on the Web is not time-based, searchers can take time to examine these materials if questions arise. In addition to tips about creating search strings, these help screens might include descriptions of databases offered by the service, lists of periodicals included or even a glossary of special vocabulary that is often preferred by professional searchers.

Some vendors provide telephonic training. At a prearranged time, a vendor representative calls and walks you through the steps required to use the product successfully. This method provides a good way to get questions answered during the training process; it usually lasts an hour or more.

Some of the largest online services maintain offices in major cities, with representatives who will visit high-volume clients, providing on-site training, new product demonstrations, etc.

The bottom line is . . . the amount and type of training should match the cost and level of sophistication of the service.

12. Ask about the availability & type of customer support

The quality of service provided to users varies by vendor. Consider some of these questions when reviewing a vendor's customer support capabilities:

♦ What hours/days of the week is the customer service/tech support department available to assist callers? Monday through Friday service during regular business hours is the norm. Be sure to note whether the service is adequate for your time zone and/or the time zones of all your potential users.

♦ Does the vendor offer subject-specific specialists? It's comforting to be turned over to someone who understands your subject matter. At DIALOG, for example, the automated telephone system instructs the caller to "Press 2 for assistance with science or technology . . ."

♦ Will the customer support representative recommend appropriate databases or help construct a good search for a tough question? At LEXIS-NEXIS, it's not unusual for the support person to say something like, "Here's a search strategy that works for your type of question. Would you like me to give it to you exactly?"

Insider Tips of the Trade — Things the Pros Watch For

You can avoid costly mistakes or misunderstandings regarding online information by thinking like a professional searcher. In addition to the selection criteria described earlier in this chapter, professional searchers have developed a "sixth sense" regarding online sources.

Beware — A Deal that Sounds Too Good to Be True

If a reference tool is sold in book form and/or CD-ROM format, is the publisher likely to make the same material available at no cost on an Internet site? Maybe, but there may be tradeoffs. To provide the product free of charge on the Web, the loss of potential sales revenue must be offset. You may be bombarded with display ads on the web pages or the publisher may charge those people or companies included in the publication to make up for lost sales.

If neither of these options has been used, the publisher is probably giving away only a *portion* of the "real thing." In some cases this is obvious because you are informed that you can only retrieve from a fixed number of records. Not all non-subscription sites make this clear, however. Here are a few tip offs:

Sudden, Repetitive Error Messages

Let's say that you've located a web site that promises to give you a very targeted list of something that you're looking for. It might be companies, industries, people, or whatever. A-Z hotlinks may be shown on the web page, and you click on "A." You're able to display a list and use your browser's "Copy" feature to copy the list to another file or to some other software program. Then you copy the "B" listing.

By the time you get to the letter "C," you may begin to receive error messages from the web site that prevent you from going further. The messages don't say "You can't have any more free information!" In fact you may not understand what the messages mean. In reality, they probably indicate that you'd better consider at ordering the publisher's CD-ROM or print product in order to have *true* access to the data. In other words, you've reached some sort of limit.

Search Results that Don't Seem Right

Suppose that you're trying to obtain a current list of companies in a particular geographic area that manufacture a specific product. You may find "no hits" are retrieved when you've carefully followed the directions on a web site search screen. Or perhaps the search results seem rather small in an industry where you know that there are many more players. If something along these lines occurs, you must begin to consider that the "free" data might not be the full version.

As a test, check the results for a company that you are confident should be on the list. If this name does not appear, you have reason to believe that the database being searched is a subset of the vendor's entire file. The next step is to call or e-mail the vendor and ask whether the entire database is available free on the Internet site or they have provided only part of the information, but failed to make it clear.

Suspicious Facts & Figures

If facts and figures that you retrieve don't go along with information you've retrieved previously, a bell should go off in your head. Check yet another source to try to validate this new information. The data may be erroneous for a number of reasons.

One measuring stick for evaluating the quality of information retrieved from electronic sources is to search your own company or to perform a similar search where you can make informed judgments regarding your findings. You will quickly recognize "bad" information. If this source is inaccurate regarding your company, question their credibility. If the source contains accurate information on your "test case," then you may have discovered valuable new information. Either way, you should still verify the data using another source.

Obvious Errors Reveal a Number of Things

It is possible to find an obvious error in almost any database. Typographical errors or errors in dates are the most common. But considering the database size (millions of records), these occurrences are rare, especially in the online services mentioned throughout this book. These services stress quality control, and a loyal customer-base that let's them know if errors are found. When anomalies are discovered, the problem very likely lies with the database producer that provided the tapes.

Thinking Like a CI Professional — The Bottom Line

Whether we're talking about commercial online sources or those found free on the Internet, if you plan to search online, choose sources carefully. Follow the guidelines above to narrow down your choices. If you subscribe to an online service, choose among those with proven track records, who will be responsive if problems are encountered.

Chapter 6

Getting the Scoop

Familiar Information Sources & Those You May Have Overlooked

Searching Newspapers

When it comes to business information, most researchers think of newspapers and wire services immediately. But not all information useful to business is printed in the Business Section. If you hope to take full advantage of the intelligence opportunities newspapers provide, you must examine the other sections of the newspaper as well.

Don't Overlook Columns

Nearly every section of the newspaper contains columns by reporters who cover a particular "beat." These writers become familiar with the people, places and companies relevant to their assigned fields. In addition, their columns are often less formal than other parts of the newspaper. Columns contain items that are not lengthy enough to justify a full-fledged article.

A now-retired Houston librarian for a major international accounting firm once helped her firm's New York office impress an important client. It seems that the client was trying to locate an elusive man, who had left town suddenly, leaving no forwarding address. Apparently, he owed the client's company a large amount of money.

The client had heard a rumor that the debtor was in Houston, but had not yet hired private investigators, or taken other measures to locate the man and collect the debt. He mentioned this situation to the New York accountants. The New York office librarian called the Houston office, asking for a search of the local newspapers. A search of the *Houston Chronicle* ensued.

Sure enough! One of the entries in the society column read something like this:

> **Mr. XXX**, Vice President of Sale & Marketing for YYY Co., celebrated his birthday Tuesday evening at XYZ [the local upscale restaurant where Houston jet-setters go to see and be seen].

Since features such as columns are included in the online version of the *Houston Chronicle* database, it took only a few seconds to locate the man's name.

From the CI perspective, this news tidbit has several potential uses. Not only does it include name, job title and company affiliation, but it also provides information about the man's personal tastes, i.e. that he likes dining in upscale restaurants that serve gourmet food.

This information could be plugged into a company personnel report (see charts for Intelligence Gathering in Chapter 15) or if your company were planning to entertain the man, you would have a clue as to his choices in restaurants.

To make a favorable impression, it is a common practice in sales and marketing, to try to learn something about a potential client's habits, preferences, etc. Similar information can be found in columns in the Business Section with titles like "On The Move . . . ," which report on individuals' progress up their respective corporate ladders.

Finding Subtle Clues in Classified Ads

Prior to the advent of the Internet, it was common for newspaper databases to omit sections like the obituaries, display advertisements, or classified ads. The old technology couldn't handle these sections easily, and database size was a concern.

Now, the contents of the classified section can provide valuable intelligence. For example, the Internet has revolutionized the process of finding a job. Online classified ad sites are proliferating. Both individual newspaper sites and specialized sites that focus on employment ads are easily located and searched for job openings. One such site at www.careerpath.com, offers three options:

♦ Search employment ads of the nation's leading newspapers

♦ Search job postings gathered from leading employers' web sites

♦ Post a confidential resume

Sites like this help you deduce another company's plans. If you read between the lines, you may learn that there are new products in development, the company is somehow expanding or improving an existing product line or they have lost people with certain expertise.

Suppose another company plans to develop a new product that, if successful, will revolutionize the market for a given product. They must hire scientists, engineers or other highly specialized employees who will engage in the research and development of the product. Existing personnel may not have the necessary skills or may not be available for the assignment.

By monitoring the classified ads, you may discover that they are advertising for people with specific skills that are not required for their existing product line. Of course, further investigation is needed to confirm your suspicions, but classifieds can act as an "early warning system" that competitors are "up to something."

DejaNews, at www.deja.com**, offers a searchable database of jobs and resumes that have been posted on Usenet groups by potential employers and employees.**

Checking Out Legal Notices Required by Law

Legal notices are usually published to meet the requirements of state or federal laws and regulations. They frequently pertain to applications for, or renewals of, permits for undertaking activities that are regulated. Alcoholic beverage licenses, zoning and building permits, and environment-related activities, such as air and water discharge permits, are typical examples.

The law generally specifies where the public notice must be published, and any time-related requirements. You can turn this legal requirement into a means of detecting the activities of competitors. Monitor the "Legal Notices" or "Announcements" section of your local newspaper, or that of the county seat, and, depending upon your business, you'll likely learn something useful.

More and more newspapers are searchable via the Internet. Searching this way reduces that likelihood that you will overlook a legal notice that was "buried."

The excerpt below addresses an application for an alcoholic beverage license. A company applying for a new or renewed permit to serve alcohol would be obliged to place a legal notice in the appropriate newspaper, announcing that they have made such an application. This notice typically would appear under the heading "Notice by Applicant," "Announcement," or similar language.

PUBLIC NOTICES - Public Notice

Notice is hereby given in accordance with the provisions of the Texas Alcoholic Beverage Code that Restaurants Unlimited LLC dba Joe's Bar & Grill is applying for an application with the Texas Alcoholic Beverage Commission for a Mixed Beverage permit & Mixed Beverage Late Hours Permit to be located at 10000 Ranch Rd 999 South, City of Austin, County of Travis, Texas. John Smith Pres; Tom Jones Sec/Treas

---

Competitors or other interested parties (such as those living in of a nearby residential neighborhood) are thereby provided notice of the company's intention and may respond by contacting the appropriate government agency, or by taking measures to counteract the effect that this license may have on their own businesses if it is granted.

The Local Angle May Prove Useful

As seen through the eyes of the local population, an incident might appear quite differently than it would in the national or international press. Local reporters have their eyes and ears on the pulse of the community and report incidents from the local perspective.

Whenever I go back to the small town in the Northeast where I was raised, I immediately go through the past week's issues of the local newspaper. Within a few minutes I am familiar with the latest "hot" issues before the City Council, state or regional topics of interest, what's going on at the high school, marriages, deaths and even how many people were discharged from the local hospital on a certain day.

Now I am ready to interact with family and old friends. I know about upcoming events of interest, and am aware of what topics, such as layoffs or planned tax increases, should NOT be discussed in certain circles. By reading the local newspaper, I see these events through the eyes of the local population, which may have a different perspective than lawmakers in the state capital or in Washington, DC. I also will find more details. I discover "who said what" during a City Council meeting, which helps me determine which side of an issue various Council members stand. This level of detail would not be found in the much larger newspaper published eighteen miles away, even though it covers news from my hometown.

Remember to check the LOCAL media closest to where an incident occurs. Lots of useful details, which didn't make it to the newswires or major newspapers, may appear there. The local story may also take a different slant, which can be essential to getting the full "picture."

Viewing news through the eyes of the local reporter is important when gathering business intelligence, too, since many stories never make it to the national newswires. Consider an unfortunate incident such as an explosion at an industrial plant. Even if this event is not significant enough to be picked up by national or international news outlets, it will probably be a front-page story in the local newspaper. Also, the local paper or trade press may add details that were omitted by writers for the newswires or the local bureaus of large regional newspapers.

The number of employees displaced by the incident may not be significant to the nation, but this information could have a significant impact on the local economy.

Dozens or even hundreds of people may be out of work for an extended period of time, and their buying power may be reduced. Restaurants near the plant, where workers create busy lunch or after-work business, may notice a significant reduction in gross sales.

The implications in this information are well understood by the company's competitors. Supply and demand for the plant's products, and ultimately, the market price for the commodity, may be affected. To meet its obligations to supply customers, the affected producer will now have to purchase the product in question on the open market. This situation could continue for months, depending upon the severity of damage to the plant.

Competitors, meanwhile, have the opportunity to charge higher prices for their products, and may find this to be an opportune time to try to increase their market share offering "deals" to the clients of the affected producer.

For assistance in determining the availability of local newspapers on the Internet, examine the *NewsDirectory: Newspapers and Media* site – www.newsdirectory.com. Here you will find a list of hotlinks to states in the US. The individual state pages are arranged according to telephone area code, making it possible to search newspapers with which you weren't familiar, but which are located in nearby cities. Many other excellent web sites are included in Bookmarks & Favorites in Part IV under the heading "News Sites."

Read Foreign Newspapers in Their Original Language

If at all possible, it is advisable to read newspapers or newswire stories in the language in which they were written. That suggestion might have resulted in hoots of laughter just a few years ago, due to the dearth of availability of foreign newspapers. But now, it is possible to obtain publications from faraway places in a relatively timely fashion.

Keeping up with happenings in a place where one does business or plans to do so is a sound practice. This strategy has saved many a businessperson from embarrassing situations that would have been caused by ignorance of another culture. But equally important, foreign research can provide hints of political and social unrest or other factors that can cost your company millions, or make the company look like a hero.

When using translations, there is always the concern that some nuance may have been lost or a word misinterpreted by the translator. It is commonly said that the so-called "English language versions" of important non-English publications are not strict translations of what was originally published. Be that as it may, using them as one information source is probably better than ignoring them. If it is *really* important, pay for a translation from a second source and compare the results. One major corporation indicates that they willingly pay for a third translation if the first two don't appear to agree.

Thankfully, there is increasing awareness of the importance of searching in a variety of languages. Two good sources for reading in the original language of publication are ISI Emerging Markets, at www.securities.com and Reuters

Business Briefs, at www.briefing.reuters.com. The ISI Emerging Market product provides full text of publications from dozens of cities and regions in countries on several continents. Publications are available in the language in which they were written. If the publisher makes a translated version available, this is also searchable on the web site. ISI also provides an e-mail newsletter for subscribers. (The Reuters service is discussed in more detail later on in this chapter.) A sampling of publications available on the ISI site, which offers thirty-day free trials, is shown below:

Representative information providers

In addition to international sources such as the Economist Intelligence Unit and BBC Worldwide Monitoring, ISI Emerging Markets publishes locally generated news, company, industry and financial data.
These are some of the more than 600 local sources available to ISI Emerging Markets subscribers:

Brazil	**Czech Republic**	**India**
Gazeta Mercantil	Czech News Agency	CMIE
CVM	Fleet Sheet	India Today
Austin Asis	Albertina Data Press Monitor	The Economic Times

ISI Emerging Markets provides access to publications from far-flung parts of the world that might otherwise be difficult to obtain.

Sections of large services like LEXIS-NEXIS are devoted to publications from Europe or Asia, many of which are available in multiple languages.

One of the newest entries into this market is the Dow Jones Web Center at www.djnr.com. The Dow Jones Web Center indexes a selection of web sites up to three times daily to gather the most recent information available. Searchers can use English, Dutch, French, German, Italian, Japanese, Portuguese, Russian and Spanish to perform searches of sites from around the world both with English and without English-language content. Searches can be performed against a single site at a time, selected categories of sites, or from the entire collection available. However, you must be a Dow Jones Interactive subscriber to use the service.

Newstrawler, at www.newstrawler.com, contains dozens of news publications in English and other languages, plus information from broadcast outlets, DejaNews (mentioned earlier) and other searchable information sites. You simply check off the titles to be included in your search. It is even possible to search ALL titles. Some documents from Newstrawler are free, while some incur small charges.

A more recent entry into the ranks of newspaper collecting sites is an Australian site called WebWombat at <u>http://www2.webwombat.com.au</u>, which has collected a whopping 3400 newspaper sites from across the world. A country-by-country list of hotlinks is provided with direct access to a state-by-state list of hotlinks for the United States. See "News Sites" in the Bookmarks & Favorites section of Part IV for many other news sites.

The important thing to remember when searching news publications is that while an online service may have a huge collection of titles, no one service includes everything. It is important to identify the key publications for a particular market or subject area, and make sure that they are included in whatever online service or services you choose.

A Word about the News Wires

You may assume that since wire services supply news to the press, you will automatically pick up the newswire stories by searching the newspapers. Not all stories filed by wire service bureaus are actually printed in newspapers, however, for at least two reasons:

1. Wire stories may take a backseat to local news stories, which will sell more newspapers.

2. The newswire "story" may be a press release sent out by a commercial service like PR Newswire or Businesswire. These organizations send to the newsroom press releases issued by companies to introduce new products or services, announce changes in executives, or to share other news that the company wishes to announce. The newspapers generally use some, but not all of these stories, depending upon space available and upon perceived interest by readers.

By searching a newswire's database you may find that a story was actually filed several times, as in the example below from AP News, File 258 on the DIALOG service (which includes stories dated as far back as July 1984):

```
DIALOG(R)File 258:AP News Jul
(c) 1998 Associated Press. All rts. reserv.

04495716 0318
Computer Associates drops $9.2 billion pursuit of Computer
Sciences
BY: ERIC R. QUINONES
DATELINE: NEW YORK  PRIORITY: Rush   WORD COUNT: 0691
THE ASSOCIATED PRESS  DATE: March  05, 1998  17:24 EST

04495692 0299
Computer Associates drops $9.2 billion pursuit of Computer
Sciences
BY: ERIC R. QUINONES
DATELINE: NEW YORK  PRIORITY: Rush   WORD COUNT: 0701
THE ASSOCIATED PRESS   DATE: March  05, 1998 16:53 EST

04495547 0173
Computer Associates backs off $9.2 billion pursuit of
Computer Sciences
BY: ERIC R. QUINONES
DATELINE: NEW YORK  PRIORITY: Rush   WORD COUNT: 0654
THE ASSOCIATED PRESS   DATE: March  05, 1998 14:25 EST
```

As reporters gather more and more information on a story, they may send corrections or additional detail in successive filings. Some of these may have arrived too late to meet the newspapers' deadlines, but they should be retrieved and examined for additional valuable intelligence.

Major newswire services like Associated Press (http://wire.ap.org) and Reuters (www.reuters.com/news/index.html) have searchable web sites. For wider coverage, at least fifteen newswire archives, from Africa, Asia, and North and South America, are available on DIALOG. While the depth of these files varies, the vendor documentation usually lists inclusive dates. The LEXIS-NEXIS service's "WIRES file" allows simultaneous searching across newswires, combining them with industry-specific services. In the fourth quarter of 1998 both LEXIS-NEXIS and Dow Jones Interactive announced the addition of searchable Associated Press *state* newswires.

Searching the Broadcast Media

Only a few years ago, it was nearly impossible to track what was being said in the electronic media. At the end of some TV shows an announcer would remind us that "For a transcript of this show, call the telephone number on your screen . . . etc," while an 800 number appeared. Listeners to public radio outlets such as National Public Radio (NPR) couldn't count the number of times they were offered taped transcripts of their favorite broadcasts. Unless you were watching or listening, and happened to jot down the ordering information, getting transcripts was not always easy.

Recently, commercial online services such as Dow Jones News/Retrieval or LEXIS-NEXIS have built searchable, full-text, electronic collections of radio and TV transcripts. These can be searched individually if you know the name of a particular program. They can also be searched globally, so that you can search for all references to a word or phrase, from dozens of broadcast sources covering a long or short period of time.

Both CNNfn, at www.cnn.com, and CNBC, at www.cnbc.com provide links to sources for transcripts of their programming. Burrelle's, a subscription service at www.burrelles.com, may be a familiar name to someone in your organization who has used their clipping services. Their offerings have expanded to include transcripts, on-demand research, and other custom services.

If you prefer to be proactive, you can subscribe to an ongoing monitoring service, such as those provided by Video Monitoring Service, www.vidmon.com. The majority of their clientele are public relations firms, advertising agencies and marketing departments, but their services can, of course, be used to monitor broadcasts for a variety of other reasons. VMS records 80,000 hours of broadcast news in over 100 top national markets every month. Provide them with date, time, station and topic and they can supply transcripts and individual videotapes. They also maintain a library of over 1 million television commercials. A search of these, for instance, could be useful to your company's Marketing Department in determining the strategies used by competitors in various markets.

In the UK, Financial Times Electronic Publishing's Broadcast Monitoring Company, at www.ftep.ft.com/bmc.htm monitors broadcast and print media in the UK, Europe, and worldwide, tracking events, brands, markets, companies, and people. The range of services includes these:

♦ UK Broadcast

♦ UK Press

♦ International Press

♦ International Broadcast

♦ Sponsorship and Media

♦ Broadcast & Press Evaluation of Exposure

For tracking competitors' activities in the international marketplace, this may prove to be a useful service.

Another approach using a commercial source would be to use a specialty vendor like Burrelle's, mentioned previously for its transcripts. Burrelle's also offers custom clip services and broadcast monitoring. Your public relations department may be interested in another Burrelle's service that helps measure the effectiveness of their efforts. Their Newsclip Analysis service evaluates press clippings with respect to such attributes as article type, and size, advertising equivalence, editorial slant, circulation and impressions, content and number of key word mentions.

Current awareness is also possible using some special Internet tools. Company Sleuth, at www.companysleuth.com, includes news stories as one category of information provided each day on companies you select. You can also monitor competitors'web sites. Chapter 11 describes a service that sends you e-mail every time specified sites or pages change.

Trade & Industry Publications

Every industry has a group of magazines, journals, newsletters and directories that are devoted to that industry. The contents of some of these publications may seem very "dry" to outsiders, but they are invaluable resources for those within the industry.

Staff members who industry insiders monitor trends, report on news in the industry and generally keep up with intelligence regarding the industry. Some trade publications also report "hot" rumors in the field that may warrant independent verification. Browsing through a few issues of such specialized periodicals is a good way to get an "instant education" on some of the basic subject matter, terminology and key players in the industry as well as the names of companies that are suppliers to the industry.

Competitors' activities, plans and strategies may be more easily ascertained in this literature than by searching mainstream news sources, because trade publications focus on details of interest primarily to the industry that they cover. In other words, trade articles are likely to be much more in-depth and informative than what would usually be found in your local paper, or even in a nationwide business newspaper.

The trade press is also a good place to identify and track the careers of executives. It may be possible to follow their employment path as they move up the corporate ladder, or from one company to another. This information may be useful to your organization's recruiters, in both identifying promising candidates for a position they wish to fill and for verification purposes.

How can you identify the trade literature for a given subject or industry? Professional searchers turn to *Fulltext Sources Online*, mentioned previously in Chapter 2. *FSO*'s Subject Index uses approximately fifty topics to organize the thousands of titles under appropriate and useful headings. The list of titles can be long under categories such as Banking/Finance/Accounting, but it's a simple job to browse the list and select titles that suit your purpose.

Some trade journals publish what are known as "special issues." These issues focus on a particular topic such as salary surveys, reviews and forecasts, lists of the "Top 100 Something-Or-Others," etc. They traditionally appear during the same month every year and are often retained by subscribers for future reference. This information is often offered in electronic format if the magazine or journal is available online in full text.

Trip Wyckoff's *Directory of Business Periodical Special Issues* is the place to go when you need to identify sources for such information. The subject index points to each publication that offers a special issue on your topic of interest. See Appendix E in Section IV for further information. See also Appendix C for lists of periodicals containing trends, forecasts, and other crucial intelligence.

Chapter 7

Deeper Sources

Off The Beaten Track

There are a number of treasure troves that may not come to mind when you think about searching for business intelligence. The Sales and Marketing Department may not think to use a source that the Human Resources Department uses frequently. Human Resources may not have discovered a source that is a basic tool for those in the Research and Development Department, and so on. Survey the different departments of your company. Find out what sources each department uses and compare. New sources may be discovered, increasing the efficiency and knowledge base for your company.

It is important to recognize that intelligence may be found in a variety of places. If you have searched in vain in the usual sources, try a fresh approach.

▬▬ Trade Associations

For nearly every cause and industry, there is some sort of association or organization. They promote and/or represent the industry or cause for which they were formed. Typically, trade associations collect data from their member companies, compile statistics and keep track of trends in the industry. As such, these organizations can be a source of intelligence.

Identifying the associations that represent a particular industry or market sector of interest is the first step toward using this resource. Once identified, it is possible to obtain the valuable data that these groups gather and disseminate.

Gale Research's *Encyclopedia of Associations* has long been a standard reference tool for identifying trade associations or other nonprofit membership organizations in the US as well as internationally. The Encyclopedia can be searched on DIALOG through an electronic service from the publisher, called *Associations Unlimited* at www.gale.com/gale/galenet/galenet.html. The print version is often available at libraries. Subscription-based *Associations Unlimited* combines the Encyclopedia of Associations with a database of additional nonprofit organizations, making it a sizeable resource of 440,000 records. *Associations Unlimited* covers US national, regional, state and local, nonprofit membership organizations in all fields, including US 501(c) nonprofit organizations.

Several good sites on the Internet can be used as alternatives to the *Encyclopedia of Associations*, but these alternatives are not as comprehensive. The American Society of Association Executives (ASAE) web site, located on the Web at `www.asaenet.org/Gateway/OnlineAssocSlist.html`, offers a searchable database that will allow you to identify associations using a keyword search. Here is what the screen looks like:

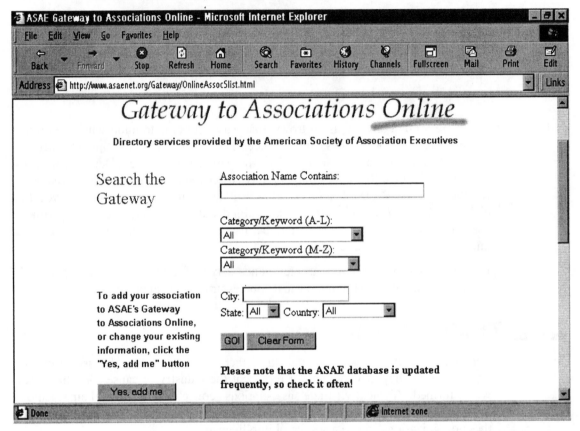

A database on the ASAE site retrieves documents of interest to executives of nonprofit organizations and associations. For industry-specific data, however, there is now a searchable database available where trade association resources can be obtained.

Obtaining Trade Association Documents

A relatively new online gold mine, called Industry Insider: The Trade Association Database, is now available from Investext at `www.investext.com`. The database contains documents from more than 175 associations, covering more than 50 industries worldwide. The records contain benchmark data, statistics and forecasts that have been compiled by industry experts. This information can be extremely useful as you analyze an industry, examine your company's market share against industry figures and learn what the experts are predicting for the next five years.

Some associations now have prepared information packages that cover "everything" they have on the industry, and they routinely send these information packages to those who inquire.

Several years ago, a client called my company to request research on the dry cleaning industry. We identified a particular trade association and called them, explaining what information we needed. The voice at the other end of the telephone line said, "I have about five pounds of paper on the subject. It will cost you $50.00."

We sent a check immediately, and in a few days our package arrived. We located the necessary statistics, prepared the report for the client, and provided them with the remaining material as an "appendix" of additional intelligence on the industry. The client couldn't believe that we had gathered so much useful data in such a short time. And the price was right!

Industry Watchers & Activist Groups

Industry watchers and activist groups have an agenda or cause as a reason for their existence. In the process of researching an issue, they may compile a great deal of material that can be useful to researchers outside of their organizations. You can capitalize on that fact by knowing that this material exists in cyberspace and going after it! But be careful – remember that the material that you retrieve may be biased.

Watching Executive Compensation

Executive compensation is a subject that may be researched for a variety of reasons. A company may wish to retain valuable employees by compensating them in line with or above the industry standard. In order to do so, the company must ask, "What is the industry standard?" By looking in the proxy statements of publicly traded companies in their industry, the company will find the information sought.

One useful tool for this purpose might be the Executive Compensation Plan Documents CD-ROM created by Global Securities Information, at www.gsionline.com/products/execcomp.html. In addition, the DIALOG service offers these databases devoted to proxy statements:

♦ EDGARPLUS - PROXY STATEMENTS (File 780)

♦ SEC ONLINE - PROXY REPORTS (File 544)

If you need a free source for proxy statements or help on how to use them, one handy source is found in Executive Paywatch, at www.paywatch.org. Click on "New CEO Pay Data," followed by "The CEO and You" to reach a database for locating the CEO's total 1997 compensation for 417 of Standard & Poor's S&P 500 companies. Along the way you will notice icons with labels like "Runaway CEO Pay" and "What You Can Do," which express the point of view of the organization that created this web site. You've already been warned about bias, but since this material comes straight from SEC filings, you are not in jeopardy.

For companies not included in their own searchable database, Paywatch recommends that you refer to the company's proxy statement, found at the US government's EDGAR site, at `www.sec.gov/edaux/wedgar.htm`.

Paywatch provides detailed step-by-step instructions for pointing your browser to the EDGAR site, selecting the Definitive Proxy Statement, performing searches on companies, and obtaining the past several years' proxy statements. Paywatch even mentions that the compensation data is likely to be found at the middle or end of the document. The instructions include a link to a worksheet for compiling a report on CEO salary data, using various tables that are part of the Proxy Statement.

Another Paywatch hotlink takes you to the *Fortune Magazine* web site that contains detailed information on the Top 1000 companies. You are instructed to download the *Fortune* database to get data and rankings on company revenues, profits, total shareholder return, and other financial indicators, to determine is the CEO's package is in line with the company's performance in the market.

What was the organization that undertook the labor needed to create the Paywatch site? You guessed it — a labor union. The AFL-CIO has provided a resource intended for use by union members, but which also can be useful to Management.

Tracking Competitors' Donations

Politics and politicians are frequent targets for interest groups. The Center for Responsive Politics offers *The Do-It-Yourself Congressional Investigation Kit*, at `www.crp.org/diykit`, subtitled *A Consumer Guide to Who's Giving the Money, Who's Getting It, and How It Affects Your Pocketbook*. Sites like this can be useful for more than what their names would indicate.

Specific issues, Political Action Committee (PAC) money, and Congressional votes are addressed individually via hotlinks provided on the homepage. An interesting collection of data can be gathered here using the site's databases:

♦ Contributions reported to the Federal Election Commission are grouped by an Interest Group Category

♦ Political Action Committees, Lobbyists or Incumbent Campaign Finance Profiles

♦ Individuals' gifts searchable by name, ZIP Code, occupation/employer, or candidate

♦ Soft money contributions of $100,000 or more

♦ Congressional travel

Data gathered to prove this watchdog group's point of view may provide your organization with valuable facts and figures. Your Government Relations Department or Law Department, for example, may monitor what is being said about the industry. Pending legislation could be of interest to your Marketing

Department, since it could affect your company's sales or those of your competitors. These departments might also be interested in issues that will impact your industry indirectly, by affecting your customers or suppliers.

The Center for Responsive Politics monitors a number of major US industries. Whether you agree or disagree with their findings connected with a given industry, it is useful to know what is being said. Their site could contain references to pertinent documents, reports, or other useful material. Here is a list of the industries which CRP monitors:

Health Care	ATM Fees
Gambling	Environment
Drunk Driving	Food Safety
Drug Safety	B2 Bomber
Phone Rates	Gun Control
Sugar Subsidies	Airline Ticket Prices
Peanut Subsidies	Smoking
Cable TV Rates	Credit Card Debt

Determining Who's Polluting the Environment

Since the Federal government requires disclosure of emissions data, it is possible to take a look at what's coming out of the stacks or otherwise being disposed of over at Competitor X's plant — or all of X's plants, for that matter. Scorecard, at www.scorecard.org, is an environmental information service provided by the Environmental Defense Fund. Hazardous air pollutants, criteria air pollutants (these include carbon monoxide, lead, nitrogen dioxide, ozone, particulate matter and sulfur dioxide), chemical releases from manufacturing facilities, and animal waste from factory farms are among the items tracked at this site.

By clicking on a state map or entering the name of company in a search box dubbed the "polluter locator", you can retrieve "the dirt" about the emission of these materials. The Toxic Release Inventory of chemicals emitted from manufacturing plants, gas stations, etc. is all there, chemical by chemical, in pounds. By examining these figures, your company's scientists and engineers may gain valuable intelligence regarding what goes on behind those closed doors at Company X, unless the site produces a number of different products.

See Chapter 11 for useful sites on the Internet where activist groups and their corresponding interests are identified.

Conference Proceedings

Papers delivered at conferences are an important and often overlooked source of valuable intelligence. They may discuss research in progress.

How to Use Them

Here are a few ways in which you can use information found in conference papers to accomplish tasks that may be crucial to your company's success:

Spot Patterns & Trends in the Industry

The same topics may appear in the proceedings of an annual conference for several years in a row. Based on this fact, you can make some logical assumptions. The subject matter is of interest to practitioners in the field, who attend this conference. Apparently, there is sustained or growing interest, since the topic is discussed again and again, perhaps in greater detail or from various perspectives.

Twenty years ago, a topic such as online information retrieval may have been addressed for an hour or two in a panel discussion with a title such as "The Company of the Future: Will the Computer Replace the File Cabinet?" A search of recent conference proceedings indicates that there are now entire three-day programs dedicated to the subject, complete with dozens of presenters and crammed exhibit halls.

Let the competition tell you what they're up to

Industry conference proceedings usually include speakers' names, affiliations and the text of the papers that they presented. Speakers often share new things they've learned, brag about how well they do something at their company or show how knowledgeable they are on a topic.

By searching on a competitor company's name and locating papers presented by their employees, you may gain valuable insights into what is going on in their labs, planning departments or other facilities. At the very least, this information may help to validate information or conclusions reached using other research methods.

Identify Experts

For recruiting purposes or for other reasons, you may wish to identify individuals with a certain expertise. Conference speakers present papers about new discoveries or other interesting information to their peers in a given profession. A person whose name appears again and again in such proceedings may be considered by some to be an expert in the field, and, therefore, worth recruiting.

Learn Names of Competitors' Employees

Your CI department may be gathering all data possible on a competitor. A search of recent conference proceedings may be useful for determining both job titles used in the competitor's organization and the names of the employees who fill those positions.

Locating Conference Proceedings Online

The two most comprehensive sources for searching across thousands of proceedings, covering dozens of subjects, are available on DIALOG. *Conference Papers Index*, File 77, and the British Library Document Supply Centre's *Inside Conferences*, File 65, contain hundreds of thousands of citations and references to conference papers. If all you want are names of presenters and an affiliation, using these resources allows you to do some of the sleuthing described above without actually reading the scientific or technical papers.

Another approach to locating conference material is to search industry or profession-specific databases that will contain conference papers along with other types of articles or documents on the subject. Even though some of these databases may contain only summaries of documents, they serve a useful purpose by *identifying* conference papers. You've quickly found out what's been written or said, and by whom.

Identifying conference papers without bothering to read the full text of what is retrieved would not be recommended for some purposes. For noting names and affiliations, however, or for tracking the frequency with which a name appears, an abstract of the paper may be sufficient.

Getting Your Hands on the Real Thing

Having located references to conference papers, the fun begins! If you need to read the full text of the conference papers, try a large research library, such as those on university campuses or in large cities. But first it may be worthwhile to stalk your prey in cyberspace. Many associations now publish their annual conference proceedings on their web sites. To find these, try a site like that of the American Society of Association Executives, at <u>www.asaenet.org</u>. You could also search the name of the association using one of the web search engines. You are very likely to locate some of the more recent material online, on the personal web site of a speaker or even on a company site.

Identifying Conferences & Tradeshows

For familiar industries or professions, you probably know the names of the important annual conferences or tradeshows. If you tried to create a comprehensive list of these events, however, you would probably be amazed, at the length and breadth of the list. Several Internet sites provide searchable databases that will be useful in your quest. Consult under the heading "Conferences/Tradeshows" in the Bookmarks & Favorites in Part IV.

Companies or services tend to announce new products at conferences or trade shows. Consult the trade press that covers the relevant industry to locate news on your competitors' offerings. Look on their web sites for press releases, and other announcements as well.

Scientific & Technical Documents

There is no underestimating the role that science and technology plays in the business of many companies. Engineers work with codes, specifications and standards. In manufacturing companies, the Research and Development Department creates inventions and better ways to do things. Everyone uses computer systems and networks put together by the Information Technology Department.

Obtaining the right information at the right time while this building, creating, or assembling is going on is crucial to getting ahead and staying ahead of the competition. Much of the necessary material is now available in electronic format, just waiting to be accessed.

Industry-specific databases abound, both on the Internet and through commercial services. Librarians know that if you name an area of science or technology, there is probably an entire database on the subject available on DIALOG, DataStar, Questel-Orbit, Ovid and other commercial online services, most of which maintain searchable web sites for subscribers.

Many of the organizations responsible for the codes and standards used in industry have web sites where you can keep up with new developments, order documents, and learn about educational opportunities. The American Society of Mechanical Engineers (ASME) ASMENET site at www.asme.org and The American Society For Testing and Materials (ASTM) at www.astm.org are two possibilities. Trade associations like the American Petroleum Institute (API) at www.api.org are also a good possibility.

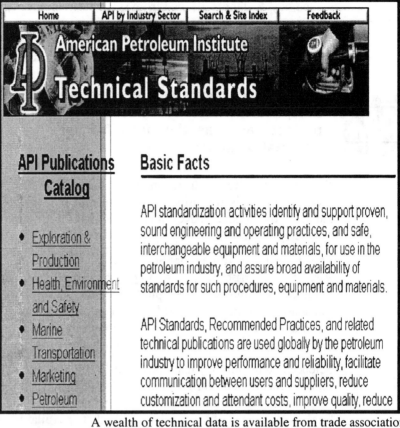

A wealth of technical data is available from trade associations,
such as the American Petroleum Institute.

**Not everything you find on the Internet should be trusted.
Always be certain that the sci/tech documents that you use are
authentic and up-to-date. Rely on recognized professional
societies, reliable document delivery companies or government
sites for obtaining them.**

Government agencies from several countries also are good sources for scientific
and technical documents.

The *National Technical Information Service (NTIS)* is a US government-related
organization that many searchers have depended on for years. It now has its own
searchable system at 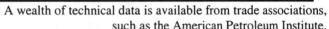www.ntis.gov/search.htm, earches the entire NTIS
web site, which contains references to 370,000 technical publications, data files,
CD-ROMs and audiovisual materials that have been collected within the last ten
years. US and non-US documents are available at reasonable prices.

Another service found through the NTIS site is Worldtec, at
http://worldtec.fedworld.gov, a subscription-based service which
offers time sensitive and retrospective information gathered from several dozen US
and non-US sources. Included are hundreds of business-related communications
from US embassies and international program offices. International science and

technology content is gleaned from speeches, seminars and workshops, internships, meetings and visits, articles, abstracts from newspapers, periodicals, and books. This extensive, in-depth collection consists of unclassified technology and scientific information briefs from Asia, Europe and US foreign missions.

NTIS subscriptions can be obtained for very brief periods of time, at low prices. You may choose to subscribe on a project-by-project basis, as the need for specific scientific or technical information arises.

The National Research Council of Canada, whose web site is located at www.nrc.ca, is the principal science and technology agency of the Canadian federal government. NRC fosters regional economic innovation through 16 research institutes located in eleven major centers across Canada.

The Canada Institute for Scientific and Technical Information (CISTI), at www.cisti.nrc.ca/cisti/cisti.html, is Canada's sci/tech and medical library, a leading scientific publisher and an information services provider in Canada and around the world. CISTI is an excellent place to start for ordering documents, searching databases, and obtaining various other services that will give you the competitive "edge" that your business needs in order to succeed.

Science and technology materials from Japan are available on the STN commercial service mentioned earlier. The Japan Science and Technology Corporation Information Center for Science and Technology (JICST) JICST-E database is an English-language subset of a larger file that is available only in Japanese. Machine translation is used to convert citations and abstracts in areas of medicine, biological sciences, chemistry and chemical engineering.

Another file, JICST-E Plus, contains the items mentioned above, plus non-indexed versions of records that will appear later in JICST-E. This source also includes coverage of more than 400 conferences not included in JICST-E. Searching here might provide a "heads up" that won't be apparent for several months in JICST-E. This could give your company an edge over competitors if you locate information that the competition doesn't know about.

Using Sci/Tech Can Win the Case!

Use of technical information isn't limited to the scientific community. Attorneys often use this type of material when trying to convince the judge or jury that their client should prevail.

A law firm represented a railroad that was sued by a driver whose vehicle was involved in an auto-train accident at a rail crossing. The driver claimed that there should have been a better warning system in place. The case was being heard before a jury in a county where it was said that juries traditionally found *against* the railroads in this type of case, granting generous awards to the plaintiffs. An attorney described the charges to the law firm librarian, expressing his desire to find some authority on warning signs.

The librarian thought of NTIS, and located a report that provided authoritative data involving the size of warning signs and distances at which they could be read satisfactorily. The information in that report was crucial to winning the case. When it was time for her next performance review, the librarian was praised for the work she had done and rewarded accordingly.

In a manner similar to the previous discussion of conference papers, scientific and technical documents or articles may be used to identify both individuals who have certain expertise and the academic institutions where research of a certain type may be taking place. If you wish to identify venture partners for scientific research projects that might have possible commercial applications, this information could be very useful toward achieving that goal.

Credit or Financial Reporting Services

The phrase "credit report" probably brings to mind names like Dun & Bradstreet, Experian or Trans Union; your company may have a direct-dial subscription to one of these services. Commercial credit report databases also are readily available on all of the major online systems, as well as on the Internet. These reports often contain more that just bill-paying information.

You may not need to check your competitors' credit, but what about learning about their collateral financial obligations? These appear in the commercial credit report under the category Public Records. You may turn up assets, such as real estate transactions, "UCCs," which are filings made under the state's Uniform Commercial Code, or adverse filings like lien records or tax liens. It's true that this information could be obtained using a public records online search, but this method can be a real time and labor saver. (Public records are explained further in Chapter 8.)

From time to time, you may spot other interesting tidbits of intelligence in commercial credit reports. A few years ago, our company worked on a CI project where one company was interested in possibly buying another. Attempts to retrieve data on the CEO of the target, a small privately held company, yielded minimal results. Retrieval of a company credit report was a "last resort." The report not only provided the company president's name, which was expected, but also the names of his alma mater and his previous employer! This background information helped our client to better understand how to approach that CEO. The leads found in the credit report helped create a successful research project out of what had looked rather bleak earlier in the day.

Other types of financial reports can be of great value in your search for business intelligence. The Dun & Bradstreet Business Information Report (BIR) can be retrieved on several of the major commercial online services, including DIALOG and Dow Jones Interactive. Professional searchers consider this report to be a basic tool for getting a concise picture of what's happening to a company. It is invaluable when researching privately held companies.

Included in the BIR, you will find detailed data regarding activities such as these:

- Special events (Earnings update, changes of officers, restructuring/reorganization, changes in Board of Directors)

- Payment summary

- Financial statement

- Cash flow

- Net worth

- Public filings (litigation, UCCs)

- Banking information

- History

- Business type

- Management background (individuals)

- Subsidiaries

- Import/export activity

A third financial report to consider is Dun & Bradstreet's Financial Profile. This is the most costly of the reports discussed here. It contains detailed financial information covering several years, and would assist your company's experts in analyzing a target company's financial strengths (or weaknesses).

Market Research Reports

Market research reports are compiled by a number of companies that make this material available both in print and via searchable databases. They have also licensed these files to major online vendors. Contents of the reports may be used to make decisions regarding new product development, sales and marketing strategies or other areas where the preferences of the buying public are important.

Entire market research reports are considered "expensive, but worth it," by those who use them. Costs may range from $1000 to $3000 each, if you purchase the print version. It is possible, however, that you don't need all of the data in the document. By accessing the reports online, you may be able to view the Tables of Contents and purchase only the pages that meet your needs, paying a fraction of the cost of the entire report! Some online services offer reports from Europe, Asia or Australia in addition to North America.

Perhaps, your company's Sales and Marketing Department is interested in consumer preferences for a product like disposable dishware. They are trying to make a decision regarding advertising: Should the emphasis in advertisements be placed on convenience (use and then throw away) or should the ads stress environmental issues (they can be recycled)? They would probably prefer to use the approach that is currently in favor with the consumers of the product, so they may try to find material that addresses the issue of convenience versus recycling.

Or perhaps the Research and Development Department is working on new product ideas. For example, has there been any research to determine whether the public has color preferences for soft drinks? Would a drink that was blue in color find a market? Would it please the beverage-buying public or would it bomb?

Are there, perhaps, cultural or language-related reasons why a product would be the new favorite in the marketplace in one country while a "dud" in another? Many people have heard the story of the General Motors company's experience years ago. Their product line included an automobile that was popular in the US, the Chevrolet Nova.

People familiar with astronomy might have interpreted the model name, Nova, as "star." But what about the Latin American market? In Spanish, Nova might be interpreted as "no va," which translates to "it doesn't go." Would you buy a car that doesn't "go"? This story illustrates the fact that market research studies contain useful background information in addition to something as specific as "Would you buy a blue soft drink?"

Two good places to find market research reports online are the DIALOG service, www.dialog.com and Investext's Research Bank Web at www.investext.com, which includes its MarkIntel service. MarkIntel offers access to market research from more than 70 sources worldwide. It is possible to purchase individual pages of your choice.

Both of these services require a subscription, but Investext offers a search-on-demand service for subscribers. This service will perform a search for you and charge accordingly, which is a convenience if you are in a hurry or short on staff.

Use a group file like DIALOG's MARKETFULL to search across the market research reports of multiple vendors simultaneously. This saves time and may turn up material that you would otherwise have missed.

A CI project from the Burwell Enterprises case files demonstrates the usefulness of market studies. A client wanted articles and other information regarding "interactive kiosks," including a list of vendors for the finished product, i.e. those companies that sold the electronic components already installed in the box or pedestal where the product was housed.

One of the most useful items retrieved was a report from Frost and Sullivan located using the DIALOG service. The abstract of the report pointed to data regarding trends and forecasts in the market for these kiosks, as well as a list of companies polled in the study itself. The client, who was familiar with Frost and Sullivan, was very pleased with the research.

A few hours later, during a visit to a neighborhood supermarket, three different interactive kiosks were spotted in the checkout area alone. Seeing these reinforced the idea that there must be a market for this product!

Be sure to look for *dates* on market studies that are located online. You probably want the most recent data that you can find, so don't waste money retrieving reports that are out of date, unless you want to observe the way that preferences have changed over time.

▬▬ Directories

Online directories are like lollipops. They come in all sizes, shapes, and colors. Many important business directories, such as Dun & Bradstreet products or the CorpTech Directory, have been available online or on CD-ROM for years. They are also available now on the Internet.

Frequent searchers know that, using these tools, they can enter keywords or an SIC code to locate companies producing or offering certain types of products or services. They also are accustomed to limiting results to a geographic area (all widget manufacturers in New York), if desired. They can even limit results to those companies with more than (or less than) X number of employees or with annual sales greater than (or less than) $Y million.

The CorpTech Directory specializes in high tech industries. Corptech's web site, at www.corptech.com, allows you to locate high tech products, view demographics within high tech industries and view projected employment trends geographically as well as by major product group, all at no charge. Subscribers get to see additional material.

Some directory databases, such as the many available from Dun & Bradstreet, have a financial perspective, providing varying amounts of data such as sales figures, credit history or even "complete financials," if your budget can afford the cost of the report. It is important to note that some sales figures are estimated (and are identified as such), and that much of the data is supplied by the subject company itself. Dun & Bradstreet products are available through most major online vendors, as well as directly from them, at www.dnb.com.

"Directory Assistance" Doesn't Always Come From the Phone Company

Directories are a key tool for gathering a great deal of business intelligence depending upon their focus. Here are a few examples of what you can learn from them:

Plant Locations

A plant need not be a large manufacturing site. Certain types of companies may have facilities where work takes place, but which are not truly branch offices. These locations may not show up in a Dun & Bradstreet file, but may appear in a directory such as the one shown in the example below, because mail is received at the site.

This type of online directory file may help you locate plant sites.

Some directories compile company data from a wide variety of sources, some of which may contain "old" information. Always search several sources and compare the results or compare the dates files were updated, if this data is available.

Corporate Family Relationships

A "tried and true" technique for identifying corporate affiliations when using Dun & Bradstreet databases is to look at the Duns Numbers. Dun & Bradstreet assigns a unique number to each company entry in its business databases like *Duns Market Identifiers*, File 516 on DIALOG. In addition to a Duns Number, a company record may show specific numbers for retrieving Duns Corporate Number, Duns Parent Number, and Duns Headquarters Number. Searching on one of these numbers could turn up a holding company with a totally different name. In reverse, you could retrieve records for all affiliated companies by searching on the Duns number of the parent company.

The Directory of Corporate Affiliations, File 513 on DIALOG, a directory file produced by National Register Publishing Company, contains business profiles and corporate linkage for 114,000 public, private, and international companies worldwide. To gather even more intelligence, follow the trail up the corporate family tree to learn sales information, number of employees, names of directors and stock-related information, if applicable.

Descriptions of Products & Services

A Standard Industrial Classification (SIC) number is not a great way to describe what a company does. The company's list of products or services may be much wider than that which is identified with a particular SIC number. In addition, the designated SIC number may be one of those extremely general designations such as "business services, nec" (not elsewhere classified).

To make matters even more complex, this is the age of the conglomerate. The "children" of the ultimate parent company may produce a wide variety of products or services that don't necessarily have a common thread. This means that each branch, subsidiary, or other corporate entity may be appropriately tagged with a different SIC code number than other members of the corporate family.

The North American Industry Classification System (NAICS) will provide much more specific categorization for businesses, and will cover many types of businesses not specifically included in the SIC system. NAICS is not entirely in use yet, however, some other measures should be considered when creating a list of companies in a specific field. Keyword searching a description of products and services may be a much better way to locate suppliers, create a list of competitors, or to see a clear picture of what a company really offers.

Using industry-specific directories, such as Ward's (www.wardsauto.com/companies), shown below, keyword searching with industry jargon will more quickly identify relevant companies than printing a long list from a directory like Yahoo! and scanning the brief description of each company in a general category.

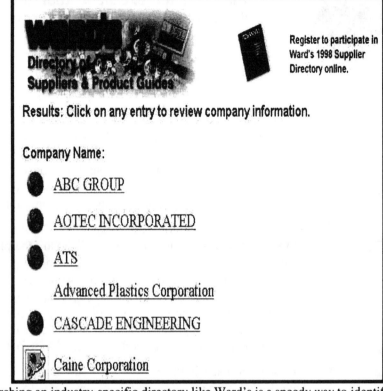

Searching an industry-specific directory like Ward's is a speedy way to identify suppliers of custom molded plastic parts to the automobile industry.

Advertising

You may be interested in how and where competitors spend their advertising budgets. *Advertiser & Agency Red Books: Advertisers*, DIALOG File 177, is a great source for this information. In addition to a great deal of detail about the company itself, its product lines and trade names, you'll learn which advertising agency it employs, the agency renewal month, approximate advertising expenditure last year and types of media used. For information on the CD-ROM version of the product, see www.redbooks.com/cd.htm.

Competitors' Service Providers

It is often very easy to learn what organizations a competitor company has retained for accounting services, legal counsel, etc. Dun & Bradstreet records, such as those in *Dun's Market Identifiers* mentioned previously, sometimes provide this information along with the name of the company's bank. In the case of very large corporations, this may be less than meaningful because various departments, subsidiaries or divisions may use the services of a number of such organizations. But for smaller companies, you may have located intelligence that will help you to make a decision or to avoid a conflict-of-interest situation.

Directories are an excellent tool for finding information on privately held companies, including some that are quite small.

For publicly traded companies, you may search filings as your primary research tool. Be sure to see the explanation of these filings in Appendix A in Section IV.

New Playing Field, New Game Plan

With the advent of the Internet, the list of possibilities for intelligence gathering has mushroomed, but the strategy has changed. Your company now has more resources available, and more options for choosing how to obtain the information they hold. Taking the direct route on the road to business success involves organization and planning, as well as implementation.

You can search an Internet directory like Yahoo! to identify competitors, possible suppliers or to answer questions like, "Who are the players in the (fill-in-the-blank) industry?" You'll retrieve a list of companies by category. You may be linked directly to company web sites. On other web sites, you may find a button that takes you to a product like Hoover's, www.hoovers.com, to retrieve company profiles containing the data you seek. Some of these types of sites even offer to compile lists of competitors, though these appear to be based on 4-digit SIC codes and may be a bit broad in their definition of "competitors."

Another approach is to search for a trade association in an industry, to see if they have linked a directory of member companies to their homepage. These also may be hot-linked to take you directly to the company's web site. It's important to check carefully, though. The list on the Internet may include only that portion of the association's membership that has web sites and *which want to be found*. Knowing that a company belongs to a certain association tells you something about their business or their interests. Some companies may not wish to broadcast all of their "connections."

When using an Internet search engine to locate directories on a topic, include "directory" as one of the keywords to be searched. Some engines allow you to require that this word be present in the search results by using a plus (+) sign. For example "+automotive +directory."

▬ Brokerage House Reports

The information in the reports created by analysts at securities firms and brokerage houses is invaluable for keeping up with or studying an industry or individual companies. You may be accustomed to telephoning a broker and requesting information, which is an economical way to tap into this expertise.

But what do you do when you're in a hurry? What if you need to compare the opinions of analysts from several different houses? How can you see if their opinions or predictions regarding a stock or an industry actually ring true months or a year after they were made?

The answer lies in searching the reports online. There are basically two good sources for analyst reports: Multexnet and Research Bank Web.

You can join Multexnet free, at www.multex.com. Their stock snapshots and consensus estimates are available free to members, and you can purchase reports at reasonable prices.

And what of the original company offering analyst reports online? They just got bigger and better. The Investext Group recently released the first upgrade to Research Bank Web at www.investext.com. The upgrade allows you to do keyword searches of thousands of reports and to buy individual pages in PDF format. Investext also offers industry studies that range from two pages upwards.

If you are a Dow Jones Interactive subscriber, at www.djnr.com, you can search and view tables of contents free, and purchase either Multex or Investext by the page. They're available on other major online services as well. The ability to tap into these high quality research products and buy pieces of them at reasonable prices makes them an invaluable resource in your arsenal of power tools.

Your CFO will know whether your competitor's CEO has met with any security analysts and should be able to provide reports resulting from the meeting. Now you'll know what your company is telling the financial world. You may be able to use the information in comparing your company with competitors or to evaluate the credibility of various analysts.

Political Risk Services

If you are considering doing business outside the US, you may need to educate yourself quickly about one or more countries. In this fast-changing world, laws, economic conditions, political and social factors contribute heavily to the potential success or failure of the undertaking. Calling the US Department of Commerce or the US Department of State will be of some help, but there are also sources in cyberspace that will prove to be very useful.

At the Economist Intelligence Unit (EIU) site, www.eiu.com, you can register free and use their archive of recent country-specific articles. These articles are current, and may be very useful.

For their subscription customers, EIU offers a variety of services, including country reports. These reports cover a general summary of events for the past quarter, political structure, economic structure, country outlook, an analysis of key political developments, and economic policies and trends, complete with statistical data. A list of their various reports can be found at www.eiu.com/catalogue/title/eiutit1.html.

Another web site to be looked at for this type of material is that of the PRS Group, at www.prsgroup.com. PRS provides political risk services in the form of country reports and forecasts covering 147 countries, market newsletters containing consumer demographic trends and analysis, and consulting services. Their various offerings can be purchased piecemeal and may be useful if you are getting acquainted with the subject.

It's not only the CIA that is interested in happenings in other countries. If your company imports, exports or otherwise does business in other countries, it may be in the company's best interests to know what's *really* going on there, and what is forecasted to happen in the forseeable future. There's nothing like having people on the scene for sensing political upheaval or similar activities and sending a warning!

Chapter 8

Public Records

A Business Intelligence Bonanza

Public Record vs. Public Information

Strictly defined, **public records** are "Those records maintained by government agencies that are open without restriction to public inspection, either by statute or by tradition." They are records of incidents or actions filed with a government agency for the purpose of notifying others.[4]

Public information is information furnished by people and businesses to contribute to the flow of business and personal communications. Your telephone number is an example of public information, unless you have made special arrangements to the contrary with your telephone company.

Some public records are also public information. An example might be the clearly posted sign found in some eating or drinking establishments, indicating maximum occupancy restrictions or the fact that this establishment is licensed to sell beer and wine. The law says that the business must have this type of license, and in posting the license or sign, the business is informing your that they meet this requirement.

There is a difference, however, between public record and public information. It is impossible to express a hard and fast rule about which is which. The fact is that access varies from state to state, county to county, depending upon the law. What is available in one place may not be available in another.

 When researching public record information in a new geographic area, always ask the "availability question." If necessary, consult your lawyer for an interpretation of the law.

Local custom can also play a role in the availability of information that, legally, is supposed to be available. Old records, which were never automated, may be stored in a sub-basement or down the street from the courthouse. These records may be unavailable — not for any legal reason, but because the courthouse is short of staff, for example. You are legally entitled to obtain these records, but doing so may

---

[4] *The Sourcebook of State Public Records*, BRB Publications, 1998, p. 2.

require asserting your rights, or using that strategy that works so well these days: "You'll hear from my lawyer tomorrow...."

There has been a growing awareness, over the past several years, of the value of using this data in the business decision-making process, as well as for tracking the activities of businesses or organizations. This is especially true when researching privately-held companies, about which it is often difficult to find accurate data.

You can avoid costly mistakes and gain a competitive advantage thanks to the increasing availability of this data in electronic format. If it's online, it doesn't matter if you are working late, on a weekend or during a government holiday — the "electronic courthouse" is open for business.

Using Public Records in Your CI Program

Whether part of a large company or on your own, you can use public record information in your business intelligence operation. The type of records used, and their application, depends upon their function. Here are a few possible applications:

Identifying corporate relationships

Official filings with the government can be used as your primary source when determining corporate parent-subsidiary relationships, or you may use this information to verify data obtained from other sources.

Certain public record filings, such as **Secretary of State Corporation** or **Limited Partnership** records, are especially important when researching privately held companies, where you can't just search for SEC documents as you can for publicly-traded companies.

Identifying affiliations of officers/directors of companies

Public records are a good source for linking people with companies. Using the major commercial online public record services, you can search by the name of an individual to learn all of their corporate affiliations in one state or across a group of states. Doing so sometimes turns up information that might otherwise have been overlooked, or which was not disclosed by the party in question.

Discovering adverse information

It's important to know the negatives and the positives when researching another company. Some public record filings appear in commercial credit reports, but under certain circumstances, it may be necessary to go to the "official" source (i.e. the government agency of origin) for information on liens, judgments or bankruptcies, as well as for possible pending litigation that could have a negative impact on the company or on its performance.

In certain cases, a judgment may have been satisfied or a lien released, but the information doesn't appear online. This is not, generally, the fault of the online vendor. Paperwork gets backlogged in many courthouses, and the release may not have been properly recorded. An on-site search will usually clear up such confusion.

Identifying and locating assets

Suppose you plan to sue a competitor. It's important to know whether they have enough assets to make the effort worthwhile. Asset information also can be useful if you are trying to determine the "value" of another company, in a merger or acquisition situation, or in litigation that is already underway.

Identifying the parties behind fictitious or assumed company names

Both the assumed or fictitious name and the responsible party will be included in the filing. Note that "fictitious" and "assumed" names are basically the same thing — the language varies from state to state.

Identifying a company's real property holdings

This information may be useful not only because real property is an asset, but also in long range planning and other strategy matters.

Depending upon your business or industry, you may think of other uses for public records. Knowing how to use the information is important — but knowing where to look is equally important.

"Where There Is Government, There Are Records"

From the highest to the lowest, all levels of government seem to collect records. Part of the skill involved in making use of these records is in knowing what information is collected at each of these levels, and then seeking it out. Public record vendors have done part of the work for us in this area, and have categorized the files nicely on menus or other types of lists.

Federal/Nationwide Level

Some public record databases are created from federal government data collected in all fifty states. Both government and commercial sources may be used to retrieve the records found in these files. Here are some examples of federal database contents:

Stock holdings

Searchable databases found on some commercial public record online services reflect stock-related transactions of officers, directors and significant shareholders in publicly traded companies. Combining search results with data found using other tools can yield a significant amount of information regarding a company's CEO, for example.

It's true that insider trading information can be found on the Internet, but some of those sites don't usually indicate the total number of shares held, as does KnowX, at www.knowx.com.

For one fee, KnowX lets you view up to 220 records in detail. The Information America online service, however, goes one step further. Searching the Stock Holdings file in IA reveals   This can reveal some other useful information that is not turned up by insider trading reports on the Internet — the names of additional companies with which a VIP's name may be connected.

> **EXAMPLE:** The typical insider trading record for John Smith, of Mega Corp. might show Mr. Smith's recent or past sales of Mega Corp. stock.

Searching Mr. Smith in the type of Stock Transactions database described above would show the recent insider trades you have already found on the Internet, but it would also show his stock transactions with **other companies where he is involved,** possibly as a director. Looking at such affiliations may provide some interesting insights into Mr. Smith's business connections, true wealth, and "pet causes."

Aircraft/watercraft ownership

These expensive items are considered assets. Identifying them can help complete a picture of a company's worth. The FAA and the Coast Guard update their files annually. Commercial sources like KnowX, CDB Infotek (www.cdb.com) or LEXIS Public Records, (www.lexis-nexis.com/ln.universe) have mounted the FAA and US Coast Guard tapes and created searchable databases for this purpose. For other aviation-related databases, check Bookmarks & Favorites in Part IV.

Bankruptcy

If a company has filed bankruptcy, the case file at the US Courthouse is usually considered public record. It contains significant detail about the organization's finances, assets, etc.

Some US Bankruptcy court records are currently searchable on the Internet free, but if a nationwide search is required, Merlin Information Services, at www.merlindata.com, may be a better source. Merlin has licensed a database containing seven years worth of bankruptcy records from across the US.

Lawsuits/Legal Opinions

Lawsuits are filed in courts at several levels of government. **The list of pending or past lawsuits provides a great deal of information about a company's history, legal problems and relationships.**

Some Federal courts have made their case records available via the Internet. Using a service called RACER. RACER provides records from the following courts:

AR	District – Eastern
AR	District – Western
ID	Bankruptcy
ID	District
NV	Bankruptcy
NC	Bankruptcy – Eastern – Raleigh Division
NC	Bankruptcy – Eastern – Wilson Division
NC	Bankruptcy – Middle
SD	District
WA	Bankruptcy – Eastern
WY	Bankruptcy

You must register to use these sites, but service is free. A warning is provided that indicates that there may be a small per-page charge at some time in the future.

In addition, some Federal courts have created their own online systems that provide Internet access. Those include:

AZ	Bankruptcy Court (limited data)
CA	Bankruptcy - Southern District
GA	Bankruptcy - Northern District
IN	District - Southern
KY	District – Western
MN	Bankruptcy
NC	Bankruptcy - Western
NY	Bankruptcy, Southern District
OH	Northern District
RI	Bankruptcy
VA	Bankruptcy – Eastern

PACER, the system that has for a number of years offered telephone dial-up access to court information, is gradually adding Internet access to some courts, but you must be a registered subscriber to PACER to gain access. See the Bookmarks & Favorites section of Part IV for URLs for the courts listed above. For a nationwide search of legal opinions, LEXIS-NEXIS or Westlaw are the online services most frequently used by the legal community.

OSHA Filings

These filings come from the US Department of Labor, Occupational Safety and Health Administration (OSHA). Searchable databases allow you to enter a business name and to retrieve records pertaining to that company.

Depending on the industry, this can be a useful tool for locating plant sites, learning about workforce size, and more. If you entered a keyword from the of a major chemical company, for example, you might identify a long list of plant sites where OSHA inspections had taken place. You can search OSHA files free at <u>www.osha.gov/cgi-bin/est/est1</u>. The information in the record would include the following:

> Business Name
>
> Address
>
> County
>
> Number of employees (at this location and nationally)
>
> Union Status (Union or non-Union)
>
> Detailed inspection information

Some public record vendors offer "nationwide" files. But read the fine print in their documentation. "Nationwide" may refer to searching the records of fifty states simultaneously, or merely those states where that vendor has access to the records. You can't assume that every state has been checked unless that is specified in the vendor's literature or on their web site.

State Level Public Records

The most frequently used state records for business applications, include these:

Corporation/Limited Partnership Records

In electronic format, Secretary of State incorporation or limited partnership records provide varying amounts of information, depending upon state law and which vendor is used.

You will usually find the corporate name, address, the names of officers and directors, as well as the Corporate Charter ID number. This number is the key to obtaining a copy of the charter from the Secretary of State's office. These documents are not available online, but may be worth obtaining manually for the extra information that they contain.

In addition, you may find Taxpayer ID Number, corporate family relationships and company assumed (fictitious) names. Inclusion of this information varies from vendor to vendor, and availability of the information varies from state to state.

Other records found at the Secretary of State's office include records for Limited Liability Companies; Assumed Name/Fictitious Name records (also available at the county level in some places); and Trademarks/Tradenames records. See Bookmarks & Favorites in Section IV for a lengthy list of these sites.

To obtain a company's corporate charter easily, search the incorporation record, obtain the company's Charter ID number, and order the document from your commercial online vendor's document retrieval service. As an alternative, find a public record retriever using www.brbpub.com, where names of retrievers can be found.

Tax records

This information is available for a few states, from commercial vendors or on a state's Internet site. Various types of state tax files are searchable. Texas, for instance, provides a searchable database of corporations that pay Franchise Tax to the state, while the state of Washington provides for searching records of companies that pay Sales Tax. Thirty-eight states will verify this information by telephone or mail.

Court documents

In the states listed below, State Court Administrators allow access to legal opinions via the Internet.

Alabama	Kentucky
Alaska	Maine
Arizona	South Carolina
Colorado	South Dakota
Florida	

For other states, state court documents are available at the County Courthouse.

Required filings with state agencies

Filings will vary, depending upon the industry involved. The important thing is to recognize that you can find state agency web sites and look for lists of forms that must be filed, or for searchable databases. Names of agencies that regulate certain industries will vary from state to state, sometimes can be puzzling. (For instance, the agency that regulates the petroleum industry in Texas is the Railroad Commission.)

Licenses

Dozens of types of businesses and professionals are required to be licensed. Licensing and certification may be managed by state agencies, professional associations, or trade associations. In California, a searchable database at `http://www2.cslb.ca.gov` allows you to check out contractors' license status. Florida, Kentucky, Massachusetts, and Vermont, among others, provide some type of online license searching.

The list below, from the state of Florida, is a good example of the types of businesses or professions that might be regulated by individual US states:

Accountant	Dentist
Acupuncturist	Deputy Pilot
Architect	Dietician/Nutritionist
Asbestos Consultant	Direct Disposer
Agent (Athletic, Talent)	Embalmer
Auctioneer	Employee Leasing
Audiologist	Engineer Business
Business Broker	Funeral Director
Chiropractor	Geologist
Cinerator Registration	Interior Designer
Contractors	Land Surveyor
Air Conditioning	Landscape Architect
Alarm	Naturopath
Building	Nursing Home Administrator
Drywall	Optometrist
Electrical	Osteopath
General	Pharmacist
Mechanical	Physician
Plumbing	Podiatrist
Pollutant Storage	Professional Engineer
Pool	Psychologist
Roofing	Real Estate
Sheet Metal	Social Worker
Specialty	Speech & Language Pathologist
Underground Utility	State Pilot
Counselors	Therapist
(Mental Health, Nutrition)	

Liens & Judgments

Lien records may be located at the state or county record levels. These would include liens filed by the Internal Revenue Service. You cannot make assumptions regarding where to find Federal tax lien records, however. In North Carolina, for example, Federal tax liens on businesses are available at the **state** level. For individual (personal) tax liens, however, you must go to the **county** courthouse. The best approach is to check an authoritative public records source like the *Public Record Research System,*[5] and let the public records experts sort it out for you.

UCC Filings

Uniform Commercial Code filings are evidence that a loan or lease has been made. UCC databases usually can be searched using the name of a debtor or creditor. Searching for a company name, may present valuable financial information, such as where the company has banking or financial relationships. The amount of the obligation will not appear, but by obtaining a number from the online record, you may request more detailed information. The majority of states make UCCs searchable at the state level. The major public record vendors provide access, but a number of states offer UCC searches at no charge. See Bookmarks & Favorites, Section IV, under the heading Public Records.

County or Local Levels

As automated records come closer to being the norm, rather than the exception, more and more county records are appearing on commercial public record services or on the Internet. The commercial services tend to seek out such records in the states or regions with the greatest population density or in what are known as the most "litigious" states.

The Corporate Information site at www.corporateinformation.com, includes a section called *Regional-based Sites* under its "US" hot link. This state-by-state listing includes many county public record sites, as well as some useful lists like "The Top 10 Private Companies in XXX County." This site is kept up-to-date and might be a good starting point when looking for county public record databases on the Internet.

Obtaining public records at the county level is more complex that at other levels because you must consider at least three different sources. To make matters even more complicated, in some states, such as Vermont, you must go to the township level, not to the county seat. In certain major metropolitan areas, you may find that the city controls certain records, rather than the county. Whether using commercial or free sources, consider looking at these records:

---

[5] BRB Publications, Tempe AZ, 1999

From the County Civil Courthouse

Court Records. Court dockets, documents and other lawsuit-related material from state courts may be viewed or photocopied at the local county courthouse, provided that you have the case number or cause number. Some jurisdictions have made court dockets available on their Internet sites.

Lawsuit records are sometimes referred to as the "defendant-plaintiff tables." These records are available on commercial public record services, for a growing number of counties. The Dallas-Fort Worth Metroplex in Texas, for example, is made up of four counties. To do a thorough search for lawsuits in the D-FW area, it would be important to include all four counties. The CDB Infotek service, found at www.cdb.com/public, makes this task much simpler. These files are important for at least three reasons:

◆ They generally point to *pending*, as well as past lawsuits.

◆ They cover the lower courts that are not routinely included in online case law services like LEXIS or Westlaw.

◆ Liens and judgments records are usually available at the county level, but as stated earlier in this chapter, it is best to determine how the various types of liens are handled in a particular state.

Probate, Family Court, Vital Records, & Voter Records are not generally available in cyberspace. The state of Kentucky, however, makes the Kentucky Vital Records Index available at http://ukcc.uky.edu/%7Evitalrec.

From the County Criminal Courthouse

Criminal or Arrest Records

Your Human Resources Department may routinely run background checks on job applicants for certain positions. In most areas of the US, these must be searched county-by-county. There are several vendors on the Internet that provide criminal record checks as part of other pre-employment screening services. You might take a look at Informus, at www.informus.com, or at Avert Inc., at www.avert.com.

From the County Recorder's Office

UCC Filings

UCC filings were described above, under the State Public Records heading. The majority of states make these records available at the state level, but in some places they may be found at the county level as well.

Real Property Transactions

Searching or monitoring real property transactions may provide advanced notice of a competitor's plans to expand a facility or build a new plant. The list of counties making this information available online is growing rapidly. See Dakota County,

Minnesota, at www.co.dakota.mn.us/depart/property/index.htm, for an example. In Maricopa County (Phoenix area) Arizona, at http://recorder.maricopa.gov/recdocdata, you can view the index of real property transactions, and view a scanned image of the actual document. It is also possible to order a certified copy, if that is called for. This is very likely the wave of the future, as scanning technology becomes available in more and more jurisdictions.

Tax Office Records

At the county level, tax office records are likely to include the real property records. Searching these records may provide evidence regarding the extent of a company's holdings or tax indebtedness. You may also obtain specific details regarding individual properties. Dozens of counties, from all over the country, are included in the Bookmarks & Favorites section of Part IV.

The County Tax Assessor — Your "New Best Friend"

The number of US county Tax Assessors that have loaded searchable databases on the Internet has skyrocketed over the past year or two. The Dallas County (TX) Central Appraisal District is a prime example of an organization that has done some of the CI Sleuth's work for you if plant information is what you need.

You might test this by entering part of the name of a major corporation headquartered in the Dallas area. For one such corporation, seven addresses for company facilities in Dallas County were located. The following categories of information are available for each property searched:

Property Location Data	Land Data
Valuation Data	Valuation Methods
Ownership Data	Taxing Jurisdictions
Legal Description	Exemption Data
Main Improvement Data	Property History

The most significant finding was listed under the following heading:

SKETCH OF THE BUILDING, INCLUDING DIMENSIONS

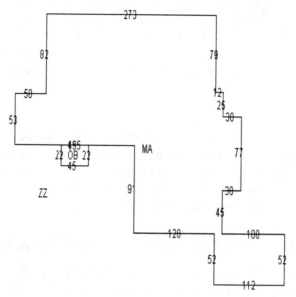

Drawing Copyright 1998, by TaxNet USA, Inc.

The inclusion of a drawing or the blueprints of the building has some interesting implications for several departments in your company. The information about plant size may be an indication of plant capacity and other manufacturing data.

HOT TIP

Not every commercial vendor offers all of the file types and services described here. It is important to ask vendors specific questions about their offerings, to be sure that they provide what you are looking for. You may find it worthwhile to use the services of several different vendors in addition to "free" files.

Options Abound, But Be Careful!

More and more government offices and agencies are making their databases searchable on the Internet. At least 32 states are among those providing a variety of records, both civil and criminal. However, the greatest amount of public record information in cyberspace is provided by commercial online services of various types. **It is extremely important, when using public records on the Internet, to choose a reputable source.** Web sites can come and go on a moment's notice, so it is crucial that you use a vendor that is a known entity, with a good track record.

Several years ago, before many of the current Internet public record vendors had mounted web sites, a search of the World Wide Web turned up a reference to a page offering public records. The "service" offered a list of record types, and made certain vague promises. They wanted a credit card number in advance, of course, and provided an e-mail order form, but crucial information seemed to be missing.

An e-mail message was sent requesting this public record vendor's company name and location. Several days later a reply arrived:

"We don't give out that type of information."

If you are going to do business with a company, you have a right to know who they are and where they are located. This organization aroused suspicion. Several months later, the site was no longer available. The moral of this story is "Caveat vendor."

Accessing Public Record Online Services

Public record services are available both on the Internet and in traditional dial-up mode. Many long-time subscribers to these services prefer dial-up access for security reasons, while others simply resist changing to the Internet while believing that, "If it's not broken, don't fix it." Still others realize that certain large Internet public records services frequently seem to have one or more files "temporarily unavailable." At other times, the telephone connection fails.

The major vendors have continued to support their proprietary software in addition to mounting Internet sites. For heavy use, this approach is definitely recommended.

Additional Services May Be Called For

Finding a record online may not be sufficient for your needs. You may need additional services from time to time. The vendor should be able to provide additional services that complement the public record search. Watch for these:

Document Retrieval

The online public record may provide an identifying number that points to a document that is available in full text only at the source, e.g. at a courthouse, the Tax Assessor's Office, etc. If the vendor offers document retrieval, you can request a copy of the full document, placing your order while at the vendor's web site or while connected to their service via dial-up. A few additional screens must be filled in to provide instructions regarding shipping method desired, address, etc.

The vendor retains correspondents, sometimes referred to as "runners," in county seats or state capitals. When your request is received electronically, the vendor contacts the runner, who is familiar with local facilities and procedures. The runner obtains the document and sends it directly to you, adhering to the delivery instructions specified.

The cost for all of this work appears in your next monthly bill. You should expect to pay for three services:

♦ The online record search, which compensates the vendor.

♦ The runner's fee, which has been paid by the vendor.

♦ Copying fees, which are levied by the office where the documents were obtained.

Search Service

You may need to order documents from jurisdictions not currently available online from your vendor. Some vendors provide this service as well. However, you must provide as much information as possible, so that the correct documents can be located.

Customer Service

Customer service should be available through a toll-free number. The customer service representative should be familiar with the types of public record files offered, the content of various types of records, and services offered by the vendor.

Some web sites that provide products or services offer support only via e-mail. You may not want to wait for several hours or overnight for an answer to your question. In that case, you may find it worthwhile to do business with a vendor that provides telephone support.

After noting the date of the last update to a database, you may wish to perform or request a manual search at the corresponding courthouse or government office for records that may have been filed since that date. You might locate new records or updates to existing ones.

Valuable Sources — A Bit of Name Dropping

Some public record vendors, like CDB Infotek, Information America and LEXIS Public Records, were among the earliest vendors in the field. These services have loaded databases of US, state, and county files from across the country. It is from these services that you will find the greatest depth and breadth of coverage. Each of these major vendors has taken a different approach to providing access to their service via the Internet.

AutoTrack

Database Technologies' AutoTrack service, at www.dbt.com, is used by many investigators and law enforcement agencies nationwide to access over 4 billion publicly available records. DBT makes available proprietary applications to help Insurance companies and other qualified gather data to solve crimes, locate people and assets, and detect and prevent fraud.

CDB Infotek

CDB Infotek provides Windows software for accessing its files through the CDB Infotek web site, www.cdb.com/public, or by direct dial. If using this software through the Internet, you aren't searching their files on the Internet, but simply placing a telephone call to their computer through your Internet connection.

Information America

Information America, while retaining its original Information America dial-up service, launched KnowX, an entirely new service. KnowX, at www.knowx.com, has become one of the most popular and powerful web sites for public record information on the Internet. Some searches can be performed at no cost, with the option of paying a fee for the detailed version of the record. Since the existence of a record may be an answer in and of itself, this can be a real information bargain. As the popularity of the site has increased, certain fees have been added for peak time use of the service.

Both "easy" and "professional" interfaces are available at KnowX, a popular
Internet source for public record information.

A real "plus" with KnowX is its approach to billing. You can charge a fixed amount of money on your credit card and search at will until that amount has been spent. Since costs are relatively low, a deposit of $200, for example, will go a long way. You are not paying monthly subscription fees that are incurred even if you don't search during some months. In addition, you don't have the headache of dealing with monthly check writing, postage, and other administrative costs. And furthermore, you are dealing with a reputable source that has a long and respected track record in the business.

It is worth examining both KnowX at www.knowx.com and the Information America site at www.infoam.com and comparing the two results. Although the two services are owned by the same organization, they use different search engines. For frequent searching, Information America may be a much better choice for your company's CI activity. The Information America search engine is intended for a more professional clientele. Search results are easier to examine because listings must begin with the business or individual name that you entered. Using KnowX, your search words appear *somewhere in the individual or company name.*

Lexis Public Records

LEXIS-NEXIS included its LEXIS Public Records service at the LEXIS-NEXIS Universe site, http://web.lexis-nexis.com/ln.universe. Record groups with CI applications include the Asset Locator, Bankruptcy, Civil and Criminal Filings, Judgments and Liens, Jury Verdicts and Settlements categories.

The **Jury Verdicts and Settlements** file, not found on most online public record services, can be a useful source of business intelligence. Suppose, for example, that you are interested in a company that manufactures motorized equipment, such as lawnmowers. A search of this database, using the company name as a search term, might indicate that the company had some problems with lawsuits involving safety issues in connection with their products. This information might not cause you to change your mind about a possible deal, but you would want to know about the lawsuits as part of your due diligence efforts, and address the subject matter during discussions with the company in question.

Merlin Information Services

Merlin Information Services, at www.merlindata.com, is an up-and-comer in the online public records business. Merlin offers a free search of thirty million names. Their "Ultimate Weapon" is a master index to the Merlin California Public Record and "Banko" National Bankruptcy databases. Merlin has been aggressively adding additional files, and appears to expanding its coverage. The company's web sites offers free trials for those who wish to try the service.

Chapter 9

Government Databases: A Wealth of Information – Free!

Distribution methods for US government information have changed radically in the past few years, as more and more agencies have created sites on the World Wide Web and CD-ROM technology has facilitated the sale of disks containing large, searchable databases. Compiled statistical data, laws and regulations, required filings, government research, and many other types of information are now available for searching and downloading.

Whether you import or export, want to sell products or services to the Federal Government, or must research laws and regulations that apply to your company, you now have easy, cost-effective or even free access to crucial data needed to survive in today's competitive environment. Government information will also help you to monitor industries or competitor companies — it's all there for the taking.

The important thing, of course, is that you take advantage of the possibilities for turning this mountain of government data in actionable intelligence. Here are some possibilities:

Finding Out Who's Selling to the Government

It's possible to find out which of your competitors is selling goods to Federal Government agencies, what they're selling, how much they're selling, and for what amount of money. You can get the information on the Internet, at the *Commerce Business Daily (CBD)* web site, `http://cbdnet.access.gpo.gov/search2.html`.

The *Commerce Business Daily (CBD)* lists notices of proposed government procurement actions, contract awards, sales of government property, and other procurement information. A new edition of the *CBD* is issued every business day. Each edition contains approximately 500 to 1000 notices, and each notice appears in the *CBD* only once.

The *CBD* offers both "Simple Search" and "Fielded Search" options. A "posted date" field can be used to search for notices placed online on an exact date, in a date range, or before or after a certain date. Notices remain in this "active" database for fifteen business days.

Here's an example of how this database can work for you. Suppose your company manufactures valves. One of your competitors is Tescom. You want to learn whether Tescom supplies valves to the Federal government, and how much these contracts are worth in dollars. By searching "Tescom" in the AWARDEE field in the *CDB*'s fielded search screen, the following would be retrieved:

PART: CONTRACT AWARDS

SUBPART: SUPPLIES, EQUIPMENT AND MATERIAL

CLASSCOD: 48-Valves

OFFADD: Defense Supply Center Columbus, PO Box 16595, DSCC-PBAB,

    Columbus, OH 43216-6595

SUBJECT: 48-PRESSURE REGULATOR

CNT SP074099D5701

AMT $27,206.00

LINE ALL

DTD 033199

TO Tescom Corp., 12616 Industrial Blvd., Elk River, MN 55330

CITE: (W-088 SN313756)

The database contains documents pertaining not only to contract awards, but also to the following:

Category: US Government Procurements

EXAMPLE: Department of Defense seeks projects to create and/or develop new products or process technologies on a 50/50 cost share basis.

APPLICATION: Your company's scientists may have ideas about products that could be developed in conjunction with the government, and you could split the development cost with the government.

Category: Sources Sought

EXAMPLE: Miscellaneous—Potential Sources Sought

OFFADD: DLA Administrative Support Center....

SUBJECT: 99—WRITING, EDITORIAL AND DESIGN SERVICES

APPLICATION: Your company may wish to bid on supplying this service to the relevant government agency. *Note: Services are purchased by the government as well as products.*

Category: Sale of Surplus Property

EXAMPLE: DESC: 1. Bid Sale No. 011-9-S0302A, Ref. PCC# 12694-370 consisting of Special Test Equipment to include B1B Aircraft, Flight Control Systems; consisting of: Automatic Test Equipment and various ATE Adapters.

APPLICATION: Certain types of equipment may be purchased from the government at great savings, and used within your company.

Category: Special Notices

EXAMPLE: NIMA intends to procure four ERDAS Imagine software licenses from ERDAS.

APPLICATION: This type of announcement may be useful both for learning what types of software a government agency uses, but also for learning who is selling, and what they are selling.

Use *Commerce Business Daily* as a business development tool. Find out what the government needs to purchase, and to then submit bids to the appropriate office.

Making the Most of SEC Filings

Publicly-traded companies in the US are required to file a variety of documents periodically with the Securities and Exchange Commission. Many of these documents are now retrievable through the SEC's Electronic Data Gathering, Analysis, and Retrieval System (EDGAR). It is possible to search the EDGAR site by company name, and to retrieve a list that company's filings, which can then be displayed in full text.

EDGAR Special Purpose Searches

As the EDGAR web site has evolved, several other types of searches, described as "Special Purpose Searches," have been added.

Category: EDGAR CIK (Central Index Key) Lookup

APPLICATION: Perform a more accurate search for a company's SEC filings without the confusion caused by similar-looking names.

You search the EDGAR Archives using a unique identifier, (e.g. 00001111) instead of searching by company name. All companies and people who file disclosure with the SEC are given such an ID.

Category: Current Events Analysis

APPLICATION: Analyze forms filed in the previous week, including 10-K, (annual) and 10-Q quarterly) reports, proxies, and others. This would allow you to keep up with a company's filings without having to look at a long list if items from previous time periods.

Category: Mutual Funds Retrieval

APPLICATION: If your company is in the financial industry, you can find several years' worth of filings by a competitor mutual fund in one easy swoop.

This search retrieves filings by a pre-written list of mutual funds. An "Exhaustive Mutual Funds Search" is available for searching, but processing is slow.

Prospectus search

APPLICATION: Monitor the competition's prospectus filings now, for the past week, last two weeks, last month, or since 1994.

Prospectus Search retrieves all "485" forms, such as the 485APOS, 485BPOS, and 485B24E.

Executive Compensation Test

APPLICATION: Extract executive compensation information for publicly traded companies in easy-to-read form. From company proxies (Form DEF 14A) that are split into two components: (1) Proxy with intra-document Executive Compensation Table Added, or (2) The Executive Compensation Table as a standalone item; with labels added to enable the user to review the entire proxy. The executive compensation information can be extracted from a proxy (DEF 14A) filing.

Required Filings Made by Competitors

Securities & Exchange Commission Filings - Required of publicly-traded companies, these documents can be searched at the SEC site, www.sec.gov/edaux/wedgar.htm. Several commercial vendors provide access to SEC filings, as well. EDGAR Online, www.edgar-online.com, and Global Securities Information, Inc.'s LIVEDGAR site, www.gsionline.com/default.htm, may be used as alternatives to the government site.

For old filings and current material, Disclosure (www.disclosure.com/disclosure), is the place to go. This company maintains archives going back many years. Their research department specializes in locating filings by insiders and other filings typically not submitted in EDGAR format, including: foreign exchange filings, company articles, bylaws and employment agreements.   Their *Worldscope* and *Canada* databases contain extensive information about companies outside the US Some, but not all, of the Disclosure files are available on major online services such as DIALOG and LEXIS-NEXIS. Most commercial vendors provide additional services such as monitoring services, non-SEC offering circulars, custom research, and more.

The 10-K Filing

Of the various SEC filings that you will want to search for business intelligence, the 10K is one of the most important. The 10K contains financial information not included in a company's annual report. This filing may also mention pending litigation, related party transactions (side deals) and audit footnotes. Conversely, the Management Discussion section found in annual reports may be useful reading material not included in the 10-K.

Companies also are required to file a 10-Q, which provides a continuing view of a company's financial position during the year. The filing is due 45 days after each of the first three fiscal quarters. It is not required that 10-Qs be audited, however, so always check the 10-K, which *is* audited. You never know what errors could have clipped into the unaudited 10-Q. Non-US companies doing business in the US must file a 20-F. which provides a continuing view of a company's financial position during the year. The filing is due 45 days after each of the first three fiscal quarters.

Other Required Agency Filings - Dozens of other government agencies offer searchable databases that may help you to uncover crucial business intelligence. Topics such as safety and hazards, disciplinary matters, and trade are included in the wealth of available data, in addition to these examples:

♦ **The Federal Election Commission**, at www.fec.gov, provides financial reports containing all receipts and disbursements committees are required to disclose under the Federal Election Campaign Act, including contributions from individuals, party committees, PACs, and candidates regardless of amount; loans received by committees; and other kinds of receipts. If you are interested in whether your competition is influencing members of Congress through financial contributions, consider these possibilities:

   ♦ **Individual Search:** Contributions made by individuals, if the gift totals more than $200 during a year, may be searched using contributor name, city, state, zip code, principal place of business, date and amount.

   ♦ **Committee Search:** Search for contributions received or made by a specific committee using committee name, city, state, zip code, Treasurer's name, party designation and committee type.

    ◆ **Candidate Search:** Search for contributions received by a specific campaign using candidate's name, state, district, party affiliation, incumbent or challenger status.

You won't find everything here, though. Campaigns for the Senate file their reports with the Secretary of the Senate — not with the FEC — so those reports are not available here. The site explains this as follows: "Reports of the National Party Senatorial Campaign Committees are, however, included in the system.(Microfilm copies of Senate reports are on file at the Commission offices in Washington, and candidates must also file copies with their state elections office.)"

◆ **The Environmental Protection Agency**

The Environmental Protection Agency offers searchable databases of intelligence from filings made by companies regulated by the agency. The Envirofacts Warehouse, at `www.epa.gov/enviro/index_java.html`, shown below, provides a single point of access to more than a dozen databases, on a variety of topics.

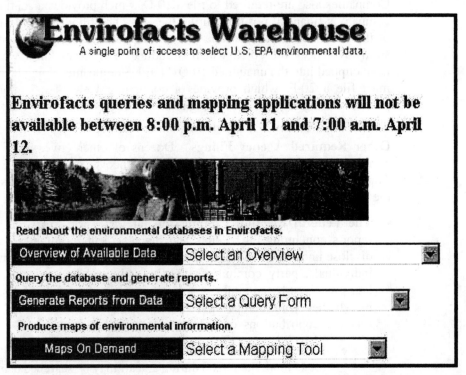

The following is a description of some of the databases searchable at The Envirofacts Warehouse:

    ◆ **Air Releases** - Contains both emissions and compliance data on air pollution point sources regulated by the US Environmental Protection Agency (EPA) and/or state and local air regulatory agencies.

- **Biennial Reporting System** - Contains data collected from generators and treatment, storage, and disposal (TSD) facilities who handle hazardous waste, which is reported to the EPA Administrator at least once every 2 years.

- **Brownfields** - Contains information on are abandoned, idled, or under-used industrial and commercial facilities where expansion or redevelopment is complicated by real or perceived environmental contamination.

- **EPA's Spatial Data Library** - Database contains the Agency's new and legacy geospatial data holdings. Users can access these data holdings through various GIS applications.

- **Facility Information** - Contains environmental data submitted by regulated facilities. Data comes from 14 national systems.

- **Hazardous Waste Data** - Records contain information provided to state environmental agencies by companies that are generators, transporters, treaters, storers, and disposers of hazardous waste (as defined by the federally recognized hazardous waste codes), concerning their activities.

- **Safe Drinking Water Info** - information about public water systems and their violations of EPA's regulations for safe drinking water

- **Superfund Data** - uncontrolled or abandoned hazardous waste sites such as abandoned warehouses, manufacturing facilities, processing plants, and landfills.

- **Toxics Release Inventory** - Contains information about releases and transfers of more than 650 toxic chemicals and compounds to the environment.

- **Water Discharge Permits** - Records reflect water discharge permit data on more than 75,000 facilities nationwide.

You might perform a Facility Information search, for example, to locate plant sites. Suppose you are interested in "everything EPA" that can be located on Company X. By entering all or part of the company name, you would retrieve the following, in tabular format:

Facility Name	Location Address	City Name	County Name	State	Zip	DUNS Number

To focus the search a bit, you could limit by geographic location (from the zip code to state level), or by database (the default is to search all of the databases.) You can also search the **Enforcement Docket System,** though that system is **not included on the *Envirofacts Warehouse* homepage**.

Another option here is to search by SIC code. This could be useful if you wished to see what companies in a certain industry sector were doing business in a particular geographic area.

Perhaps your company manufactures emissions control equipment, for instance. You might build a list of plants that are in violation, and sell them the solution to their problem.

If you are examining certain types of companies for merger or acquisition purposes, you would definitely want to know all about their track record with the EPA. Otherwise, you could be acquiring more than you bargained for!

♦ **The Federal Deposit Insurance Corporation** Bank Data Institution Directory, at `http://192.147.69.50/id` offers searches for institutions or bank holding companies. Data is searchable going back as far as 1992, and can be accessed by ID number, name, city, or state. The site also allows you to compare two institutions, groups, or holding companies, providing detailed data on assets and liabilities, income and expenses, and performance and condition ratios. Information is updated on a quarterly basis. Whether financial institutions are part of your company's competition, or whether you use this information in other ways, retrieving the information in electronic format is very useful.

For a handy starting place when searching for Federal government agency web sites and those of Federal independent establishments and government corporations, see this site from The Center for Information Law and Policy at Villanova University: `www.cilp.org/Fed-Agency/fedwebloc.html`. **Government offices are constantly adding new pages and adding features and functionality to those that already exist, so periodically exploring sites connected with agencies that regulate an industry is recommended.**

Intellectual Property Information

You may use the patent, trademark, or copyright laws to protect your own company's intellectual property, or you may be interested in these topics in the context of competitors. The material can be very complex, and may require assistance from your attorney or legal department. For an introduction, however, the government offices have published much useful material on the Internet:

Trademarks - The US Patent and Trademark Office produces *Basic Facts About Registering A Trademark*, which may be downloaded in word processor formats, or ordered in printed format from its web site, `www.uspto.gov/web/offices/tac/doc/basic`. A great deal of other useful information regarding trademarks is also available at this site, including forms, which are available for you to download, fill out, and turn in. Instructions are provided.

The USPTO's free trademark database, at `www.uspto.gov/tmdb/index.html`, includes the full bibliographic text of pending and registered trademarks published in the Official Gazette. Pending trademark applications are usually entered in the PTO database one to two months after filing.

Limitations regarding the database, database contents, database currency, and sources of more current data are published on the USPTO Web site. This information should be reviewed before interpreting the results of searches of PTO's Web Trademark Database.

You may wonder how to put this knowledge to use. Trademarks are a hot item of intellectual property, and as such, they are guarded carefully by those who have registered them.

> **EXAMPLE:** Suppose your company plans to market a new type of snack food. The Advertising and Marketing Department is trying to develop a "catchy" phrase to use in advertising — something using the words "the health food that tastes good."

A quick check of the USPTO trademark database produces the news that at least twelve registered trademarks already contain the phrase "tastes good." It would now be very wise to involve the Legal Department in determining whether to go forward with the plan, or to choose new wording for this trademark.

Patents - The US Patent and Trademark Office site also provides detailed information regarding many aspects of the patent process on a page titled *General Information Concerning Patents*, at `www.uspto.gov/web/offices/pac/doc/general/index.html`.

Descriptions of US patents granted since January 1971 by the US Patent & Trademark Office (USPTO) as well as the last 23 years of images are searchable on a site created by IBM, at `www.patents.ibm.com`. Several commercial vendors also offer this material in database form.

It is possible to get a quick and dirty estimate of a company's intellectual property assets using the USPTO patent database.

> **EXAMPLE:** Search the database by Assignee Name. This will provide the total number of patents assigned to that company, and a hot-linked list of the patents. Remember, however, that some of this property could have been included in the sale of part of the company, and is no longer an asset of the company searched.

Copyright – General information, legislation, publications, announcements, and international copyright law are among the topics addressed by the United States Copyright Office at the agency's site: `http://lcweb.loc.gov/copyright`.

Other Resources

Like many other US Government agencies, the Patent and Trademark Office provides a FOIA Reading Room, at www.uspto.gov/web/offices/com/sol/foia/readroom.htm. FOIA refers to the *Freedom of Information Act*, a federal law which provides access, by request, to a great deal of information collected by government.

Statistical Reports

The Federal Interagency Council on Statistical Policy maintains an Internet site at www.fedstats.gov that is intended to provide easy access to the full range of statistics and information produced by more than 70 US Government agencies.

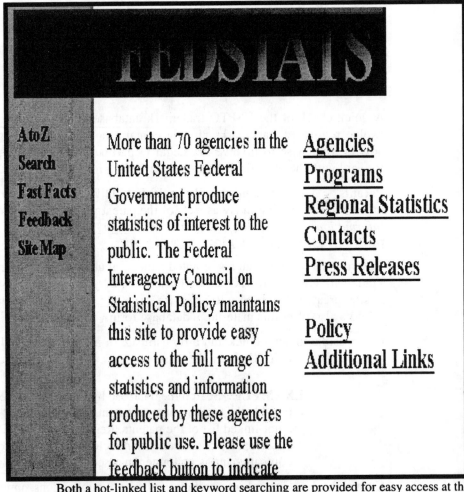

FEDSTATS

AtoZ
Search
Fast Facts
Feedback
Site Map

More than 70 agencies in the United States Federal Government produce statistics of interest to the public. The Federal Interagency Council on Statistical Policy maintains this site to provide easy access to the full range of statistics and information produced by these agencies for public use. Please use the feedback button to indicate

Agencies
Programs
Regional Statistics
Contacts
Press Releases

Policy
Additional Links

Both a hot-linked list and keyword searching are provided for easy access at the FedStats site.

The detailed data that can be retrieved here may be used for a variety of different purposes. Suppose, for example, that your company plans to market a new product aimed at a particular segment of the population. The demographic data, available down to the lot and block level, may help you to decide which neighborhoods or larger geographic areas will provide the market you seek. The 1990 census is the most recent available.

If, on the other hand, income level would be the deciding factor in determining how or where to market the product, something like Statistics of Income (SOI), retrievable from the Internal Revenue Service might be of more use. SOI provides annual income, financial, and tax data based on individual and corporate tax returns and returns filed by tax-exempt organizations.

Extensive regional statistics, covering several general topics, can be obtained easily from the FEDSTATS site. The list below contains a few samples:

Category	Topic	Source
Agriculture	Crops County Data	National Agricultural Statistics Service
	Farm Characteristics, Financial Indicators, and Top Agricultural Commodities	Economic Research Service, USDA
	Livestock County Data	National Agricultural Statistics Service
Demographic and Economic	Country Profiles	Central Intelligence Agency
	State and County Profiles	Bureau of the Census
	Demographic Indicators for Countries	Bureau of the Census
	State Data Centers	Bureau of the Census
	Science and Engineering State Profiles	National Science Foundation
Crime	Crime and Justice	Bureau of Justice Statistics
Education	Public School Student, Staff, and Graduate Counts by State	National Center for Education Statistics

Category	Topic	Source
	International Comparisons	National Center for Education Statistics
Energy & Environment	Commodity Minerals Information	US Geological Survey
	Country Analysis Briefs	Energy Information Administration
	Environmental State & County Profiles	Environmental Protection Agency
	International minerals information	US Geological Survey
	State energy data	Energy Information Administration
	State minerals information	US Geological Survey
Health	Atlas of the United States Mortality	National Center for Health Statistics
Income	Corporation tax returns Estate/Wealth tax returns Excise taxes Exempt organizations Bond tax returns Individual tax returns International or Foreign Related tax returns Sole proprietorships tax returns	Internal Revenue Service
Labor	Regional Information	Bureau of Labor Statistics
National Accounts	Personal income and gross product, by State	Bureau of Economic Analysis

Government statistics can be valuable in dozens of ways when studying industries, planning market strategies, importing and exporting, or various other business activities. Suppose, for example, that you are considering building a new domestic manufacturing plant. Labor costs could be a significant expense. It would be important to compare average wages, along with other costs, when selecting the state where you plan to build. By using the detailed statistical tables that are available from the Bureau of Labor Statistics, state by state or nationwide, you can make a more informed decision. Here is a tiny sample, comparing New York and Alabama in one job category:

Comparison of 1997 State Occupational Employment & Wage Estimates:

New York

OES Code	Occupation Title	Employment	Mean Wage Hourly	Mean Wage Annual
56002	Billing, Posting, and Calculating Machine Operators	6,590	$10.22	$21,260
56005	Duplicating Machine Operators	3,490	$10.51	$21,850
56008	Mail Machine Oper. Prep. & Handling	5,040	$8.82	$18,350

Alabama

OES Code	Occupation Title	Employment	Mean Wage Hourly	Mean Wage Annual
56002	Billing, Posting, and Calculating Machine Operators	1860	$8.88	$18,470
56005	Duplicating Machine Operators	380	$8.29	$17,230
56008	Mail Machine Oper. Prep. & Handling	470	$7.43	$15,460

Detailed statistics regarding numbers of people employed, and hourly and annual wages for the fifty US states is available for hundreds of job titles. See Bureau of Labor Statistics site.

The examples above involved wages. The Bureau of Labor Statistics also provides statistics on a number of other areas worth looking at:

Compensation	Job injuries
Consumer expenditures	Labor force
Consumer Price Index	Locality pay
Contingent workers	Longitudinal surveys
Displaced workers	Occupational projections
Employee benefits	Producer Price Index
Employer provided training	Productivity
Employment	Real earnings

Employment cost trends	State and area employment
Employment projections	Unemployment
Foreign labor	Union members
Import-export prices	Wages
Industry employment	Weekly earnings

Statistical data on the topics listed above can be used to determine what is happening or is likely to happen in an industry. This may impact your company's planning as well as that of competitors. The data can also be used to estimate competitors' costs in various labor-related areas.

Finding Business Information From State Government Sources

For an easy way to locate US State government web sites, look at. the National Association of State Information Resource Executives (NASIRE) site, at www.nasire.org/stateSearch. The screen captures that follows shows the hotlinks found at the NASIRE site, provides an idea of the subject matter that can be found. This should be very useful when you need to investigate matters that will impact doing business in other states.

STATE SEARCH

StateSearch is a service of NASIRE and is designed to serve as a topical clearinghouse to state government information on the Internet. If you have information you feel should be added to StateSearch, please notify us.

There are currently 2167 entries in 33 categories.

Agriculture	Governor's Offices	State Auditors
Arts Councils	Health & Human Services	State Constitutions
Corrections	Information Technology	State Homepages
Criminal Justice	Judicial	State Legislatures
Disability Agencies	Legal Opinions	State Libraries
Economic Development & Commerce	Lieutenant Governors	State Police
Education	Other Links	State Statutes
Employment Services	Purchasing/Procurement	Tourism
Energy & Environmental Resources	Regulation & Licensing	Transportation
Executive Branch	Revenue	Treasurers
Finance & Administration	Seniors & Aging	Year 2000 Efforts

The National Association of State Information Resource Executives (NASIRE) web site provides links state sites covering a wide variety of topics. This list is especially useful if you plan to compare the way the several states address an issue or handle a process.

Identifying State Government Agencies Where the Competition Sells Goods & Services

Every state in the US has a special office that manages the process of buying goods and services. Many of them now make a great deal of information regarding this process available on web sites. You may be able to learn several useful facts regarding your competitors:

♦ Lists of companies selling to a particular state.

♦ What goods and services that a given company is selling.

♦ Names of state agencies involved.

◆ Location where goods and services will be used (sometimes).

Another application for state procurement information your company is to add state government agencies to your own client list. Clicking on "Procurement" in the screen above would take you to another hot-linked list of Procurement Offices for the fifty US states. By selecting a state, you can quickly gather what it takes to learn how the procurement system works in that state.

Here is a summarized sample of what's available regarding procurement at the Texas Procurement Information site, just to give you a feel for the type of intelligence to be found here:

Announcements / Notices

Find out, among other things, the identities of suspended vendors at the state level, and a similar list at the federal level.

> **APPLICATION:** This information could shed light on a competitor's activities, or provide you with hints on doing business with the state.

General Services Commission Contracting Bid Opportunities

Find out what items will be coming up for bid a year or two from now, and how to bid. Areas covered include open market purchases, lease space, construction, purchasing, travel, and architect/engineering services.

> **APPLICATION:** Consider whether to bid for supplying goods or services to the state. Decide whether your company has products or services that are sought by the state.

Bid Tabulations and Award Information

Find out about bids and awards that have been made. Both tabulations and awards information are available for Open Market, Contract, and Schedule purchasing activity.

> **APPLICATION:** Use previous bid information for pricing on future bids for similar products or services.

How the State of Texas Procures Commodities & Services

Learn the definitions of the terms used to categorize the various arrangements for purchasing goods and services.

GSC Commodity Book (Version 10.1, September 1998)

Learn about the Commodity Book, which is a guide to identifying classification codes for goods and commodities on which you might bid.

> **APPLICATION:** Use these codes during the bidding process.

GSC Term Contracts

Learn the state's established rules and procedures for procuring goods and services.

APPLICATION: Avoid delays or wasted efforts by preparing your bid according to the established procedures.

QISV Catalogue Purchasing Information (includes online access to QISV List)

Learn how the state purchases certain products that may be require exceptions to their normal procurement procedures, (This allows qualified entities (state agencies and political subdivisions) to purchase automated information systems products and/or services in a efficient, cost effective, and competitive procurement method.)

APPLICATION: Get your company on the Qualified Information Systems Vendors list, or search your competitors' names to see if they are likely to be selling to the state.

New Centralized Master Bidders List (All vendors, including HUBs)

Learn who is registered to sell to the state, including name, address, and contact person.

APPLICATION: Build a list of companies that provide certain goods or services.

Historically Underutilized Business (HUB) Information

Learn all about the HUB classification.

APPLICATION: Apply for HUB status, if you qualify.

GSC Purchasing Specifications Library

Learn the purchasing specifications that are in place.

APPLICATION: Plan your bid around these specifications.

GSC Procurement Related Files for Download

Download files for list creation.

APPLICATION: Learn names or job titles of contact persons at various state agencies, for marketing purposes.

As you can see, a wealth of information is now a few mouse clicks away. Note the **Centralized Master Bidders List** in the group above. This is searchable by vendor name, city, and class, among other data types, and search results can be limited in various ways. You can view entire sections of this list by simply indicating the desire to see the list of companies with names that start with a particular letter of the alphabet.

Not every state has a web site for every category of information on the NASIRE State Search screen, and not every site has searchable databases. It is important to note, however, that the number of intelligence-laden sites is constantly increasing. You should revisit these state pages periodically if the information is the type that you need.

Searching various competitors' names to see if they are on a state's approved list may be worthwhile when you are working on a market strategy or trying to determine where a competitor sells products or services.

The amount and type of information available from state government varies extensively, since each state in the US makes its own laws and creates departments or agencies at will. By searching your own state's site, you may find some headings that are more specific than those mentioned above. The list below provides some typical organizations that you can seek out in your own state. Some of these may offer searchable databases:

Secretary of State

Florida, for example, offers SUNBIZ, a service offers access to documents filed with the Secretary of State. Searchable databases include Corporations, Trademarks, & Limited Partnerships; UCC & Federal Lien registrations; Fictitious Names; and Limited Liability & General partnerships. Included in the detail of the data record is the ability to display the actual document image that was submitted to the Division.

> **APPLICATION:** Learn detailed information about companies registered to do business in the state. (Florida offers more of this information than most states.)

Industry-Specific Regulatory Agencies

Visit your state's web site and look for links to agencies such as the State Department of Environmental Affairs, Banking Department, Department of Transportation, etc. California, as an example, has lists of banks, thrifts, etc. at the Department of Financial Institutions web site

State Comptroller or Comparable Office

This office handles subjects such as Licensing and Registration, Unclaimed Property, and other matters related to state finance. Databases are provided in some states, such as Florida and Washington.

APPLICATION: Use this type of database to check the professional licensing credentials of individuals in regulated professions or businesses.

Many state web sites do not yet feature detailed information from state agencies where databases are not yet common. Keep your eyes open for databases in the future, from agencies like these:

♦ State Securities Board

♦ State Labor Commission

♦ State Environmental Office

See Bookmarks & Favorites in Part IV, under the heading "Public Records" for state sites that will allow you to search their databases free on the Internet.

Chapter 10

Letting "The Other Guy" Do the Work for You

Starting Points for Business Research Using the Internet

Searching for useful web sites is like hunting for sunken treasure in the ocean from a rowboat. Even if you are an experienced searcher, you can spend hours looking at dozens of sites without finding the "gold" you seek. Therefore, web surfing may not be the most productive use of your time online.

Fortunately, there is help at hand! Some great web sites have been compiled by individuals with the experience and knowledge to gather the best of the thousands of possible sites that mention your topic, organize them and present them in a useful, readable interface, complete with site search engines and hot-links for easy access.

Many of these meta-sites are the product of schools of business or library science at major universities in the US and abroad. Therefore, some of them may reflect the specialty, interests and/or curriculum of the institution. It is possible to determine any special emphasis of a site by reading the mission statement or reviews included on the main page.

This chapter is your introduction to some of the best of these sites. By visiting them and choosing from the categories presented, you can more quickly decide whether a particular site suits your purpose.

To decide where to start, it's best to begin by examining your question (i.e. your reason for the search). If you need more detail about the types of company or industry reports to create, and what goes into them, see the checklists provided in Chapter 16.

Defining the Need Helps Define Your Search

Your question could be a broad one, such as "What's happening in the Widget industry?" Or you may be researching a more focused question, such as "Is the SOHO (Small Office/Home Office) market for PC's growing? If so, at what rate? What's driving the growth?"

Using the Internet search engines to research these questions may take a lot longer to identify relevant sites and locate documents that will help answer the question. You may find links that use your search terms, but which are totally off of the subject. Using the sites mentioned below to begin your research, you reduce the likelihood of having to wade through a long list of "false hits." The sites' creators have focused on business applications. As you visit what can be large and complex sites, keep these questions in mind:

◆ Does the question involve a specific industry?

◆ Is the question related to technology? If so, what type?

◆ Are you researching specific companies?

◆ Are management issues involved?

◆ Should the topic be covered from a US or an international perspective?

Look at broad categories first and "drill down" by choosing more narrow topics. You may need to explore more than one category, but at least you'll know that the material has been screened and selected by someone with business applications in mind.

Business Sites on the WWW

The World Wide Web is filled with business sites of all kinds. The sites below are some good examples of the useful collections of material that have been put together, and which are among the author's favorites for business information research.

BRINT

A Business Researcher's Interests (BRINT), at www.brint.com, touts a long list of favorable reviews from well-respected sources. The site has changed significantly over time, becoming more "commercial" in appearance, but if you drill down to www.brint.com/business.html, you'll see the screen capture that follows:

A Business Researcher's Interests

BizTech Research Library & Searchable Knowledge Map

"Premier Collection of Contemporary Business, Management & Technology Issues" -- *Wall Street Journal*

"Thumbs Up for this Serious Surfer's Tool Useful for Managers" -- *Fortune*

"Best Source for Information Technology & Business Information" -- *Computerworld*

"Unparalleled in Depth & Relevance for Business Research" -- *Information Week*

| Business & Technology ▼ | Go! |

Highlight Your Choice and Click 'Go!' or **Scroll Down for Details**

Information Search Search
Engines & Directories, Reference, Travel,
Weather, Government, Yellow Pages...

Business & Technology
Company & Industry Info, Accounting,
Finance, Economics, Marketing, HR,
Sciences, Strategy, Telecom, Law...

International Countries,

Knowledge Management
WWW Virtual Library of Knowledge
Management, Online Discussion Forums,
Organizational Learning, Intellectual
Capital, Change Management...

Reengineering (BPR)
Business Transformation, TQM, Enterprise
Architecture, Workflow, ABC,
Benchmarking, Tools, Methods, Cases..

Web Strategy & Design
Basics, Surveys, Demographics,
Marketing, Advertising, Internet Service
Providers (ISPs), Domain Names,
Security, Free Software, Techniques...

Intellectual Property
Copyrights, Patents, Trademarks, Internet
& WWW, Trends & News, Governance,
Laws, Infringements, Security, Fair Use

The hot-linked categories shown above lead to pages with dozens of links to related material.

Following the Business & Technology hotlink shown on the screen above brings you to the area that you will likely wish to explore in greater detail. Here is what you will see:

Company & Industry Information

General Indices for Business & Technology

Business Schools & Business Education

Subscription Based Business & Technology Resources

Accounting, Finance & Investments

Business & Technology Law

Business Strategy

Computers & Telecom

CIS / MIS
(Information Systems)

<u>Economics</u>

<u>Human Resources & Organizational Development</u>

<u>International Business</u>

<u>Marketing</u>

<u>Operations Management</u>

<u>Philosophy</u>

<u>Social Sciences</u>

Under the link <u>Company & Industry Information</u>, for instance, BRINT provides links to most of the "Top This and That" lists referred to in Chapter 14, along with additional links to information such as sources for company profiles, industry news and information as well as sector information. Be prepared to invest some time in using this site for the first time. Its breadth and depth can seem overwhelming.

As you begin to locate the sources that seem be strongest for the type of information you seek, BE SURE TO BOOKMARK THEM OR ADD THEM TO YOUR LIST OF FAVORITES! By doing so, you will prevent a great deal of future aggravation when you can't seem to remember the web address for that "great" source.

Business Information Sources On the Internet

This site, also an award winner, from the University of Strathclyde in Glasgow, is found at <u>www.dis.strath.ac.uk/business/index.html</u>. The site is a combination of links to useful Internet resources that contain company, business news or market information as well as sites that provide significant guides to these types of resources. There is an emphasis on UK and European resources, which makes it especially useful for those researching non-US companies or industries. There is good coverage of the US as well.

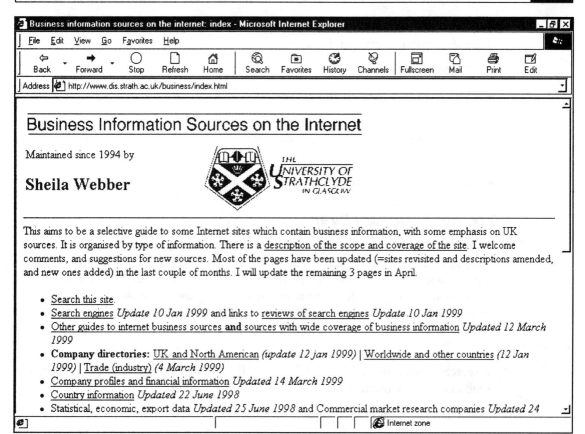

Sheila Webber's Business Information Sources on the Internet site is well organized and easy to use.

This web site's organization is simple and straightforward. Each reference is annotated. The site appears to be updated regularly. Headings include:

◆ Company directories (UK, North America and worldwide as well as other countries — Trade or industry specific)

◆ Company profiles & financial information

◆ Country information

◆ Statistical, economic, export data

◆ Commercial market research companies

◆ News sources (in general)

◆ News sources published in the UK

◆ Search engines

Ms. Webber's search engine page is a good place to start if you are want to get a "big picture" of the search engines available to you on the Internet. The page contains links to three different groups of sites, with brief descriptions covering features, coverage, and similar details:

- ◆ Major Internet search engines.

- ◆ Multiple (meta) search engines that search using several individual search engines.

- ◆ Long lists of search engines, generally categorized into groups. (Several of these are described below.)

- ◆ Search engines are discussed in more detail later in this chapter.

Internet Business Library

The Internet Business Library (IBL), at `www.bschool.ukans.edu/intbuslib/virtual.htm`, has been designed to provide a selective, current, subject-oriented guide to business information on the Internet. The IBL links only to those sites that provide information that is freely available on the Internet. Some sites may have a tiered service, but to be included in the IBL, a substantial amount of information must be available without paying a fee.

A table on the homepage provides links on a variety of topics useful to the business researcher. Suppose you needed a concise list of links on international trade topics. One mouse click produces the following list of hot links:

- ◆ Country & Regional Profiles

- ◆ European Union & Related Documents

- ◆ Guides to International Business

- ◆ Bibliographies of countries and regions

- ◆ International Company Directories

- ◆ International Markets & Trade Opportunities/Statistics

- ◆ International Statistics (Both economic and demographic)

- ◆ International Trade Organizations

- ◆ North American Free Trade Agreement (NAFTA) & related documents

- ◆ Trade & International Law

- ◆ Travel Guides, World Maps & Currency Converter

- ◆ World News (Includes an index to current news by country and region)

International Business Resources on the WWW

The Michigan State University Center for Business Education and Research sponsors the MSU CIBER site, at `http://ciber.bus.msu.edu/busres.htm`. The site's index includes a *long* list of the headings that you would expect, involving news sources, government material, country or regional links, etc. These are "free" sites, created by identifiable sources. How can you turn this list into actionable intelligence?

Suppose that your company is becoming interested in investing in Africa, one of the emerging markets of the world. The hot-link Regional or Country Specific Information (Africa) would take you to a page of annotated links to government and non-government sources for African countries. Follow these links to sites that provide much of the information needed to gather in-depth data on many of the important considerations that must be undertaken if you wish to do business in these countries. Here are some of the links that would be uncovered:

Africa: Africa Business Network

The Africa Business Network is a new and developing site serving the sub-Saharan Africa countries. The site will contain a wealth of country and investment information, for now available only for a couple countries. There is already some information about investing in Africa in general. The site will also facilitate trade and discussion through numerous mailing lists.

Africa: MBendi - Countries of Africa

The site provides a country profile for most of the African countries. Each country profile includes general information, economic information, financial information, as well as detailed industry analyses and company listings.

Africa: Lex Africa Business Guides

Lex Africa is a network of law firms in Africa. This site features business guides prepared by member law firms for 11 African countries. Each business guide features investment information, forms of business organizations, taxation, exchange control, tariffs, intellectual property issues, privatization issues and more.

Africa: Ernst & Young - A guide to investing in Africa

A separate investment profile exists for each African country. Prepared by Ernst and Young, these guides cover a wide variety of topics from a general overview to tax issues, investment incentives, types of business establishments, exchange control regulations and more. However, these guides are dated August 1996 and considering the volatility of political climate in most of these nations users should be cautious in using the information.

Egypt: Technology Development Program of Egypt

Includes information about The Egyptian Cabinet Information & Decision Support Center (IDSC) Technology Development Program (TDP) which is a government initiative. There is also a search engine for the High-Tech Business Directory (listed separately in the company listings section).

Egypt: Egypt Business Information Center

Economic indicators, business directory, information about investing in Egypt, company profiles, projects for promotion and much more...

South Africa: Big Emerging Markets Country Guide

Provided by the US Department of Commerce, this guide explains why South Africa is a big emerging market. Includes information on key economic indicators, big emerging sectors, market access (tariffs, barriers) and competition.

LANIC Search

The University of Texas LANIC site, at `http://info.lanic.utexas.edu/business` contains links to Latin American search engines (in Brazil, Chile, Mexico etc.). You can search a number of country or region-specific search engines, retrieving document descriptions in either Spanish or English. There are links to other Latin American Studies sites as well.

Institute of Latin American Studies
UT-LANIC Joint Projects and Hosted Databases

Newsroom: Earthquake in Colombia

Country Directory

Argentina	Bahamas	Barbados	Belize	Bolivia
Brazil	Chile	Colombia	Costa Rica	Cuba
Dominican R.	Ecuador	El Salvador	Guatemala	Guyana
Haiti	Honduras	Jamaica	Mexico	Nicaragua
Panama	Paraguay	Peru	St. Lucia	Suriname
Trinidad & Tobago		Uruguay	Venezuela	Other Caribbean

Both Caribbean and Latin American countries are included in the LANIC web site's coverage.

The LANIC Newsroom is a collection of links on major current events in Latin America. The inaugural page, in November 1998, covered the devastation caused in Central America by Hurricane Mitch. Companies that will be involved in the massive reconstruction as a result of events such as this will likely find the in-depth and localized coverage useful, as was discussed in Getting the Scoop, Chapter 6.

Dow Jones Interactive's Web Center

Dow Jones Interactive's Web Center links the searcher with thousands of general, business, market, government and industry news sites from the US and around the world. It also includes reviews of high-quality web sites, written by Dow Jones editors. Searches can be performed against a single site at a time, selected categories of sites or from the entire collection available. Available categories include these:

Top News Sites	Non-English Language Sites
Regional Sites	Industry-Specific Sites
Reference & News Sites	

You can choose among non-English language sites, regional sites and industry-specific sites (50+ industry groups). An alphabetical listing of sites is also available. Custom site lists can be created for easy searching.

Storing searches that you wish to run periodically is a timesaver. At the Dow Jones Web Center the search string and list of sites to be searched can be stored and edited at will.

Suppose, for example, that you wish to monitor forecasts and trends in the wireless telecommunications industry. After choosing the industry category labeled **"Telecommunications — Wireless,"** a search strategy as simple *as "trends or forecasts"* yields several interesting documents, including a government report and a press release mentioning a trade association study:

> **Statistical Trends in Telephony**, US Federal Communications Commission (English). Last Updated: Friday, November 13, 1998. (You can read this document online or download in PDF or ZIP formats.)

> Telecommunications Resellers Association (English) Last Updated: Wednesday, November 04, 1998 NEWS RELEASE For Immediate Release Contact: Julie Hill Director of Communications 202-835-9898, ex. 3009 October 9, 1998. **Slowdown in Local Resale Noted in Telecommunications Resellers Association Study (Washington, DC).**

The Dow Jones Web Center identifies and reviews web sites in a number of categories.

CI-Oriented Web Sites

A number of large consulting companies specializing in competitor/competitive intelligence have mounted complex and sophisticated web sites. As you might expect, these commercial operations contain information about upcoming seminars and speaking engagements, books by principals and the company's products and services. See Bookmarks & Favorites in Part IV, under the heading "Competitive Intelligence," for examples.

You may not need to consult one of these companies today, but they hope to keep their names in your mind for future use. To do this, some of them provide useful articles, tips, and hotlinks to sites that you will find invaluable. As in the case of the award-winning and favorably reviewed sites described previously, the web sites mentioned by these CI consultants have been examined and deemed to be of value for the business intelligence function.

The **Society of Competitor Intelligence Professionals (SCIP)** web site, www.scip.org, offers several forums on CI-related topics. To participate in discussions, registration is required. Read access is available, however, on a guest basis. Another useful feature of this site is the searchable list of experts.

You could also check this site to identify upcoming conferences or seminars that are offered in various parts of the world. You can learn a great deal about sources and applications for online information (as well as other aspects of CI). The exhibit halls at these conferences are always filled with vendors offering a variety of cyber-tools.

Fuld & Company, Inc

Fuld & Company, Inc's web site at www.fuld.com is one of the best examples of sites mounted by CI consulting companies. The homepage indicates that the *New York Times* praised their Internet Intelligence Index, calling it a "good place to start a web tour of competitive-intelligence sites." The index contains more than 300 links, including a long list that are industry-specific. The site is updated quite frequently.

Among the useful treasures located here is a page called ***Internet Searching Tip Sheet,*** located at www.fuld.com/i3/searchtips.html, which was compiled by the Fuld & Company Library. This sheet is a summary of the basic commands used by many of the search engines mentioned elsewhere in this chapter. It is worth printing and placing to the bulletin board near your PC, for handy reference when searching the Internet.

How About a Game of "40 Questions"?

The Corporate Evaluation Questionnaire might be another useful item to look at while examining the Fuld site. The questionnaire consists of a series of questions that you or your company could use to evaluate whether you use intelligence "expediently and decisively." This evaluation is designed to answer that question by examining your ability to handle and apply vital intelligence.

This site has several other links that you might investigate to find equally useful information on the subject of CI.

Fuld & Dow Jones Interactive — A Dynamite Combination

In May 1999, a press release announced plans to develop a program that will "help DowJones Interactive subscribers leverage business information to build competitive advantage."

Fuld & Company will now partner with Dow Jones Interactive to combine with the online resources available at Dow Jones Interactive. The program is aimed at business information users who aren't professional searchers, and it sounds like just the "hand holding" tool that some searchers new to CI will welcome Clicking on a link at the Dow Jones site will take you to a special Fuld web page. Once there, the procedure is as follows:

- Select the type of business question you are trying to answer.

- Follow a step-by-step procedure that will help refine the question.

- Follow additional steps to identify sources within Dow Jones Interactive.

Plans call for the development of additional CI training tools by Ironhorse Multimedia, in conjunction with Fuld, as well as the introduction of CI modules into training provided by Dow Jones Interactive to its enterprise clients.

Iron Horse Multimedia, an electronic publisher of interactive competitive intelligence training programs, is expected to contribute web-based training modules on competitive intelligence. "An alliance with Fuld and Iron Horse will take business intelligence to the next level by bringing together Dow Jones Interactive's powerful content and ease of use, Fuld's depth of experience in competitive intelligence analysis and research techniques, and Iron Horse's customized Web-based training programs," said Timothy M. Andrews, vice president and editor, Dow Jones Interactive. "Armed with targeted information, tools and training found in one central location, our customers will be able to conductthorough competitive intelligence research and make even better business decisions."

BiTE

The Institution of Electrical Engineers, of London, UK, located on the Web at `www.iee.org.uk/Bite/comp-int.htm`, provides a useful overview of what you can look for in CI work, by describing their services, which are provided in the detailed description of a series of 18 searches. If you're preparing to do some mergers and acquisitions research, consider examining another page on this site, at `www.iee.org.uk/Bite/m-and-a.htm`.

By looking at what IEE will do for you, you may avoid overlooking crucial data in your own research. You may, of course, end up hiring them, after examining the list of data that you will need to collect.

The research service represents only a portion of the activity of this large and well-known institution. According to their homepage, The Institution of Electrical Engineers represents the "public, professional and educational interest of over 140,000 electrical, electronic and manufacturing engineers world-wide. Key activities include publishing, the organization of conferences, the maintenance of technical standards, interaction with government departments and the provision of scientific and technical information services."

IEE is the organization that produces the *Inspec* database, which is searchable as File 4 on the DIALOG service.

Search Engines & Internet Directories

Search engines are an important key to searching the Internet successfully. Quality, search algorithms and coverage varies, so it is best not to depend on one of them if trying to do an extensive search on a topic.

Some of the search engines or locators in the lists below may be new ones for many some searchers. Note that several European search engines are included. These could be especially useful if you are gathering intelligence using non-US sites or if you wish to search using languages other than English.

Searching foreign databases and reading documents in their native languages may yield intelligence that is not apparent in translated versions. Idioms or cultural nuances may escape the translator or be misinterpreted.

Meta search engines are so called because they offer the ability to enter a search once, but to execute the search across multiple search engines. Some of them are "smart" enough to translate your wishes into the commands expected by the individual engines. This means that you spend less time trying to remembering each search engine's individual search instructions.

Some meta sites search more than just the World Wide Web. Dogpile, a personal favorite, is a good example. It "fetches" answers from half a dozen different places in cyberspace, allowing you to do many types of searches from one "jumping off place." It may search some places you would use only occasionally, such as archived conversations that appeared in Usenets several years ago.

Here is a list of Dogpile's search capabilities, and some possible applications for the information. By now, you can probably think of others. A list of some other meta search engines follows.

The Web:

Yahoo!, Thunderstone, Lycos' A2Z, GoTo.com, Mining Co., Excite Guide, PlanetSearch, What U Seek, Magellan, Lycos, WebCrawler, InfoSeek, Excite and AltaVista.

> *CI Application:*
>
> *Search for company web sites, industry or trade association homepages, documents on topics of interest.*

Usenet:

Reference, DejaNews, AltaVista and Dejanews' old Database.

> *CI Application:*
>
> *Monitor what's being said about your company or about others in which you have an interest. Gather public opinion on a topic.*

FAST FTP Search:

(Only the first word will be passed on to FTP Search.)

CI Application:

> *Locate and read files located on servers worldwide,   that are not loaded on the WWW. Example: conference agendas, which contain names of speakers and their topics. Use the information to identify experts or to see what new developments or topics are beginning to be talked about by presenters.*

Other NewsWires:

Yahoo News Headlines, Excite News and Infoseek NewsWires.

CI Application:

> *Keep up with current news about companies, industries, developments in science or technology.*

BizNews:

Search for Business News from various sources.

CI Application:

> *As above, but with a business slant to the story.*

Stock Quotes:

Enter Tickers or Company Name.

CI Application:

> *Track your stock or "theirs."*

Weather:

Enter City, State or Enter ZIP Code

CI Application:

> *Make marketing decisions regarding products or services.*

Yellow Pages:

Enter Business Name, City State

CI Application:

> *Identify companies offering products or services within a geographic area.*

White Pages:

Enter First Name Last Name, City State

CI Application:

> *Locate addresses, telephone numbers for individuals - possibly someone you wish to interview, without calling them at work.*

Maps:

Enter Street Address, City State

> *CI Application:*
>
> *Study competitors' plant locations, in terms of proximity to highways, railroads, or other modes used to transport goods.*

Meta Search Engines

Language	Site Name	URL (World Wide Web Address)
English	**All4one**	www.all4one.com
English	**Dogpile**	www.dogpile.com
English	**Go2net**	www.go2net.com/search.html
English French German	**InferenceFind**	www.infind.com
English	**Mamma**	www.mamma.com
English	**Metacrawler**	www.metacrawler.com
English	**Profusion**	www.profusion.com

The list below provides will assist you in identifying language availability and URL's for many popular individual search engines. Check them out individually for features that would be useful in your particular type of searching. Some of these engines offer unique features. Alta Vista, for example, offers translation for many foreign language documents that you might retrieve.

Machine translations may be useful for getting the "gist" of a foreign language document, but they sometimes read rather strangely. If you plan to use the document's contents for decision-making, be sure to use a competent human translator who will be aware of multiple meanings for words or phrases.

Search Engines

Language	Site Name	URL (World Wide Web Address)
English	**AltaVista**	www.altavista.com

Search Engines

Language	Site Name	URL (World Wide Web Address)
English	**Ask Jeeves**	www.askjeeves.com
English (UK)	**Euroferret**	www.euroferret.com
Numerous European Languages	**EuroSeek**	www.euroseek.com
English (UK, US, AU, NZ) Chinese French German Italian Japanese Dutch Swedish UK and Chinese	**Excite**	www.excite.com
English	**GoTo**	www.goto.com
Dutch English Finnish French German Italian Portuguese Spanish Swedish	**HotBot**	www.hotbot.com
Danish Dutch English French German Japanese Portuguese (Brazil) Spanish (Spain, Mexico) Swedish	**Infoseek**	www.infoseek.com
English	**Livelink Pinstripe**	http://pinstripe.opentext.com

Search Engines

Language	Site Name	URL (World Wide Web Address)
English Numerous European Languages	**Lycos**	`www.lycos.com`
English (UK)	**Mirago**	`www.mirago.co.uk`
English	**Microsoft Network**	`http://msn.com`
English	**Northern Light**	`www.northernlight.com`
English	**searchUK**	`www.searchuk.com`
English	**Thunderstone**	`http://dwarf.thunderstone.com/texis/websearch`
English	**UKMax**	`www.ukmax.com`
English	**WebCrawler**	`www.webcrawler`
English	**WebSitez**	`www.websitez.com`

For more search engines, see Bookmarks & Favorites, Section IV, under the heading "Search Engines."

That popular Internet service called **Yahoo!** is a classification system rather than a search engine. There are **Yahoo!** sites in many countries, all over the world. To facilitate locating business intelligence in foreign countries, use the list below. The advertisements, yellow pages, etc. on these sites will generally pertain to the country where the site is located, or in a group of countries identified on the home page.

Yahoo! Sites

Language	Site Name	URL (World Wide Web Address)
English	**Yahoo!**	`www.yahoo.com`
English	**Yahoo! Asia**	`http://asia.yahoo.com`
English	**Yahoo! Australia & New Zealand**	`www.yahoo.com.au`

Yahoo! Sites

Language	Site Name	URL (World Wide Web Address)
English French	**Yahoo! Canada**	www.yahoo.ca
Danish	**Yahoo! Denmark**	www.yahoo.dk
French	**Yahoo! France**	www.yahoo.fr
German	**Yahoo! Germany**	www.yahoo.de
Chinese English	**Yahoo! Hong Kong**	www.yahoo.com.hk www.english.yahoo.com.hk
Italian	**Yahoo! Italy**	www.yahoo.it
Japanese	**Yahoo! Japan**	www.yahoo.co.jp
Korean	**Yahoo! Korea**	www.yahoo.com.tw
Norwegian	**Yahoo! Norway**	www.yahoo.no
Spanish	**Yahoo! Spain**	www.yahoo.es
Spanish	**Yahoo! in Spanish (Latin America)**	http://espanol.yahoo.com
Swedish	**Yahoo! Sweden**	www.yahoo.se
Chinese	**Yahoo! Taiwan**	www.yahoo.com.tw
English (UK)	**Yahoo! UK and Ireland**	www.yahoo.co.uk

Tools for Finding the Right Search Engine

The search engines and other tools described thus far could be considered "generalists." They index web sites and then search across them using keywords. This means that you may retrieve documents that contain those keywords, but which are not even close to the topic of your research.

In business, one key to success is to identify a need, and then to create and offer the product or service that meets the need. A number of web sites have been created to do just that. These sites gather together and organize search engine lists, usually by type.

Using a specialized search engine may be a great time-saver when looking for particular types of material on the Internet. The list that follows identifies some of the major players in this group:

Search Engines Locators

Language	Site Name	URL (World Wide Web Address)
French	**7Alpha**	www.7alpha.com
English	**All-in-one**	www.albany.net/allinone
Dutch English French German Japanese Spanish	**Beaucoup**	www.beaucoup.com
English Spanish	**LANIC**	http://lanic.utexas.edu/world/ search
English	**Virtual Search Engines**	www.dreamscape.com/ frankvadsearch.html

To keep up with developments regarding Internet search engines, visit and bookmark http://searchenginewatch.com. **If you wish, you can request a free subscription to** *Search Engine Report Mailing List.*

Chapter 11

Staying on Top of the Subject

Tracking Your CI Targets Automatically

The ongoing business of gathering data and analyzing the competitive situation in your industry, related industries, or within your own market sector can be extremely labor intensive and time consuming. Timeliness is crucial, since certain news could require an immediate response or reaction. Under certain circumstances, skipping even one day's search could put your company at a disadvantage.

One good way to keep up to date is to have a tracking mechanism in place. For that purpose, there are several types of cyberspace tools that can be used to make the job easier. These tools allow you to use a proactive, rather than reactive, approach.

Custom News Services — Track Companies, Industries, & Trends

Commercial online vendors have offered current awareness services for years. With the advent of the Internet, however, a new class of products entered the marketplace. Custom news services are used to put news, stock quotes, and other timely information on desktops across Corporate America. Researchers now have access to at least three categories of products or services:

♦ PUSH Technology

♦ Alert Services

♦ Vertical Market Products

Each of these types of services fills a need in the information gathering process. Many companies use all three options, either on a regular basis, or as needed.

PUSH Technology

PUSH technology has proliferated thanks to the Internet. Using the combined resources of multiple vendors, these services bring information right to your computer desktop in the form of a direct feed, e-mail or as an icon that runs your searches on demand.

In general, PUSH services allow you to customize your news by choosing from a list of topics. The list of subjects varies from service to service, as do the features. Some may even highlight the keywords you are looking for within the articles.

These services are frequently sold as enterprise packages, which makes them available to your organization on a company-wide basis. Others may be available at no charge, but are advertising supported. Although some sources may be on a service's "free" list, you may be asked to pay for other articles if you want them full text.

The variety of choices means that even the smallest companies, or those with small budgets for information tracking, can still take advantage of automated company or industry tracking. In general, the more costly services are the ones that offer more features, greater customization, and fewer, if any, additional costs.

NewsEdge, located at www.newsedge.com, is a good example of PUSH technology. Their web page claims to deliver more than 50,000 stories per day from over 2,000 global information sources from over 120 of the world's leading publishers.

Free Services

NewsEdge offers a free service called NewsPage where you can track the exact topics, companies and even investments that are of greatest interest to you. A list of headlines and lead sentences for documents or articles is delivered via e-mail every business morning. Some of the articles on your topics may come from a "premium" list, which may even advise you of patents that have been granted.

Internet Services like PUSH tools can monitor the patents received by a competitor company as well as pertinent news articles. You might choose this method as a reminder, or as a complement to other methods used to monitor intellectual property.

This free subscription can be very useful for keeping up with developments, especially if you don't have time to read lots of full-text articles. Some CI searchers use free services to cross-check against the results they obtain from expensive subscriptions or monitoring services.

The Excite NewsTracker, at www.excite.com, has 300+ sources. You can customize the service by choosing your own topics. For each article retrieved, you will see the title, the Web site on which the article appeared, a brief summary of its contents, and the date the article was first posted. The source list at http://nt.excite.com/sources.html will give you an idea of NewsTracker's scope of coverage. You must sign on and retrieve the results of your custom news search. It's easy to forget to do this on a busy day, so the e-mail approach used by NewsEdge is considered by many searchers to be the preferable approach.

Commercial Sources

There are also commercial current awareness tools available. These could bring business intelligence to every desktop in your company, if that is your plan. One of the best-known of these is Inquisit, at www.inquisit.com. This popular and relatively low-cost system offers approximately 600 sources. Inquisit delivers your business intelligence by e-mail.

For a comparison of some of the various PUSH products available, look at http://idm.internet.com/tools-km.shtml. This site contains a table that categorizes these products by product name, company, platforms, highlights and price, with links to sites that provide more detail on each product.

Alert Services

All of the large commercial online vendors offer their Web or direct access subscribers current awareness or alert services in one form or another. In some environments the phrase "selective dissemination of information," or SDI, is used to describe the process.

Assuming that you are a subscriber, you can contact your designated representative or call the vendor's Customer Support Department. The vendor's personnel should be able to help you construct searches that are run automatically, by the system, every time a database is reloaded — daily, weekly, or annually. The vendor sends you relevant documents or articles that have been added to the system since the last reload, by e-mail, fax or whatever method has been agreed upon. You are charged a modest fee for storage of the query on the vendor's computer, plus a fee for each item retrieved. If you prefer, you may set up such alert services by filling in forms available on some vendors' web sites.

Your Sales & Marketing Department may wish to keep abreast of the market strategies of a dozen companies in the US and abroad. Think how much time and labor could be saved if you automate the process. Rather than try to read and clip dozens of newspapers, trade publications, newswires and other sources, let the online vendor's computer do the work for you.

If you opt to receive the articles by e-mail, you will have relatively timely information. Of course, *how* timely depends upon the frequency with which the vendor updates and reloads the database. You may find that Vendor A reloads a certain database more frequently than Vendor B. If talking with vendors about their services, be sure to ask these and other questions discussed in Chapter 5.

Using another approach, **Dow Jones Interactive's Custom Clips** allows you to set up as many as five clip folders, covering companies, industries, news topics, investment topics, or custom selections of words, terms, and sources to be searched. You can run these searches on demand, searching a list of publications that you select, by industry, region, title, or type. You are, of course, charged for each article retrieved, but the cost is moderate.

In addition, you can set a relevance ranking that will find news with at least a relevance score that you have specified. The score can be raised to get a smaller result, or lowered to get more. If you use a company's ticker symbol as a search term in Dow Jones Interactive, the search engine retrieves relevant articles and omits those that coincidentally contain words that are part of the target company's name.

You can search across broad categories like "All Newswires," or select particular sources. Suppose, for example, that you wish to monitor Texas newspapers for articles that mention both of the two PC manufacturers based in the state, Dell Computer and Compaq. By choosing a tab marked "Regional," a list of Texas newspapers is available either individually, or as a group. You can create a search strategy and run it as frequently as desired. When you no longer need this folder, it can be discarded.

The vendor's staff should be able to help you to choose the best sources and to construct optimal search strategies. They can also advise you of additional files that were recently added to their service, which may yield new and valuable intelligence.

Constantly monitoring your company's competitors, industry, or topics of interest, is a major undertaking. To do this efficiently, you need an electronic helper, which will monitor particular sources for any references to items of interest, even if you are on vacation, taking a "sick day," or are just too busy to take the time to do so.

DIALOG and LEXIS-NEXIS are popular sources for this type of alert service. Here is how the system works, assuming that you are a subscriber:

◆ You follow instructions on the vendor's web site, contact your designated representative or call the vendor's Customer Support Department.

◆ You construct one or more searches that are run automatically, by the system, **every time a database is reloaded — daily, weekly, or annually**.

◆ Using e-mail, fax or whatever method has been agreed upon, the vendor sends you relevant documents or articles that have been added to the system since the last reload.

◆ You are charged a modest fee for storage of the query on the vendor's computer, plus a fee for each item retrieved.

At Dow Jones Interactive, the approach is slightly different. The *Custom Clips* feature allows you to set up your choices as follows:

◆ Add an Industry Topic Folder - Select from 400 industries.

◆ Add a Company Topic Folder - Select from 5,000 major companies.

◆ Add a News Topic Folder - Select from 50 news subjects.

♦ Add an Investing Topic Folder - Select from 50 investing subjects.

♦ Add a Custom Folder - Cover any subject using your own words and publication selections.

Search results can be delivered by email if desired.

There are plenty of applications for these types of services. Your Sales and Marketing Department may wish to keep abreast of the market strategies of a dozen companies in the US and abroad. Research & Development may be interested in new patents filed by a competitor. The Ppublic Affairs Department may be interested in what Competitor X is saying in print on an issue of importance to the entire industry. Think how much time and labor could be saved if you automate the process. Rather than try to read and clip dozens of newspapers, trade publications, wires and other sources, let the vendor's computer do the work for you.

Vendor A may reload a file more frequently than Vendor B. Be sure to compare database update schedules. This and other important questions to ask when choosing online vendors are discussed in Chapter 5.

Current awareness is also possible using some special Internet tools. Company Sleuth, at www.companysleuth.com, includes news stories as one category of information provided each day on companies you select. You can also monitor competitors'web sites. Chapter 11 describes a service that sends you e-mail every time specified sites or pages change.

Consider PUSH technology, discussed further in Chapter 11, for alerting purposes, as well. With this method, news and other stories on previously selected topics or industries are brought to the desktop, automatically. But remember that those services may not search all of the sources that you consider important. You may need a combination of several alerting tools to feel comfortable that you are monitoring *all possible outlets* for business intelligence.

Vertical Market Products

Vertical market online services focus on providing products and services that meet the information needs of specific markets or industries. **Reuters** is a good example of a provider in the news area because of the large variety of subject matter in their vertical offerings, which may be obtained directly, or through the Internet.

Their specialty services run the gamut from geographically oriented collections like their Latin American Business report, to entertainment or similar general topics. Data can be received via satellite dish, FM antenna or leased phone lines. Internet delivery is possible through Newscom, www.newscom.com, or Presslink — www.presslink.com.

The Reuters Business Briefs Select Services are available through several Internet services, including NewsEdge at www.newsedge.com, and Wavephore at www.wavephore.com or through Windows software that is available in four languages and provides articles in at least twelve languages. This product replaces Reuters Textline, a very popular database file that formerly was available on LEXIS, DIALOG and other sources.

Though Reuters services are marketed chiefly to the media, the rapid access to information inherent in a service like this has attracted many large corporations who consider it a worthwhile investment. Special services have been developed for the insurance, advertising and transportation industries, as well as health and other corporate and professional sectors. These services may be very useful for keeping in touch with what's happening in faraway places where you may have a significant investment in material or personnel.

Not all stories of potential interest to your company are picked up on vertical market wires. They may be important to you, but would not have been categorized as "industry specific." You may find that you need to search general sources as well, on a regular basis, to avoid missing such items.

Keeping Tabs on Competitors' Web Sites

Suppose that you would like to monitor the web sites of several companies or organizations. This means investing significant time in visiting each web site, looking at key areas, or perhaps browsing the entire site, looking for new material — unless you can find an easier way to do the job! For starters, it would be very useful to know when your competitor's web site has been updated.

How to Know When Your Competitor's Web Site Changes

You can't exactly call NetMind, at http://netmind.com, the best-kept secret on the Internet, because they claim to have four million users, including 100 Fortune 500 companies. NetMind's free online service, Mind-It, tracks changes to any Web-based information, either at the site level or page level. It checks the Web at least once every 24 hours.

When your target sites or pages are updated, you are notified via an e-mail containing a link to the changed site or page, so that you are "instantly" informed of the change. There is also a link back to NetMind so that you can make additions, modifications, or deletions to your instructions for monitoring. Use of this type of tool helps you to stay more informed and significantly reduces time spent checking web sites where the information has not changed.

The following list of possibilities may provide some useful site research suggestions:

ACTIVITY: Track sections of a competitor's site. Some large corporations may have hundreds of separate web pages on their sites, while you may be interested only in particular parts of it.

Application: Select the page where a company lists its *press releases*. Each time new press releases are added, you will be alerted, and you can click your way directly to the release you wish to read.

Application: Monitor new products that are added to a competitor's site by clicking on their "Products" button and setting the tracker to the resulting page.

Application: Keep an eye on *job openings* that the target company puts on its web site. This could alert you to someone's departure, or perhaps give you an idea about a new direction the company intends to take in product development, R&D, etc. Sometimes the fact that they are hiring or not hiring is useful information.

ACTIVITY: Highlight a portion of the text on a page and ask to be alerted to changes *only* in the highlighted area.

Application: Watch for evidence that a company *repositioning* itself in the market. For example, a software developer might have chosen to stop marketing certain products individually. They may now use new language such as "interactive system" in the section of their site that formerly touted the features of the individual products. This may be of great interest if you are trying to determine their marketing strategy.

ACTIVITY: Highlight the pertinent regulatory section on a government agency site.

Application: If *the regulations change*, you will be made aware of the publication of the new regulations, and you can then adjust your activities accordingly.

ACTIVITY: Set keywords to be used against a page, so that you can be notified when certain words are added to a site.

Application: Add a keyword tracking *your company name* to appropriate news site pages. As a result, if the news site mentions your company, you will know it. You may also be able to see which of the press releases your company issues are being picked up, and where.

Application: Add keywords tracking *a competitor's name* to a government agency's public calendar page. You'll be made aware of meetings between that company and regulatory agencies such as the Food & Drug Administration (FDA).

Using a tool like Mindit! for keyword tracking may be sufficient for some companies, while for others it may supplement or back up larger, more sophisticated monitoring operations.

This Site Even Works on Weekends!

A new addition to your CI resources might be Company Sleuth, at www.companysleuth.com, the brainchild of Infonautics Corporation. After registering, you may choose to monitor a list of *public* companies as investments, competition, prospects, or clients. You receive daily (including weekends) reports that cover a number of the areas you've decided are important to watch. New items in each category are flagged daily.

One of the most useful reasons for using a site like Company Sleuth, however, is to keep an eye on the message boards. Present employees are likely to exercise caution when commenting on company matters, but former employees may feel less constrained. Your Public Relations department is very aware of the company's image, and may wish to keep track of what these people have to say.

Other departments within your company also may wish to monitor the message boards or Usenets for commentary by certain activist groups. For example, this could provide early warnings for your company regarding protests planned by such organizations. This type of information regarding your company also may provide useful intelligence to your competitors, so it is wise to know what is being said.

Here are the categories included in each day's Company Sleuth report for tracking publicly held companies:

Company Brief	Analyst Reports
Patents granted within the past month	Earnings Whispers
Trademarks granted within the past month	Message Boards Summary
Federal Litigation	Job Postings
Broker Reports	SEC Filings
Internet Domains	Stock Quote
Insider Trading Information	Short Interest
News	

The graphic below shows a portion of a report on Dell Computer Corporation.

COMPANY SLEUTH

Helen's Personal Report

Dell Computer Corporation

Investments   Competition   Prospects   Clients   Other

(Dell Computer Corporation)

check 7 days prev 11/19/98 next today

open all   close all   edit companies   preferences   top ten   more options   logout

▶ Patents   0 new ⑦

▶ Trademarks   10 new ⑦

▶ Internet Domains   0 new ⑦

▶ Insider Trading Information   0 new ⑦

▶ Analyst Reports   0 new ⑦

Company Sleuth tracks up to ten companies, retrieving information from public records, message boards, etc. to keep users abreast of new filings or messages on their target companies.

Before registering at this site, be sure to take a look at the <u>More Options</u> hotlink. In addition to changing passwords and other "housekeeping" options, several interesting lists are available under the heading "Top Ten":

<u>Who is Watching Me?</u>

<u>Top Ten This Week</u>

<u>All Time Top Ten</u>

This site may be one where you might choose to perform Defensive CI, as described in Chapter 4. You will know on a daily basis what competitors can learn about your company's activities, to the extent that articles about companies appear in the site's list of news sources, or if your company's activities fall into the categories covered by each report:

Monitoring Reloads of Your Favorite Government Site

Suppose that your company needs to answer questions like these:

♦   Is this a good time to borrow money?

♦   Should we make that capital investment?

♦ Should we expand the business?

The company's corporate planning department or comptroller might use certain government figures as part of their effort to make decisions that are in the company's best interests. They would, of course, want the latest information. They also would want to monitor trends or changes in these figures over time.

All of this and more is available in sources such as the *Government Printing Office's Economic Indicators Monthly* (`www.access.gpo.gov/congress/eibrowse/99febbro.html`), which contains month-by-month links to the past three years' reports. To give you an idea of the type of data that is available here in PDF format, some of the headings found in the February 1999 monthly are summarized below:

ECONOMIC INDICATORS - FEBRUARY 1999

TOTAL OUTPUT, INCOME, AND SPENDING	Gross Domestic Product
	Real Gross Domestic Product
	Implicit Price Deflators for Gross Domestic Product.
	Gross Domestic Product & Related Price Measures: Indexes & Percent Changes.
	Nonfinancial Corporate Business— Output, Costs, & Profits.
	National Income
	Real Personal Consumption Expenditures.
	Sources of Personal Income.
	Disposition of Personal Income.
	Farm Income.
	Corporate Profits
	Real Gross Private Domestic Investment.
	Real Private Fixed Investment by Type.
	Business Investment
EMPLOYMENT, UNEMPLOYMENT, AND WAGES	Status of the Labor Force
	Selected Unemployment Rates
	Selected Measures of Unemployment & Unemployment Insurance Programs.
	Nonagricultural Employment
	Average Weekly Hours, Hourly Earnings, & Weekly Earnings—Private Nonagricultural Industries.
	Employment Cost Index—Private Industry.
	Productivity & Related Data, Business Sector.
PRODUCTION AND BUSINESS ACTIVITY	Industrial Production & Capacity Utilization.
	Industrial Production—Major Market Groups & Selected Manufactures
	New Construction

ECONOMIC INDICATORS - FEBRUARY 1999

	New Private Housing & Vacancy Rates.
	Business Sales & Inventories—Manufacturing & Trade.
	Manufacturers' Shipments, Inventories, & Orders.
PRICES	Producer Prices
	Consumer Prices—All Urban Consumers.
	Changes in Producer Prices for Finished Goods.
	Changes in Consumer Prices—All Urban Consumers.
	Prices Received & Paid by Farmers
MONEY, CREDIT, AND SECURITY MARKETS	Money Stock & Debt Measures
	Money Stock & Debt Measures
	Aggregate Reserves & Monetary Base.
	Bank Credit at All Commercial Banks
	Sources & Uses of Funds, Nonfarm Nonfinancial Corporate Business
	Consumer Credit
	Interest Rates & Bond Yields
	Common Stock Prices & Yields
FEDERAL FINANCE	Federal Receipts, Outlays, & Debt
	Federal Receipts by Source & Outlays by Function.
	Federal Sector, National Income Accounts Basis.
INTERNATIONAL STATISTICS	Industrial Production & Consumer Prices—Major Industrial Countries.
	US International Trade in Goods & Services.
	US International Transactions.

One convenient site for locating and monitoring this information is through the University of California's GPO Gate site, at www.gpo.ucop.edu/catalog/econind.html. US Depository Libraries at other academic institutions may also offer access. By setting NetMind's Mind-It, mentioned previously, to monitor this page, you will receive an e-mail when the succeeding month's figures have been added.

A similar strategy might be wise for the MANUFACTURERS' SHIPMENTS, INVENTORIES, AND ORDERS "M3" report that is issued periodically at www.census.gov/ftp/pub/indicator/www/m3/index.htm.

Researching the Competition Anonymously

If your company maintains a web site, your computer services department may monitor the site to see who visits. Just as you visit competitors' sites, they visit yours. Knowing this, you may wish to visit them anonymously.

EXAMPLE 1: Suppose that you are interested in what a competitor is saying about a particular topic on their web site. You may not care if they know you visited their site, but you don't want them to know exactly which pages interest you. An anonymous visit is what is called for.

EXAMPLE 2: Suppose you are considering electronic commerce at your web site. You visit Internet sites offering this service because you'll soon be their competitor. You want to see what's being offered, and how matters such as accepting credit cards, placing orders, etc. are handled. If you can make it easier, more secure, or otherwise more attractive for Internet shoppers to do business at your site, your site will likely be a "winner." If, however, the competition can see that it was *you* who has visited so many times recently, they may guess what you are planning and speed up plans to revamp their own sites. You could lose that competitive advantage! Again, an anonymous visit may be called for.

The Anonymizer, at <u>www.anonymizer.com</u>, allows you to do just that.

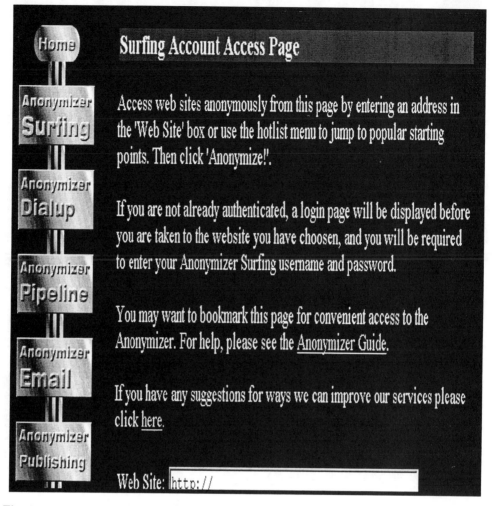

The Anonymizer keeps your identity from being disclosed while you visit competitors' sites.

What happens once on Anonymizer's access page, you enter the URL of the site you wish to visit. The site is displayed on your screen and you view, search or print it as you normally would. Your competitor's tracking software learns that their site was visited by Anonymizer, and your identity is not disclosed.

You many not consider this procedure necessary for all of your Internet research, but it is a handy tool to have available for those times when you need it.

Anonymizer informs you up front that paying customers are first in line, so to expedite service, a subscription is a good idea. You can use the free service as much as you like, as often as you like, and if you try their free service you may find that the time element is satisfactory for your needs.

Chapter 12

Looking at the Big Picture

Examining an Industry

Competitor/competitive intelligence involves much more than looking at individual companies in a given market or comparing one company's market share with that of another. It is often important to examine the industry in which your company is involved, and possibly to study others, for several purposes:

♦ **Keeping up with developments or trends in your industry** - To compete successfully within your own industry, your company must aim for competitive advantage in one area or another. To do this, it is necessary to know what has happened in the past, what is currently happening, and to be able to predict the right moves for the future.

♦ **Watching developments or trends in another industry** - These may have a direct impact on your company. This information is taken into consideration by those involved in strategy or planning the direction in which your company will move. It is also of interest to those in the sales and marketing area.

♦ **Moving into a new industry** - To keep a company viable over time, it is often decided to move into new product areas, which possibly will make you a player in a totally different industry from that in which your company is now active. Before making that decision, it is important to have researched the "new" industry carefully.

♦ **Considering an acquisition or merger** - Mergers or acquisitions are not undertaken lightly. Considerable research goes into the big decision, and a thorough understanding of both the present and the future of one or more industries is crucial in the due diligence process that accompanies this type of undertaking.

Hard Facts & Figures Abound Online & Elsewhere

For most industry categories, it is not difficult to gather statistics. The challenge lies in whether the analysts and strategists in your company can use the data to create knowledge. The information will come from several sources:

Government Agencies

Government sources are an invaluable resource in this undertaking, since they collect data so widely. Much of the important statistical data from dozens of agencies is now available on the Internet. In many cases it can be downloaded and loaded into your company's software for further analysis. The Bureau of the Census provides detailed data which can be viewed or downloaded in PDF format, ASCII, or worksheet format at its Current Industrial Reports site, `www.census.gov/pub/cir/www/index.html`. Format and frequency of update vary by industry.

One of the more traditional government sources is the Statistical Abstract of the United States, at `www.census.gov/statab/www`. Statistics abound on on social and economic conditions in the United States, and selected international data are also included. The Abstract also points you to additional data from the US Census Bureaumentioned above, from other Federal agencies, and from private organizations.

The LEXIS-NEXIS Universe site provides searching of Economic Indicators from its Industry News page. A number of other useful government statistics sites can be located in the Bookmarks & Favorites section of Part IV, under the heading "Statistics."

Finding the "Softer" Information

Soft information about an industry is generally considered to be non-statistical intelligence gleaned from non-traditional sources. Some of this intelligence can be gleaned using cyber-tools to learn what is being said by people, in print or on electronic format.

Changes in public sentiment may have a dramatic impact on an industry. This could mean, therefore, that the trends observed during the past five years are *not* a true picture of where the industry is going, or that forecasts for the industry are impacted by certain unforeseen events, and therefore invalid.

The tobacco industry is an example. Health-related lawsuits against this industry have been big news for several years. At one point rumors have begun to appear in print regarding the sell-off of their tobacco units by some large companies involved in both the tobacco and food industries. "Letters-to-the-Editor" from corporate watchdog groups calling for boycotts of these companies appeared in major US newspapers.

Trends and forecasts in the tobacco industry prior to the filing of these lawsuits did not reflect changes in public opinion in more recent years. Unless industry analysts or others creating such prognostications could look into a "crystal ball," they were unable to predict the saga that would unfold.

Searching the Editorial Pages

Searching for an industry topic and the words "op-ed" or "letters" in commercial vendors' newspaper files is a good research strategy. Visiting the Web sites of various newspapers and searching archives also works well, and is less costly. (A number of individual newspapers web sites are included in Bookmarks & Favorites, under the heading "Newspapers.")

A search of the *San Francisco Chronicle*, at www.sfgate.com/search is an example:

Search strategy: tobacco and op-ed

Results: 86 articles in 1998, including Letters to the Editor and other material.

Usenets & Listservs: Cyber Listening Posts

Another place to look for soft information would be the listservs and Usenets on the Internet. Dejanews, at www.deja.com or Dogpile, at www.dogpile.com, offer you the opportunity to search the archives of these types of files to gather public opinion as expressed in cyberspace by list members - you are "taking the pulse of the nation," so to speak. The various lists available through Yahoo! at www.yahoo.com would provide another access point for this type of search.

Pre-Packaged Reports From Commercial Vendors

Several reputable commercial vendors package industry studies of various types. At times, it may be cost-effective to take this route toward studying an industry. You might choose to supplement what is learned from a packaged study, using the categories of information described in the next chapter. The list below is a sampling of sources for industry studies:

Dow Jones Interactive - The Company & Industry Center on the Dow Jones web site offers Company-to-Industry and Industry-to-Industry comparison reports, formatted or ASCII delimited for downloading into other software programs. Industry categories are as defined by Dow Jones' company-to-company reports are also available.

Investext - Investext's *Research Bank Web* page includes an Industry Monitor which provides Investment Research, Market Research, and Trade Association reports on industry-specific topics. The box that follows demonstrates the citation for a report on the petroleum industry:

WORLD INDUSTRIAL RAW MATERIALS -
CRUDE OIL
Report #: 5171870   Pages: 11 pgs
Date: 19 Jun 98
Contributor: Economist Intelligence Unit

FINDEX - DIALOG File 196, FINDEX, is a database of industry and market research reports and studies, consumer studies, major multi-client studies, surveys and polls, audits, and industry or company reports issued by investment brokerage firms. Using FINDEX, you could receive comprehensive analyses of markets, industries, products, and companies. Ordering information is included, for both US and non-US sources. FIND/SVP's reports are also available in LEXIS-NEXIS in the MKTRES library, along with market research reports from other sources.

When searching for industry reports in a broad database such as FINDEX, include the word "industry" as part of your search string to "zero in" on the industry studies and avoid other types of reports.

Frost & Sullivan Market Intelligence - DIALOG File 765, the Frost & Sullivan file, contains in-depth analyses and forecasts of technical market trends. Reports contain five-year forecasts of market size by product category and end-user application. Marketing and distribution strategies are discussed, and assessments of the competitive and legislative environment are also provided. European, US, and worldwide studies are organized by geographic region. Reports include the following elements:

- Executive Summary
- Introduction
- Scope and Methodology
- Technical Review
- Current Product Characteristics
- End-user/Application Analysis
- Competitor Market Shares and Profiles
- Five-Year and Interim Forecast by Major National Market
- Product Group and End-user/Application
- Trends and Opportunities
- Company names and addresses.

Industries covered by Frost & Sullivan include:

Aerospace & Defense	Industrial Automation
Automotive	Instruments & Controls
Biotechnology	Medical Devices
Data & Telecommunications	Pharmaceuticals
Data Processing & Office Automation	Paper & Packaging
Diagnostic Equipment & Reagents	Plants & Machinery
Energy	Plastics
Electro-medical Instrumentation	Security & Access Control
Environmental Controls	Textiles
Fast-moving Consumer Goods	Veterinary Medicine & Agriculture
Food & Beverages	

Market research studies from other sources are likely to contain similar categories of information from a variety of industries. But if a prepackaged study is not in the budget, if you're researching an unusual industry, or if you just want the fun of a "do it yourself" project, read Chapter 16 carefully. You'll learn what to look at and where to start looking.

Chapter 13

Information Gold vs. Fool's Gold

Mining Company Web Pages

One of the first thoughts that comes to mind these days when searching for factual information on a company is to check the company web site to see if the answers are there. This is often the first and best route to finding what you want to know, especially when researching privately held companies.

Internet sites are designed to present a company in the best possible light. Since it is *their* site, they can brag, if they choose to, about products, services, accomplishments and so on. You'll want to keep that thought in mind as you read what they're presenting. Reputable companies usually present accurate information, generally choosing to ignore topics that they consider negative. You'll have to find *that* material elsewhere.

The Major Benefits of Searching Company Web Sites

Company web sites can be an extremely useful and convenient research tool. Searching these sights offers several advantages over other methods of information retrieval when you need to gather intelligence on a particular company or small group of companies. Here's why they are useful:

♦ **You may find the hard-to-find.**

> Suppose that you are trying to create a list of the countries where a multi-national competitor operates. You may find that their web site provides not only a numeric answer, for example, *"We operate in 75 countries,"* but it may also include world maps that show where the corporation does business. This information is probably updated as they move into additional countries.

♦ **There is probably no cost involved.**

> If what you seek is basic information about products, services, ordering and directories, then using company sites can save you money since that information is gathered for free. For in-depth data, such as financials, however, you may still need to supplement

this basic information with additional details that are likely to be obtained by searching a commercial source.

♦ **It's convenient.**

> It may be a simple matter to "copy and paste" the data you find, adding it to a report created in a word processing program, for instance, or attaching it to an e-mail.

♦ **The material is likely to be up-to-date.**

> You'll probably find that the information on the company web site is more timely than that obtained from certain other sources, such as printed directories.

> Most directory publishers update their records annually, or even less frequently. The company's webmaster, on the other hand, is probably charged with keeping the site up-to-date, making changes as frequently as daily. (Daily updates are often the case on web sites that include news coverage on their homepages.)

How to Use What You Find on a Company's Web Site

Touring a number of company Internet sites can provide insights into the types of information that is often included on other sites in that same genre. Larger companies may spend more money on web site projects than smaller companies. Larger companies tend to use sophisticated or eye-catching graphics, and make available archives of company publications, or educational material aimed at teachers and students. On some sites, the page count may number in the hundreds. These sites may attract thousands of online visitors daily.

You will find that the types and amount of information found on company web sites varies greatly. A certain amount of "copy cat" behavior occurs, however, so it may be worth checking competitors' sites frequently to see what's new there.

The alphabetical list that follows will give you an idea of the types of information that you may find, and some hints about how the information can be useful. Remember that if you don't want them to know that you visited, you can search anonymously, as described at the end of Chapter 11.

Community/Charitable Activities

Looking at a company's charitable activities may give you a "tip-off" about their corporate philosophy toward such activities. The site may actually list groups or organizations that the company supports. Your strategists may take this into consideration when entering a marketplace in which a competitor is already active. **Seeing what a competitor is doing in this area may provide ideas about projects that your company might undertake in its own Community Relations efforts.**

Company History

Company history is often useful in assessing an organization's corporate culture. If a company has existed for decades, or even longer, its management or Board of Directors may be very aware of what the company founder would have done or said in certain situations. They may make decisions that reflect that knowledge or follow that precedent. **If you are familiar with the company's history, you may be able to predict corporate behavior.**

On the other hand, high tech start-up companies founded within the past twenty years may reflect a totally different culture, which may be much easier to discern. The company founder may have been interviewed extensively in newspapers or the trade press, as examples. And, as examined in Chapter 11, you can find this information quite readily.

Whichever best describes your target company, knowing their history can prove useful, and their web site may be a good starting point for obtaining that information.

Company Magazines

Most companies publish magazines or newsletters for stockholders and employees. To the extent that the company considers them to be useful public relations or marketing tools, you may find them in an archive that is available from their web site.

These publications may contain photographs of work sites and equipment, descriptions of projects, or other useful intelligence information. Usually, the content is carefully screened during the editorial process, so it is not likely that you will find the company's strategic marketing plan for the next five years. Still, you will find a lot of information about people, places and things.

Corporate Philosophy/Beliefs

Words like "environment" and "diligence" appear frequently on the sites of companies in certain industries. We assume that they will say "politically correct" things, so you won't find a statement like "We don't care..." **But, determining what they have said may help your company to market products or services to them.**

While a company's "Position Statement" on important issues may be useful to your company in reaching conclusions about their strategy, that information may also be useful as you plan your own company's position statements, and as you consider whether or not it is to your advantage to concur with the competition's positions on issues.

Customer Endorsements

Any endorsements or success stories included on a company's web site are bound to be favorable, but reading them may not be the waste of your time you may at first think it is. Looking at these items can **provide insights into areas where the competitor is strong; i.e., satisfied customers rave about customer support, a money-back guarantee or other replacement policy.** Endorsements may provide insights into their customer or client base, particularly if the happy customer's age, gender, profession, employer, or similar information is included.

Employment Opportunities

The amount and types of employment opportunity information on corporate web sites runs the gamut from very general to the extremely detailed.

Some companies state that there are openings for recent graduates with degrees in ... (fill in the blank). The site may include a hot-link to their Human Resources Department's page, which may accept e-mailed resumes, which, if not read directly, may be scanned electronically and pre-screened automatically. Other companies may provide lists containing details such as job title, skills required, and location of the opening. These, of course, provide the greatest amount of business intelligence as **they point out which people the company is in need of.**

Executive Speeches

Some company web sites contain the text of a selected group of speeches by company VIPs. These may vary in value in terms of competitive intelligence, yet you can't judge their value until you read them.

Honors, Awards, Achievements

If a company has received prestigious honors or awards, they are likely to mention them somewhere on the company web site. Important industry awards generally receive significant coverage in the trade press, and the programs or activities that helped garner the honor may be described in detail. Local newspapers should also be searched for this type of story.

Investor Information

Facts and figures intended to provide information to shareholders also provides information to competitors! Among the items that you might expect to find in this area of a company web site are the Annual Report to Shareholders, stock prices, dividend information, links to the SEC, and that ubiquitous Internet phenomenon, "frequently asked questions."

Miscellaneous Publications

A "miscellaneous" category may include many different publications, such as reports on the company's operations in another part of the world, topic-oriented position papers, or brochures. Checking these items carefully can yield tidbits of intelligence that may be of interest to you, their competitor.

News/Media Coverage

Although, you hopefully have one or more monitoring mechanisms in place (see Chapter 11), a periodic run through of your competitors' web sites could provide links to articles that you had not seen previously. Articles on that web site may have come from a location or source not covered in your monitoring activity.

You may even find a few press releases that never made it into print due to more important news events at the time. These may have been passed up by the Business Editor at the newspaper, but **they may provide you with valuable intelligence such as the name of the new Vice President of X Company.**

Operations Locations

A competition's web site may provide numbers on, or better still, lists of plant locations and other facilities. These should not be considered complete, however, and more research may be called for if you need a list that includes all company facility locations. However, **lists found on the web site can be used for validating or augmenting existing information.**

Product Manuals & Documentation

These publications may provide detailed product descriptions or diagrams that could be of interest to your company's R&D or engineering departments. Often, you may have to be a registered owner of a specific product to gain access to this data. At other companies, you may not.

Products/Services

A company's listing of products and services on their web site gives you an indication of the way they are positioning those products or services. This information can be quite useful to your company in **positioning your own products, developing new ones, or evaluating what the competition is offering.**

Research & Development Activity

While it is highly unlikely that a company web site will provide information about products still in development, some sites offer lists of general areas where the company is engaged in research and development. These lists can be used to guide you in further research about such activity.

SEC Filings (Publicly Traded Companies)

Company web sites of publicly-traded companies often contain hot-links to the full texts of the Annual Report to Shareholders or SEC filings such as 10-K Reports. Some sites also list additional filings of various types. It is not unusual to find hot-links to the US government's EDGAR site, where a more comprehensive search can be run. Refer to Appendix A for a detailed list of these filings, including descriptions of their contents.

The filings listed on a company web site may represent only a portion of those actually available. If you are interested in all filings for a publicly-held company, to obtain them consider going directly to the SEC's EDGAR site or using commercial online sources.

Subsidiaries/Affiliated Companies

A company web site may include references to or lists of related companies. These may be a useful reference, but should not be trusted as a comprehensive listing of all divisions, subsidiaries, affiliates, or other members of the corporate family, if that is what you are seeking. It is recommended that other resources be used to create such a list, and that you cross check what you have found.

Trademarks/Tradenames

Some web sites contain extensive lists of a company's trademarks or tradenames. There is often a warning, however, that such lists may not be complete. More research may be called for if you require a comprehensive list of such intellectual property. But, the web site's list can be used for cross-checking or validating information located previously.

Finding Subsidiary, Division or Affiliate Web Sites

Finding all Internet sites connected with a competitor can be a bit of a challenge. Some corporate web sites provide links to related sites, but that list may be incomplete. It may be necessary to try several different approaches to locating those elusive site, including these:

♦   Search the company name using your favorite search engine.

> This can be very problematic, however, because some company names contain familiar words that have been used across corporate America. The word "sun," for example, appears in the names of hundreds of companies large and small across the country. Locating "all" web sites for "Sun Microsystems" using one of the popular web search engines could become a time-consuming task, requiring that searcher dig through a long list, and still not being guaranteed that the list is complete.

> In addition, Sun Microsystems could be responsible for some sites that do not use the word "sun" as part of the web address. These sites would be more difficult to identify.

♦   Consult one of the Internet sites that identify web sites connected with a company.

Company Sleuth, described previously in Chapter 11, provides users with a daily e-mail report that includes a list of company web sites, including those sites whose names might not be automatically associated with the company name. This service currently covers only publicly-traded companies, however.

Websitez, at www.websitez.com, contains over one million web sites in a searchable database of domain name owners. For identifying company web sites, Websitez works best where the company name contains a word with a unique spelling, such as "Compaq" or Texaco. Even using this technique, search results may include web sites for stores selling Compaq computers, or your local Texaco service station.

Searching companies whose names begin with common words such as "sun," for example, retrieves a long list of hits. Be sure to examine the list of sub-categories provided by Websitez to focus on an industry or market sector, as this will reduce the number of sites you must check.

Part III:

Finding Business Intelligence on People, Companies & Industries

Chapter 14

Using the Internet to Locate Information About People

The CI Perspective

▬ Scoping Out a Competitor's Personnel

The World Wide Web is used constantly by individuals seeking to find other individuals, for a variety of reasons. The same approach can be used to locate important business intelligence by gathering information on a competitor's key personnel. Knowing the CEO's career experience, politics, family background, favorite "causes" or charities, likes and dislikes, hobbies, personality quirks, etc. can be useful when doing business with that person or in predicting the direction in which he or she will take the company.

Such detail may not always be the goal of your search. If you are planning to market products or services to another company, it may be the name and job title that you need. Directing a mailing to "Occupant," Vice President of Sales, would be a waste of postage. Obtaining "Occupant's" name may be possible with a telephone call, but suppose you are compiling a list of a hundred companies to contact? Under these circumstances, the telephone approach would be expensive and time-consuming.

So whether it's compiling a dossier on the competitor's CEO or generating a list of their personnel, online information sources can help. The secret to finding this information lies in knowing where to begin looking, and in not giving up if at first you don't find much. If this happens, you simply dig wider and deeper — all in publicly available sources, of course — no engaging in unethical behavior! Here are some places to look:

Using SEC Filings to Identify Affiliations & Holdings

Although the Securities & Exchange Commission (SEC) had made public company filings available via the Internet, it is the private sector that has made it possible to search the filings for documents related to company personnel. *EDGAR Online* offers a people search feature at <u>www.edgar-online.com/people</u>. The database allows you to search an *individual's* name and see the companies with which he or she is connected as an officer or director. Hot-links allow you to get further data on filings, company information, or to perform searches using additional hot-linked research tools.

The site compiles data from SEC Form 144, which must be filed by certain "insiders" prior to their intended sale of restricted stock. Form 144 is filed by the seller in paper at the SEC. EDGAR Online adds all of the current day's Form 144 paper filings to their database at the end of each business day.

You can get a report on your competitors' insider trading at www.insidertrader.com. Search by *company name* and see the list of corporate officers who have filed Form 144s, complete with the number of shares held. Free data includes 13-months worth of Detailed Form 4 and 144 data, as well monthly summaries. The Premium Service has three years' worth of 13Ds, 144s, 3s and 13Gs along with the Form 4 data. "Pay-per-view" access is available if desired. This is very convenient if you are an occasional user of this type of information. Portfolio Alerts can be set up to monitor companies on which you are compiling data. Insider trading information is also one of the segments in the daily report provided by Company Sleuth at www.companysleuth.com.

The Top "This & That" Lists

Several popular business magazines offer lists that track successful people. Whether it's wealth, power, or gender, these lists can provide some insights into the positions of these people within their companies, along with indirect clues about other corporate matters. Here are several of the most recent of these lists:

Forbes 400 Richest People in America at www.forbes.com/tool/ toolbox/rich400/index.htm, allows you to create a custom list from The Forbes Four Hundred database. This means that you can determine something about source of wealth, industry in which the individual is involved, state where he or she lives, or search several searchable fields.

The Forbes Daily Wealth Index, found at www.forbes.com/gates/ daily.asp, is a ranking of the ten richest members who made their money in the technology sector. Another sight pertaining to the high tech industry is *ASAP Technology's Wealthiest 100*, available at www.forbes.com/asap/tech100.

Forbes CEO 1998: Corporate America's Most Powerful People 1998 at www.forbes.com/tool/toolbox/ceo is self-explanatory.

At the *Fortune* magazine site, you will find *The 50 Most Powerful Women in American Business* at www.pathfinder.com/fortune/mostpowerful. This ranked list provides names, corporate affiliation and job titles, education, and career description.

"Who's Who" Publications

The Internet abounds with sites that contain directories of members or searchable directories of people that meet some type of criterion — they are in a particular industry, live in a certain place, etc. While some of these sites initially sound promising, you may find that in reality, they are commercial web sites that want businesses to register, rather than providing some sort of authoritative list.

Others, on the other hand, may be an electronic version of a recognized hardcopy publication. Canadian Who's Who on the World Wide Web, at www.utpress.utoronto.ca/cww/cw2w3, is an example of the latter. Here you can search the Canadian Who's Who database compiled by the University of Toronto Press, allows you to search the biographies of more than 15,000 prominent Canadians by name, date of birth, city, or full text. Chances are that you will find more than a few corporate CEO's among the listings in this directory.

Trade Publications

The trade press is also a good place to identify and track the careers of executives. It may be possible to follow their employment path as they move up the corporate ladder or from one company to another. This information may be useful to your organization's recruiters, in both identifying promising candidates for a position they wish to fill and for verification purposes.

The names and other data found in industry-specific newspapers or magazines supply crucial intelligence that is needed to build or complete your "picture" of a competitor's organization or of its staffing. Thousands of these publications are searchable in databases throughout the ranks of commercial online services.

Specialized reference books exist in many industries, and some of the most important can be found on the Internet. In the broadly defined high tech industry, for instance, the Corptech Directory's free search at www.corptech.com/ResearchAreas/PeopleSearch.cfm can be useful for connecting a person and a company. The profile that is retrieved is that of the company, but the target person's affiliation is made clear. For a fee, you can access either the Standard Profile (includes multiple executives), or the Extended Profile (Standard Profile plus 10 years' corporate and executive history). Another potentially useful list found here includes Previously Listed Executives. This list includes the date the listing was deleted (translate that as the time when the person left the company).

See Chapter 11 for references to some tools that may help you to track high-profile individuals on an on-going basis.

Industry Directories

Directories like the *Thomas Register of American Manufacturers* or the various Dun & Bradstreet databases frequently list job titles as well as the names of the people filling those positions. At the very least, it provides you with a starting place when contacting individuals within a company. The job title can be very useful, since the person filling the position may have been reassigned.

Watch the officers and directors and other personnel listings in records found in company directories. You may occasionally notice that one or two individuals appear to carry several titles. You may interpret this fact in various ways, but it usually means that a small group of people is in charge.

Search Engines

The powerful Hotbot search engine at www.hotbot.com provides a drop-down box that will limit search results. Instead of choosing "all of the words," "any of the words," or "exact phrase" as your search criterion, choose "the person." This feature work's quite well, and will definitely cut the search results down to a manageable level – unless you search for a person who is an icon, like Elvis Presley!

Commercial Vendors' Web Sites

Commercial sources are another valuable resource for locating information on people. Here is a sampling, by vendor, that should give you some ideas about places to search as you begin to build your company's knowledge base regarding competitors' personnel:

DIALOG

The DIALOG service, at www.dialog.com, contains many science and technology files that can be searched for biographical articles. For the strictly biographical approach, DIALOG offers these files, among others:

MARQUIS WHO'S WHO - File 234. Marquis Who's Who contains detailed biographical information on "outstanding achievers worldwide in a wide variety of professions and virtually every important field of endeavor." The file contains over 790,000 profiles drawn from the entire 19-volume Marquis Who's Who library since 1985.

STANDARD & POOR'S REGISTER - BIOGRAPHICAL - File 526 contains extensive personal and professional data on approximately 70,000 key business executives. Most officers and directors included in the file are affiliated with public or private, US or non-US companies with sales of $1 million dollars or more.

EUROPEAN RESEARCH & DEVELOPMENT DATABASE - File 113 - Separate profiles are available for professionals currently engaged in research. Detailed biographies give information on the career history of over 85,000 heads of organizations, senior researchers, research directors, and managers.

Dow Jones Interactive

Dow Jones Interactive offers a Search By Person feature in the site's extensive Publications Library. Search By Person Find allows you to limit search results to articles that mention this person at least n times (where n equals a number selected by you). You may also specify words or phrases that also must appear in articles.

You can search all 6000+ newswires, newspapers, magazines and trade journals, or through select groups such as Energy Industry, Financial Services Publications, *New York Times,* etc.

Electric Library

At the useful Electric Library site, at www.elibrary.com, you can search broadly, or limit by one of a dozen or more subject categories. "People" is not a category, but the search results can be quite good if you are searching an uncommon name. In addition, a sidebar provides additional "themes" connected with the name searched. "Unlimited access" subscriptions are available for both monthly and annual subscriptions. A search on a corporate CEO using Electric Library is illustrated in the following screen capture:

TI names president, chairman: New leader was protege of firm's previous chief
Score: 100; The Dallas Morning News; *Alan Goldstein, Jim Mitchell / Staff Writers of The Dallas Morning News;* 06-21-1996 Size: 9K ; Reading Level: 6.

Calm approach to being 'it' at TI: New president Engibous sees mandate for speeding things up
Score: 100; The Dallas Morning News; *Alan Goldstein / Staff Writer of The Dallas Morning News;* 06-22-1996 Size: 5K ; Reading Level: 6.

A Leaner TI Sharpens Focus On Chips, Lets Engibous Lead Way – But Makeover Isn't Complete Yet, Analysts Say
Score: 100; Electronic Buyer News; *Darrell Dunn;* 02-24-1997 Size: 11K ; Reading Level: 10.

Electric Library's Major Themes sidebar is useful for retrieving articles about people connected with your target individual. Note also, that references are provided to variations in the subject's first name.

Electric Library Business Edition is available on the World Wide Web at www.business.elibrary.com. This service is available for a flat annual fee. Its Business Archive contains seven million articles, transcripts, books, CorpTech and Hoover's.

LEXIS-NEXIS

The LEXIS-NEXIS Universe site offers a hot-link to its "People" files at http://web.lexis-nexis.com/ln.universe/page/content. This extensive list of sources may prove fruitful when searching for corporate executives and employees. Even the elusive personnel connected with privately held companies may appear if they made Duns Decision Makers list, which is part of the list below:

Almanac of American Politics	Judicial Staff Directory
The Almanac of the Unelected	Judicial Yellow Book
American Medical Information	Kaleidoscope
American Men and Women of Science	Marquis Who's Who Biographies
The Associated Press Candidate	Martindale-Hubbell Law Directory
Biographies	Practice Profiles
Civil Servants (UK)	The Official American Board of

Congressional Member Profile

Congressional Yellow Book

Directory of Bankruptcy Attorneys

Directory of Hospital Personnel
Dun's Decision Makers

European Research & Development
Database
Executive Changes, Promotions, Appts,
& Resignations
Federal Staff Directory
Federal Yellow Book
Financial Post Directory of Directors

Gale Biographies
Peers & Members of House of Lords

Medical Specialists
Member of European Parliament
and Candidates
National Directory of Law
Enforcement Administrators
New York Times Government
Biographical Stories
Obituary Information
Standard & Poor's Register of
Corps, Directors & Executives
State Legislative Directory

Washington Post Biographical
Stories
Who's Who in American Art
Who's Who in American Politics
Who's Who in European Business
& Industry
Who's Who in Russia & the
Commonwealth of
Independent States

Internet Address Books

There are various "people finder" services available on the Internet. You can enter a name and possibly retrieve an address or e-mail address. These services will not likely yield addresses of VIPs at major companies. These people generally don't register for this type of service. In addition, their Security Departments may frown on distribution of such information.

One problem with Internet address books is that they can be sadly out of date. Some of them are built by allowing people to register themselves. Since many individuals change internet service providers (ISPs) frequently, the e-mail address that you locate for them simply not work. Don't try to reach this author using the CompuServe address shown on one of the Internet Address books. It hasn't been active in over a year! (Information on contacting the author is included in the About the Author Section inside the back cover.)

It is useful to know that these services are there, for occasional use. Some of them also are useful for locating businesses. See the Bookmarks & Favorites section in Part IV for a current selection of these sites.

Focused Databases from Specialty Vendors

Putting directories on the Internet is a natural for some companies who have been building databases for years. Some of these companies offer high quality information, but it's not free.

IdEXEC, formerly known as Finex On Demand, is an example. The database contains contact information, title and job responsibility for almost 400,000 business decision-makers from over 60,000 of the world's largest public, private, government, and nonprofit organizations. idEXEC tracks US organizations reporting revenues of more than $30million; international organizations reporting over $50 million in revenue, or asset based firms with over $200 million. Company executives are categorized by 40 different functional responsibility types. A two-day free trial is available, but first you'll have to complete a detailed form and wait for a sales person to contact you by telephone.

Chapter 15

Organizing CI Research

What's In a Company Report on a Competitor Company?

It depends upon the task at hand. The content of a Company Report reflects the context of the requestor. If your work involves a specific function within the company, you may have a more or less standard template that is used to gather information on competitors. But if you field questions from many directions, or address a new subject, the assignment becomes much more complex. You could spend hours creating something that lacks a crucial "ingredient," rather like simmering a pot of soup all day, but forgetting to season it.

The templates provided in this chapter are intended, therefore, to help you to know what to look for when you try to examine a company from a particular perspective. Some examples of electronic sources are provided, but many more may be found by consulting Bookmarks & Favorites and the Resource List in Part IV at the back of this book. Vendor contact information is also available there. In some cases no specific source has been recommended. Certain information may be confidential, or just not the type of thing that gets published. This information may be obtained through interviews, observation, or other legal and ethical methods, however, so it remains in the template to serve as a reminder.

The Company Profile Report

The quality of company "profiles" varies extensively, depending upon their source. The accuracy and timeliness of the data and the amount of detail included are important considerations. Some Internet sites that promise free company profiles provide only sketchy data, while others are excellent resources. In some cases, online sources provide a brief company profile at no charge, but if you're willing to subscribe, or to take out your credit card, you may save a good deal of time.

The list below provides a means of getting a good look at what a company is all about. You may access several sources to locate all of the required information. Also, you might combine this report with one of those that follow, since they address specific aspects of the competitor's operations.

Company Profile

Data Elements	Types of Information Sources	Online Information Sources
BASIC DETAILS		
Company Name	Company Profiles	Dun & Bradstreet
Company Address		Hoover's
Description of Business		Bookmarks & Favorites: COMPANY PROFILES
Public or Privately Held		
Ownership, Percent (if Privately Held)		
Year established, or Year Acquired	Public Records - Secretary of State	DATABASE FILES: CDB Infotek www.KnowX.com LEXIS Public Records service
Headquarters state of incorporation		
Technological Developments / Intellectual Property	Patents Databases	Derwent Inpadoc (DIALOG, STN) www.uspto.gov
MANAGEMENT ISSUES		
Management - Quality, Style	Business Management Files	ABI Inform BAMP
Community Involvement, Reputation	Local, Regional Newspapers	Bookmarks & Favorites: NEWS SITES
Company Competitors	Directory	Hoover's
Bill Payment History	Credit Reports Credit Bureau Web Sites	Dun & Bradstreet Equifax Experian TransUnion
PERSONNEL		
Key personnel Changes	Newspapers, Trade Publications	Dialog Dow Jones Interactive - Publications Library NEXIS
Where They Went	Newspapers Trade Publications	Bookmarks & Favorites: NEWS SITES
Sales force: Size, Organization, Compensation		
VIPs: Track Records, Stock Transactions		www.companysleuth.com
INDUSTRY-RELATED DATA		
Impact of Industry Mergers/Joint Ventures	Trade Publications	
Other companies in the industry	Directories	Hoover's

Data Elements	Types of Information Sources	Online Information Sources
Other firms entering the industry	Newspapers Trade Publications	Bookmarks & Favorites: NEWS SITES
Social Concerns, Similar Issues		DATABASE FILES: IAC MARS
Trends affecting industry	Business Databases Government Data Trade Publications	DATABASE FILES: Globalbase IAC PROMT IAC Trade & Industry TableBase
	Trade Associations	Bookmarks & Favorites: ASSOCIATIONS
Laws and regulations that affect the industry	State & Federal Laws & Regulations	Bookmarks & Favorites: LEGAL INFORMATION - MISC.
	State & Federal Agencies	Individual States Web Sites Individual Agency Web Sites
	Trade Associations	Bookmarks & Favorites: ASSOCIATIONS
Significant events in recent history: major developments	Newspapers Trade Publications	Bookmarks & Favorites: NEWS SITES

SALES & MARKETING

Data Elements	Types of Information Sources	Online Information Sources
Major Products/Services	Trade Publications Newspapers	Bookmarks & Favorites: INDUSTRIES & PROFESSIONS - ADVERTISING
		Bookmarks & Favorites: NEWS SITES
Customers/Clients		
Market Share	Business Databases Trade Publications	DATABASE FILES: Business & Industry Datamonitor Market Research TableBase
Threats of substitutes		
Market Inroads By Foreign Competitors		
Dependence on Suppliers		
Dependence On Other Products		
Media Used in Promotions (Past & Present)	Advertising Trade Publications	DATABASE FILES: Advertiser and Agency Red Books
Advertising & Marketing Spending		
Ad Campaigns		
Marketing & Promotion Practices Used In This Industry	Business Databases Trade Publications	DATABASE FILES: ABI Inform IAC Trade & Industry MARS
New Distribution Channels In Use		
Price Structures, Margins and Mark-ups, Past & Present		

Data Elements	Types of Information Sources	Online Information Sources
Pricing Changes	Business Databases	DATABASE FILES: BCC Datamonitor Euromonitor IAC New Products Plus PROMT TableBase
Comparison With Competitors: 　Age, Size, Sales/Income, 　Products/Services		

TECHNOLOGY ISSUES

New technologies: Do They 　License or Develop	Newspapers Trade Publications	DATABASE FILES: DIALOG Dow Jones Interactive NEXIS
Cost Structure: Production, 　Distribution, Overhead		
New Patent/Trademarks Registrations	Patents Databases	DATABASE FILES: Derwent Inpadoc (Dialog , STN) www.uspto.gov
New Technologies In Use	Newspapers Trade Publications	Varies By Industry
Downsizing/Re-engineering 　Taking Place		
Impact On Rivals' Strategies		
Special Expertise Required		
Age of Technology or Equipment		

▬ Mergers & Acquisitions

Before considering any sort of merger, acquisition, or joint venture, you no doubt check out a target company carefully. The information referenced below, if gathered and analyzed, will give you a good picture of that company's structure, history, and current activity. This will help determine whether there is a good "fit" between your company and theirs.

Company Mergers & Acquisitions Checklist

Data Elements	Types of Information Sources	Online Information Sources
CORPORATE STRUCTURE		
Divisions, Subsidiaries	Company Profiles Directories	Dun & Bradstreet DATABASE FILES: SDC DIALOG (File 551)
Branch locations		
Public or Privately Held		
OWNERSHIP		
Ownership Structure		
Other Companies Held By Owner	Public Records	DATABASE FILES: CDB Infotek www.KnowX.com LEXIS Public Records
POSSIBLE ADVERSE ITEMS		
Hazardous Waste Issues, If Any	Environmental Protection Agency (EPA) State Environmental Agency	Bookmarks & Favorites: ENVIRONMENT Bookmarks & Favorites: GOVERNMENT SITES - US
Labor Problems or Issues	Newspapers Trade Publications	Bookmarks & Favorites: NEWS SITES
Lawsuits, Past and Pending - Company	Public Records	DATABASE FILES: CDB Infotek Bookmarks & Favorites: PUBLIC RECORDS KnowX
	Case Law	LEXIS Public Records BRAINWAVE LEXIS-NEXIS Universe WESTLAW
Lawsuits, Past/Pending - Officers		
Negative Media Coverage	Newspapers, Radio, TV	BOOKMARKS & FAVORITES: NEWS SITES Burrelles www.vidmon.com
SALES & MARKETING		
Annual Sales	Company Profiles Trade Publications	DATABASE FILES: Dun & Bradstreet Hoover's
Current Products/Services		DATABASE FILES: Hoover's IAC New Product Announcements/Plus

Data Elements	Types of Information Sources	Online Information Sources
Former Products/Services		Bookmarks & Favorites: COMPANY PROFILES
Product market - Industrial/Consumer	Business Databases Trade Publications	BUSINESS & INDUSTRY MARS PROMT
Customers		
Relationship With Customers		
Reputation in Industry		
Strategic Physical Location, If Relevant	Industry Directories Trade Publications	
Regulated By - State	State Laws & Regulations State Agencies	Bookmarks & Favorites: LEGAL INFORMATION - MISC. Individual States' Web Sites
Regulated By - Federal	Federal Laws & Regulations Federal Agencies	Bookmarks & Favorites: LEGAL INFORMATION - MISC Individual Agency Web Sites
MISCELLANEOUS		
Management - Quality, Style	Business Management Files	ABI Inform BAMP
Community Involvement, Reputation	Local, Regional Newspapers	BOOKMARKS & FAVORITES: NEWS SITES
Company Competitors	Directory	Hoover's
Bill Payment History	Credit Reports Credit Bureau Web Sites	Dun & Bradstreet Equifax Experian TransUnion
Key personnel Changes	Newspapers, Trade Publications	Dialog Dow Jones Interactive - Publications Library NEXIS
Where They Went	Newspapers Trade Publications	Bookmarks & Favorites: NEWS SITES
TECHNOLOGY ISSUES		
Special Expertise Required to Operate	Trade Publications	Varies By Industry
Age of Technology or Equipment	Trade Publications	Varies By Industry
New technologies: Licensed/Developed		
Cost Structure: Production, Distribution, Overhead		
New Patent/Trademarks Registrations		
New Technologies In Use		
Downsizing/Reengineering Taking Place		
Impact On Rivals' Strategies		

▬ Useful Labor-Related Information

Retrieving labor information from cyberspace regarding a competitor company may be more challenging than simply checking a few routing sources such as directories.

Company Labor Information Checklist

Data Elements	Types of Information Sources	Online Information Sources
State-sponsored retraining programs	Business Databases Newspapers Trade Publications	DATABASE FILES: ABI Inform Bookmarks & Favorites: NEWS SITES
Wages in relation to other regions and competitors		
Number of hourly employees by job classification		
Number of unionized employees		
Wages by job category		
Wage trends		
Benefit packages		
Retirement		
Insurance		
Incentive		
Stock options		
Longevity of employees		
Hiring and layoff history		
Union contracts, past and current history		
Organization and structure of middle management		
Track record of management		
Numbers of:		
Management		
Professional		
Technical		
Support		
Salaries of management	Proxy Statements	
Management's benefit packages		
Internal or external promotion to upper management	Newspapers Trade Publications	

More Company Reports

The issues mentioned in the Company Strategy Report below are topics that must be considered as a company develops its strategy in various areas. By gathering information on what is going on within the industry, or by researching and/or deducing competitors' strategies, it may be possible to develop strategies that will out-perform competitors, or at least allow you to gain competitive advantage.

Note that not all of the blanks have been filled in on this and the additional company reports in this chapter. This allows them to be used as templates. The sources described in other forms in this chapter (and the next) should provide you with good ideas for choosing the types of sources to search.

Company Strategy Report

Company's Strategy	Content	Online Information Sources
Markets/Marketing Issues		
Has anyone in the industry tried a new distribution channel; results?		**Trade Publications** Business & Industry (Dialog File 9) IAC Trade & Industry Index (Dialog File 148)
Are foreign competitors moving into the domestic market?		**Trade Publications** **Newspapers**
Advertising and promotion spending by competitors.		
Any changes in ads or marketing strategies of competitors?		**Advertising Media** MARS (Dialog File 570)
Infrastructure supports of marketing staff?		
Pricing Issues		
Competitor prices - are any changes anticipated?		
Competitors' cost structure: production, distribution, overhead?		
Technology Issues		
How are new technologies being used by others in industry?		**Trade Publications**
Are new technologies being acquired or developed?		
New patents and trademarks registrations, pending expirations?		**Current Awareness Service:** CompanySleuth: www.companysleuth.com

Company's Strategy	Content	Online Information Sources
Customers		
Competitors' main clients or customers?		
Personnel Matters		
Competitors' top executives and their track records?		**Company Profiles** **Trade Publications**
Staffing cuts, downswing, or re-engineering strategies?		**Newspapers** **Trade Publications**
Sales force size; how are they organized?		
Industry compensation; how do they compare?		**Industry Directories**
Competitors, firm and industry large stock transactions?		**Newspapers** **Trade Publications**
Miscellaneous		
Product or service share being purchased?		
Mergers or joint ventures in the industry?		**Newspapers** **Trade Publications**
Impact on rivals' strategies?		

Company Report - Products & Services

Company Products and Services	Content	Online Information Source
Description of Products or Services		
Description of the major products and services		**Directory Record** Corptech Directory (Dialog File 559)
Description of minor product lines		
List of products and services		Company Website
Scope and limitation of products and services		
Additional product distinctions; key features		
Full product range vs. Limited product range		
Advanced technology vs. Basic (low) technology		

Company Products and Services	Content	Online Information Source
Product and services differentiation		
Product and services key innovation		
Product and services performances		
Product and services features		

Sales of Products or Services

Dollar sales of all products and services		
Sales dollars by products and services		
Unit sales of all products and services		
Sales of key products and services		
Sales by company, by product line		
Sales of units by products and services		
Retail prices for products and services		
Prices for key products and services		
High price vs. Low price		

Market/Marketing Issues

Market Position of Products and Services by Industry		
High quality vs. Low quality perception of products		
Perceptions in marketplace of product and services		
Market position of key products and services		

Miscellaneous Issues

Services and maintenance provided to support the products		
Training requirements of products and services		
Quality ratings of products and services		

Company Report - Finances

Company Finances	Content	Online Information Sources
Company Name		**Company Profiles** **Industry Directories** Hoover's Dun & Bradstreet
Sales/Revenues		
Sales of company or division		
Sales of individual business unit		
Trends: historical, future outlook		
Total company revenues		
Costs		
Direct costs		
Indirect costs		
Cost relevant to success		
Earnings/Profits		
General profitability of the company		
Profits by branch, division or business units		
Assessment of overall profitability		
Dividends paid		
Growth		
Revenue growth / past three years		
Revenue growth / past five years		
Major factors affecting revenue growth		
Asset data on company and industry		
Factors affecting growth		
Liability information		

Data Downlink's XLS service (www.xls.com) provides a number of specialized databases that could be useful in compiling the data needed for this report.

Company Report - Plant Site Locations

The list below specifies the data needed to create a detailed analysis of plant sites. Not all of this information can be expected to be found in online sources, but with diligent searching, and monitoring the media for references to the company or to a specific plant, a great deal of intelligence can be compiled over time. This information gathering process can be supplemented with telephone interviews, visits to local government offices, and other manual or onsite research.

Identity of Plant Sites	Content	Online Information Sources
List of all facilities		**Online Directories** American Business Directory (Dialog File 531) Duns Market Identifiers (Dialog File 516)
Function served by each		**Online Industry Directories** Examine descriptions of listed plants.
Location of all facilities		**Online Directories** American Business Directory (Dialog File 531) Duns Market Identifiers (Dialog File 516)
Description of Plant Sites		**Tax Assesor's Office Online** (Many now include drawings)
Equipment used		
Number of shifts		
Production capacity		
Products manufactured		**Local, Regional Business Directories**
Manufacturing equipment		**Equipment Manufacturers' homepages** (Check for lists of customers
Region served by facility		**Thomas Register**
Number of production lines		
Square footage of facility		Duns Market Identifiers (Dialog File 516)
Production utilization rate		
List of parts purchased from suppliers		

Description of Major Distribution Facilities of Company	**Industry Directories**
Proximity to suppliers	
Description of facilities	
Flexibility for product production	
Location of distribution facilities	
Geographic region served by facilities	
Sophistication, safety and efficiency of plant	**OSHA** http://www.osha.gov/oshstats/

PC Industry & Blank Industry Analysis Report

This industry report on the PC Industry contains brief information of the type needed to "fill in the blanks" in the Industry Report form. A list of citations to articles follows. (Form begins on the following page.)

Industry Analysis Report - The PC Industry

Data Category	Content	Source	Ref #
Status of the Industry — Relative size and scope of the industry - growing, stable, or declining?	Industry growing, per shipment information below. China PC industry growing rapidly, may out-do Japan by year 2000.	Economic Daily News	13
History of industry	Detailed series of articles, one year at a time, chronicling events in the industry during that year.	Electronic Engineering Times	15
Trends in industry	Moving from PC's for Internet access to use of "information appliance" More low-cost PC's being made/sold Shipments up, revenues down.	Financial Times	2

Forecasts regarding size of the industry	Personal Computers Shipments
	Yr. 1998: 12,800,000
	     1999: 14,850,000
	     2002: 23,050,000
	     2003: 26,900,000
	     2004: 31,000,000
		Tablebase	1

	CONFLICTING INFORMATION[1] US figures for 1998 : 35,200,000, up 16% from 1997	Computer Reseller News	8
SIC or NAICS Codes	SIC=3571; NAICS=334111	http://www. census.gov/ epcd/naics/	

Customers For Products or Services

Data Category	Content	Source	Ref #
Customers	Home market expected to grow slightly faster than business sector. Buyers will be lower-income households and two-PC households.	Newsbytes News Network	14
Size of Market	Computer and office equipment shipments for Feb. 1999, $11,225,000	http://www.ce nsus.gov/ftp/p ub/indicator/ www/m3/inde x.htm	9
Potential New Buyers	Customers for PC-based control systems used in industrial control.	Process Engineering	4
Directions in the market	"There is a big move toward growth," concurs John Mariotti, IW columnist and president of The Enterprise Group, a manufacturing consulting	Industry Week	23

---

[1] It will be necessary to study both information sources carefully, and to possibly seek out other sources to determine which of two seemingly conflicting numbers is accurate.

Data Category	Content	Source	Ref #
	Group, a manufacturing consulting business, "mainly because people feel that they have wrung everything they can out of downsizing.		
Import penetration	Hewlett-Packard offering its HP Pavilion PC in the Philippines. To gain market penetration in the home PCs segment, the company will address operational excellence, customer and channels satisfaction, and integrated product/technology offering.	Newsbytes News Network	
Forecasts for market	China PC sales to grow 35%	Singapore Business Times	10
Distribution methods	Wholesale Distributors are growing faster than the PC industry. Attributed in part to growth of Small Business, partly to value-added services offered.	Computer Reseller News	8
	Dell Computer called an anomaly; other vendors moving away from selling direct.		

Market/Marketing Issues

Data Category	Content	Source	Ref #
Scope of products	Home/business PC's		
	More emphasis on servers, to centralize IT operations and build systems such as intranets and web sites.	Financial Times Surveys Edition	9
	Supercomputers		
Brand loyalty	According to the Ziff-Davis 1998 Technology User Profile, 3 out of 4 people who purchased a Gateway computer in 1997 were repeat purchasers.	Des Moines Register	18
	Apple computer users said they would consider another brand only if the price were at least $606 less.	USA Today	17
	Brand loyalty might be the major reason notebook leaders Toshiba America Information Systems Inc., The IBM PC Co. and Compaq Computer Corp. have held on to market share despite across-the-board shortages last year, analysts said.	Computer Reseller News	19

Data Category	Content	Source	Ref #
Product leader description	Compaq and IBM dominate nearly all major markets except Japan.	Nikkei Weekly	5
Product differentiation	Becoming harder for manufacturers to come up with a leap in performance to justify upgrading hardware. Consumers less willing to upgrade.	Wall Street Journal	7
Alternate products/services	Moving from PC's for Internet access to use of "information appliance"	Financial Times	2
Complementary products	Palm computer market grew 60% in 1998, compared with 15% for PC's.	Globe & Mail	3
Quality continuum	Concern about Y2K issues may slow sales, study shows.	Computer Reseller News	12
Marketing media used	N/A		
Price structure	Compaq, H-P, IBM cut prices, offered monitor promotions in 1998 to clear excess inventory and affect market share.	Computer Reseller News	8
Price margins	Shrinking, with demand for low-cost PC's	Computer Reseller News	8

Manufacturing Goods Issues

Technology in Use	N/A		
Technological trends	CD-ROM vs. DVD-ROM transition will be slower than originally projected.	Electronic Buyers News	6
Industry innovations	N/A		
Emerging technologies	Intel Corp.'s 100 MHz system bus and 440BX core-logic chip. PC-100 memory spec. may be a concern.	Computer Reseller News	

Service Business Issues

Scope of services	N/A		
Level of services	N/A		

Fiscal Matters

Changes that may impact supplier prices	N/A		
Legislation/Regulations	FTC, Intel to square off over interpretation of law (Intel, computer chip firm, facing FTC antitrust charges for abusing 80% market share to harm 3 computer companies)	USA Today	20

Data Category	Content	Source	Ref #
Availability of raw materials	N/A		
Other Sales by major product type	Servers: $10.5bn in 1997; projected to be $21bn in 2001	Financial Times Surveys Edition	9

Productivity -Related Matters

Manufacturing rates	N/A		
Efficiency levels	N/A		
Product innovation	...the launch of the world's first flat monitor will help the company in	BusinessLine	21
	maintaining the premier position in terms of product innovation and market share.		
	(Apple Computer interim CEO Steven Jobs introduces fastest Mac ever, powered by IBM PowerPC microprocessor using copper-metalization)	Newsbytes News	22

Industry Analysis: References to Articles

1. US shipments of business appliances in units for 1998 and forecast for 1999, with shipments breakdown by each of 18 alphabetically-listed appliances
Journal: **Appliance** , v 56 , n 1 , p 52 Publication Date: January 1999 Document Type: Journal; Time Series ISSN: 0003-6781(United States)

2. INSIDE TRACK: Battle to bridge the information gap: IT VIEWPOINT STEVE FRANCE: The PC will be soon be challenged as a way to access the internet by information appliances', bringing two industry sectors into direct conflict. (It is predicted that there will be 200 Internet connections worldwide by 2002, with 60 mil online households in the US)
Financial Times London Edition , p 16 March 30, 1999

3. BOOM IN PALM COMPUTER NOT LIKELY TO SUBSIDE (According to Dataquest Inc, the market for palm computers grew by more than 60% last year, compared with a 15% growth for the entire PC industry)
Globe & Mail , p R5   February 26, 1999

4. PC -based control set for growth (By 2004 the European market for PC -based control systems will be valued at more than UKPd80 mil; potentially lucrative opportunities exist in the food and beverage industry)
Process Engineering , v 79 , n 6 , p 9   June 1998

5. Industry sees Windows of opportunity (Personal computer makers expect growth in market with introduction of Windows 98 in July)
Nikkei Weekly , v 36 , n 1,824 , p 4 May 11, 1998

6. PC makers delay move to DVD-ROM (Industry watchers and suppliers rethink transition from DC to DVD and readjust forecasts for sales to 5 mil units this year)
Electronic Buyers News , p 1 November 30, 1998

7. Upgrade Fatigue Threatens PC Profits (Unwillingness to upgrade PCs looms a big issue for the industry)
Wall Street Journal , v CCXXXI , n 94 , p B1+ May 14, 1998

8. Distributors Outrun Industry In Growth (Distributors continue to grow faster than PC industry , thanks to increasing number of vendors and products selling through two-tier channels)
Computer Reseller News , p 71 May 04, 1998

9. **Financial Times Surveys Edition** , p 05 March 04, 1998
Document Type: Business Newspaper; Industry Overview ISSN: 0307-1766 (United Kingdom)

10. **Newsbytes News Network** , p N/A January 26, 1998 Document Type: Journal; Ranking ISSN: 0983-1592 (United States)

11. China PC sales to grow 35% (China Ministry of Information Industry forecasts 35% increase in PC market to Yuan50 bil in 1999)
Singapore Business Times , p 9
January 25, 1999

12. Vendors, VARs React To Study Findings (Some personal computer vendors are expecting some slowdown in the industry because customers might hesitate to upgrade systems not affected by the year 2000 bug)
Computer Reseller News , p 115
November 30, 1998 , Document Type: Journal; Survey ISSN: 0893-8377 (United States)

13. Mainland China's PC Industry Explodes. (Mainland China's personal computer production will reach 7.6 mil/yr by the year 2000)
Economic Daily News , p N/A June 01, 1998 Document Type: Newspaper (Taiwan) Language: Chinese Record Type: Abstract

14. PC Shipments Up, Revenue Growth Down - Dataquest Forecast (A new study by Gartner Group division Dataquest says worldwide PC shipments will be up 15.6 percent in 1998 but industry revenues will be up only 6.4 percent)
Newsbytes News Network , p N/A April 20, 1998. Document Type: Journal ISSN: 0983-1592

15. DIALOG(R)File 148:IAC Trade & Industry Database (c) 1999 Info Access Co. All rts. reserv. 1996. (a history of the electronics industry)(EE Times Chronicles: 1972-1997) (Industry Trend or Event) Rostky, George
Electronic Engineering Times, n978, p244(1)

16. HP Pavilion PCs Enter Philippines Market (Hewlett-Packard is now offering its HP Pavilion PC in the Philippines)
Newsbytes News Network, p N/A
February 26, 1999
DOCUMENT TYPE: Journal ISSN: 0983-1592 (United States)

17. Computer users display brand loyalty (Apple computer owners express greater brand loyalty then IBM users in   survey of 1,600 home and office computer users)
USA Today, v 13, n 40, p B1, Nov. 9, 1994
DOCUMENT TYPE: National Newspaper; Survey ISSN: 0161-7389 (United States)

18. Gateway muffling its (sacred) cow. Is abandoning folksy, Midwestern image in hopes of continuing growth and carving out bigger slice of the corporate computer mkt
Ridgeway, Michael **Des Moines Register (IA)**
Sept 14, 1998 p. B4

19. Resellers enter 'notebook zone': Logical Solutions finds what works for desktops does not always work for notebooks
Bliss, Jeff
Computer Reseller News Feb 10, 1997 p. 81 ISSN: 0893-8377

20. FTC, Intel to square off over interpretation of law (Intel, computer chip firm, facing FTC antitrust charges for abusing 80% market share to harm 3 computer companies)
USA Today, v 17, n 121, p 1B+, March 05, 1999
DOCUMENT TYPE: National Newspaper; Cover Story ISSN: 0161-7389 (United States)

21. India: 100 pc flat monitor from LG Electronics (LG Electronics is debuting the zero deflection 15-inch TFT LCD monitor and the 17-inch Flatron monitor in India)
Business Line , p N/A June 15, 1998
DOCUMENT TYPE: Journal ISSN: 0971-7528 (India)

22. Apple Products At Seybold (Apple Computer interim CEO Steven Jobs introduces fastest Mac ever, powered by IBM PowerPC microprocessor using copper-metalization)
Newsbytes News Network, p N/A
March 17, 1998
DOCUMENT TYPE: Journal ISSN: 0983-1592 (United States)

23. GOING FOR GROWTH (IBM, a computer giant, hired 26,000+ employees in 1996 to propel growth; the firm had reduced its staff to 225,000 employees in 1995)
Industry Week, v 246, n 11, p 32+ June 09, 1997
DOCUMENT TYPE: Journal; Geographic Profile ISSN: 0039-0895 (United States)

Chapter 16

Industry Studies, Revisited

The "Do-It-Yourself" Approach

To accurately size up an industry it is should be examined from a number of different perspectives. To determine where the answers might be found for your industry, consider these broad topics and suggested sources. They are intended as a guide, to get your research started. Some sources will be more useful than others. You will notice that certain key business databases appear over and over, because they cover many industries or are considered basic tools for this type of research.

Online research may be only one of the tools needed to find the information included in the outline at the end of this chapter. To learn more about other means for gathering this business intelligence, consult the articles and books mentioned in the Appendix E of Part IV.

As you begin to identify key sources for an industry, study the vendor's documentation or click on the Search Tips button on a web site. You can usually narrow or focus the research easily by taking advantage of suggestions provided there. Most expert searchers have a few "tried and true" favorite sources that are used over and over.

Is the industry growing, stable, or declining? To make this determination, look at the following:

History of the Industry

The depth and amount of information available will vary according to the specific industry under consideration. For high tech industries, this material will be available in electronic format. For long-established industries such as meatpacking, oil, or automobiles, it may be possible to locate printed histories that will provide the necessary background. Economics-oriented sources could also be useful.

General Sources

Trade publications

Search industry-specific publications. To identify key publications, consult *Fulltext Sources Online* or *Net.Journal*.

Trade associations

Identify relevant trade associations using the Bookmarks & Favorites section in Part IV and search their web sites.

Specific Sources

Industry-specific databases

Consult commercial vendor documentation or the Bookmarks & Favorites section in Part IV.

Resources List

See sources listed under "Industry History" in the Data Elements list in Part IV.

Trends in the Industry

What has been happening in an industry may help your company's planners and strategists to make crucial decisions regarding new products, new markets, or possibly what company to acquire. In some cases the decision might even be made that it's best to be acquired! Decisions of this magnitude involve the investment of money and resources, so it's important to research developments in the field and "educate" the decisionmakers.

General Sources

Trade publications

Search industry-specific publications. To identify key publications, consult *Fulltext Sources Online* or *Net.Journal*.

Trade associations

Identify relevant trade associations using the Bookmarks & Favorites section in Part IV and search their web sites.

Specific Sources

Industry-specific databases

Consult commercial vendor documentation or Bookmarks & Favorites.

Other Sources

Resources List - See sources listed under "Industry Trends" in the Data Elements list in Part IV. Also, check out Industry Insider at www.investext.com.

Forecasts Regarding Size of the Industry

Government sources provide data regarding the size of many industries. Trade associations also collect this information. By examining this type of data for a period of years, it is possible to make observations about growth patterns, or the lack thereof.

General Sources

Trade publications

Search industry-specific publications. To identify key publications, consult Fulltext Sources Online or Net.Journal.

Trade associations

Identify relevant trade associations using the Bookmarks & Favorites section in Part IV and search their web sites.

Specific Sources

Industry Insider

www.investext.com

Bookmarks & Favorites

Look in "Industry & Research" under the subheading "Forecasts."

Industry-specific databases

Consult commercial vendor documentation or the Database Coverage of Industries Section in the Resources List of Part IV

Customers for Products or Services

The customer base for products or services provides crucial intelligence needed to understand the industry. Gather the data below to examine customer issues:

Size of market

Knowing the size of the market will help you to determine where your company stands in relation to the rest of the companies in the industry, and to make crucial decisions regarding bringing new products or services to market.

General Sources

Trade publications

Search industry-specific publications. To identify key publications, consult *Fulltext Sources Online* or *Net.Journal*.

Trade associations

Identify relevant trade associations using the Bookmarks & Favorites section in Part IV and search their web sites.

Government Statistical Sources

Market research reports & analyst reports

Specific Sources

Resources List

See sources listed under "Market Size" in the Data Elements List of Part IV.

Bookmarks & Favorites

Look at site listed under heading "Statistics."

Potential New Customers

Learning about possible new customers for an industry's products is crucial to increasing sales. Your company's Sales & Marketing department is always looking for this type of information.

General Sources

Trade publications

Search industry-specific publications. To identify key publications, consult *Fulltext Sources Online* or *Net.Journal* in the Data Elements List of Part IV.

Specific Sources

Resources List

See sources listed under "Consumer Trends" and "Emerging Markets."

Changes that Affect the Market

Activity in the market is affected by a number of factors. Here are some ideas for examining several of the things that can impact the market for and industry's products.

Import Penetration

Have foreign imports affected the market for an industry's products in your country? Is the trend expected to continue? What effects can be expected?

General Sources

Trade publications

Search industry-specific publications. To identify key publications, consult *Fulltext Sources Online* or *Net.Journal*.

Government Statistics

Search the Bookmarks & Favorites section in Part IV under heading "Industry Research."

Industry-specific Databases

Consult vendor's documentation for appropriate files. Search using terms like "market" and "penetration" and "imports." Also see Database File Coverage of Industries in the Resource List.

Specific Sources

Resources List

See sources listed in the Data Elements List under the heading "Market Penetration." Within the database files listed, search using terms like "market" and "penetration" and "imports." Add name of industry.

Market Forecasts

General Sources

Trade Associations

Identify relevant trade associations using the Bookmarks & Favorites section in Part IV and search their web sites.

Specific Sources

Bookmarks & Favorites

Look in "Industry Research" under the subheading "Forecasts," for both government and non-government sources. Look specifically for market forecasts.

Resources List

See sources listed in the Data Elements List under the heading "Forecasts" and "Product Forecasts." Within the referenced database files, search on keywords like "market" and "forecasts" with name of a specific industry. Also consider sources listed under "Market Research."

Distribution Methods

Changes or innovation in distribution methods within an industry can result in new leadership among the companies vying for success when it comes to the bottom line. Locating examples of success stories may provide your organization with inspiration for similar undertakings.

General Sources

Trade Publications

Include "distribution" in keywords searched. You may not want to limit to one industry, however. Look at examples in other industries that might work in your own. Consider using words like "innovative" to narrow search results.

Specific Sources

Industry-specific Databases

Consult vendor's documentation for appropriate files. Search using terms like "distribution." See also Database File Corver of Industries in the Resources List section of Part IV.

Resources List

See sources listed under "Distribution Methods" under the Data Elements list.

Market & Marketing Issues

Markets and marketing issues cover a wide span of topics, as is evidenced in the list below.

Scope of products

The scope of products in the industry in question may be broader than expected. Likewise, it could contain some surprises. It is crucial, from the CI perspective, to know what is being offered by those in the industry.

General Sources

Newswires

Product announcements generally are made using a press release. Search by company or type of product.

Company web sites

Search company web sites under hotlinks like "Products" to gain insight into the types of products offered by companies in an industry.

Specific Sources

Industry-specific Databases

Searching in these focused files using keywords like "products" yields good results. Searching for "product line" in article titles can work well, too.

Resources List

See sources listed under "Product Introductions" and "Product Forecasts" in the Data Elements List within the Resources List Section of Part IV.

Brand Loyalty

Brand loyalty means continuing business. It can vary from industry to industry and from market to market.

General Sources

Trade publications

Search industry-Specific Sources publications. To identify key publications, consult *Fulltext Sources Online* or *Net.Journal*.

Specific Sources

Resources List

See sources listed under "Brand Share" and "Brand Loyalty" in the Data Elements List. Use those terms as keywords when searching the databases.

Product Leaders

This distinction will, of course, vary by geography and by market segment.

General Sources

Trade Publications

Having identified the key publications in the industry, try searching for words like "product or brand" in titles, along with "leader or leading."

Specific Sources

Resource List

See sources listed under the heading "Market Share" in Data Elements List. Combine the keywords "market share" with the name of a product, such as "coffee."

Product Differentiation

Differentiating its products from "the rest of the pack," whether because of quality, features, or other means, may be crucial to the growth of an industry.

General Sources

Trade Publications

Search for words like "product" near "differentiation."

Specific Sources

Resource List

See sources listed under the heading "Product Differentiation" in the Data Elements list.

AdWeek

www.adweek.com

BrandWeek

www.brandweek.com

Substitute or Complimentary Products or Services

These products or services may co-exist with products or services already available. Over time, they may supplant them, due to changes in consumer preferences, or other factors.

General Sources

Trade Publications

Identify the industry's key publications and search using terms like "alternate" or "substitute" with the name of a product or service.

Specific Sources

Resource List

See sources listed in the Data Elements List under the heading "Product Differentiation" or similar topics.

Quality Continuum

General Sources

Trade Publications

Identify the industry's key publications and search using terms like "quality" with the name of a product or service.

Marketing Media Used

The media used to market an industry's products varies greatly from industry to industry. Consumer products are aimed, for example, at a much different market than raw materials or industrial products.

General Sources

Trade Publications

Search by industry name with additional keywords like "marketing" and "media."

Specific Sources

Resource List

See sources listed in Data Elements list under headings that start with the word "marketing."

AdWeek

www.adweek.com

BrandWeek

www.brandweek.com

Advertising Age

www.adage.com

Price Structure

Learning about the price structure in an industry will aid your organization in both pricing its products competitively, and in developing alternative pricing strategies.

General Sources

Trade Publications

Search by industry name with additional keywords like "price" or "pricing."

Specific Sources

Resource List

See sources listed under headings in Data Elements list that start with the word "price," or under "product pricing."

Price Margins

General Sources

Trade Publications

Search by industry name with additional keywords like "price" or "pricing."

Trade associations

Identify relevant trade associations using the Bookmarks & Favorites section in Part IV and search their web sites.

Specific Sources

Industry Insider

www.investext.com

Resource List

See sources listed in Data Elements list under headings that start with the word "price trends."

Manufactured Goods Issues

Examine the various subtopics listed below to help build the company's knowledge base regarding manufacturing industries.

Technology in Use

The technology in use may be high-tech or antiquated. These factors affect the bottom line of the companies in the industry, or the life or death of the industry itself.

General Sources

Trade publications

Search industry-Specific Sources publications. To identify key publications, consult *Fulltext Sources Online* or *Net.Journal*.

Trade associations

Identify relevant trade associations using the Bookmarks & Favorites section in Part IV and search their web sites.

Specific Sources

Industry-Specific Databases

Consult vendor's documentation for list of databases or click on a hotlink like sources on a web site. Look for a subject-oriented list of sources. See also Database File Coverage in the Resources List of Part IV.

Bookmarks & Favorites

Examine sites bookmarked under the heading "Industries & Professions," subheading "Manufacturing."

Resources List

See sources listed under "Manufacturing" in Data Elements List.

Industry Insider
www.investext.com

Technological Trends

General Sources

Trade publications

Search industry-specific sources publications. To identify key publications, consult *Fulltext Sources Online* or *Net.Journal*.

Trade associations

Identify relevant trade associations using the Bookmarks & Favorites section in Part IV and search their web sites.

Specific Sources

Industry-Specific Sources databases

Consult commercial vendor documentation or the Bookmarks & Favorites section in Part IV.

Resources List

See sources listed in Data Elements list under "Industry Trends."

Industry Insider

www.investext.com

Industry Innovations

General Sources

Trade publications

Search industry-Specific Sources publications. To identify key publications, consult *Fulltext Sources Online* or *Net.Journal*.

Trade associations

Identify relevant trade associations using the Bookmarks & Favorites section in Part IV and search their web sites. Trade associations monitor what is going on in the industry, and which companies are moving forward with innovation.

Specific Sources

Industry-Specific Databases

Consult commercial vendor documentation or the Bookmarks & Favorites section in Part IV.

Industry Insider

www.investext.com

Emerging Technologies

General Sources

Trade publications

Search industry-Specific Sources publications. To identify key publications, consult *Fulltext Sources Online* or *Net.Journal*.

Specific Sources

Resources List

See sources listed in Data Elements list under "Emerging Technologies or Patents."

Knowledge Express

This web-based commercial online service specializes in new technologies. Explore it at www.KnowledgeExpress.com.

Service Business Issues

Service business issues are often quite different from those which must be addressed in the manufacturing or product-oriented environment. Measurement and evaluation are much more subjective than in product-oriented industries, and an industry may be more dependent upon feedback from its clientele.

Scope & Level of Services

Consider these as "quality" and "quantity" questions. What types of services are being offered in various types of service industries? What level of service is provided? Is the industry responding to the wants and needs of its market?

General Sources

Trade Publications

Search industry-Specific Sources publications. Use *Fulltext Sources Online* or *Net.Journal* to identify titles.

Trade Associations

Identify relevant trade associations using Bookmarks & Favorites in Part IV and search their web sites.

Specific Sources

Resources List

See sources listed in the Data Elements list under the headings such as "Service Industries" or "Service Introductions"

Fiscal Matters

In one way or another, money drives most industries. As a matter of fact, it *is* an industry, if you consider banking and related industries. At the same time, fiscal matters can involve that which is impacted by the presence or absence of money. A variety of sources are available for obtaining this information.

General Sources

Business Newspapers/Trade Publications

Search industry-Specific Sources publications. Use *Fulltext Sources Online* or *Net.Journal* to identify titles.

Trade Associations

Identify relevant trade associations using the Bookmarks & Favorites section in Part IV and search their web sites.

Specific Sources

Dow Jones Interactive

This commercial online service is noted for coverage of financial business matters of all sorts: www.djnr.com.

The Census Bureau

Manufacturers' Shipments, Inventories, and Orders - www.census.gov/ftp/pub/indicator/www/prel.html

Bookmarks & Favorites

Choose from the wide variety of financial sites listed under "Financial Information Sites" and "Financial Media." Also look at government sites included under "Economics/Economic Data" and under "Statistics."

Resource List

Search the databases reference under "Financial Information" in the Data Elements List.

Impact of New Laws on Regulations

It is important to determine which level of government regulates the industry in question. Industries such as finance, telecommunications, and transportation are subject to both federal and state regulation, while education, finance, franchising, health, insurance, and professional services are regulated by the states.

Certain industries are not subject to such regulation, which is in itself an important fact. Since there is so much variation in state laws, if there is any question regarding this matter, it is best to check with your company's legal department as to whether a particular industry is regulated by your state.

General Sources

Newspapers & Trade Press

Search industry-Specific Sources publications. Use *Fulltext Sources Online* or *Net.Journal* to identify titles. The issues of interest to the industry will be covered in depth. Search on name of bill or law, or on name of regulating agency, as well as by keywords that identify the industry, such as "telecommunications."

Trade Associations

These organizations can provide the industry's perspective on the laws and regulations that govern the industries that they represent. Seek out web sites for an industry and then look for appropriate hotlinks.

Case Law

In some cases, the legality of laws or regulations governing an industry has been tested in federal or state courts. Search the industry name in case law databases like LEXIS or WESTLAW. (Remember that for credit card access, the LEXIS case law files are available on Winstar's Brainwave site, www.n2kbrainwave.com.)

Specific Sources

Bookmarks & Favorites

Examine the links under the heading "Activist/Interest Groups." These organizations often provide copies of laws or regulations, as well as position papers and other explanatory materials. Try to find sites that are non-partisan. At other sites, remember the "bias factor" as you explore the material or hotlinks provided.

Also consult bookmarks under the heading "Legal Information." In some cases, Specific Sources :headings like "Government/Legal/Regulatory" are provided for industries included under "Industries & Professions." The telecommunications industry is an example.

▬▬ Availability of Raw Materials

General Sources

Trade Publications

Search industry-Specific Sources publications. Use *Fulltext Sources Online* or *Net.Journal* to identify titles.

Business Newspapers

If raw materials come from foreign countries, check that country's media.

Specific Sources

Bookmarks & Favorites

Examine bookmarks under heading "Economics/Economic Data" or "Statistics." Government sites are a good source.

Resource List

Search databases listed in the Data Elements List under "Raw Materials (Availability)."

▬▬ Sales By Major Product Type

General Sources

Trade Publications

Search industry-Specific Sources publications. Use *Fulltext Sources Online* or *Net.Journal* to identify titles.

Trade Associations

Identify relevant trade associations using Bookmarks & Favorites in Part IV and search their web sites.

Market Research Reports

Choose among many databases available on major commercial online services. Search by product or industry and keyword "sales."

Specific Sources

Resource List

Search the database sources listed in the Data Elements List under headings "Sales By Product" and "Sales Volume."

Bookmarks & Favorites

Look for government sites whose agencies deal with this information e.g. the Bureau of Economic Analysis, www.bea.doc.gov. See the heading "Government Sites."

Productivity-Related Matters

Is this industry productive? Is it vegetating or adjusting to the times? By examining productivity-related matters, and combining your findings with other material in your organization's knowledge base, you may reach a more clear understanding the industry's productivity level.

Manufacturing Rates

General Sources

Trade Publications

Search industry-Specific Sources publications. Use *Fulltext Sources Online* or *Net.Journal* to identify titles.

Trade Associations

Identify relevant trade associations using the Bookmarks & Favorites section in Part IV and search their web sites.

Specific Sources

Resource List

Search the database sources listed in the Data Elements List under "Manufacturing Industries."

Efficiency Levels

General Sources

Trade Publications

Search industry-Specific Sources publications. Use *Fulltext Sources Online* or *Net.Journal* to identify titles.

Specific Sources

Resource List

Search the database sources listed under headings "Efficiency Levels."

Product Innovation

General Sources

Trade Publications

Search industry-Specific Sources publications. Use *Fulltext Sources Online* or *Net.Journal* to identify titles.

Trade Associations

Identify relevant trade associations using the Bookmarks & Favorites section in Part IV and search their web sites.

Specific Sources

Resource List

See headings in the Data Elements List beginning with "Product" and search the resources listed there, using keywords "product" and "innovation."

Bookmarks & Favorites

See the web site entitled Business Research Reports at www.saibooks.com.

What About Other Topics?

For other topics, use the Industry Study template shown below:

Industry Study Template

STATUS OF THE INDUSTRY

Relative size and scope of the industry -
growing, stable, or declining?   _____

History of industry   _____

Trends in industry   _____

Forecasts regarding size of the industry   _____

SIC or NAICS Codes   _____

CUSTOMERS FOR PRODUCTS
OR SERVICES

Customers   _____

Size of market   _____

Potential new buyers   _____

Directions in the market   _____

Import penetration   _____

Forecasts for market   _____

Distribution methods   _____

MARKET/MARKETING ISSUES

Scope of products   _____

Brand loyalty   _____

Product leader description   _____

Product differentiation   _____

Alternate products/services   _____

Complementary products   _____

Quality continuum   _____

Marketing media used   _____

Price structure   _____

Price margins   _____

MANUFACTURED GOODS ISSUES

Technology in Use   _____

Technological trends   _____

Industry innovations   _____

Emerging technologies   _____

SERVICE BUSINESS ISSUES

Scope of services   _____

Level of services   _____
_____

FISCAL MATTERS

Changes that may impact supplier prices   _____

Legislation/Regulations   _____

Availability of raw materials   _____

Other Sales by major product type   _____

PRODUCTIVITY-RELATED MATTERS

Manufacturing rates   _____

Efficiency levels   _____

Product innovation   _____

Part IV

References & Appendices

Bookmarks & Favorites

The CI Sleuth's Guide to the Universe

▬▬ Do It Like a Pro

Nearly every week the Internet listservs frequented by professional searchers contain several "Does anybody have a good site for (fill in the blank)" questions. Essentially, the searcher has been asked for something on an unfamiliar topic or has "struck out" searching the usual sources, so he or she has posted a message asking for assistance.

Invariably several colleagues quickly reply, providing one or more hot-links to sources on the topic. How do they do this so quickly? The answer, of course, is obvious:

BOOKMARKS (ALSO KNOWN AS FAVORITES)

The pros know that they will need certain material repeatedly or that particular sites may be useful again. Thus, with one or two fast mouse clicks, they perform the equivalent of the following:

◆ Writing down a name and web address (the URL)

◆ Going to the supply cabinet and taking out a manila folder

◆ Labeling the folder appropriately

◆ Tossing in the slip of paper containing the valuable information

◆ Walking to the file cabinet, opening a drawer, and placing the folder carefully in its place alphabetically.

Because they've stored important Internet sites as bookmarks/favorites, they can easily take a minute to make suggestions to a colleague, even on a busy day. All they do is open their browser, examine their bookmarks list, and use the copy and paste features to add the sites' Internet addresses (URLs) to an outgoing e-mail message.

On the commercial online side, the process may be a bit more complex, since the reference may be to a source that requires a subscription.

Once inside of a vendor's site, you must know which of the many files available should be searched for the intelligence that is needed. The next search may take you back to the same vendor's site, but to a different file or group of files, containing material relevant to the project or question in hand. Frequent searchers can develop and save mental or written lists consisting of points like these:

♦   What files are available on my topic?

♦   Which vendor(s) offer the file for searching?

♦   Where can I get the best price and/or greatest efficiency?

♦   Do I have a subscription to the necessary service?

♦   If not, is there an Internet source that offers that the database on a pay-as-you-go basis?

If bookmarks or the list above does not provide answers, we are back to the top of this section — the pros ask their colleagues to check *their* bookmarks.

Managing Your Bookmarks/Favorites File

Your bookmarks files may be varied or highly focused, depending upon your job. Librarians, for example, will collect bookmarks for a wide variety of subjects, while others in the company may concentrate on information sources suited to their department's activities.

The remainder of this chapter consists of bookmarks chosen over several years, but checked and re-evaluated frequently. The intent is to provide a skeleton framework to get you started, and to provide some examples for categorizing what could become hundreds or thousands of individual bookmarks. The categorizing provides greater efficiency and prevents overlooking a "great site" because its name is not a clear indicator of its contents.

When you find a useful site for business intelligence, or even a particular page buried somewhere on a larger site, remember to BOOKMARK IT IMMEDIATELY, preferably in a folder with a meaningful heading. Otherwise, you may not easily find it again.

Examine the name of a site when you bookmark it, and edit if necessary, using language that will give a clear indication of the site's contents. Delete words before the name of the site, like "Welcome to...," for more effective alphabetizing.

Web pages disappear and relocate frequently. Run your browser's program for checking bookmarks monthly and try to visit those that are marked unavailable when the check was performed. The server may merely have been busy. If the site has moved, a new address may be available for a limited period of time. Follow the link to the new site, create a bookmark and save it in the appropriate folder within your bookmark file. If you receive a "404" message, delete the bookmark from your list.

The Usual Disclaimer...

These Internet addresses were last updated in late March 1999 and were current at that time. Sites containing searchable databases were sought out. For the most part, personal pages or sites of particular companies within an industry are not included. The list is not comprehensive — creating such a list would be an impossible task. This list is a starting point. To help with the thought process, notes about applying certain information when performing CI have been included. Many of the sites included here can serve as "jumping off places" to further research a topic. A number of award-winning or favorably reviewed Internet sites offer collections of links to dozens of other valuable sites, a fact which is made clear by the name used so frequently to describe this key part of the Internet: the World Wide Web. To locate additional bookmarks and other useful material, visit the Burwell Enterprises web site at www.burwellinc.com.

Activist / Interest Groups

Some of these groups may have an impact on your company or industry, so it is important to know who they are and what they are up to. They also may be valuable sources of information — providing documents, copies of laws (or proposed legislation), hot-links on their web sites, names and addresses or other useful intelligence. It is important to remember that although they have an opinion, or an "axe to grind," they do a great deal of research that can save you time and may be useful to your company.

Catherwood library: NYS School of Industrial & Labor Relations
www.ilr.cornell.edu/library/reference/Guides/LUI.html

Center for Responsive Politics
www.crp.org

Center for Responsive Politics: Database Index
www.crp.org/databases.htm

EFFweb - The Electronic Frontier Foundation
www.eff.org

Executive PayWatch
www.paywatch.org/paywatch/index.htm

FACSNET: Reporter's Cardfile
www.facsnet.org/sources_online/cardfile.htm

Greenpeace USA
www.greenpeaceusa.org

Multinational Monitor Online
www.essential.org/monitor

Political Science Resources: United States Politics
www.lib.umich.edu/libhome/Documents.center/psusp.html#activ

Scorecard
www.scorecard.org/env-releases

SPJ: FOI Resource Center: Federal Advocacy Group Contacts
www.spj.org/foia/foiresources/advocacy/adindex.htm

Associations

Trade associations may provide a wealth of material on the industry they represent. Searching some of the sites below may point to associations that you had not identified previously.

AcqWeb's Directory of Associations & Organizations
www.library.vanderbilt.edu:80/law/acqs/assn.html

AeroWorldNet • Aviation & Aerospace Associations
www.aeroworldnet.com/indass.htm

American Petroleum Institute
www.api.org

American Society for Testing and Materials (ASTM)
www.astm.org

American Society of Assn Executives Database
www.asaenet.org/Gateway/OnlineAssocSlist.html

ASMENET: Home Page for ASME International
www.asme.org

Association of Advertising Agencies
www.ara.cz/engl/arahome.htm

Association of Private Pension and Welfare Plans (APPWP)
www.appwp.org

Auto-Links TRADE PAGE - Associations
www.findlinks.com/autolinks.html#asns

Bevier Engineering Library: Associations, Societies & Organizations
www.pitt.edu/~engrlib/associations.html

Brainstorm business bookmarks (Trade Association sites)
www.brainstorm.co.uk/TANC/Bookmarks/
Associations.html

Canada Info: Canadian Associations Online
www.clo.com/~canadainfo/associations.html

Federation of International Trade Associations: Import Export Trade Leads
www.fita.org/fita.html

GaleNet (Encyclopedia of Associations)
www.gale.com/gale/galenet/galenet.html

Hoover's UK
www.hoovers.co.uk

International Organization / NGO Web Sites
www.uia.org/website.htm

Internet Public Library: Associations on the Net (AON)
www.ipl.org/ref/AON

Manufacturing Central: Hot Links to Associations Council Members
www.nam.org/Bulletin/AC/acmember.html

PhRMA (Pharmaceutical Research & Mfr. of America) - Members Only
www.phrma.org

Professional Associations
http://freeweb.pdq.net/ennis/ih/professi.htm

Professional Organizations in the Information Sciences
http://witloof.sjsu.edu/peo/organizations.html

Telecoms Virtual Library: Associations
www.analysys.com/vlib/assoc.htm

US Department of Commerce: Metals Industry Trade Associations
www.ita.doc.gov/metals/assoc

Yahoo! Business & Economy: Organizations: Professional
www.yahoo.com/economy/organizations/professional

Yahoo! Business & Economy: Organizations: Trade Associations
www.yahoo.com/Business_and_Economy/
Organizations/Trade_Associations

Bookstores

Search these sites to identify books written about your industry or your competitors. You can also use their search engines to identify the newest CI books.

Amazon.com
www.amazon.com

Barnesandnoble.com
www.barnesandnoble.com

Powell's Bookstore-used, new, and out of print books
www.powells.com

Broadcast Monitors

Track new products, competitors' ad campaigns or coverage of media companies.

Video Monitoring Services of America LP (VMS)
www.vidmon.com

Business Sites - Compilations & Reviews

Use these sites to identify other sites of interest in your research. BRINT is a favorite in the US. Sheila Webber's site from the University of Strathclyde in Glasgow is especially strong for UK and European information; it is annotated, and is a personal favorite at Burwell Enterprises.

BRINT - A Business Researcher's Interests: Business Research, Management Research & Information Technology Research
www.brint.com/interest.html

BUBL LINK: Browse by Subject
www.bubl.ac.uk/link/subjects

Business Information Sources on the Internet: Index
www.dis.strath.ac.uk/business/index.html

Direct Search: Search Tools & Directories
http://gwis2.circ.gwu.edu/~gprice/direct.htm

EARLweb: Business Intelligence
www.earl.org.uk/earlweb/busns.html

ENTERWeb The Enterprise Development Web Site
www.enterweb.org

Global Business Centre
www.euromktg.com/gbc

Hieros Gamos • The Comprehensive Law & Government Site
www.hg.org/guides.html

Spire Project
http://cn.net.au

The Biz
www.thebiz.co.uk

Virtual International Business & Economic Sources (VIBES)
www.uncc.edu/lis/library/reference/
intbus/vibehome.htm

Business Sites - General

These general business sites will provide you with an overview of what's out there, and how it is generally categorized. Non-US sites are included. Some of these sites are updated frequently, and are worth repeat visits to keep on top of what new sites are out there.

BUBL LINK: Business
http://link.bubl.ac.uk/business

Business in Latin America - LANIC
http://lanic.utexas.edu/la/region/business

Business information sources on the internet: Guides to business sites
www.dis.strath.ac.uk/business/general.html

Downsizing the American Dream
www.house.gov/democrats/research/downsize.html

Global Business Centre
www.euromktg.com/gbc

Government & Contract Bids from BidNet
www.bidnet.com

International Business Directory
http://msm.byu.edu/c&i/cim/ibd/Dir.htm

International Business Guide: Worldclass Supersite
http://web.idirect.com/~tiger/supersit.htm

International Business Resources on the WWW
http://ciber.bus.msu.edu/busres.htm

Internet Business Library
www.bschool.ukans.edu/IntBusLib

Prices's List of Lists
http://gwis2.circ.gwu.edu/~gprice/listof.htm

The Economist Intelligence Unit
www.eiu.com

Webliography: A Guide to Internet Resources
www.lib.lsu.edu/weblio.html#Business

Yahoo! Infodesk
http://howto.yahoo.com/infodesk/yahoo_finance.html

Classification Systems - Business

Use these systems to identify competitors by searching for companies that are classified under the same number that your company uses to describe what it does. NAICS is the newer of the two system, and is more specific. The first bookmark on this list cross references the two systems.

Download NAICS and SIC tables
www.census.gov/epcd/www/naicstab.htm#download

NAICS Implementation Schedule
www.census.gov/epcd/naics/timeschd.html

North American Industry Classification System (NAICS) (Georgetown Univ.)
    http://gulib.lausun.georgetown.edu/swr/business/
    naics.htm

North American Industry Classification System (NAICS)
    www.census.gov/epcd/www/naics.html#fedreg

OSHA: Standard Industrial Classification Search
    www.osha.gov/oshstats/sicser.html

SIC (6 digit) plus NAICS Database
    www.env-sol.com/solutions/SIC.HTML

Company Information

Industry-specific - Worldwide

Keep up with the players in worldwide markets by looking for sites like these. Many of the sites contain searchable databases or company profiles that may be especially useful for finding and learning about privately held companies. If your competition happens to be a multi-national corporation, locate addresses of foreign offices using some of the country-specific files.

AeroWorldNet • Aerospace Companies
    www.aeroworldnet.com/companie.htm

Association of Advertising Agencies Members- Czechoslovakia
    www.ara.cz/engl/clenove.htm

Banking Institutions in Slovenia
    www.tradepoint.si/Banke/Institutions.htm

Chambers County Appraisal District
    www.chamberscad.org

CorpTech Database of 50,000 U.S. Technology Companies
    www.corptech.com

Directory of All Swiss Banks
    www.swissbanknet.ch

Egypt's Pharmaceutical Companies
    www.idsc.gov.eg/health/pharm.htm

Energiearchiv : Inhaltsverzeichnis (In German)
    http://dynamik.fb10.tu-berlin.de/~borg_pc2/stein/
    archiv/eaindex.htm

Global 250 - Europe (Food)
    www.foodexplorer.com/BUSINESS/Companies/
    Global250/Europe.htm

Industry List Page
    http://profiles.wisi.com/profiles/indsrch.htm

Industry Medicinal Chemistry Company Sites
    www.phc.vcu.edu/link/industrylinks.html

LeatherIndia - Home Page
    www.leatherindia.com

LinkGuide Business Information Centre
    http://www-linkguid.enst-bretagne.fr

List of Banks for Czechoslovakia
    www.mpo.cz/english/g/gb/page0111.htm

LOTUS INTERGATE - Die Energie Datenbank (In German)
www.lotusintergate.at/energiedatenbank

Pharmaceutical Company Sites
www.nwkinetics.com/phrmlnks.htm

Report on Banks in Nigeria
www.afbis.com/vanguard/banks/index.htm

Swissbanknet: Directory of All Swiss Banks
www.swissbanknet.ch/html/bank_directory.html

Tennessee High Tech Company Database
www.state.tn.us/ecd/scitech/index.htm

Trade Point: Slovenia: Insurance
www.tradepoint.si/Zavarovalnice

US Department of Energy Homepage
http://198.124.130.244

WARS-Pharmaceuticals on the 'Net
http://pathit.clever.net/wars/war_phrm.htm

Who Makes Machinery in Germany
http://wbm.hoppenstedt.com/Englisch/index.html

Non-US Public Company Filings

Filings made by public companies are available in some countries. These provide valuable intelligence, but the amount will vary from country to country.

Australian Securities & Investments Commission
www.asic.gov.au

Canada - Search for Public Company Documents
www.sedar.com/search/search_form_pc.htm

Carlson Online Services Inc
www.fin-info.com/index.html#basicsearch

Cerved S.p.A. - Italian Companies (In Italian)
www.cerved.com

Cerved SpA • Italian Companies (In Italian)
www.cerved.com

Companies House (UK)
www.companies-house.gov.uk/frame.cgi?OPT=ddir

Global Register: New Zealand Companies
www.globalregister.co.nz/nzcomp.htm

Japan Company Records
www.japancompanyrecord.com

Non-US Public / Private

These sites may refer to public or privately held companies outside the US. Many can be searched by company name. Also consider the venture capital information web sites, listed under the Financial Information heading below.

:// YELLOWWW - The Big German Business Directory in the Internet
http://english.branchenbuch.com

1998 Forbes International 800 Search Page
www.forbes.com/tool/toolbox/int500

Asiaweek Offers
www.pathfinder.com/asiaweek/newoffer/index.html

Canadian Corporate Information
www.corporateinformation.com/cacorp.html

CAROL - ASIA
www.carol.co.uk/reports/asia/index.html

CAROL (UK)
www.carol.co.uk/reports/index.html

ChinaBig Yellow Pages
www.chinabig.com

Comissão de Valores Mobiliários - Brazil
www.cvm.gov.br/indexi.htm

Companies in Bulgaria
www.eunet.bg/catalog/index.html

Corporate Reports Ltd (UK)
www.corpreports.co.uk

Corporations Database Online (Canada)
http://strategis.ic.gc.ca/sc_mrksv/corpdir/
engdoc/corpns.html

COSMOS Online (Mexico)
www.cosmos.com.mx

Credit Information Reports from Business Credit Management UK
www.creditman.co.uk

Executive PayWatch • The Ceo and You
http://aflcio.paywatch.org/ceopay/ceoyou/
ceolist.html

French Companies - DAFSA (In French)
www.dafsa.fr/cgi-bin/Dafsa/dafsa.pl

Global 500 | 500 List
http://pathfinder.com/fortune/global500/index.html

Hoppenstedt (Germany)
www.hoppenstedt.com

Indonesia Net Exchange
www.indoexchange.com

InfoCamere (In Italian)
www.infocamere.it

Israel Export Institute's Bookmarks
www.export.gov.il/bookmark.html

Japan Company Records
http://japanfinancials.com

Juniper from ICC Information (UK)
www.icc.co.uk

Kobmanstanden
www.kob.dk/english

Kompass Ireland - Company Register
www.kompass.ie

Kompass
> www.kompass.com

Liquidations Search, Insolvency (UK)
> www.insolvency.co.uk/liq/liqfind.htm

Mexican Corporate Information
> www.corporateinformation.com/mxcorp.html

Orient Business Express (ASIA)
> www.accessasia.com/
> cgi-win/imagemap.exe/newmap?152,212

Perfect Information (UK)
> www.perfectinfo.com

PJ Online: Philanthropy Links : Meta Index of Non-Profit Sites
> http://204.243.96.61/links_metaindex.cfm

SKATE: Online Company Data (Russia)
> www.skate.ru/rcd/ruscompdata.html

Teikoku Databank America Inc
> www.teikoku.com

The UK Business Directory
> www.milfac.co.uk/milfac/bisindex.html

Thomas Register Europe
> www.tipcoeurope.com

Wright Research Center: Country List Page (Multiple Countries)
> http://profiles.wisi.com/profiles/cntrysrch.htm

Yahoo! UK & Ireland Company Index
> www.yahoo.co.uk/finance/profiles/alpha

US Company Profiles - Public/Private

These sites have been identified as containing searchable databases or lists of company profiles. The quality and quantity of information will vary from site to site, so it will be important to obtain several profiles on the companies that are searched, and to compare their contents. Some sites are updated more frequently than are others. Be sure to read the fine print regarding the source of the information, as well.

Companies Online - Deja News
> http://in-123.infospace.com/_1_94327698__info.deja/
> bizweb.htm

Company profiles & financial information from the University of Strathclyde
> www.dis.strath.ac.uk/business/financials.html

Corporate Financials Online
> www.cfonews.com

Corporate Information Bank
> www.dir.co.jp/Affiliates/DaiwaSec/
> IR/CIB/welcome.html

Corporate Information
> www.corporateinformation.com

Dallas Central Appraisal District
> www.dallascad.org

Dun & Bradstreet CompaniesOnline Search
www.companiesonline.com

Dun & Bradstreet Reports
www.dnb.com

Electric Library - Business Edition
www.business.elibrary.com

Fortune 500 | 500 List
www.pathfinder.com/fortune/fortune500/500list.html

Hoover's Company Capsules
www.nytimes.com/partners/quote/hoovers.html

Hoover's Online
www.hoovers.com

Infoseek Industrywatch
www.industrywatch.com

invest-o-rama
www.investorama.com/cosearch.html

MedNet Interactive - a service of COR Healthcare Resources
www.mednet-i.com

NASDAQ-100 Index
www.nasdaq.com/asp/nasdaq100_activity.stm

NewsEdge: NewsPage - Companies: Company Lookup
http://companies.newspage.com

OneSource Information Services
www.onesource.com

Platt's on the Internet
www.platts.com

Red Herring Online - Company Profiles
www.herring.com/profiles/home.html

Standard & Poor's Compustat PC Plus
www.compustat.com/products/pcplus/bw_archv.htm

Star-Telegram Online Services: Top 100 Employers
http://startext.net/today/news/business/
tarrantb/top100.htm

TechWeb Finance - Quotes & Data
www.techweb.com/wire/finance/quotes

The PRS Group
www.prsgroup.com

The Ultimate Directory - ThomWeb
www.infospace.com/uk.thomw

Thomas Register of American Manufacturers
www.thomasregister.com/index.html

Transium Corporation
www.transium.com

VaultReports.Com
www.vaultreports.com

Worldwide banking guide
www.qualisteam.com/eng/conf.html

Yahoo! Business & Economy: Companies
www.yahoo.com/Business_and_Economy/Companies

US Private Companies

These are the most difficult types of companies to research. In addition to sites like those listed below, remember to search public records and local or regional newspapers by company name. One of the best spots in cyberspace for collective sources of information on private companies is the Corporation Information site. The Venture Capital sites, listed under financial information sites, also cover private companies.

Denver Business Journal - Private Companies
www.amcity.com/denver/stories/041398/list.html

Denver Business Journal - Private Companies
www.amcity.com/denver/stories/041398/list.html

Export Market Information Centre (EMIC) - Home
www.dti.gov.uk/ots/emic

Forbes: The 500 Top Private Companies, 1998
www.forbes.com/tool/toolbox/private500

Greater Washington: Top Private Companies
www.greaterwashington.org/be_pr.htm

Largest Private Companies Headquatered in Los Angeles
www.svmf.org/svif/report/tanigawa/lapriv97.htm

Red Herring: Top 50 private companies - 9/97
www.herring.com/mag/digital/private.html

Regional Career Guide: Private Companies in Maryland, Virginia & Washington, DC Metro Area
www.firstmagnitude.com/career/regional.htm

The Inc 500
www.inc.com/500

Top Triad Private Companies
www.greensboro.com/97top50/private.htm

US Corporate Information • Privately Held Companies
www.corporateinformation.com/uspriv.html

US Public Company Filings

Even though everyone says that public companies are the "easy ones" to research, it's nice to have a handy collection of sites for filings by public companies. Both government and commercial sources are included here. To collect annual reports on competitors without ordering directly, consider one or more of the Annual Report services listed below. For older filings, Disclosure is a tried and true source used by librarians. That source also provides non-US material as well as the required SEC filings by US companies. Also, remember that not all filings are required to be made electronically, so checking EDGAR may not be sufficient.

Annual Reports

Annual Report Gallery
www.reportgallery.com/index.htm

Public Register's Annual Report Service
(PRARS) NASDAQ, NYSE, AMEX, OTC
`www.prars.com`

The Annual Reports Library
`www.zpub.com/sf/arl`

Wall Street Journal: Annual Reports Service
`www.icbinc.com/cgi-bin/wsj`

Miscellaneous Reports

10-K Wizard
`www.10kwizard.com`

aRMadillo Company Database
`www.rmonline.com/pr2.htm`

BvD Suite
`http://suite.bvdep.com/cgi/template.dll?product=2`

Company Annual Reports Online (CAROL) - UK & Asia
`www.carol.co.uk`

Directory of OTC Bulletin Board Companies
`www.proinvestor.com/pub/maccess/index.html`

Disclosure
`www.disclosure.com/disclosure`

Disclosure-Investor.com
`www.disclosure-investor.com/retail/helps/`
`sec_guide.cgi?VENDOR=INTERNET`

EDGAR
`www.sec.gov/edaux/wedgar.htm`

EDGAR Online
`www.edgar-online.com`

EDGAR, Important Information About
`www.sec.gov/edaux/wedgar.htm`

EDGAR-Online the Source for Today's SEC Filings
`www.edgar-online.com/bin/esearch`

Facts Online: Hot Technology Companies
`www.FACTS-ONLINE.COM/FACTSS.HTM`

FreeEDGAR.com: Companies - Today's filings
`www.freeedgar.com/companies/todays.htm`

FreeEDGAR.com: Companies.
`www.freedgar.com/companies/index.htm`

Global Securities Information
`www.gsionline.com`

Investor Communications Business
`www.icbinc.com`

InvestQuest Annual Reports
`Data Element' www.investquest.com/iq_annual.htm`

InvestQuest - DRIPs & DSPPs
`www.investquest.com`

Moody's Investors Service
`www.moodys.com`

Partes FreeEDGAR: Free Real-Time SEC EDGAR Filings - Today's Filings
`www.FreeEDGAR.com/Search/TodaysFilings.asp`

US Regional Sites

Some regional sites also are included under other headings in this list.

Apparel.net: The Online Guide for the Apparel Industry
`http://apparel.net/index.cgi`

Chicago Fact Book: Business
`www.ci.chi.il.us/wm/dpd/ChgoFacts/Business.html`

Cinncinnati Enquirer 1997: Greater Cincinnati 100
`www.enquirer.com/editions/1997/10/05/`
`bus_cincy1-22.html`

City of Farmers Branch, TX: Directory of Manufacturers
`www.ci.farmers-branch.tx.us/econdev/`
`manufdir/manufdir.html`

D-FW Top 200
`www.nordby.com/regions/dallas/top200/200home.htm`

Ellis County Appraisal District
`www.elliscad.org`

Hometown Dallas - Top 100 Companies
`www.hometowndallas.com/top100.html`

newsday.com / Long Island 100
`www.newsday.com/az/100biz10.htm`

NJO BUSINESS Top 100
`www.nj.com/business/top100/listindex.html`

North Dakota's Largest Employers By Total Payroll
`www.state.nd.us/jsnd/rankp3.htm`

Oregon Business Channel
`www.oregonbusiness.com`

Regional Career Guide: Private Companies in Maryland, Virginia and Washington, DC Metro Area
`www.firstmagnitude.com/career/regional.htm`

The Hale & Dorr LLP New England IPO Report, 1990-96
`www.haledorr.com/publications/ipo/IPO_9096/`
`Contents.html`

Thomas Regional Directory
`www.thomasregional.com/newtrd/c_home.html`

Triangle's Top Technology Companies
`http://cgi2.nando.net/newsroom/nao/biz/`
`030297/tech.html`

US Corporate Information: Regional Sites
`www.corporateinformation.com/usstates.html`

Washington Top 100 Companies
`www.kent.wednet.edu/KSD/KR/WA/ECON/100list.htm`

Competitive Intelligence Sites

These sites are a combination of web pages of CI consulting companies and sites that address the concept of CI. There is overlap, so they have been combined into one list. At the Fuld site, pay particular attention to the Internet Intelligence Index.

BiTE Competitive Intelligence: Information Product Details
> www.iee.org.uk/Bite/comp-int.htm

Cipher Systems
> www.cipher-sys.com

Company Sleuth
> www.companysleuth.com/
> my-page.cfm?CFID=56459&CFTOKEN=34864225

Competitive Intelligence Handbook
> www.combsinc.com/handbook.htm

Competitive Intelligence on the Web - Web Search - 08/14/98
> http://websearch.miningco.com/library/
> weekly/aa081498.htm

Fuld & Company Inc: Competitive Intelligence Guide
> www.fuld.com

Global Integrity Corporation Packages
> www.globalintegrity.com/info/services/packages.html

Internet Resources for the Competitive Intelligence Professional
> http://dspace.dial.pipex.com/aware/
> competitive-intelligence.shtml

NetBrief: Your Own Strategic Intelligence Service
> www.netbrief.com

Second Sight Internet Intelligence LLC
> www.2s2i.com

Society of Competitive Intelligence Professionals (SCIP)
> www.scip.org

Sun Tzu & the Art of Business
> http://cazmedia.com/suntzu

The Benchmarking Exchange (TBE)
> www.benchmarking.org

WebMaster: July 1996 Click & Dagger [Peer Counseling]
> www.cio.com/archive/webbusiness/
> 0796_click_peer.html

Conferences/Trade Shows

Conferences and trade shows can be useful sources of business intelligence for different reasons, depending upon your company's interests. As mentioned in earlier chapters, these sources are useful for finding experts, identifying topics of competitors' speakers, or learning about competitors' new products.

EventSeeker The World Events Calendar
> http://w3.eventseeker.com

EventSource
> http://eventsource.com

Trade Show Directory
www.industry.net/tools/tradeshows.htm

Trade Show News Network (TSNN)
www.tsnn.com

Country/World Regional Sites

Search these web sites when interested in business intelligence outside of the US. Many of them contain links to various general topics, such as finance, laws, industries, etc. in the specific country or region. Government sources have been included.

AFRICA

Ananzi: Catalogue: Industry Manufacturing & Mining
www.ananzi.co.za/catalogue/industry.html

Mbendi: Information for Africa
http://mbendi.co.za

Orientation Africa
http://af.orientation.com

The Bureau of Financial Analysis Network
www.bfanet.com

ASIA

AIT's Asia Information Page
www.ait.ac.th/Asia/asiamap.map?49,73

Asia Inc Online
www.asia-inc.com

Asia Inc: Who's Who in Asia
www.asia-inc.com/who.htm

Asia Internet Directory: Main Index
www.asia-inc.com/dir.htm

Asia Pacific Chamber of Commerce
http://oneworld.new-era.com/apcc

Asian Business Watch
www.webcom.com/darrel

Asian Sources Online
www.asiansources.com

Asian Studies WWW VL
http://coombs.anu.edu.au/WWWVL-AsianStudies.html

Asia-Pacific Information
http://sunsite.sut.ac.jp/asia

Orientation Asia
http://as.orientation.com

Virtual Library: Asian Studies
http://vlib.stanford.edu/AsianStudies.html

CANADA

Agriculture & Agri-Food Canada's Electronic Information Service (ACEIS)
www.agr.ca

BC OnLine • Access to Government Information
www.bconline.gov.bc.ca

Canadian Council of Ministers of the Environment
www.mbnet.mb.ca/ccme

Canadian Industry Statistics for Trade, Finance, Economics, etc.
www.msnbc.com/news/254376.asp

CANUTEC – The Canadian Transport Emergency Centre
www.tc.gc.ca/canutec

CCN NewsNet
www.cdn-news.com

Corporations Database Online (Canada)
http://strategis.ic.gc.ca/sc_mrksv/corpdir/
engdoc/corpns.html

Environment Canada's Green Lane
www.doe.ca

National Energy Board
www.neb.gc.ca

Natural Resources Canada
www.nrcan.goc.ca/homepage

Strategis - Canada's Business Information Site
http://strategis.ic.gc.ca/engdoc/main.html

Technical Standards & Safety Authority
www.tssa.org

CHINA

China Council For The Promotion of International Trade
www.ccpit.org/engVersion/index.html

China Information
http://sunsite.sut.ac.jp/asia/china

ChinaBig Yellow Pages
www.chinabig.com

ChinaOnline
www.chinaonline.com/sitemap.html

Finding News About China
http://freenet.buffalo.edu/~cb863/china.html

SurfChina.com
www.surfchina.com

CZECH REPUBLIC

Open for Business in Central Europe • Czech Republic
www.dti.gov.uk/ots/centeuro/czech_republic.html

HEALTH RELATED

Pan-American Health Organization: Country Health Profiles Information
www.paho.org/english/country.htm

Travel Health Online: Directory of Country Summary Profiles
www.tripprep.com/country/country.html#a

ISRAEL

Israel Export Institute's Bookmarks
www.export.gov.il/bookmark.html

Israel's Infomedia
www.infomedia.co.il

JAPAN

Bridge to Japan
www.daiwa-foundation.org.uk

Japan - General Information
www.stat.go.jp/16.htm

Japan - General Information
http://SunSITE.sut.ac.jp/asia/japan/general

Japan in Figures 1999
www.stat.go.jp/16.htm

Japan Information
www.ntt.co.jp/japan

Japan Information - Government Sites
http://SunSITE.sut.ac.jp/asia/japan/gov

Japanese Public Opinion
www.ropercenter.uconn.edu/JPOLL/home.html

LATIN AMERICA

Business in Latin America - LANIC
http://lanic.utexas.edu/la/region/business

Central American Report
www.worldcom.nl/CAR

Inter-American Understanding
www.erols.com/iauinc

Orientation Latin America & the Carribean
http://la.orientation.com

WWW Virtual Library: Latin American Studies
http://lanic.utexas.edu/las.html

MIDDLE EAST

ArabNet - The Resource for the Arab World in the Middle East and North
Africa
www.arab.net

Association for International Business (AIB): Middle Eastern Links
http://earthone.com/middleast.html

MIDDLE EAST STUDIES RESOURCES
www.columbia.edu/cu/libraries/indiv/area/MiddleEast

MULTI-COUNTRY

1997 World Factbook
www.odci.gov/cia/publications/factbook/index.html

Association for International Business Country & Region Links Page
http://earthone.com/country.html

Australian Department of Foreign Affairs & Trade
www.dfat.gov.au

Bank of America: World Information Services
www.bankamerica.com/econ_indicator/wis.html

FCO Online (British Travel Advice)
www.fco.gov.uk/reference/travel_advice/
countries.html

Library of Congress / Federal Research Division / Country Studies / Area Handbook Series
http://lcweb2.loc.gov/frd/cs/cshome.html

Orientation Central & Eastern Europe
http://eeu.orientation.com

The Economist Intelligence Unit
www.eiu.com/latest

US State Department - Services - Background Notes
www.state.gov/www/background_notes/index.html

USPTO Upcoming Opportunities - Information Technology
www.uspto.gov/web/offices/ac/comp/proc/upopp.htm

POLAND

POLAND '98 • Business Information Service
www.bmb.com.pl/MainFrameE.dbi

RUSSIA

American Chamber of Commerce in Russia
www.amcham.ru

Governments on the WWW: Russian Federation
www.gksoft.com/govt/en/ru.html

Investment Guide to Russia
www.fipc.ru/fipc

Russian Internet
www.neystadt.org/russia

Russian Legal Server
www.friends-partners.org/partners/fplegal/main.html

Russian News from EurasiaNews – Eurasia Research Center
http://eurasianews.com/erc/00rusnews.htm

The List of Russian Web Servers – Weblist
http://weblist.ru

THAILAND

Thailand Web Directory
www.okeydonkey.com/donkey1

UNITED KINGDOM

CCTA Government Information Service
www.open.gov.uk

Database Vendors

The major commercial online vendors' Web sites have been collected here. If you don't subscribe to a service, check the group marked "Pay By Credit Card." Brainwave, for example, allows pay-as-you-go access to many files contained on major subscription services, such as DIALOG or LEXIS.

PAY BY CREDIT CARD

Basic Facts about Registering a Trademark
www.uspto.gov/web/offices/tac/doc/basic

Business Information from Brainwave - The Business Information Resource for Company, Industry and Market Research
www.n2kbrainwave.com/
cgi-bin/scribe/index.htm[BOUNTY]

Business Information from Brainwave
www.n2kbrainwave.com

CorpTech Database of 45,000 US Technology Companies
www.corptech.com

infoMarket search page
www.infomarket.k-link.com

Information Please Home Page
www.infoplease.com

KnowX | Home
www.knowx.com

Multex: Institutional Investment Research, Earnings and Equity Reports
www.multex.com

Online Sleuth
www.inc.com/online_sleuth

POWERIZE.com
www.powerize.com/index.htm

Standard & Poor's Ratings Services
www.ratings.com

VISTACheck
www.vistacheck.com

WestDoc
www.westdoc.com

SUBSCRIPTION REQUIRED

Asia Pulse
http://203.63.165.109/asiapulse/home.nsf

Companies House
www.companies- house.gov.uk/frame.cgi

Disclosure
www.disclosure.com/disclosure

Electric Library - Business Edition
www.business.elibrary.com

Equifax
www.equifax.com

EuropeanInformafionNeworkServices(EINS)
www.equifax.com

Experian Uniform Commercial Code sample report
www.experian.com/product/pubrec/uccsample.html

H.W. Wilson Co.
www.hwwilson.com

Harris Info Online
www.HARRISinfoonline.com

IRSC
www.irsc.com/home.htm

Knowledge Express
www.knowledgeexpress.com

LEXIS-NEXIS Universe - Sign-On
http://web.lexis-nexis.com/ln.universe

Manning & Napier
www.mnis.com

NTIS Online Subscriptions
www.ntis.gov/online.htm

OPEN - Ohio (No search engine)
www.OPENOHIO.com

Public Affairs Information Service (PAIS)
www.pais.inter.net

Responsive Database Services, Inc.
www.rdsinc.com

STINET: Scientific & Technical Reports Collection
www.dtic.mil/stinet/str/index.html

Teikoku Databank America Inc
www.teikoku.com

Thomson & Thomson
www.thomson-thomson.com

US Industry & Trade Outlook '98 - Business Forecasts ....
www.ntis.gov/yellowbk/1nty752.htm

USPTO Upcoming Opportunities - General Procurement
www.uspto.gov/web/offices/ac/comp/proc/upopp1.htm

Westlaw
www.westlaw.com

XLS
www.xls.com

Demographics

Data contained in some of these sites can be invaluable to your company's Sales and Marketing department. For new businesses, this data will be needed in the company's business plan. There is some duplication of information among the sites, but some of them are often quite busy. If that is the case, try another URL.

FFIEC Geocoding System
www.ffiec.gov/geocode

Internet Business Library: Demographic & Census Data
www.bschool.ukans.edu/intbuslib/census.htm

Population Index
http://popindex.princeton.edu

US Census Data at Lawrence Berkeley National Laboratory
http://cedr.lbl.gov/mdocs/LBL_census.html

US Census Bureau: County Business Patterns
www.census.gov/epcd/cbp/view/cbpview.html

US Demography
www.ciesin.org/datasets/us-demog/us-demog-home.html

Directories

Some of these links point to membership lists for certain organizations. Search those to identify directories in an industry or topic of interest. Still others list companies or organizations that can be contacted directly.

American Association of Advertising Agencies (AAAA) Membership List
www.commercepark.com/AAAA/members/memhome.asp

American Hospital Directory (AHD) Guest Services
www.ahd.com/guest1.html

American Institute of Architects' ProFile Search
www.cmdg.com/profile/search.html

Burwell World Directory of Information Brokers Search (Free)
www.andornot.com/ibdb/quick.html

Business Information Sources on the Internet: Directories: UK/North America
www.dis.strath.ac.uk/business/directoriesUK.html

Business Information Sources on the Internet: Directories: Worldwide & Other Countries
www.dis.strath.ac.uk/business/directories.html

Business Information Sources on the Internet: Trade Directories
www.dis.strath.ac.uk/business/trade.html

CorpTech Database of 50,000 U.S. Technology Companies
www.corptech.com

Direct Search: Search Tools & Directories
http://gwis2.circ.gwu.edu/~gprice/
direct.htm#Business/Economics

Directory of Public Relations Agencies & Resources on the Web
www.impulse-research.com/impulse/usa.html

Find: Financial Information Net Directory
www.find.co.uk

Economics/Economic Data

This group of links points to a wide variety of resources for gathering statistical economic data needed to make good business decisions. Some sites contain files for downloading into spreadsheets or other software for further manipulation or analysis. Government sites are included. Cost of living web sites have been grouped under a separate heading for convenience.

BUBL LINK: Economics
    http://link.bubl.ac.uk/economics

Business Information Sources on the Internet: Statistical,
    Economic & market information
    www.dis.strath.ac.uk/business/market.html

Census Bureau - Economic Clock
    www.census.gov/ftp/pub/econ/www

Census Bureau - Economic Indicators
    www.census.gov/indicator/www/table1p.txt

Cleveland Federal Reserve Bank Research Department Home Page
    www.clev.frb.org

County Business Patterns, 1977-1995
    www.lib.virginia.edu/socsci/cbp/cbp.html

Economic & Commercial Information (France)
    www.ccip.fr/uk/die/bdd.html

Economic Information Systems, Inc.
    www.econ-line.com

Economic Report of the President, Statistical Tables
    www.gpo.ucop.edu/catalog/erp.cta.html

Economic Statistics Briefing Room (US)
    www.whitehouse.gov/fsbr/esbr.html

Federal Reserve Bank - Atlanta
    www.frbatlanta.org

Federal Reserve Bank - Chicago
    www.frbchi.org

Federal Reserve Bank - New York
    www.ny.frb.org

Federal Reserve Bank of Dallas: Economic Data
    www.dallasfed.org/econdata/econdata.html

Federal Reserve Bank of Kansas City
    www.kc.frb.org

Federal Reserve Bank of Minneapolis
    http://woodrow.mpls.frb.fed.us

Federal Reserve Bank of San Francisco - Economic Research
    www.frbsf.org/econrsrch/index.html

Federal Reserve Bank of San Francisco - Economic Research
    www.frbsf.org/econrsrch/index.html

Federal Reserve Bank of San Francisco: Pacific Basin Center
    www.frbsf.org/econrsrch/pbc/index.html

Federal Reserve Bank of St. Louis
    www.stls.frb.org

FRB Industrial Production and Capacity Utilization Data
    http://bos.business.uab.edu/browse/frbg17.htm

FRB: Beige Book (Current Economic Conditions)
    www.bog.frb.fed.us/FOMC/BeigeBook/default.cfm

FRED • Federal Reserve Economic Data
    www.stls.frb.org/fred

GPO Gate, GPO Gate, Economic Indicators Monthly
www.gpo.ucop.edu/catalog/econind.html

Handbook of International Economic Statistics, 1997
www.odci.gov/cia/publications/hies97/index.htm

Latin America Research Group - Atlanta Federal Reserve Bank
www.FRBATLANTA.ORG/research/larg/index.htm

National Bureau of Economic Research (NBER)
www.nber.org

National Bureau of Economic Research
www.nber.org

NBER Macrohistory Database
www.nber.org/databases/macrohistory/
contents/index.html

Office of Trade & Economic Analysis
www.ita.doc.gov/tradestats

Regional Indicators: Asia Pacific Econonic Cooperation
www.eia.doe.gov/emeu/cabs/apec.html

STAT-USA
www.stat-usa.gov

US Census Bureau - Economic Clock
www.census.gov/ftp/pub/econ/www

US Census Bureau - Economic Indicators
www.census.gov/indicator/www/table1p.txt

US State Department - Policy - Economic and Trade Policy
www.state.gov/www/issues/economic/index.htm

Virtual International Business & Economic Sources (VIBES)
www.uncc.edu/lis/library/reference/intbus/
vibehome.htm

WebEc - WWW Resources in Economics
www.helsinki.fi/WebEc

WEFA
www.wefa.com

WWW Virtual Library: Economics
www.hkkk.fi/EconVLib.html

COST OF LIVING

ACCRA
www.accra.org

Consumer Price Indexes
http://stats.bls.gov/cpihome.htm

NCS Home Page
http://stats.bls.gov/comhome.htm

Regional economics, Demographics & Statistics: The Dismal Scientist
www.dismal.com/regions/regions.stm

Relocation: Best places To Live: Cost of Living
www.virtualrelocation.com/Relocation/
Best_Places/Cost_Of_Living

Statistical Resources on the Web/Cost of Living
    www.lib.umich.edu/libhome/Documents.center/
    steccpi.html

The International Salary Calculator: Relocation, Cost of Living, Real Estate
    http://www2.homefair.com/calc/salcalc.html

US Cost-of-Living Comparisons
    www.mazerecruiters.com/job.htm

Employment/Want Ads

Search sites like these for job openings and job descriptions that may indicate a competitor's plans. Check also, for legal notices published in compliance with state or federal law. They also point to a company's planned actions.

AdQuest Classifieds - Currently Updating Ads
    www.adquest.com/sorry.asp

BioSpace: The Hub Site For Biotechnology and Pharmaceutical News, Jobs, Companies, Stocks
    www.biospace.com

Career Resources @ JobBank USA
    www.jobbankusa.com

CareerCast Job & Resume Search
    www.careercast.com

CareerCity Jobs and Employment
    www.careercity.com

CareerMosaic
    www.careermosaic.com

CareerPath.com
    www.careerpath.com/res/owa/home.display_rblogin?

Communcations Week International (CWI) Online: World News
    www.totaltele.com/cwi

DejaNews
    www.deja.com

Employer & Company Search / Query - TOPjobs USA
    www.topjobsusa.com/employer

International Foundation of Employee Benefit Plans
    www.ifebp.org

Internet Career Connection
    HTTP://iccweb.com

jobEngine
    www.jobengine.com

JobOptions
    www.joboptions.com/esp/plsql/espan_enter.espan_home

Monster.com
    www.monster.com

Monster.com
    www.occ.com

Search Engines • Beaucoup! (Employment)
www.beaucoup.com/1empeng.html

True Job Search Engine
www.jobsearchengine.com/cgi-bin/jbsearch

Westech Virtual Job Fair Search on Deja News
www.deja.com/=vjf/search.shtml

Yahoo! Classifieds
http://classifieds.yahoo.com

Environment

Some of these sites, such as the EPA's Envirofacts, may be searched by competitors' names to learn about "incidents" involving their companies. Environmental impact statements can be located using the Northwestern University's Transportation Library site.

BUBL LINK: Environment & Economics of Land & Energy
http://link.bubl.ac.uk/environment

Eldis - Electronic Development and Environment Information System
http://nt1.ids.ac.uk/eldis/eldwhat.htm

ENDS Environment Daily - European environmental news
www.ends.co.uk/envdaily

Envirofacts Query Form
www.epa.gov/enviro/html/multisystem.html

Environmental Reporting Clearinghouse • Corporate Environmental Reports by Sector
http://cei.sund.ac.uk/envrep/corprepS.htm

National Environmental Data Index (NEDI) Catalog
www.nedi.gov/NEDI-Catalog

National Oceanic & Atmospheric Administration: Environmental Information Services
www.esdim.noaa.gov

NUL • Transportation Library Environmental Impact Statement Collection
www.library.nwu.edu/transportation/tleis.html

RTK NET Environmental Databases
www.rtk.net/www/rtknet/webpage/databas3.html

Scorecard Home
www.scorecard.org

US Environmental Protection Agency (EPA)
www.epa.gov

VISTACheck
www.vistacheck.com

European Union

If your company is multi-national, you may need to be familiar with the various implications of formation of the EU. These sites will get you started.

Chambers of Commerce of the EU Members in the US
www.eurunion.org/infores/business/chambers.htm

ETHOS: Structural Funds:Sweden, United Kingdom
www.tagish.co.uk/ethos/tap/seuklu.htm

Euro Links
HTTP://europa.eu.int/euro/html/liens5.html?lang=5

Europa
http://europa.eu.int

European Union Information Resources
www.eurunion.org/infores/home.htm

Exeter Subject Tree - European Information
www.ex.ac.uk/~pcovery/lib/eurostudies.html

Telematics Applications Programme Projects By Country
www.tagish.co.uk/ethos/tap/country.htm

Executive Compensation

Executive compensation may be of interest to those researching the CEO of a competitor company, or by your own Human Resources department to determine competitive compensation for a particular job title. This list contains both general and industry-specific web sites.

1997 Gaming Industry CEO Compensation Rankings • Top 59
www.hotel-online.com/Neo/Trends/HVS/Kefgen/
1997GamingIndustryTop59.html

Executive Compensation Examples
www.sec.gov/edaux/ec.htm

Executive PayWatch • The Ceo and You
http://aflcio.paywatch.org/ceopay/
ceoyou/ceolist.html

Executives' Pay
www.stlnet.com/postnet/news/execpay.nsf

Forbes CEO 1998: Corporate America's Most Powerful People 1998
www.forbes.com/tool/toolbox/ceo

Fortune: 6.8.98 Proxies: The Treasure Is Still Buried
www.pathfinder.com/fortune/1998/980608/tri.html

Special Report E - Main • WSJ Interactive Edition
http://wsj.com/public/current/articles/
SB860673047472625500.htm

The 1997 Hotel Industry CEO Survey / HVS Executive Search / June, 1997
www.hotel-online.com/Neo/Trends/HVS/Kefgen/
CompensationSurvey_1997.html

The Top 1000
www.robmagazine.com/top1000

US Economy Is Neither Leaner nor Meaner for Investors or CEOs
www.house.gov/democrats/research/6ceopay.html

Experts – Locating

FACSNET: News Sources
www.facsnet.org/sources_online/
facs_source/main.html

How to locate a speaker
> www.montague.com/review/speaker.html

NRC Expertise Database
> www.nrc.ca/expertise

Financial Information Sites

This group of financial sites has been subdivided for convenience. Locate profiles, track competitors, etc. on foreign companies by visiting stock exchange sites.

FINANCE - GENERAL SITES

ADRs (American depositary receipts), global shares and foreign shares from J.P. Morgan
> www.adr.com

Fisher College of Business Financial Data Finder
> www.cob.ohio-state.edu/cgi-bin/DB_Search/
> db_search.cgi?setup_file=finance.setup.cgi

Index of World Finance (A)
> www.qualisteam.com/eng/catal.html

J.J. Kenny
> www.jjkenny.com/index.htm

Moody's Investors Service
> www.moodys.com

New York Times: Financial Index
> www.nytimes.com/yr/mo/day/news/
> financial/indext.html

Standard & Poor's Ratings Services
> www.ratings.com

The OSU Virtual Finance Library
> www.cob.ohio-state.edu/dept/fin/overview.htm

Virtual Finance Library
> www.cob.ohio-state.edu/dept/fin/overview.htm

Worldwide Directory: The Best & Banking Resources on the 'Net
> www.qualisteam.com/eng/catal.shtml

WWW Virtual Library: Finance & Investments
> www.cob.ohio-state.edu/dept/fin/overview.htm

Yahoo! Finance
> www.yahoofinance.com

FINANCIAL MARKETS - WORLDWIDE

Amex: The American Stock Exchange
> www.amex.com/cgi-bin/WebObjects/AmexWeb

Australian Stock Information
> www.asx.com.au/asx0.htm

Bolsa - Madrid Stock Exchange
> www.bolsamadrid.es

Bonds in the World
> www.qualisteam.com/eng/obl.html

Bourse de Paris
www.bourse-de-paris.fr

CBS MarketWatch - Global Markets
http://cbs.marketwatch.com/data/
gfa.htx?source=htx/http2_mw

Center for Latin American Capital Markets: Exchanges
www.netrus.net/users/gmorles/exchange.htm

Chicago Board of Trade
www.cbot.com

Chicago Mercantile Exchange
www.cme.com

LatinStocks.com: Latin American Financial Markets & Business
www.latinstocks.com

London Stock Exchange
www.londonstockex.co.uk/left.htm

NASDAQ
www.nasdaq.com

New York Stock Exchange
www.nyse.com

SKATE – Your Key to Russian Financial Markets
www.skate.ru

Standard & Poor's MMS
www.globalmarkets.com

Stock Exchanges in the United States
www.qualisteam.com/aactusa.html#Ari

TeleStock
www.teleserv.co.uk/stock

The African Stock Exchange Guide
http://africa.com/pages/jse/page1.htm

Tokyo Stock Exchange
www.tse.or.jp/eindex.html

Worldwide Guide: Online Stock Exchanges
www.qualisteam.com/eng/act.shtml

FINANCIAL MEDIA

Financial Media on the 'Net
www.qualisteam.com/eng/docu.html#base

IPOs

Be sure to search these sites to see if a company is planning to do an Initial Public Offering. Keep abreast of rumors and new developments using them, as well. IPOs can also be identified through S&P files and Investext; both are on several systems. Dialog and Lexis-Nexis offer EdgarPlus Prospectus files. Additionally, Dialog offers the SDC Initial Public Offerings File and IPO Maven.

Disclosure, Inc
www.disclosure.com

EDGAR Online IPO Express
`www.edgar-online.com/ipoexpress`

Facts-Online Hot Technology Companies
`www.facts-online.com/factss.htm`

Hoover's Edgar Online: IPO Central
`www.ipocentral.com`

Initial Public Offerings, Mergers, Acquisitions, & Spin-Offs
`www.stocksmart.com/ows-bin/owa/ssd?pg=newsipos`

INVESTools: Trusted Advice for Independent Investors
`www.investools.com/cgi-bin/Library/mavn.pl`

IPO Data Systems Inc
`www.ipodata.com`

IPO Intelligence Online - Rennaisance Capital
`www.ipo-fund.com/cgi-bin/SoftCart.cgi/`
`INDEX2.html?E+aa0008740`

IPO Interactive - Federal Filings, Inc.
`www.fedfil.com/ipo/index.html`

SciWeb - IPO & Public Financing Activity
`www.sciweb.com/home/eddyjake/ipo/ipo_4_3_98.html`

Securities Data Company
`www.secdata.com/home.html`

The Hale & Dorr LLP New England IPO Report, 1990-96
`www.haledorr.com/publications/ipo/`
`IPO_9096/Contents.html`

MERGERS & ACQUISITIONS

M&A Impact
`www.computerwire.com/ma/about.html`

Mergerstat
`www.mergerstat.com`

Stock Smart
`www.stocksmart.com/ows-bin/owa/ssd?pg=newsipos`

NON-US FINANCIAL INFORMATION

Thanks to the World Wide Web, you can research financial topics and financial markets for many parts of the world. Here are a few places to get started.

Beurs Bedrijven in Beeld
`www.aex.nl/finance/aex0.html`

Electronic Share Information Ltd
`www.esi.co.uk`

Financial Information Warehouse (In German)
`www.financial.de/index.htm`

Financial Interactive Services Hub
`www.infront.com.sg`

find: financial information net directory
`www.find.co.uk`

Global Investor: Global Investor Directory
```
www.global-investor.com/dir/index.htm
```

Investment Trusts & Offshore Funds
```
www.trustnet.co.uk/general/trust00.html
```

Japan Financials
```
http://japanfinancials.com/#JAPAN FINANCIALS
```

Mutual Funds in the World
```
www.qualisteam.com/eng/opcvm.html
```

US FINANCIAL INFORMATION

Some of these sites are also listed under Economics / Economic Data, since there is some overlap between the two categories of information. This list will point you to the major US government and non-government sites for such financial matters as the markets, mutual funds, and that bastion of financial news, Dow Jones. Search using competitors' names or analyze the industry using these tools.

10-K Wizard
```
http://beta.tenkwizard.com
```

ABI World (Bankruptcy Information on the Web)
```
www.abiworld.org
```

Cleveland Federal Reserve Bank Research Department: Economic Research
```
www.clev.frb.org/research/index.htm
```

DailyStocks
```
www.dailystocks.com
```

DBC Market Monitor
```
URL www.dbc.com/cgi-
bin/htx.exe/dbcfiles/indicators.html
```

DJIA Search
```
http://averages.dowjones.com/screen1.htm
```

Fast Quote - Quote.com
```
http://fast.quote.com/fq/excite/quote
```

Federal Reserve Bank of New York: Links to Federal Reserve Banks
```
www.ny.frb.org/links.html
```

Federal Reserve Bank of St. Louis
```
www.stls.frb.org/general/fedsystem.html
```

Fidelity Investments • Your Personal Investing Resource
```
http://personal31.fidelity.com/index.html
```

Financial Statistics
```
www.dfi.ca.gov/stats/stats.htm
```

Futures & Options at the Chicago Mercantile Exchange
```
www.cme.com
```

Insider Trading Monitor
```
www.wsdinc.com/products/p1470.shtml
```

InsiderTrader: Profiting Legally From Insider Trading
```
www.insidertrader.com
```

Internet Bankruptcy Library - Distressed Securities
```
http://bankrupt.com/newgen.aug97.html
```

Microsoft Investor
> http://investor.msn.com/home.asp?newguid=1&

Money Financial Tool Kit
> www.pathfinder.com/@@L3r5qQQAMMF6bP2q/
> money/lincoln/toolkit.html

Money Online
> www.money.com

Morningstar.Net
> www.morningstar.net

Morningstar.Net - Fund Screens
> www.morningstar.net/nd/ndNSAPI.nd/
> Research/FundInterim

Morningstar.Net - Quicktake
> www.morningstar.net/nd/ndNSAPI.nd/
> General/EnterQuicktake

New York Stock Exchange
> www.nyse.com

OneSource Information Services
> www.onesource.com

Quote.com – Quotes, News, Investment Research & More
> www.quote.com

Stock Exchanges in the United States
> www.qualisteam.com/aactusa.html#Ari

Stock Quotes
> http://fast.quote.com/fq/excite/quote

StockMaster Stocks By Name
> www.stockmaster.com/sm/stocks/C.html

Streeteye: Indexes of Financial Links
> www.streeteye.com/toplevel/tables/indexfin.html

US Securities & Exchange Commission
> www.sec.gov

***USA Today* Mutual Funds**
> http://167.8.29.47/cgi-bin/ndCGI.exe/lipper/pgMain

USA: Online Stock Exchange
> www.qualisteam.com/eng/actusa.shtml

Wall Street Directory: Insider Trading Monitor
> www.wsdinc.com/products/p1470.shtml

Wall Street Research Net
> www.wsrn.com

Yahoo! US Stock News & Report Company News
> http://biz.yahoo.com

Zacks Investment Research, Inc.
> www.ultra.zacks.com

VENTURE CAPITAL

Learn where privately-held competitor companies get their funding by searching these venture capital sites. Note that some regional and non-US sites are included.

American Venture Capital Exchange & M&A Service
www.avce.com

Boston.com / Business / Emerging / Venture capital update
www.boston.com/business/emerging/capital

European Private Equity & Venture Capital Association (EVCA)
www.evca.com

PricewaterhouseCoopers: Global: Insights & Solutions: MoneyTree Survey
http://209.67.194.61/index.asp

SciWeb - The Life Science Home Page - Venture Capital Gateway
www.sciweb.com/home/eddyjake/vc.html

Geographic Searching Sites

Once you've identified competitor's plant sites and other business locations, these sites may help to find them on the map - and to learn more about the communities where they are located. This intelligence may be plugged in to your analysis of a competitor's labor force, potential for expansion, etc.

American Community Network
www.acn.net

International Chamber of Commerce & City-State-Province Directory
www.chamber-of-commerce.com

Government Sites - US

The amount of information here is unbelievable! Finding what you want is sometimes confusing, because the name of the agency is not a clear indication of the scope of the information it may provide. Some data can be downloaded into spreadsheets and databases for further analysis.

A tour of these sites may be in order, with the question "How can our company use this data?" clearly in mind as you drill down through it all. Note also that government sites have been included under general subject headings eslewhere in this list of bookmarks and favorites.

MISCELLANEOUS

This is a collection of additional useful federal government sites - you could find some surprising intelligence sources here.

1997 World Factbook
www.odci.gov/cia/publications/factbook/index.html

Committee on Government Reform & Oversight: Policy & Supporting Positions (Plum Book)
www.access.gpo.gov/plumbook/toc.html

FACS Home page
http://procurement.nasa.gov/facs/html

Federal Aviation Administration Search
www.faa.gov/search.html

Federal Information Center
http://fic.info.gov

Federal Web Locator
www.law.vill.edu/Fed-Agency/fedwebloc.html

FedWorld Information Network
www.fedworld.gov

GAO/OSI-97-2 Investigators Guide to Sources of Information
www.gao.gov/special.pubs/soi/soi_ch5.htm

GovBot - Government Search Engine
http://ciir2.cs.umass.edu/Govbot

Government Information Exchange
www.info.gov

Government Information from UT Library Online
www.lib.utexas.edu/Libs/PCL/Government.html

Government Information Sharing Project
http://govinfo.kerr.orst.edu/index.html

GPO Gate, Select Databases by Subject
www.gpo.ucop.edu/dbgsearch.html

Information Collections Under Review/Approvals Expired
http://library.whitehouse.gov/omb/OMBPPRWK.htm

Investigators Guide to Sources of Information
www.gao.gov/special.pubs/soi/contents.htm

Material Safety Data Sheet Searches
www.epa.gov/superfund/sites/index.htm

SBA - PRO-Net - What is PRO-Net? (Procurement Search Engine)
http://pro-net.sba.gov/index2.html

Search Engines • Beaucoup! (Politics/Government/Law)
www.beaucoup.com/1poleng.html

State & Local Government on the 'Net
www.piperinfo.com/state/states.html

US Department of Agriculture
www.usda.gov

US Securities & Exchange Commission
www.sec.gov

CENSUS BUREAU

Check out the offerings at the Censtats site in addition to the free sites listed below. Your Sales & Marketing department may be very interested in the M3 report as they engage in strategic planning regarding market-related issues.

American FactFinder
http://factfinder.census.gov/java_prod/dads.ui.homePage.HomePage

M3 Report - Shipments, Inventories, Orders
www.census.gov/ftp/pub/indicator/www/m3/index.htm

US Census Bureau
www.census.gov/index.html

US Census Bureau - FERRET Login Form
http://ferret.bls.census.gov/cgi-bin/ferret

US Census Bureau - New Retail/Wholesale Page
www.census.gov/econ/www/retmenu.html#WHOL

US Census Bureau - UPDATING THE 1990 CENSUS/POPULATION
www.lib.umich.edu/libhome/Documents.center/
cenupdem.html

US Census Bureau: CENSUS • Lists of Metropolitan Areas
www.census.gov/population/www/estimates/
metrodef.html

CONGRESS

Here are several sites for the US Congress. The University of Michigan has a searchable database for locating hearing transcripts. This material can be searched by competitor company or individual's name to locate their testimony.

Congress • THOMAS • US Congress on the Internet
http://thomas.loc.gov

Congressional Hearings on the Web
www.lib.umich.edu/libhome/Documents.center/
hearings.html

House of Representatives (UniPress W3's Will T. Bill)
www.unipress.com/will-t-bill.html

US Congress (GPO Access)
www.access.gpo.gov/congress/index.html

DEPARTMENT OF COMMERCE

Look here for trade or commerce related sites. You may find that Stat-USA, this department's subscription service, is a very good investment because of its customer support feature which allows you to discuss questions with a staff member familiar with government information sources.

GovCon - Commerce Business Daily, FACNET, Government Regulations & Databases
www.govcon.com

Office of Trade & Economic Analysis
www.ita.doc.gov/tradestats

STAT-USA/Internet Site Economic, Trade, Business Information
www.stat-usa.gov

DEPARTMENT OF ENERGY

Information Bridge
www.doe.gov/bridge/home.html

OpenNet
www.doe.gov/opennet

US Department of Energy National Laboratories & Programs
www.gpaa.dec.usc.es/ENGLISH/CS-topics/local/
doe-labs.html

US Department of Energy Homepage
http://198.124.130.244

DEPARTMENT OF LABOR

Many business decisions require the kind of data that may be retrieved from these sites.

1996 National Industry Staffing Pattern Data (US)
http://stats.bls.gov/oes/oes_ispd.htm

1996 Occupational Employment & Wage Data (US)
http://stats.bls.gov/oes/oes_data.htm

Bureau of Labor Statistics
http://stats.bls.gov

Bureau of Labor Statistics: Economy At A Glance
http://stats.bls.gov:80/eag.table.html

Davis-Bacon Wage Determination Database
http://davisbacon.fedworld.gov

DEPARTMENT OF STATE

The Department of State offers pages covering contract opportunities, country commercial guides and economic and trade policy pages among the sites listed below. The page offering links to related foreign affairs sites may also prove useful if your country does business outside of the US.

US State Department - Index
www.state.gov/www/ind.html

US State Department - Official Web Site
www.state.gov

US State Department - Policy - Business Services
www.state.gov/www/about_state/business/index.html

US State Department - Related Foreign Affairs Sites
www.state.gov/www/websites.html

US State Department - Services - Contracting Opportunities & Related Information
www.state.gov/www/services_admin.html

US State Department - Services - Country Commercial Guides Index
www.state.gov/www/about_state/business/
com_guides/index.html

ENVIRONMENTAL PROTECTION AGENCY

See the general heading Environment above for additional environment-related sites. Also look at the Public Records category for US government databases.

Superfund Search
www.epa.gov/superfund/sites/index.htm

US Environmental Protection Agency
www.epa.gov

FEDERAL AVIATION ADMINISTRATION

The FAA's Corporate Search Facility may turn up a variety of interesting intelligence if your business intelligence quest involves aviation or aerospace matters.

FAA • Federal Aviation Administration
www.faa.gov

FEDERAL COMMUNICATIONS COMMISSION

FCC ID Search Form
www.fcc.gov/oet/fccid

Federal Communications Commission (FCC) Home Page
www.fcc.gov

FEDERAL ELECTION COMMISSION

The FEC's Direct Access Program means that you can download and search files of contributions data to learn about your competitors' donations to political campaigns. You might also look under the Public Records heading in this bookmark list for a FECInfo, a non-government source for this information.

FEC Image/Query System
www.fec.gov/1996/sdrindex.htm

FECInfo
www.tray.com/fecinfo

Federal Election Commission: Direct Access Program
www.fec.gov/info/dapbroch.htm

FOOD & DRUG ADMINISTRATION

Be sure to use the SEARCH facility and examine ARCHIVES to calendars at the FDA to find out the who/what/when/where information regarding competitors' activities with this agency. The see the agency's FOIA reading room or consider a FOIA request for further information.

Food & Drug Administration (FDA)
www.fda.gov

US Food and Drug Administration Archives
www.fda.gov/opacom/archives.html

US Food and Drug Administration FDA Search Page
www.fda.gov/search.html

GOVERNMENT PRINTING OFFICE

Use these two links to locate government publications on almost any topic, or use the GPO Check page to find where to access the government information you seek.

GPO Access, Search Online Databases via
www.access.gpo.gov/su_docs/dbsearch.html

GPO Monthly Catalog
www.lib.iastate.edu/scholar/db/gpoxxx.html

LIBRARY OF CONGRESS

Library of Congress
http://lcweb.loc.gov

OCCUPATIONAL SAFETY & HEALTH ADMINISTRATION

Occupational safety and health issues, as they pertain to your competitors, could be of great interest within your own company. These records may also provide the addresses of plants or other company facilities.

Occupational Safety & Health Administration - OSHA
www.osha.gov

POSTAL SERVICE

USPS ZIP+4 Code Lookup
www.usps.gov/ncsc/lookups/lookup_zip+4.html

SOCIAL SECURITY ADMINISTRATION

Social Security Online
www.ssa.gov

Human Resources

Benefits - Human Resources Net Links
http://humanresources.miningco.com/msub2.htm

Industries & Professions

These bookmarks are a "tip of the iceberg" list, with a few government sites included for regulated industries such as banking. To see a more comprehensive collection, see the Internet Intelligence Index at the Fuld.com site listed under Competitive Intelligence. That page contains links to a list of individual industries.

MULTIPLE INDUSTRY LINKS SITES

Competitive Intelligence Guide - Fuld & Company Inc
www.fuld.com/i3/index.html

Hoover's Industry Snapshots
www.hoovers.com/features/industry/industries.html

Industry Home Pages
www.virtualpet.com/industry/mfg/mfg.htm

ACCOUNTING

Accounting in France
http://msm.byu.edu/c&i/cim/account/France.htm

Accounting in Germany
http://msm.byu.edu/c&i/cim/account/Germany.htm

Accounting in Hungary
http://msm.byu.edu/c&i/cim/account/Hungary.htm

Accounting In Italy
http://msm.byu.edu/c&i/cim/account/Italy.htm

Accounting in Japan
http://msm.byu.edu/c&i/cim/account/Japan.htm

Accounting in Korea
http://msm.byu.edu/c&i/cim/account/Korea.htm

Accounting in New Zealand (v1.0)
http://msm.byu.edu/c&i/cim/account/
newzealand/nz_homep.htm

Accounting in Norway
www.csom.umn.edu/WWWPages/COURSES/
ACCT/5310/Norway.htm

Accounting in Poland
http://msm.byu.edu/c&i/cim/account/Poland.htm

Accounting in Singapore
http://msm.byu.edu/c&i/cim/account/Sing.htm

Accounting in Slovakia
www.slovak.sk/business/legislation/
accountancy_act_1.htm

Accounting in Spain
http://msm.byu.edu/c&i/cim/account/Spain.htm

Accounting in Sweden
www.csom.umn.edu/WWWPages/COURSES/
ACCT/5310/Sweden.htm

Accounting in Switzerland
http://msm.byu.edu/c&i/cim/account/Swiss.htm

Accounting in the Czech Republic
http://msm.byu.edu/c&i/cim/account/czech/czech.html

Accounting in the United Kingdom
http://msm.byu.edu/c&i/cim/account/UK.htm

ADVERTISING

Ad Council
www.adcouncil.org

Ad Track
www.usatoday.com/money/index/ad001.htm

Advertising Age • Ad Age Dataplace • AGENCY REPORT
www.adage.com/cgi-bin/genDPcat.pl?cat=AGENCY_REPORT

Adweek Online
www.adweek.com

American Advertising Federation
www.aaf.org

International Advertising Association
www.iaaglobal.org

The Advertising Research Foundation
www.arfsite.org

AEROSPACE/AVIATION

AIR - Aircraft Information Database Search Engine
http://AIR-online.com/aircraft/search.shtml

AIR: Airport Website Search Engine
http://AIR-online.com/Airport/Search.shtml

Aircrafat Register
www.casa.gov.au/lic_cert/Register/REG_HOME.HTM

Aircraft Performance
www.risingup.com/planespecs

Aviation Internet Resources
http://AIR-online.com/AIRcontents.shtml

Bermuda Department of Civil Aviation - Register of Aircraft & Flight Crew
www.dca.gov.bm

Civil Aviation Aircraft Register Query
www.caa.govt.nz/Scripts/Air_Reg_Query.asp

EX: English - Aircraft Registration and Leasing Index
www.tc.gc.ca/aviation/general/ccarcs/index.htm

Irish Aviation Web Site - Irish Register
http://homepages.iol.ie/~markzee/eirereg.htm

Landings: Aviation Search Engines: FARs, N-Numbers, NTSBs, SDRs, ADs, AMEs, Pilots, Medical Examiners, Regulations
http://www1.drive.net/evird.acgi$pass*8099593!mtd*7
!map*_landings/images/landings-strip.map?51,40

Landings: Search for Certified Pilots
www.landings.com/_landings/pages/search_amd.html

Scramble on the Web
www.scramble.nl/civ/ph/nedreg_main.htm

Singapore Changi Airport
www.changi.airport.com.sg

Spotters' Nest
www.spotters.it/en/database.htm

World Wide Web Aerospace Business Development Center
http://arganet.tenagra.com/Tenagra/aero_bd.html

APPAREL

Apparel.net: The Online Guide for the Apparel Industry
http://apparel.net/index.cgi

ARCHITECTURE

PlanetAEC: Architect Homepage
www.planetaec.com/architects

ProFile on the Web
www.cmdg.com/profile

AUTOMOBILES

Kelley Blue Book New Car Pricing and Bluebook Values
www.kbb.com

Ward's Directory of Suppliers & Product Guides
www.wardsauto.com/companies

World Wide Web Virtual Library: Autos
www.cyberauto.com/vl/autos.html

BANKING

Bank for International Settlements
www.bis.org

Banking - General Resources (Britain)
http://link.bubl.ac.uk/banking

Banking in Slovenia
www.tradepoint.si/Banke/Institutions.htm

Banking on the WWW • Guides
www.gwdg.de/~ifbg/bank_1.html

BankWeb: International Banks
www.bankweb.com/international.html

Business Compass Banking Database
http://kelsey.abcompass.com/abc/abs/ind/ba.html

Central Banks of the World • Central Banking Resource Center
http://patriot.net/~bernkopf

Directory of All Swiss Banks
www.swissbanknet.ch

Federal Deposit Insurance Corporation (FDIC)
www.fdic.gov

Internet Banking - Banks on the Net - Directory of banks on the Web
www.qualisteam.com/eng/conf.shtml

Internet Banking: Directory of Banks on the Web
www.qualisteam.com/eng/conf.shtml

National Information Center (NIC)
www.ffiec.gov/nic/general_information.htm

OCC Weekly Bulletin Search
www.occ.treas.gov/weekly/wkblsrch.htm

Online Banking Database
www.qualisteam.com/database_search/db_search.cgi

Report on Banks in Nigeria
www.afbis.com/vanguard/banks/index.htm

Research: The Bank of New York
www.researchmag.com/company/alpha.htm

World Bank Group
www.worldbank.org

Worldwide Banking Guide
www.qualisteam.com/eng/conf.html

BEER/BREWING

WWW Virtual Library: Beer & Brewing
www.beerinfo.com/vlib/index.html

BIOTECHNOLOGY

ABC Biotechnology Sites
http://kelsey.abcompass.com/abc/abs/ind/bi.html

Biological Data Transport Biotech Registry
www.data-transport.com/q/@041080xrxvcb/
registry.html

Biological Data Transport
www.data-transport.com

BioSpace.com: The Hub Site for Biotechnology & Pharmaceutical News,
Jobs, Companies, Stocks
www.biospace.com

Connections, Networks & Links
www.raucon.com/businet/index.html

Knowledge Express
www.knowledgeexpress.com

Recombinant Capital (ReCap)
www.recap.com

CHEMICALS

ChemConnect: Chemical Suppliers
www.chemconnect.com/directory

ChemConnect: Chemical Trading Exchange
www.chemconnect.com/ctx

ChemConnect: Reference Library
www.chemconnect.com/library

Chemical Marketing Online
www.chemon.com/chemon.htm

Internet Chemistry Resources
www.chem.rpi.edu/icr/chemres.html

Plastics Network
www.plasticsnet.com

PlasticsNet Forums
www.plasticsnet.com/scripts/Forums/index.cfm

COMPUTER TECHNOLOGY

ABC Computer/Electronics Sites
http://kelsey.abcompass.com/abc/abs/ind/co.html

Processors
www.pricewatch.com/attdocs/3cat.htm

The Burton Group
www.tbg.com

The Computer Information Centre (CompInfo)
www.compinfo.co.uk/index.htm

Yahoo! Business & Economy: Companies: Computers
www.yahoo.com/Business_and_Economy/
companies/computers

CONSTRUCTION

BUILDER Online: Guide to Building Products
`http://builder.hw.net/guide`

Construction Market Data Inc
`www.cmdonl.com`

ConstructionNet: Comprehensive Directory
`www.constructionnet.net/dashboard`

Construction Site
`www.emap.com/construct/a-z.htm`

PlanetAEC: Contractors Homepage
`www.planetaec.com/contractors`

The Construction Site - Construction's Best Directory
`www.constr.com/tcs.htm`

DEFENSE

Jane's Information Group
`www.janes.com`

ELECTRONICS

Electronic Industries Alliance
`www.eia.org`

ENERGY

Country Analysis Briefs - No Frames Version
`www.eia.doe.gov/emeu/cabs/contents.html`

Dwights Petroleum Industry Related Links
`www.dwights.com/misc/links.htm`

Energysearch: Energy Links
`www.energysearch.com/links.html`

Energysearch: Search
`www.energysearch.com`

EPRI
`www.epri.com`

Espicom Business Intelligence Power and Energy
`www.energybase.com/index.html`

Gov.Research-Center: Energy Science and Technology Database
`http://grc.ntis.gov/energy.htm`

IHS Energy Group
`www.ihsenergy.com`

International Energy Agency
`www.iea.org/homechoi.htm`

Petroleum Pages: Index
`www.pe.utexas.edu/Departmental_Information/`
`Reading_Room_Information/petroleum.html`

Platt's on the Internet
`www.platts.com`

Propane Gas Association of Canada Inc
www.propanegas.ca/related_sites.html

ENGINEERING

Edinburgh Engineering Virtual Library (EEVL)
www.eevl.ac.uk

Internet Connections For Engineering (Cornell)
www.englib.cornell.edu/ice/ice-index.html

PlanetAEC: Engineer Homepage
www.planetaec.com/engineers

Virtual Library: Engineering
http://vlib.stanford.edu/Engineering.html

Webliography: A Guide to Internet Resources
www.lib.lsu.edu/weblio.html#Engineering

Yahoo! Science:Engineering
www.yahoo.com/Science/Engineering

HEALTHCARE

Clinical Trials

CenterWatch Clinical Trials Listing Service Home Page
www.centerwatch.com

Clinical Trial Posting!
www.clinicaltrials.com

Clinical Trials Resource Center
http://pharminfo.com/conference/
clintrial/ct_rsc.html

Consumer Health

Consumer Health
www.ahcpr.gov/consumer

Healthfinder - a gateway consumer health and human services information
web site from the United States government
www.healthfinder.gov

Health Related Search Engines

MedWatch: The FDA Medical Products Reporting Program
www.fda.gov/medwatch

Search Engines - Beaucoup! (Science/Nature/Technology)
www.beaucoup.com/1scieng.html

Miscellaneous

(7/28/97) 1997 Best Hospitals
http://www4.usnews.com/usnews/nycu/hosphigh.htm

1996 New Drug Application (NDA)
www.fda.gov/cder/foi/nda/index96.htm

Academy for International Health Studies: International Resources
www.aihs.com/resources.html

Achoo Healthcare Online
www.achoo.com

Additional Resources for Industry Professionals
www.centerwatch.com/PRORESRC.HTM

American Cancer Society
www.cancer.org/frames.html

American Hospital Directory
www.ahd.com/guest1.html

BioMedNet
www.biomednet.com

BioSpace News: Phase I • Safety
www.biospace.com/b2/news_category.cfm

Center for Devices and Radiological Health MDR Data Files
www.fda.gov/cdrh/mdrfile.html

Clinical Research Studies Protocol Database
http://clinicalstudies.info.nih.gov

CPSNet
http://pmd@cpsnet.com

Drug Enforcement Administration (DEA) Controlled Substances Act Registration Database
www.ntis.gov/yellowbk/1nty088.htm

EMEA • The European Agency for the Evaluation of Medicinal Products
www.eudra.org

Frost & Sullivan - Healthcare Market Engineering
www.frost.com/healthcare

Hardin MD - Hardin Meta Directory of Internet Health Sources
www.lib.uiowa.edu/hardin/md/index.html

Health Information Resource Database
http://nhic-nt.health.org/Formsrch.htm

Health On the 'Net Foundation
www.hon.ch

Healthtouch • Online for better health
www.healthtouch.com

HealthWeb
www.healthweb.org

Hospitals
http://mel.lib.mi.us/health/health-hospital-hospitals.html

InteliHealth - Home to Johns Hopkins Health Information: Health Library
www.intelihealth.com/IH/ihtIH?t=331&r=WSIHW000&st=408

International Health Resources
www.aihs.com/resources.html

Medical Device Reporting Search
www.accessdata.fda.gov/cfDOCS/cfMDR/Search.CFM

Medical Equipment and Hospital Equipment Classified Ads - Medmatrix!
www.medmatrix.com

Medical, Pharmaceutical, Managed Health Care, Alternative Medicine & Associations Sites
www.erols.com/inteltek/pharm.html

Medicine on the 'Net
    www.mednet-i.com

Mediconsult.com Inc
    www.mediconsult.com

MEDLINE: PubMed & Internet Grateful Med (Free)
    www.nlm.nih.gov/databases/freemedl.html

MedNet Interactive - a service of COR Healthcare Resources
    www.mednet-i.com

MedWatch: The FDA Medical Products Reporting Program
    www.fda.gov/medwatch

MGH Neurology - Neurology Web-Forum
    http://neuro-www.mgh.harvard.edu/forum

National Cancer Institute: CancerNet
    http://cancernet.nci.nih.gov

National Center for Biotechnology Information
    www.ncbi.nlm.nih.gov

National Library of Medicine (NLM):
    Health Services/Technology Assessment
    http://text.nlm.nih.gov

Net Medicine
    www.netmedicine.com

Online Medical Dictionary
    www.graylab.ac.uk/omd

Organizing Medical Networked Information (OMNI)
    http://omni.ac.uk

PDQ Clinical Trial Search
    http://cancernet.nci.nih.gov/cgi-bin/cancerform

PSL Group
    www.pslgroup.com

Robbie Dewey's Home Page (Medical Links)
    www.servtech.com/public/robbie

Search Engines • Beaucoup! (Science/Nature/Technology)
    www.beaucoup.com/1scieng.html

TeleSCAN: Telematics Services in Cancer
    http://telescan.nki.nl/index.html

The Virtual Hospital: Information for Healthcare Providers
    http://vh.radiology.uiowa.edu/Providers/
    Providers.html

US Medicine Information Central
    www.usmedicine.com

Virtual Library: Medicine
    http://vlib.stanford.edu/Medicine.html

Regulatory Resources

FDA Dockets Management
    www.fda.gov/ohrms/dockets/default.htm

LAW ENFORCEMENT

Police Officer's Internet Directory
www.officer.com

MANUFACTURING

Appliance Manufacturer Online
www.ammagazine.com

Manufacturing News, Manufacturing Update by MEP - Manufacturing Extension Partnership
www.mep.nist.gov/mfgupdate

R&D 100 Awards
www.manufacturing.net/magazine/rd/rd100/100award.htm

Machinery Manufacturers - Germany
http://wbm.hoppenstedt.com/Englisch/index.html

Manufacturing News, Manufacturing Update by MEP - Manufacturing Extension Partnership
www.mep.nist.gov/mfgupdate

Thomas Regional Directory
www.thomasregional.com/newtrd/c_home.html

Thomas Register Europe Home Page
www.tipcoeurope.com

Thomas Register of American Manufacturers
www.thomasregister.com/index.html

PHARMACEUTICALS

1996 New Drug Application (NDA)
www.fda.gov/cder/foi/nda/index96.htm

BioSpace.com - The Hub Site for Biotechnology
www.biospace.com

New Products, Markets, Opportunities
www.raucon.com/busidev/1.1.html

pharmatrends.com: Search
http://pharmatrends.com/search.html

WARS-Pharmaceuticals on the 'Net
http://pathit.clever.net/wars/war_phrm.htm

PUBLIC RELATIONS

Directory of Public Relations Agencies & Resources on the Web
www.impulse-research.com/impulse/usa.html

O'Dwyer's Inside News of PR
www.odwyerpr.com

PR Central Reputation Management
www.prcentral.com

Public Relations Society of America (PRSA)
www.prsa.org

RETAIL / WHOLESALE

Corporate Intelligence On Retailing
www.cior.com

US Census Bureau: Retail & Wholesale Trade
www.census.gov/econ/www/retmenu.html#WHOL

TELECOMMUNICATIONS

Company Web Sites

Cascade: Company
www.casc.com/company/index.html

Ericsson
www.ericsson.se

InterDigital
www.interdigital.com

Electronic Commerce

Global Information Infrastructure Commission (GIIC)
www.gii.org

Information Infrastructure Task Force
www.iitf.doc.gov

Government / Regulatory Sites

Federal Communications Commission (FCC)
www.fcc.gov

Federal Standard 1037C: Glossary of Telecommunications Terms
www.its.bldrdoc.gov/fs-1037

International Telecommunication Union (ITU) Home Page
www.itu.ch

National Telecommunications & Information Administration
www.ntia.doc.gov

TelecomPolicy.net: The History of the Telecommunications Act of 1996
www.callthemonit.com/history

Listservs

Telecom Mailing Lists Available on the Internet
www.spp.umich.edu/telecom/maillists.html

Miscellaneous

Glossary of Telecommunications Industry Terms: A to B
www.bell.ca/bell/eng/library/glossary/gtit1.htm

internetTelephony
www.internettelephony.com

Technical & Regulatory Issues
www.industry.net/c/orgunpro/tia/issues

Telecom AM: Daily Telecommunications News
www.telecommunications.com/am

TELECOM Digest & Archives
http://hyperarchive.lcs.mit.edu/telecom-archives

Telecom Information Resources
http://china.si.umich.edu/telecom/telecom-info.html

Telecommunications Magazine
www.telecommagazine.com

Telecoms Virtual Library
www.analysys.com/vlib

Telephone History Web Site
www.cybercomm.net/~chuck/phones.html

Telstra Corporation: {Tele}Communications Information Sources
www.telstra.com.au/info/communications.html

TPG's Telecom Lingo Guide Online
www.telecommunications.com/pages/guide.htm

TRANSPORTATION

Directory of Transportation Resources
http://dragon.princeton.edu:80/~dhb

Institute of Railway System Engineering & Transportation Planning
www.uibk.ac.at/c/c8/c819/p0005.html

World Wide Web Virtual Library: Transportation Page
www.bts.gov/smart/links/transportation.html

UTILITIES

HandiLinks to Electric Companies
www.ahandyguide.com/cat1/e/e12.htm

Power Online Services Ltd
http://pos.net/guest/m_benefit.htm

Industry Research

One of the key items in industry research is forecasts for an industry for the next few years. This information is needed for crucial decision making. The G2R site contains some free forecast information. For other sources of forecast information see sources described under that heading in the next section of this book.

FORECASTS

Bureau of Land Management FY99APP
www.blm.gov/natacq/app99.html

Computer Industry Forecasts
www.cif1.com

Defense Special Weapons Agency Forecast to Industry - FY '98
www.dna.mil/dswaproc/forecast/forecast.htm

Department of Energy - FORECAST
www.hr.doe.gov/ed/ftoc1.htm

Department of Interior FY '99 Forecast
www.doi.gov/osdbu/welcome.htm

Department of Transportation Contracting and Procurement Opportunities
http://osdbuweb.dot.gov/conop1.html

EPA Acquisition Forecast
www.epa.gov/oam/main/forecast

Federal Aviation Administration Procurement Forecast
www.faa.gov/sbo/fore2.htm

Federal Highway Administration-EFLHD Bid Solicitation Schedule for future projects
www.efl.fha.dot.gov/procurement/fpstate.htm

FEMA- Business and Finance Forecast
www.fema.gov/ofm/forecast.htm

Food and Nutrition Service FY 1999-2000 Acquisition Forecast
www.usda.gov/fcs/contract/foreca~1.htm

G2R, Inc Free Forecasts
www.g2r.com/Business_Perf/forecast/forecast.asp

NASA Acquisition Forecast
http://ec.msfc.nasa.gov/hq/forecast/index.html

Naval Air Warfare Center Training Systems Division - Business Forecast
www.ntsc.navy.mil/bf/business.htm

Office of Personnel Management
www.opm.gov/procure/HTML/RECURNG.HTM

Procurement Forecast - HUD
www.hud.gov/cts/cts4cast.html

Small & Disadvantaged Business Utilization Program
www.nrc.gov/ADM/CONTRACT/forclist.html

Small Business Forecast - National Institutes of Health
www.niehs.nih.gov/omcpmb/general/fy99sbfo.htm

Treasury Bureau - Forecast of Contract Opportunities
www.treas.gov/sba/getsic.html

UNICOR (Forecast 1999)
www.unicor.gov/procurement/fcast99.html

US Air Force - Long Range Requirements
http://sirius.eiw38.af.mil/contracting/
lgcx_csa/long-range.htm

US Army Engineering & Support Center FORECAST '99
www.hnd.usace.army.mil/contract/fcast.htm

US Army HW TRADOC Acquisition
www.tradoc-acq.army.mil

US Department of Agriculture Food Safety & Inspection Service
www.usda.gov/da/smallbus/99fsis.htm

US Department of Education Contract Opportunities
http://gcs.ed.gov/CONINFO/Forecast.htm

US Industry and Trade Outlook '98 - Business Forecasts
www.ntis.gov/yellowbk/1nty752.htm

USAID Forecast Reports - Procurement
www.info.usaid.gov/procurement_bus_opp/
procurement/forecast

USDOT - Central Federal Lands Highway Division Solicitation Schedule
www.cflhd.gov/Edi/pna/sched.htm

USDOT:FRA:HSGT Research Projects and Technology 98-01
www.fra.dot.gov/o/hsgt/baa/baapack.htm

USGS Acquisition Planning Forecast
www.usgs.gov/contracts/app99.html

USPTO Upcoming Opportunities - General Procurement
www.uspto.gov/web/offices/ac/comp/proc/upopp1.htm

USPTO Upcoming Opportunities - Information Technology
www.uspto.gov/web/offices/ac/comp/proc/upopp.htm

MISCELLANEOUS

Current Industrial Reports - Production, Inventories, & Orders
www.census.gov/pub/cir/www/index.html

Electric Library - Business Edition
www.business.elibrary.com

FindLinks - Industry-Specific Web Links
www.findlinks.com/index.html

Industry Information: Hoover's Industry Snapshots
http://home.sprintmail.com/~debflanagan/
indust01.html

Industry Information: Dow Jones Business Directory
http://home.sprintmail.com/~debflanagan/
indust04.html

Industry Research Desk
www.virtualpet.com/industry

Industry Research Desk: Industry Home Pages
www.virtualpet.com/industry/mfg/mfg.htm

Industry-Occupation Employment Matrix
http://stats.bls.gov/../oep/nioem/empiohm.asp

Internet Business Library: Industry Reports
www.bschool.ukans.edu/intbuslib/industry.htm

Information Brokers

Information brokers are information professionals or information research consultants worldwide, who perform online searching, library research, competitor intelligence, and similar services for business, industry, government, academia and the scientific communities. The companies listed on the sites below subscribe to codes of ethics of professional associations such as the Society for Competitive Intelligence Professionals or the Association of Independent Information Professionals. Search the Burwell World Directory to identify a company to assist with your information research.

Burwell Enterprises, Inc: Focus on Information Brokering
www.burwellinc.com

Pastel Programming Co
www.netins.net/showcase/trhalvorson

Association of Independent Information Professionals
www.aiip.org

Burwell Enterprises, Inc: Focus on Information Brokering
www.burwellinc.com

Pastel Programming Home Page
www.netins.net/showcase/trhalvorson

Yahoo! - Business & Economy:Companies:Information:Information Brokers
www.yahoo.com/Business_and_Economy/
Companies/Information/Information_Brokers

International Organizations

This is a brief list of such organizations. See links on sites below for locating additional organizations.

NAFTA Home Page
www.iep.doc.gov/nafta/nafta2.htm

Spire Project: United Nations Information
http://cn.net.au/un.html

The World Bank Group
www.worldbank.org

United Nations
www.un.org

United Nations System
www.unsystem.org

US Department of State: Organization of American States
www.state.gov/www/background_notes/
oas_0398_bgn.html

Internet Tools

A wide variety of useful tools is represented in this group of bookmarks. Several of them are described earlier in this book in Chapter 16.

Alexa Internet
www.alexa.com

Anonymizer Inc
www.anonymizer.com

BullsEye
www.intelliseek.com/be/bullseye.htm

Daily Diffs Free Web Page Change Monitoring
www.dailydiffs.com

DaveCentral: Show-URL
www.davecentral.com/1442.html

InterNIC
www.internic.net

Javalink - Monitor the Web Daily
www.javelink.com/cat2main.htm

Netcom
www.netcom.com/access/index.html

NetMind
www.netmind.com

NetPartners Internet Solutions: Resources: Company Locator
www.netpart.com/resources/search.html

Show-URL Bookmark Utility
http://netvigator.com/~godfreyk/showurl

Statistics Toolbox
www.iw.com/daily/stats/index.html

The Nymserver
www.nymserver.com

Traceroute: Internetica - December 1996
www.boardwatch.com/mag/96/dec/bwm38.htm

Voice E-Mail 4.0 for Netscape
www.bonzi.com/netscape/voicenet.htm

WebSitez - Search engine for domain name addresses!
www.websitez.com

Legal Information

Use these bookmarks to locate laws and regulations of the US and other countries around the world.

MISCELLANEOUS

AALLNET WEB • American Association of Law Libraries
www.aallnet.org/aallnetweb.html

Business Resources on the Web: Economic Statistics, Government Statistics, and Business Law
www.idbsu.edu/carol/busness2.htm

Center for Information Law & Policy
www.cilp.org/newhome/welcome.html

HG
www.hg.org/hg.html

Hiieros Gamos: Law Library
www.hg.org/lawlibrary.html

Verdict Search
www.verdictsearch.com

VersusLaw
www.versuslaw.com

WashLaw WEB: Law Journals
http://lawlib.wuacc.edu/washlaw/lawjournal/
lawjournal.html

CASE LAW

Business Information from Brainwave - The Business Information Resource for Company, Industry and Market Research
www.n2kbrainwave.com/
cgi-bin/scribe/index.htm[BOUNTY]

LEXIS-NEXIS Universe - Sign-On
http://web.lexis-nexis.com/ln.universe/page/content

westlaw.com
www.westlaw.com

CRIMINAL LAW-RELATED

Cecil Greek's Criminal Justice Page: Law Indexes
www.fsu.edu/~crimdo/law.html

Criminal Law Links
http://dpa.state.ky.us/~rwheeler

NON US / INTERNATIONAL LAW

Foreign & International Law Web
http://lawlib.wuacc.edu/forint/forintmain.html

International Trade Law Monitor
http://itl.irv.uit.no/trade_law

Law-On-Line / APOL [Asia/Pacific, including CHINA] Free
www.lawhk.hku.hk/dbmenu/freeserv.shtml

US LAW / REGULATIONS

DocLaw Web
http://lawlib.wuacc.edu/washlaw/doclaw/
doclawnew.html

FedLaw
www.legal.gsa.gov

FindLaw: Supreme Court Opinions
www.findlaw.com/casecode/supreme.html

GPO Access at PALNI (Search Federal Register)
www.palni.edu/gpo

NARA: Code of Federal Regulations
www.access.gpo.gov/nara/cfr/index.html

US Code Table of Popular Names
www.law.cornell.edu/uscode/topn

US House of Representatives - Internet Law Library - US Code (Searchable)
http://law.house.gov/usc.htm

US Federal Courts Finder
www.LAW.emory.edu/FEDCTS

US STATE LEGAL SITES

Full-text state statutes and legislation on the Internet
www.prairienet.org/~scruffy/f.htm

PaLAWnet - Pennsylvania's Legal Information Network
www.legalcom.com

StateLaw: State & Local Government
http://lawlib.wuacc.edu/washlaw/uslaw/statelaw.html

Full-text State Statutes & Legislation on the Internet
www.prairienet.org/~scruffy/f.htm

Pennsylvania Law - Legal Communications Ltd.
www.legalcom.com

StateLaw: State & Local Government - Executive, Legislative, & Judicial Information
http://lawlib.wuacc.edu/washlaw/uslaw/statelaw.html

Libraries

These are a few of the many library sites on the Internet. Most major universities have excellent sites, as do some public and special libraries.

CARRIE: A Full-Text Electronic Library
http://history.cc.ukans.edu/carrie/carrie_main.html

Repositories of Primary Sources
www.uidaho.edu/special-collections/
Other.Repositories.html

Research-It! - Your one-stop reference desk
www.iTools.COM/research-it

University of Michigan: Documents Center
www.lib.umich.edu/libhome/Documents.center

webCATS: Library Catalogues on the World Wide Web
www.lights.com/webcats

Maps

Many of these map sites will be useful in pinpointing the location of competitors' business operations. Your Sales and Marketing department may find them useful for reaching your clients' sites.

Map Collections: 1597-1988
http://lcweb2.loc.gov/ammem/gmdhtml/gmdhome.html

MapBlast! BlastOff
www.mapblast.com

MapQuest!
http://mapquest.com

Maps On Us: A Map, Route and Yellow Pages Service
www.mapsonus.com

Microsoft Expedia Maps - Place Finder
www.expediamaps.com/PlaceFinder.asp

SEARCH.COM - Vicinity MapBlast Map Launcher Page
www.search.com/Single/0,7,0-350474,00.html

TheTrip.com Professional Flight Tracking Tools
http://flightpro.thetrip.com/pro

Market Research

These web sites supplement the many market research sources available on commercial vendors' sites.

FIND/ SVP: Business Research
www.find.com

Frost & Sullivan - Industrial Market Engineering
www.frost.com/industrial

iMarket Inc.: Direct Marketing, Database Marketing, Mailing Lists and Market Analysis Software Products.
www.imarketinc.com

New York AMA GreenBook - Greenbook Search
www.greenbook.org/greenbook/search.cfm

USADATA Custom Reports Form
www.usadata.com/usadata/masub.htm

News Sites

These sites contain links to multiple news information sources from around the world as well as to individual newspapers' sites are listed further down this list. Newswires and other news sources are included here as well. Some of these sites allow searching many sources simultaneously, which can facilitate retrieving business intelligence.

AILEENA - Media-Index
www.aileena.ch/linknav.htm

AJR NewsLink
www.newslink.org/biz.html

All the World's Newspapers
www.webwombat.com.au/intercom/newsprs/index.htm

BBC News
http://news.bbc.co.uk

Bourque NewsWatch Canada
www.bourque.org

Business Week Online
www.businessweek.com

Business Wire 1998
www.businesswire.com

Canada NewsWire
www.newswire.ca

Central Europe Online
www.centraleurope.com

CNNfn • The Financial Network
www.cnnfn.com

Ecola: Newsstand
www.ecola.com/news

Editor & Publisher: MediaINFO Links
www.mediainfo.com/emedia

Excite's NewsTracker
http://nt.excite.com

Financial Media on the 'Net
www.qualisteam.com/eng/docu.html

Forbes Digital Tool
http://forbes.com

Fortune
http://cgi.pathfinder.com/fortune

Geographic Location & Media Category Search
www.mediainfo.com

Library of Congress: Lists of Newspapers, Periodicals & News Resources
http://lcweb.loc.gov/rr/news/lists.html

Library of Congress: Newspaper Indexes
http://lcweb.loc.gov/rr/news/oltitles.html

Lookout Point Links to Online Newspapers
www.lookoutpoint.com/linknews.html

Mario's Cyberspace Station: News & Information
http://mprofaca.cro.net/search2.html

MediaFinder from Oxbridge Communications, Inc.
www.mediafinder.com

MediaINFO Links - Search Page
www.mediainfo.com/emedia

MSNBC
www.msnbc.com/news/default.asp

National Newspapers Related Internet Resources (UK)
www.strath.ac.uk/Interest/papers.html

News Index
www.newsindex.com

NewsCentral: North America
www.all-links.com/newscentral/northamerica

NewsCom
www.newscom.com

NewsDirectory.com
www.newsdirectory.com

NewsLibrary
www.newslibrary.com

Newspaperlinks
www.newspaperlinks.com/framesFiles/
framesContent.asp

NewsTrawler
www.newstrawler.com/nt/nt_home.html

NPR Online
http://iris.npr.org

Online Newspapers
www2.hawaii.edu/~rpeterso/newspapr.htm

Online Newspapers - 2250 listings
www.webwombat.com.au/intercom/newsprs/index.htm

PR Newswire
www.prnewswire.com

Reuters News
www.reuters.com/news/index.html

Russian Story - Russian Periodicals Online
www.russianstory.com

Search Engines - Beaucoup! (Media)
www.beaucoup.com/1medeng.html

The Wire
http://wire.ap.org

Time Warner's Pathfinder!
www.pathfinder.com/welcome/?navbar

US News Archives on the Web (Special Libraries Associations)
http://sunsite.unc.edu/slanews/internet/
archives.html

WavePhore Inc
www.wavephore.com

Wired News
> www.wired.com/news

Yahoo-News and Media
> www.yahoo.com/News_and_Media/Newspapers

Newspapers

Individual newspapers' sites have been collected here. You'll want to add bookmarks for newspapers in cities where you or your company's competitors do business. Some of them may not be included in the group files offered by News Sites, above, or by commercial online vendors' collections.

Africa Press International
> http://home.global.co.za/~boervolk/index2.htm

American City Business Journals
> http://amcity.com

Business Day
> www.bday.co.za

Kansas City Star
> www.kcstar.com

New York Times on the Web
> www.nytimes.com

Shanghai Daily
> http://china-window.com/shanghai/sstr/sst.html

Straits Times Interactive
> http://straitstimes.asia1.com

The Economist
> www.economist.com

Wall Street Journal Interactive Edition
> www.wsj.com

WashingtonPost.com: The Interactive Post 200
> www.washingtonpost.com/wp-srv/business/longterm/post200/post200.htm

Nonprofits & Charities

These sites could occasionally be useful to the CI researcher. Some charities may mention names of VIP's on their Board of Directors, for example, which may provide more background details on a competitor's CEO.

Better Business Bureau Business and Charity Reports
> www.bbb.org/reports/index.html

Charity Search
> http://209.96.199.3/search/search.cfm

Chronicle of Philanthropy
> http://philanthropy.com

Corporate Grantmakers on the Internet (no frames)
> http://fdncenter.org/grantmaker/gws_corp/corp2.html

Exempt Organizations Search - IRS
www.irs.ustreas.gov/prod/bus_info/eo/eosearch.html

Grant Award Action Database 1997
http://web99.ed.gov/grant/grtawd97.nsf

Grantmaking Public Charities on the Internet (no frames)
http://fdncenter.org/grantmaker/gws_pubch/
pubch2.html

GuideStar - The Donor's Guide to Charities & Nonprofits
www.guidestar.org

Idealist Home
www.idealist.org

INDEPENDENT SECTOR Home Page
www.indepsec.org

Indiana University Center on Philanthropy
www.tcop.org

Internet Nonprofit Center
www.nonprofits.org

Internet Prospector Reference Desk
http://w3.uwyo.edu/~prospect

IU Center on Philanthropy
www.tcop.org

Literature of the Non-Profit Sector
http://fdncenter.org/onlib/lnps/index.html

National Center for Charitable Statistics at The Urban Institute
http://nccs.urban.org

NonProfit Times
www.nptimes.com

Notices of Funding Availability
http://ocd.usda.gov/nofa.htm

PJ Online: Philanthropy Links : Meta Index of Non-Profit Sites
http://204.243.96.61/links_metaindex.cfm

Private Foundations on the Internet (no frames)
http://fdncenter.org/grantmaker/gws_priv/priv2.html

Real Estate
www.people.Virginia.EDU/~dev-pros/Realestate.html

The Foundation Center
http://fdncenter.org

The Foundation Center - Community Foundations on the Internet
http://fdncenter.org/grantmaker/gws_comm/comm.html

The Foundation Center's Foundation Finder
http://lnp.fdncenter.org/finder.html

The Rich List
www.richlist.com/jewish.htm

Patents / Trademarks

A variety of US and non-US sources have been collected here. The Media Advisory from USPTO may provide some interesting intelligence about your competitors' research and development activity.

Copyrights

Thomson & Thomson
www.thomson-thomson.com

Miscellaneous

Manning & Napier
www.mnis.com

MicroPatent
www.micropat.com

Patent Explorer
https://www.patentexplorer.com/secure/
details/default.htm

Search the PTO Web Server
http://www1.uspto.gov/web/menu/search.html

USPTO FOIA Reading Room
http://www1.uspto.gov/web/offices/com/sol/
foia/readroom.htm

World Intellectual Property Organization
www.wipo.org/eng/dgtext.htm

Patents

Canadian Intellectual Property Office - Canadian Patent Database
http://Patents1.ic.gc.ca/intro-e.html

CPP: Locate US Patents
http://casweb.cas.org/cgi-bin/demo_cpp

Derwent Scientific and Patent Information
www.DERWENT.com

esp@cenet
http://ep.dips.org

European Patent Office
www.european-patent-office.org

General Information Concerning Patents
www.uspto.gov/web/offices/pac/doc/
general/index.html

IBM Patent Server Home Page
http://patent.womplex.ibm.com

Information Research: Commercial Database List - Patents
http://cn.net.au/
cgi-bin/cd_find.pl?search=US+and+Patents

Japan Patent Office Home Page
http://www2.jpo-miti.go.jp

Media Advisory - August 19, 1997
http://www1.uspto.gov/web/offices/com/
speeches/98-01.htm

Patent Bibliographic and AIDS Databases
http://patents.uspto.gov

Patent Cooperation Treaty Electronic Gazette
http://pctgazette.wipo.int/eng/index.html

QPAT-US
www.qpat.com

STO's Internet Patent Search System
http://sunsite.unc.edu/patents/intropat.html

United States Patent and Trademark Office
www.uspto.gov

US Patent Database Access
http://patents.cnidr.org/access/access.html

Trademarks

Basic Facts About Registering a Trademark
www.uspto.gov/web/offices/tac/doc/basic

Domain Name, Trademark, & Competitive Intelligence Services
www.namestake.com

Final Decisions - Trademark Trial & Appeal Board
http://www1.uspto.gov/web/offices/com/sol/
foia/ttab/ttab.htm

Researching Trademarks
www.info-law.com/tmsearch.html

Thomson & Thomson
www.thomson-thomson.com

Trademark Database
www.uspto.gov/tmdb/index.html

People Locators

These sites may be useful in gathering biographical information about a competitor's personnel. They should, of course be supplement by the use of newspapers and magazines and other types of sources mentioned earlier in this book.

AMA Physician Select
www.AMA-ASSN.ORG/aps/amahg.htm

Bigfoot
www.bigfoot.com

Canadian Who's Who 1997: Search
www.utpress.utoronto.ca/cww/cw2w3.cgi

Congressional Biographical Directory
http://bioguide.congress.gov/biosearch/
biosearch.asp

CorpTech People Finder
www.corptech.com/ResearchAreas/PeopleSearch.cfm

Database America
www.databaseamerica.com

EDGAR Online: People
http://people.edgar-online.com/people

E-Mail Directory
www.Four11.com/login?HBURWELL@IX.NETCOM.COM&roosia

Fortune: 50 Most Powerful Women in Business
www.pathfinder.com/fortune/mostpowerful

InfoSpace.Com
www.infospace.com

Insider Trader
www.insidertrader.com

Insider Trading Monitor
www.wsdinc.com/products/p1470.shtml

Landings: Search for Certified Pilots
www.landings.com/_landings/pages/search_amd.html

LEXIS-NEXIS Universe - Sign-On
http://web.lexis-nexis.com/ln.universe/page/content

Martindale Hubbell Lawyer Locator
www.martindale.com

MetaEmail Search Agent (MESA)
http://mesa.rrzn.uni-hannover.de

Tele-Info OnLine (German)
www.teleinfo.de

The Noble Group: Internet Directories
www.experts.com

The Ultimates
www.theultimates.com

Yahoo! People Search
www.yahoo.com/search/people/email.html

Political Risk

These sites provide a great deal of intelligence for companies doing business in other countries. In addition to advising on the stability of the business environment in these countries, they provide detailed country reports and data on licensing and related business issues.

International Credit Reports, Collection Svcs & Marketing
www.kreller.com

The Economist Intelligence Unit
www.eiu.com

The PRS Group
www.prsgroup.com

Products

Your Sales and Marketing or Research and Development departments are always interested in what your competition is doing regarding product development. Here are a couple of sites that may be useful in their quest.

New Products, Markets, Opportunities
> `www.raucon.com/busidev/1.1.html`

PNN - Product News Network
> `http://productnews.com`

Product ReviewNet
> `www.productreviewnet.com/home.html`

Productscan
> `www.productscan.com`

Public Records

This large collection of public record sites on the Internet has been subdivided for more efficient use. The initial group contains both commercial and free sites, containing various types of information.

ASSORTED SITES & VENDORS

AccuSearch Inc
> `www.accusearchinc.com`

American Information Network
> `www.ameri.com/sherlock.htm`

American University's Campaign Finance Data on the Internet
> `www.soc.american.edu/campfin`

Arizona Central | Arizona Inc
> `www.azcentral.com/depts/work/azinc97/rep100.shtml`

Avert Inc - Pre-Employment Screening Services
> `www.avert.com`

Campaign Finance
> `http://campaignfinance.org/states.html`

CDB Infotek - The Public Records Information Company
> `www.cdb.com/public`

City-County Directory (Yahoo!)
> `http://local.yahoo.com/bin/get_local`

County Information Address Locator
> `www.familytreemaker.com/00000229.html`

CourtLink
> `www.courtlink.com`

CRP: Federal Lobbyist Database
> `www.crp.org/lobby`

Dataquick Real Estate Information
> `http://products.dataquick.com/consumer`

Experian Credit & Real Estate Information
> `www.experian.com`

Experian: Uniform Commercial Code Sample Report
www.experian.com/product/pubrec/uccsample.html

Fair Credit Reporting Act
www.camel.com/fulltext.htm

Family Tree Maker's Genealogy Site: Resources by County
www.familytreemaker.com/00000229.html

FECInfo
www.tray.com/fecinfo

Federal Reserve Press Releases - Enforcement Actions
www.federalreserve.gov/boarddocs/press/enforcement

Genealogy Gateway: Gateway to Military Sources & Searches
http://polaris.net/~legend/milifile.htm

Genealogy Gateway: The Largest Online Newspaper Obituary Search
Listing On The Web!
www.polaris.net/~legend/gateway5.htm

How to Obtain Birth, Death, Marriage & Divorce Certificates
www.cdc.gov/nchswww/howto/w2w/w2welcom.htm

Information America
www.infoam.com

KnowX | Home
www.knowx.com/home/home.exe?

KOMO 4 News - Disciplined Doctors
http://komotv.com/news/doctors

Landings: Aviation Search Engines: FARs, N-Numbers, NTSBs, SDRs, ADs,
AMEs, Pilots, Medical Examiners, Regulations
http://www1.drive.net/evird.acgi$pass*8099593!mtd*7
!map*_landings/images/laURL ndings-strip.map?51,40

Landings: Search for Certified Pilots
http://www1.drive.net/evird.acgi$pass*8099593!_h-
www.landings.com/_landings/pages/search_amd.html

line Web Outpost
www.militarycity.com

Merlin Information Services
www.merlindata.com

miliarycity.com
www.militarycity.com

Military Searches Genealogy Gateway
http://polaris.net/~legend/milifile.htm

NASD-R Public Disclosure Program [Broker Search]
http://pdpi.nasdr.com/pdpi/broker_search_frame.asp

National Public Records Research Association (NPRRA)
www.nprra.com/default.htm

Nebraska Secretary of State: Services
www.nol.org/home/SOS/htm/services.htm

New Generation Research (Bankruptcy Publications)
www.turnarounds.com

OPEN - Online Professional Electronic Network
www.openohio.com

OSHA Statistics & Data - Searchable
www.osha.gov/oshstats

Privacy Act
http://foia.state.gov/privacy.htm

PublicRecordSources.Com
www.publicrecordsources.com

Real Estate Inquiry - Dakota County, Minnesota
www.co.dakota.mn.us/depart/property/index.htm

Social Security Administration & Genealogy FAQ
http://members.aol.com/rechtman/ssafaq.html#11

Social Security Death Index
www.ancestry.com/ssdi/advanced.htm

State Bar of California Member Records Online
www.calsb.org/MM/SBMBRSHP.HTM

State Privacy Laws
www.epic.org:80/privacy/consumer/states.html

The Daily Watch
www.dailywatch.com

The Largest Online Newspaper Obituary Search Listing on the Web!
www.polaris.net/~legend/gateway5.htm

US Corporate Information • Regional Sites
www.corporateinformation.com/usstates.html

USDatalink
www.usdatalink.com

Vital Records Information - United States
www.inlink.com/~nomi/vitalrec

CREDIT RECORDS

Dun & Bradstreet Reports
www.dnb.com

National Credit Information Network
www.WDIA.com

FOIA REQUESTS

Department of Justice: Other Agencies' FOIA Web Sites
www.usdoj.gov/foia/other_age.htm

Freedom of Information Act (FOIA)
http://foia.state.gov/foia.htm

Freedom of Information Act Group Inc.
www.foia.com

SPJ: FOI Other Resources
www.spj.org/foia/foiresources/resourcelist.htm

SPJ: FOI Resource Center
www.spj.org/foia/index.htm

SPJ: FOI Resource Center: Driver Records
www.spj.org/foia/drivers/drivindex.htm

State & National Freedom of Information Resources
www.reporters.net/nfoic/web/index.htm

US Department of State Electronic: Reading Room: Reference
http://foia.state.gov/refer.htm

INDIVIDUAL STATES/COUNTY FILES - FREE

Alaska

ALASKA Corporations Database
www.commerce.state.ak.us/com/owa/comdata.bus

Aurora Query for Dial-In Users
www.co.fairbanks.ak.us/database/aurora

Arizona

ARIZONA Campaign Finance
www.sosaz.com/scripts/cfs_contributions.cgi

ARIZONA Lobbyists
www.sosaz.com/scripts/lobbyist_engine.cgi

ARIZONA Uniform Commercial Code Filings
www.sosaz.com/ucc.htm

Maricopa County
www.maricopacounty.com

Maricopa County Assessor
www.maricopa.gov/assessor/default.asp

Maricopa County Recorder
http://recorder.maricopa.gov/recdocdata/
GetRecDataSelect.asp

Maricopa County Superior Court
www.supcourt.maricopa.gov

Pima County Courts
http://iissvr.jp.co.pima.az.us/webinfo/findcase.asp

Arkansas

ARKANSAS Banks & Insurance Zip File
www.sosweb.state.ar.us/corp.html

ARKANSAS Cooperatives Zip File
www.sosweb.state.ar.us/corp.html

ARKANSAS Corporations Zip File
www.sosweb.state.ar.us/corp.html

ARKANSAS Notaries
www.sosweb.state.ar.us/corp.html

ARKANSAS Secretary of State Search: Incorporations
www.sosweb.state.ar.us/corps/incorp

ARKANSAS Secretary of State Search: Trademarks
www.sosweb.state.ar.us/corps/trademk

ARKANSAS Trademarks Zip File
www.sosweb.state.ar.us/corp.html

California

CALIFORNIA Department of Real Estate: Public License Information
http://www2.dre.ca.gov/I_Licensee_list.qry

CALIFORNIA DocFinder
www.docboard.org/ca/df/casearch.htm

CALIFORNIA Secretary of State - Lobbyist Directory - Contents
www.ss.ca.gov/prd/ld/contents.htm

CALIFORNIA Secretary of State - Voluntary Electronic Filing
http://reform.ss.ca.gov

CALIFORNIA Southern Bankruptcy Court
www.casb.uscourts.gov/html/fileroom.htm

CALIFORNIA State Bar Members Online
www.calsb.org/MM/SBMBRSHP.HTM

Contractors - License Status Inquiry Request
http://www2.cslb.ca.gov

Directory of Facilities (Banking)
www.dfi.ca.gov/directry/fac.htm

Directory of Foreign Banks
www.dfi.ca.gov/directry/fbc.htm

Directory of Premium Finance Companies
www.dfi.ca.gov/directry/fin.htm

Directory of Representative Offices
www.dfi.ca.gov/directry/rep.htm

Directory of State Chartered Banks
www.dfi.ca.gov/directry/state.htm

Directory of State Chartered Credit Unions
www.dfi.ca.gov/directry/cu.htm

Directory of State-Chartered Savings & Loan Associations
www.dfi.ca.gov/directry/S&L.htm

Directory of Thrift & Loan Companies
www.dfi.ca.gov/directry/thrift.htm

Directory of Transmitters of Money Abroad
www.dfi.ca.gov/directry/tma.htm

Issuers of Payment Instruments
www.dfi.ca.gov/directry/pi.htm

Issuers of Travelers Checks
www.dfi.ca.gov/directry/tc.htm

Los Angeles Trial Courts
www.latriacourst.org/civil.htm

State Bar of California
www.calsb.org

Trust Companies
www.dfi.ca.gov/directry/trust.htm

Colorado

Arapahoe County Assessor
`www.co.arapahoe.co.us/AS/index.htm`

Assessor's Office Real Estate Property Search • El Paso County, CO
`www.co.el-paso.co.us/assessor/asr_main_srch.htm`

Park County Colorado Assessor's Office
`www.parkco.org`

Pitkin County Assessor
`www.aspen.com/aspenonline/dir/gov/sponsors/`
`assessors/index.html`

Connecticut

CONNECTICUT Sex Offender Registry
`www.state.ct.us/dps/Sor.htm`

Florida

FLORIDA Campaign Finance - About the Database
`http://election.dos.state.fl.us/`
`campfin/CFININFO.HTM`

FLORIDA Corporate Inquiry Search
`http://ccfcorp.dos.state.fl.us/COR_menu.html`

FLORIDA Department of Business & Professional Regulation
`www.state.fl.us/dbpr`

FLORIDA Ficticious Company Name Inquiry Menu
`http://ccfcorp.dos.state.fl.us/FIC_menu.html`

FLORIDA General/Ltd. Liability Partnerships Inquiry Menu
`http://ccfcorp.dos.state.fl.us/GEN_menu.html`

FLORIDA Inmate Population Information Search
`www.dc.state.fl.us/activeinmates/inmatesearch.asp`

FLORIDA Lien Inquiry Menu
`http://ccfcorp.dos.state.fl.us/LIEN_menu.html`

FLORIDA Professional Licenses
`http://fcn.state.fl.us/oraweb/owa/`
`dbpr2.qry_lic_menu`

FLORIDA Report on Physician Discipline & Malpractice
`www.fdhc.state.fl.us/hpcc/hpolicy/malpractice/medrp`
`t.html`

FLORIDA Sexual Offenders/Predators
`www.fdle.state.fl.us`

Jacksonville Public Data Depot
`www.ci.jax.fl.us/pub/depot.htm#prop`

Orange County
`www.property-`
`appraiser.co.orange.fl.us/ocpa/owa/disclaimer`

Orange County Florida Comptroller
`www.comptroller.co.orange.fl.us`

Pinellas County
http://pao.co.pinellas.fl.us/search2.html

Georgia

GEORGIA Secretary of State: Search the Corporations Database
> www.sos.state.ga.us/corporations/corpsearch.htm

Illinois

Cook County Assessor's Virtual Office
> www.assessor.co.cook.il.us

ILLIINOIS Department of Corrections Inmate Locator
> www.idoc.state.il.us/inmates

ILLINOIS Corporate Name Search
> www.sos.state.il.us/cgi-bin/corpname

Macon County Illinois Circuit Court
> www.court.co.macon.il.us

Indiana

INDIANA Sex Offender Registry
> www.ai.org/cji/html/sexoffender.html

INDIANA Southern District US Courts
> www.insd.uscourts.gov/casesearch.htm

INDIANA Trademarks Database: Search
> www.ai.org/cgi-bin/icpr/cgi-bin/trademarks.pl

Iowa

Pottawattamie County Courthouse
> www.pottco.org

Kansas

KANSAS Doc Finder
> www.docboard.org/ks/df/kssearch.htm

Kentucky

KENTUCKY Corporation Search - List Business Entity by Name
> www.sos.state.ky.us/corporate/entityname.asp

KENTUCKY Real Estate Brokerage Database Search
> www.krec.net/Tango/Bsearch1.qry?function=form

KENTUCKY Real Estate Licensee Search
> www.krec.net/Tango/Lsearch.qry?function=form

KENTUCKY UCC Lookups
> www.sos.state.ky.us/cclix/default.htm

KENTUCKY Vital Records Index
> http://ukcc.uky.edu/%7Evitalrec

Louisiana

LOUISIANA Secretary of State/Corporations Database
> www.sec.state.la.us/crpinq.htm

Maine

MAINE Corporate Name Search
> www.state.me.us/sos/corpinfo.htm

MAINE Doc Finder
> www.docboard.org/me/df/mesearch.htm

Maryland

City of Boston: Assessor's Office - Query Property Values
    www.ci.boston.ma.us/assessing/search.asp

MARYLAND SDAT: Real Property Search
    www.dat.state.md.us/realprop

MARYLAND Doc Finder
    www.docboard.org/md/df/mdsearch.htm

State of Maryland Department of Assessments & Taxation
    www.dat.state.md.us/bsfd/UCC/search.html

Massachusetts

Home Improvement Contractors (HIC) Lookup
    www.state.ma.us/bbrs/hic.htm

Licensed Contractor Lookup
    www.state.ma.us/bbrs/cntrctrs.htm

MASSACHUSETTS Lobbyist & Employer Search System
    www.state.ma.us/scripts/sec/pre/search.asp

MASSACHUSETTS Physician Profiles
    www.docboard.org/ma/ma_home.htm

Minnesota

Charities
    www.ag.state.mn.us/home/charities/default.shtml

Hennepin County Property Information Search
    http://www2.co.hennepin.mn.us

US Bankruptcy Court – District of Minnesota
    www.mnb.uscourts.gov/cgi-bin/mnb-450-main.pl

Missouri

MISSOURI Corporations Database Query
    http://168.166.2.55/corporations

Nebraska

Lancaster County InterLinc: County Assessor: Property Information
    http://interlinc.ci.lincoln.ne.us/InterLinc/
    cnty/assess/property.htm

Nevada

Clark County, NV: Official Records Inquiry System
    www.co.clark.nv.us/recorder/or_disc.htm

Douglas County Assessor Parcel Menu
    www.co.douglas.nv.us/assessor/menu.html

Douglas County Sales Data Bank Inquiry
    www.co.douglas.nv.us/sales

Douglas County Treasurer
    www.co.douglas.nv.us/treasurer

NEVADA Secretary of State: Corporation Searches
    http://sos.state.nv.us/default.asp

New Hampshire

Portsmouth, NH - Assessed Property Values
www.portsmouthnh.com/realestate/index.htm

New Jersey

Center for Analysis of Public Issues (CAPI)
www.crp.org/capi

NEW JERSEY Charitable Registration Directory
www.state.nj.us/lps/ca/charfrm.htm

New Mexico

Dona Ana County Real Property Records Search
www.co.dona-ana.nm.us/assr/txparcel.html

NEW MEXICO Corporation Information Inquiry
www.state.nm.us/scc/sccfind.html

NEW MEXICO UCC Search
http://web.state.nm.us/UCC/UCCSRCH.HTML-SSI

New York

NEW YORK Southern Bankruptcy Court
www.nysb.uscourts.gov

NEW YORK State Department of Health: Professional Misconduct &
Physician Discipline
www.health.state.ny.us/nysdoh/opmc/main.htm

Office of the New York State Attorney
www.oag.state.ny.us/moneymatters/charities/
pennies97/index.html

Property Assessments for Schenectady County, New York
www.scpl.org/assessments/index.html

North Carolina

Apex Planning Department: Town of Apex Parcel Search
www.2isystems.com/parcels/sparcels.htm

Cabarrus County GIS Public Access
www.co.cabarrus.nc.us/pages/maphelp.html

NORTH CAROLINA Corporation Names Directory
www.sips.state.nc.us/secbin/search.ptr

NORTH CAROLINA Medical Board DocFinder
www.docboard.org/nc/df/ncsearch.htm

NORTH CAROLINA Registered Lobbyist Search
www.secstate.state.nc.us/secstate/lob.htm

Ohio

US Court - Northern District of Ohio
www.ohnd.uscourts.gov

Oklahoma

OKLAHOMA TEST Physician Search
http://osbmls.state.ok.us/physrch.html

OKLAHOMA County Assessor
www.oklahomacounty.org/assessor/default.htm

OKLAHOMA Osteopathic DocFinder
www.docboard.org/ok/df/oksearch.htm

Oregon

OREGON Department of Justice: Charities Database
www.state.or.us/cgi-bin/OrgQuery.pl

UCC Record Search
www.sos.state.or.us/cgi-bin/uccsrch.htm

Pennsylvania

Register of Wills
www.berksregofwills.com

Rhode Island

RHODE ISLAND Corporations Listing
www.state.ri.us/submenus/corpindex.htm

US Bankruptcy Court - Rhode Island
http://top.usbcri.ids.net/ebr

Texas

Agent & Company List in Self-Extracting Files from TX Dept of Insurance
www.tdi.state.tx.us/general/forms.html

Archer County Central Appraisal District
www.taxnetusa.com/archer

Bexar County Appraisal District
www.bcad.org/property.htm

Brazoria Central Appraisal District
www.brazoriacad.org

Brazos County Appraisal District
www.taxnetusa.com/brazos

Caldwell County Central Appraisal District
www.caldwellcad.org

Cameron Appraisal District.
www.cameroncad.org

Central Appraisal District of Taylor County
www.taylorcad.org/page2.htm

Chambers County Appraisal District
www.chamberscad.org

Collin County Appraisal District
www.taxnetusa.com/collin

Dallas Central Appraisal District
www.dallascad.org

Denton County Tax Roll Search
www.taxnetusa.com/denton

El Paso Central Appraisal District
www.elpasocad.org

Ellis County Appraisal District
www.elliscad.org

Franklin Central Appraisal District
www.taxnetusa.com/franklin

Galveston Central Appraisal District
www.galvestoncad.org

Gregg County Appraisal District.
www.gcad.org

Guadalupe Central Appraisal District
www.guadalupecad.org

Hardin County Appraisal District
www.taxnetusa.com/hardin

Harris County Appraisal District
www.hcad.org

Harrison Central Appraisal District
www.harrisoncad.org

Hays County Tax Roll Search
www.taxnetusa.com/hays

Henderson County Appraisal District
www.hendersoncad.org

Hidalgo County Appraisal Roll Search
www.taxnetusa.com/hidalgo

Jack County Appraisal District
www.taxnetusa.com/jack

Jefferson County Appraisal District
www.jcad.org

Kendall Appraisal District
www.kendallcad.org

Lubbock Appraisal District
www.lubbockcad.org

McLennan Appraisal District
www.taxnetusa.com/mclennan

Potter Randall Appraisal District
www.prad.org

Rockwall County Tax Roll Search
www.taxnetusa.com/rockwall

Rusk Central Appraisal District
www.taxnetusa.com/rusk

Smith County Appraisal District
www.taxnetusa.com/scad

Tarrant Appraisal District
www.tad.org

TEXAS Corporation Taxpayer Search
http://open.cpa.state.tx.us

TEXAS DocFinder
www.docboard.org/tx/df/txsearch.htm

TEXAS Harris County - Personal Property Search
www.hcad.org/Appraisal/Personal.htm

Travis County Appraisal District
www.traviscad.org

Van Zandt County Appraisal District
www.vanzandtcad.org

Webb County Appraisal District
www.webbcad.org

Williamson Appraisal District
www.taxnetusa.com/williamson

Utah

Disciplinary Actions & Citations
www.commerce.state.ut.us/web/commerce/DOPL/disc.htm

FirmFind: Main Menu
http://udese.state.ut.us/cgi/foxweb.exe/firmfind

Vermont

VERMONT Business Registry Database Download
www.sec.state.vt.us/seek/download.htm

VERMONT Business Registry Database Individual Person Name Search
www.sec.state.vt.us/seek/name.htm

VERMONT Licensing - Professional Regulation Database
http://170.222.200.66/seek/lrspseek.htm

VERMONT Medical Board DocFinder
www.docboard.org/vt/df/vtsearch.htm

VERMONT Secretary of State . . . Licensing & Registration Name Finder
http://170.222.200.66/seek/lrspseek.htm

VERMONT Secretary of State . . . Lobbyist Name Finder
www.sec.state.vt.us/seek/lbylseek.htm

VERMONT Secretary of State . . . Notary Public Name Finder
www.sec.state.vt.us/seek/not_seek.htm

VERMONT Secretary of State . . . Tradename Data Download
www.sec.state.vt.us/corps/trade.htm

VERMONT Secretary of State . . . UCC Debtors Name Finder
http://170.222.200.66/seek/ucc_seek.htm

VERMONT Secretary of State: Searchable Databases
www.sec.state.vt.us/seek/database.htm#lobby

Virginia

Wise County Virginia
www.courtbar.org

Washington

Charities Registration Data Lookup
http://207.153.159.68/sec_state/charities98/
quick.tmpl

WASHINGTON State Dept of Revenue - PRD Search Page
www.wa.gov/dor/prd

Yakima County Assessors Office
www.pan.co.yakima.wa.us/assessor/assessor.htm

Wisconsin

Assessor's Office, Milwaukee, WI • Property & Assessment Data Inquiry
www.ci.mil.wi.us/citygov/assessor/assessments.htm

Dane County Land Information Office: Main Search Page
> http://170.125.12.32/lio/lis/date_update.idc

Wyoming

100% Wyoming
> www.me.uwyo.edu

WYOMING Secretary of State: Public Access to Corporations
> http://soswy.state.wy.us/corps1.htm

NON-US PUBLIC RECORD SITES

aRMadillo
> www.rmonline.com/pr2.htm

BC OnLine - Access to Government Information
> www.bconline.gov.bc.ca

Canada - Search for Public Company Documents
> www.sedar.com/search/search_form_pc.htm

Industry Canada Corporations Database
> http://strategis.ic.gc.ca/cgi-bin/corp-bin/corpns_s

Japan Company Records
> http://japanfinancials.com

Liquidations Search, Insolvency (UK)
> www.insolvency.co.uk/liq/liqfind.htm

Register of Charities
> www.charity-commission.gov.uk/cinprs/first.asp

Teikoku Databank America Inc
> www.teikoku.com

UK Data Ltd (UK Company Information)
> www.ukdata.com/ukcompanyinformation.htm

Yahoo! UK & Ireland Company Index
> www.yahoo.co.uk/finance/profiles/alpha

YELLOWWW • The Big German Business Directory in the Internet
> http://english.branchenbuch.com

JUMPING OFF PLACES FOR OTHER PUBLIC RECORD SITES

Consumer Business DB Link Page
> www.security-online.com/info/baddebt.html

Find it on StateSearch
> www.nasire.org/ss/STcriminal.html

Property Assessment Files Online
> www.people.Virginia.EDU/~dev-pros/Realestate.html

The State Court Locator
> www.cilp.org/State-Ct

US Corporate Information • Regional Sites
> www.corporateinformation.com/usstates.html

Webgator Page70-State Parole Boards, Inmates, Sex Offenders, & Prison
> www.inil.com/users/dguss/gator70.htm

SUBSCRIPTION OR FEE REQUIRED

American Information Network - A nationwide information provider.
www.ameri.com/sherlock.htm

Aristotle Online
http://products.aristotle.org/pages/online.htm

Avert, Inc - Pre-Employment Screening Services
www.avert.com

CDB Infotek - The Public Records Information Company
www.cdb.com/public

CourtLink Home Page
www.courtlink.com

DAC Services
www.dacservices.com

Database Technologies (AutoTrack)
www.dbt.net

DCS Information Systems
www.dnis.com

Experian Credit and Real Estate Information
www.experian.com

IRSC
www.irsc.com/home.htm

KnowX
www.knowx.com

LEXIS-NEXIS Universe - Sign-On
http://web.lexis-nexis.com/ln.universe

Merlin Information Services
www.merlindata.com

Services of the Office of the Secretary of State
www.nol.org/home/SOS/htm/services.htm

Superior Information Services
www.superiorinfo.com

The Daily Watch Home Page
www.dailywatch.com

UNCLAIMED PROPERTY

This is a combination of commercial and government sites. Although usefulness as business intelligence is limited, unclaimed property generates public records, which is why they have been retained in this list.

FindCash.Com - UNCLAIMED MONEY Database
www.findcash.com

Foundmoney.com
www.foundmoney.com

It'$ Your Money - National Unclaimed Property Database
www.unclaimed-property.com

Louisiana Unclaimed Property
http://neworleans.miningco.com/msubg1d.htm

NAUPA: Unclaimed Property
www.unclaimed.org/offices/index.html

Nevada County California Unclaimed Property
http://treas-tax.co.nevada.ca.us

Rhode Island Unclaimed Property
www.state.ri.us/treas/treas.htm

US GOVERNMENT SEARCHABLE PUBLIC RECORD SITES

A number of US government databases have been made available for searching on the Internet. Competitors' names may appear on any of these, and you may therefore add this data to your knowledge base.

Employer Sanctions Database
www.cis.org/search.html

Envirofacts Query Form
www.epa.gov/enviro/html/multisystem.html

Exempt Organizations Search - IRS
www.irs.ustreas.gov/prod/bus_info/eo/eosearch.html

Fannie Mae - Search
www.fanniemae.com/Homebuyer/REO/index.html

FDIC: Bank Data
www.fdic.gov/databank/index.html

IRS: Search for Exempt Organizations
www.irs.ustreas.gov/prod/bus_info/eo/eosearch.html

OSHA Statistics & Data
www.osha.gov/oshstats

US Department of Education: Grant Award Action Database 1997
http://web99.ed.gov/grant/grtawd97.nsf

Publishers

Dozens of publishers maintain homepages on the Internet. This short list includes publishers whose materials facilitate successful online searching, and therefore more successful competitor intelligence gathering.

Bibliodata
www.bibliodata.com

BRB Publications Inc
www.brbpub.com

Burwell Enterprises
www.burwellinc.com

Hermograph Press - Net.Journal Directory
www.hermograph.com

Information Today - Fulltext Sources Online
www.INFOTODAY.COM

Information Today Inc
www.infotoday.com

Online Inc
www.onlineinc.com

Push Technologies

This technology may be useful for gathering business intelligence as it becomes news. The Intranet Content Management site contains a survey of current PUSH products, with pricing information.

Inquisit
www.inquisit.com

Intranet content management and push products
http://idm.internet.com/tools-km.shtml

NewsEdge Corporation
www.newsedge.com

The PointCast Network (Download)
http://pioneer.pointcast.com/download/dwnwin.html

WavePhore, Inc
www.wavephore.com

Reference Tools

These sites contain a variety of information that may be useful in many types of research, not strictly limited to business intelligence.

All Yellow Pages
www.allyellowpages.com

Biographical Dictionary Search Page
www.s9.com/biography/search.html

CCFINDER
www.flash.net/~coxsw/ccfinder.htm

City-County Directory (Yahoo!)
http://local.yahoo.com/bin/get_local

Embassy & Consulate Directory of Embassy & Consulate Addresses & Websites
www.embassyworld.com

FedEx | Tracking
www.fedex.com/us/tracking

Information Please Home Page
www.infoplease.com

Ira Sterbakov's All-in-one Search & Link Page
www.erols.com/irasterb

J.P. Morgan & Co Incorporated
www.jpmorgan.com/cgi-bin/HolidayCalendar

News, Weather & Sports Headlines & Links from all the major news services
www.moose-jaw.com/news

NewsEngin Inc.
http://newsengin.com/newsengin.nsf

NewsEngin's Cost-of-Living Calculator
http://newsengin.com/nefreetools.nsf/cpicalc

OANDA Currency Converter, Historical Charts, Current Exchange Rates, and Forex Forecast
www.oanda.com

Online Dictionaries and Translators
http://rivendel.com/~ric/resources/dictionary.html

Online Medical Dictionary
www.graylab.ac.uk/omd

Open Stacks -Best Bet Internet
www.ala.org/editions/openstacks/bestbet/index.html

POSTINFO : World-Address postal information service
http://postinfo.net

Prices's List of Lists
http://gwis2.circ.gwu.edu/~gprice/listof.htm

SPIRE Project
http://cn.net.au

The Inflation Calculator
www.westegg.com/inflation

The National Address Server
www.cedar.buffalo.edu/adserv.html

The Quotations Page
www.starlingtech.com/quotes/index.html

UPS Package Tracking
www.ups.com/tracking/tracking.html

USPS ZIP+4 Code Lookup
www.usps.gov/ncsc/lookups/lookup_zip+4.html

Sales Leads

Harris Info Online
www.harrisinfoonline.com

infoUSA
www.imarketinc.com

Science/Technology

Although there is a great deal of material available on the Internet that falls under the heading "science and technology," these sites may have some application in the process of determining what is happening in an industry of interest where science or technology is a key component.

BIOTECHNOLOGY

BUBL LINK: Biotechnology
http://link.bubl.ac.uk/biotechnology

HMS Beagle
www.biomednet.com/hmsbeagle

CHEMISTRY

SciFinder
http://info.cas.org/SCIFINDER/scicover2.html

World Wide Web Virtual Library: Chemistry
www.chem.ucla.edu/chempointers.html

DOCUMENTS / REPORTS

Canada Institute For Scientific and Technical Information (CISTI)
www.cisti.nrc.ca/cisti/cisti.html

Canadian Federal Government Research Agencies
http://strategis.ic.gc.ca/sc_innov/tech/
engdoc/2a2.html

CASI Technical Report Server
www.sti.nasa.gov/casitrs.html

DOE Reports Bibliographic Database
www.osti.gov/html/dra/dra.html

Gov.Research-Center: NTIS Database
http://grc.ntis.gov/energy.htm

Information Bridge
www.doe.gov/bridge/home.html

NASA Technical Report Server (NTRS)
http://techreports.larc.nasa.gov/cgi-bin/NTRS

Networked Computer Science Technical Reports Library
http://sunsite.berkeley.edu/ncstrl

OpenNet
www.doe.gov/opennet

Science & Technology Documents & Subscription Information
www.pub.whitehouse.gov/WH/EOP/OSTP/html/pub.html

STINET: Scientific & Technical Reports Collection
www.dtic.mil/stinet/str/index.html

UCSD Engineering Library - Technical Reports
www.sti.nasa.gov/casitrs.html

US Government Laboratories
http://info.er.usgs.gov/network/gov.html

Yahoo! Science: Computer Science: Technical Reports
www.yahoo.com/Science/Computer_Science/
Technical_Reports

MISCELLANEOUS

Community Research and Development Information Service (CORDIS)
www.cordis.lu

Federal Laboratory Consortium (FLC): Resource Directory Search
www.federallabs.org/flc/flcrd2.htm

IDRIS - Inter-Agency Development Research Information System
www.minweb.idrc.ca/idrislog.htm

National Research Council Canada
www.nrc.ca

Science and Engineering Indicators: 1998
www.nsf.gov/sbe/srs/seind98/start.htm

Web of Science : Institute for Scientific Information
www.isinet.com/prodserv/citation/websci.html

Search Engines & Internet Directories

These tools are often considered the backbone of the Internet. The list below includes both meta search engines, that search multiple search engines at one time, and the more traditional search engines. The Beaucoup sites are a favorite of this author because they gather so many specialized search engines together on one page. This is a great way to manage an organized search across many search engines since the links on the list change color after you've accessed them.

META SEARCH ENGINES

All4One
www.all4one.com

Ask Jeeves
www.askjeeves.com

Debriefing
www.debriefing.com

Dogpile, the Friendly Multi-Engine Search Tool
www.dogpile.com

Go2Net
www.go2net.com/search.html

Internet Sleuth
www.isleuth.com

MAMMA
www.mamma.com

MetaCrawler
www.metacrawler.com

Metasearch
http://metasearch.com

One Search
www.onesearch.com

ProFusion
www.profusion.com

Savvy Search
www.savvysearch.com

MISCELLANEOUS

All-in-One Search Page
www.albany.net/allinone/all1desk.html#DeskRef

Alta Vista
www.altavista.com

Beaucoup! (English)
www.beaucoup.com/engines.html

Beaucoup! (Main Menu)
www.beaucoup.com

BUBL LINK: Browse by Subject
www.bubl.ac.uk/link/subjects

Inference Find!
www.infind.com

Internet Searching Center
www.clearinghouse.net/searching/index.html

Internet Sleuth (iSleuth.com)
www.isleuth.com

Northern Light
www.northernlight.com

ProFusion
http://profusion.ittc.ukans.edu

Search Engine Watch: News, Tips and More About Search Engines
http://searchenginewatch.com

Spider's Apprentice
www.monash.com/spidap5.html

Spider's Apprentice - How to Use Web Search Engines
www.monash.com/spidap.html

Starting Point
www.stpt.com/default.asp

Starting Point: PowerSearch
http://pwrsrch.stpt.com/cgi-bin/pwrsrch/ms1a.cgi

Yahoo!
www.yahoo.com

Euroferret
Www.euroferret.com

EuroSeek
Www.euroseek.net/page?ifl=uk

Livelink Pinstripe
http://pinstripe.opentext.com

Lycos
www.lycos.com

Lycos Top 5%
http://point.lycos.com

MiningCo
http://home.miningco.com

Mirago - The UK Search Engine
www.mirago.co.uk

searchUK
www.searchuk.com

Thunderstone
http://search.thunderstone.com/texis/websearch

Web Site Search Tools
Www.searchtools.com

Webcrawler
www.webcrawler.com

whatUseek
www.whatuseek.com

SPECIALIZED SEARCH ENGINES

Beaucoup! (Arts/Music/Graphics)
www.beaucoup.com/1artseng.html

Beaucoup! (Computers/Internet/WWW/Programming)
www.beaucoup.com/1comeng.html

Beaucoup! (E-mail)
www.beaucoup.com/1emaeng.html

Beaucoup! (Employment)
www.beaucoup.com/1empeng.html

Beaucoup! (Geographically Specific)
www.beaucoup.com/1geoeng.html

Beaucoup! (Health/Medicine/Foods)
www.beaucoup.com/1heaeng.html

Beaucoup! (Media)
www.beaucoup.com/1medeng.html

Beaucoup! (Politics/Government/Law)
www.beaucoup.com/1poleng.html

Beaucoup! (Science/Nature/Technology)
www.beaucoup.com/1scieng.html

Beaucoup! (Social/Environmental/Political Concerns)
www.beaucoup.com/1enveng.html

Beaucoup! (Software)
www.beaucoup.com/1softeng.html

Beaucoup!
www.beaucoup.com/1refeng.html

SBA - PRO-Net (Procurement Search Engine)
http://pro-net.sba.gov/index2.html

Software

Software found on some of these sites may prove useful in massaging or manipulating business intelligence gathered elsewhere in electronic format.

Adobe Acrobat Reader Download Page from CARRIE: An Electronic Library
http://history.cc.ukans.edu/carrie/acroread.html

CWSApps - 32-bit Internet Agents
http://cws.internet.com/32agents.html

DOWNLOAD.COM • List of Tools & Utilities
www.download.com/PC/Result/TitleList/
0,2,0-d-37-49,00.html

FerretSoft - Free Downloads
www.ferretsoft.com/netferret/download.htm

Jumbo! Download Network
www.jumbo.com

Statistics

Statistics of all types are required for building the knowledge base in your company. Information gathered using this data is crucial for making good business decisions, but must be updated periodically.

COUNTRY-SPECIFIC STATISTICS SITES

1996 National Industry Staffing Pattern Data (US)
http://stats.bls.gov/oes/oes_ispd.htm

1996 Occupational Employment & Wage Data (US)
http://stats.bls.gov/oes/oes_data.htm

Centraal Bureau voor de Statistiek/Statistics Netherlands
www.cbs.nl

Economic Statistics Briefing Room (US)
www.whitehouse.gov/fsbr/esbr.html

Instituto Nacional de Estadistica (Spain)
www.ine.es

Office for National Statistics (UK)
www.ons.gov.uk/ons_f.htm

Statistics Canada
www.stat.can.ca

Statistical Links (Links to many countries)
www.cbs.nl/eng/link/index.htm

Statistical Office of the Republic of Slovenia
www.sigov.si/zrs/index_e.html

Statistical Profile of Canadian Communities
http://ww2.statcan.ca/english/profil

Statistics Bureau & Statistics Center (Japan)
www.stat.go.jp/1.htm

Statistics Bureau & Statistics Center
www.stat.go.jp/1.htm

Statistisk sentralbyrõ (Norway)
www.ssb.no

MISCELLANEOUS

BUBL LINK: Statistical Mathematics
http://link.bubl.ac.uk/statistics

Business information sources on the Internet: Statistical, economic and market information
www.dis.strath.ac.uk/business/market.html

EUROSTAT
http://europa.eu.int/en/comm/eurostat/serven/home.htm

FedStats • One Stop Shopping for Federal Statistics
www.fedstats.gov

FedStats: A to Z
www.fedstats.gov/key.html

International Business Resources on the WWW: Statistical Data & Information Resources
http://ciber.bus.msu.edu/busres/statinfo.htm

Internet Business Library: Economics & Statistics
www.bschool.ukans.edu/intbuslib/economic.htm#reports

National Bureau of Economic Research (NBER)
www.nber.org

NSF • Division of Science Resources Studies
www.nsf.gov/sbe/srs/stats.htm

OECD Statistics
www.oecd.org/statlist.htm

Other Statistical Sites on the World Wide Web
http://stats.bls.gov/oreother.htm

Statistical Abstract of the U.S.
www.census.gov/statab/www

Statistical Resources on the Web
www.lib.umich.edu/libhome/Documents.center/stats.html

Standards & Specifications

BUBL LINK: 389.6 Standardisation
http://link.bubl.ac.uk/standards

ISO Online
www.iso.ch/welcome.html

Safety Link
www.safetylink.com

World-Wide Web Resources - Shaver Engineering Library - Standards
www.uky.edu/Subject/standardsall.html

Yahoo! Reference: Standards
www.yahoo.com/Reference/Standards

Telephone Information

These tools can be used in every department that makes long distance telephone calls. They save time, thereby increasing productivity.

Area Code Changes LinkPage
www.aim-corp.com/swbull/wwareacode.htm#us

Telephone Area Code Finder by MMIWORLD
http://mmiworld.com/statelis.htm

TELEPHONE LOOKUPS

Locate the correct telephone numbers for clients or competitors using tools such as these.

555-1212.com
www.555-1212.com

GTE SuperPages: Interactive Yellow Pages
http://yp.gte.net

International Directories
> www.eu-info.com/inter/world.asp

Telephone Directories on the Web
> www.contractjobs.com/tel

Trade

All aspects of trade can benefit from one or more of these sites. Locating new sources for raw material may improve your company's bottom line, as could locating new markets for finished products. Government import/export related sites have been included here, as well.

Asian Sources Online
> www.asiansources.com

British Exports Interactive – General Information
> http://193.128.244.175:7001/docap/start.html

Business information sources on the internet: Trade directories
> www.dis.strath.ac.uk/business/trade.html

CCx Consignment Tracking Request
> www.ccx.com/cx/vafsr1

Chamber of Commerce (Israel)
> www.chamber.org.il

Commerce Business Daily - Fielded Search via GPO Access
> http://cbdnet.access.gpo.gov/search2.html

Conduct a Fielded Search of the CBD via GPO Access
> http://cbdnet.access.gpo.gov/search2.html

COSMOS
> www.cosmos.com.mx/#trade

Export@ll.net - Your Trade Gateway
> www.exportall.net

Government Information Sharing Project: US Imports/Exports History
> http://govinfo.kerr.orst.edu/impexp.html

Harmonized Tariff Schedule of the United States
> www.customs.ustreas.gov/imp-exp/rulings/harmoniz

IIEINet - Resources - International Trade Links
> www.intlimport-export.com/IIEI%20Links.html

IMF International Monetary Fund
> www.imf.org

Imports: Select Commodity
> http://govinfo.kerr.orst.edu/import/import.html

International Business Resources on the WWW: International Trade Leads
> http://ciber.bus.msu.edu/busres/tradlead.htm

International Trade Administration - Trade Information
> www.ita.doc.gov

Journal of Commerce Online
> www.joc.com/web_indx.htm

Journal of Commerce Top 100
> www.joc.com/special/joc100/index.htm

Schedule B - Commodity Classification - Browse & Search
www.census.gov/foreign-trade/schedules/b

SICE - Foreign Trade Information System
www.sice.oas.org

STAT-USA Internet
www.stat-usa.gov

Trade Data Online
http://strategis.ic.gc.ca/sc_mrkti/tdst/engdoc/tr_h
omep.html

Trade Information Center
www.ita.doc.gov/tic

Trade Leads On Line -Argentina - Business Opportunities - Exporting to or Importing from Argentina and the Mercosur
www.tradeline.com.ar

TradePort - International Trade & Export Assistance
www.tradeport.org

US Department of Commerce: State Exports to Countries and Regions
www.ita.doc.gov/cgi-bin/otea_ctr?task=readfile&file=state-re

US Global Trade Outlook
http://sys1.tpusa.com/dir03/mrktinfo/usglobal

US International Trade Commission: Tariff Database Search
http://205.197.120.17/scripts/tariff.asp

USITC: Trade Resources
www.usitc.gov/tr/tr.htm

IMPORTS/EXPORTS INCLUDING GOVERNMENT SITES

American Export Register
www.aernet.com/english

Bureau of Export Administration Home Page
www.bxa.doc.gov/#index

Canadian Exporters Catalogue
www.worldexport.com

Cd. Juárez, Chihuahua México - Import Export (In Spanish)
www.mexguide.net/cd_juarez/cat_fra/19.html

Ex-Im Bank
www.exim.gov:80/country/country.html

EXIM HomePage (Japan)
www.japanexim.go.jp

Export Administration Regulations Marketplace (EAR)
http://bxa.fedworld.gov

Export Market Information Centre (EMIC) - Home
www.dti.gov.uk/ots/emic

ExporTel
www.exporthotline.com/filefind.htm

Export-Import Bank Home Page
www.exim.gov

INTERDATA Import Export Publications
www.export-leads.com/index.html

Iowa Exporter's Directory
www.state.ia.us/international/expdir/index.html

Serra International, Inc Freight Forwarder
www.serraintl.com

The Commercial Service of the US Department of Commerce
www.ita.doc.gov/uscs

The IEBB Import and Export Trade Leads
www.iebb.com

US Imports/Exports History
http://govinfo.kerr.orst.edu/impexp.html

Travel

If you're in the transportation industry, these sites may provide the scoop on what deals a competitor is currently offering. If you're not in that industry, you may reduce costs by taking advantage of some of the deals found on these sites.

American Airlines
www.americanair.com

Arthur Frommer's . . . Best Current Air Fare Bargains
www.mcp.com/frommers/hottest/airfare

Arthur Frommer's Budget Travel Online
www.mcp.com/frommers

Southwest Airlines Home Gate
http://southwest.com

Travel Microsoft Expedia Travel
http://expedia.msn.com/daily/home/default.hts

Travelocity
www.travelocity.com

US Airways: Low Fares
www.usairways.com/travel/fares/specoff.htm

World Wide Travel Exchange
http://wwte.com

Usenets/Listservs

Monitor these groups to find out what is being said about your company or your competitors. This list of sites will help you to identify lists of interest.

CataList, the official catalog of LISTSERV lists
www.lsoft.com/lists/listref.html

Deja News
www.deja.com

Information Research: Special Interest Groups
http://cn.net.au/sigs.html

Liszt, the mailing list directory
www.liszt.com

Reference.Com Search
www.reference.com

Tile.Net
http://tile.net

Yahoo! Computers & Internet: Internet Mailing Lists

```
www.yahoo.com/computers_and_internet/
internet/mailing_lists
```

Resource List

Locating Data, Databases, or Vendors

Finding Who Has What

After awhile, choosing which source to use becomes second nature. You learn which source would work best for the question at hand. There are times, however, when you need to do one of the following:

♦   Determine (before going online) whether a database file on a service to which you subscribe actually offers the *facts* you need.

♦   Find an alternative source for a database file that you know is available on an "expensive" service.

♦   Validate information already found, using another source.

♦   Locate pieces of information not explicitly required by the project description, but that will be needed to provide a satisfactory answer.

♦   Answer the "Friday Afternoon Question."

To librarians, the "Friday Afternoon Question" is that tough question that comes along when they don't have time to spend hours finding the answer, or boning up on a new subject or industry. It happens something like this:

You (or your team, or the Boss) need the information by (fill in blank with short deadline). You're under a time crunch, just as you might be on Friday afternoon, when your colleagues are leaving for the weekend. There's no "tomorrow" because tomorrow is Saturday, and you can't work late because you have plans for the evening. Nonetheless, you need the answers quickly.

This Resource List is designed to come to your aid. It contains a **sampling** of the resources available in cyberspace for locating intelligence.

The list is divided into four sections:

♦   Data Elements - Look in the alphabetical list for the type of fact you need, and quickly learn the names of database files that contain that type of data, along with the names of one or more online services that offer that database file.

♦   Database Files - This list provides brief descriptions of the database files mentioned in the Data Elements list.

♦ Industry List - This list provides the names of one or more database files that cover each industry, with the names of the online services where the files can be found.

♦ Vendors List - Here you will find contact information for the database vendors mentioned above and for publishers of print materials mentioned elsewhere in the book.

The Resource List will be updated - where else? In cyberspace, of course, at the Burwell Enterprises Web site, www.burwellinc.com. Bookmarks & Favorites will be found there, as well.

Data Elements List

Accountant (Independent) Voting Results
LIVEDGAR   www.gsionline.com

Accountant Opinions
LIVEDGAR   www.gsionline.com

Accountants, Change Of
LIVEDGAR   www.gsionline.com

Advertising /Marketing Firm
Advertiser & Agency Red Books   DIALOG (File 177, 178)

Marketing & Advertising Reference   DIALOG (File 570)
Service (MARS)   InSite Pro
                                           LEXIS-NEXIS

Standard Directory of Advertisers   LEXIS-NEXIS

Advertising Campaigns
Globalbase   DataStar (EBUS)
                                           DIALOG (File 583)

Marketing & Advertising Reference   DIALOG (File 570)
Service (MARS)   InSite Pro
                                           LEXIS-NEXIS

Predicasts Overview of Markets &   DataStar (PTSP)
Technology (PROMT)   DIALOG (File 16)
                                           InSite Pro
                                           LEXIS-NEXIS

Advertising Media
Business & Industry   DIALOG (File 9)
                                           XLS

Marketing & Advertising Reference   DIALOG (File 570)
Service (MARS)   InSite Pro
                                           LEXIS-NEXIS

Advertising Spending
Beverage Marketing   DIALOG (File 770)
                                           Investext: Research Bank Web
                                           Profound

Communications Industry Forecast   XLS

Marketing & Advertising Reference   DIALOG (File 570)
Service (MARS)   InSite Pro
                                           LEXIS-NEXIS

MarketTrack   LEXIS-NEXIS (MKTRES)

Advertising Strategy

Marketing & Advertising Reference   DIALOG (File 570)
Service (MARS)   InSite Pro
                                                              LEXIS-NEXIS

Advertising Techniques

Marketing & Advertising Reference   DIALOG (File 570)
Service (MARS)   InSite Pro
                                                              LEXIS-NEXIS

Analyst Reports

CompanySleuth   www.companysleuth.com

Investext Analyst Reports   Dow Jones Interactive
                                                              DIALOG (File 545)
                                                              Investext: Research Bank Web

Multex Analyst Reports   Dow Jones Interactive
                                                              www.multex.com

Analyst Specialty

Nelson s Specialty Regional Analyst   LEXIS-NEXIS (NELSPE)
Coverage

Analysts (Fixed Income/Securities)

Nelson's Analyst Company Coverage   LEXIS-NEXIS (NELANC)

Annual Meeting Proxy Statements

EDGARPlus - Proxy Statements   DIALOG (File 780)

LIVEDGAR   www.gsionline.com

Annual Reports

EDGARPLus - Annual Reports   DIALOG (File 777)

Awards

Small Business Innovation Research   Knowledge Express
Awards (SBIRs)

Balance Sheets

MG Financial/Stock Statistics   DIALOG (File 546)

MGFS Common Stock Database   XLS

Bank Assets

    Bankstat   XLS

Bankruptcy 8-Ks

    LIVEDGAR   www.gsionline.com

Bankruptcy Records

Bankruptcy File (CBKF)	Infomart Online
CourtLink	Courtlink : www.courtlink.com
New Generation Research	XLS

Banks - Financial Information

    Bankstat   XLS

Best Efforts

    LIVEDGAR   www.gsionline.com

Betas (Stock)

BARRA Global & Single Country Equity Models	www.xls.com
Financial Snapshot	Dow Jones Interactive
Stocksite	www.stocksite.com; See company profile

Board - Classified / Staggered

    LIVEDGAR   www.gsionline.com

Board Size-Increase

    LIVEDGAR   www.gsionline.com

Brand Loyalty

ABI/INFORM	DIALOG (File 15) LEXIS-NEXIS (ABISEL)
Business & Industry	DIALOG (File 9) XLS
IAC: Newsletter Database	DIALOG (File 636)
Marketing & Advertising Reference Service (MARS)	DIALOG (File 570) InSite Pro LEXIS-NEXIS
Predicasts Overview of Markets & Technology (PROMT)	DataStar (PTSP) DIALOG (File 16) InSite Pro

LEXIS-NEXIS

Brand Share

TableBase

DIALOG (File 93)
XLS

Bridge Loans

LIVEDGAR

www.gsionline.com

Broker Reports

CompanySleuth

www.companysleuth.com

Budget Activity

Jane's Information Group

DIALOG (File 587)
DOW JONES (PUB LIBRARY)
LEXIS-NEXIS (JANDEF)

Business Partners

Company Needs/Capabilities

Knowledge Express

Capital Spending

Predicasts Overview of Markets &
Technology (PROMT)

DataStar (PTSP)
DIALOG (File 16)
InSite Pro
LEXIS-NEXIS

Cash Flow

MG Financial/Stock Statistics

DIALOG (File 546)

MGFS Common Stock Database

XLS

Change in Control Tender

LIVEDGAR

www.gsionline.com

Collaborative Research & Development Agreements (CRADAs)

Federal Bio-Technology Transfer
Directory

Knowledge Express

Company History

ABI/INFORM

DIALOG (File 15)
LEXIS-NEXIS (ABISEL)

Hoover's Company Profiles

www.hoovers.com

Company Information

Canadian Corporate Names (CCCN)	Infomart Online
Delphes European Business	DataStar (DELP) DIALOG (File 481) Questel (DELPHES)
FP Corporate Survey (CFPS)	Infomart Online
Toolbox	www.hoovers.com

Company Profiles

Beverage Marketing	DIALOG (File 770) www.investext.com Profound
Bio Pharma Surveys	Knowledge Express
Business Communications Company BCC	DIALOG (File 764); MARKETFULL Investext: Research Bank Web LEXIS-NEXIS Profound
Canadian Corporate Profiles (DCCP)	Infomart Online
Canadian Federal Corporations & Directors (DCFC)	Infomart Online
CorpTech	Internet
Corptech	Knowledge Express
Hoover's Company Profiles	www.hoovers.com
IAC Trade & Industry Database	DIALOG (File 148) InSite Pro LEXIS-NEXIS
Marketline International Market Research Reports	LEXIS-NEXIS (MKTLIN) DataStar (MKTL)
NELCOM Nelson's Public Company Profiles	LEXIS-NEXIS (NELCOM)

Competitive Analysis

Marketline International Market Research Reports	LEXIS-NEXIS (MKTLIN) DataStar (MKTL)

Competitive Intelligence

ABI/INFORM	DIALOG (File 15) LEXIS-NEXIS (ABISEL)
Company Intelligence Database	DIALOG (File 479) InSite Pro LEXIS-NEXIS

Competitive Strategy

Business Trend Analysts (BTA)	www.investext.com
IAC Trade & Industry Database	DIALOG (File 148) InSite Pro LEXIS-NEXIS

Competitors

Asian Business Intelligence	DIALOG (File 568) LEXIS-NEXIS (MKTRES)
Business Trend Analysts (BTA)	www.investext.com
FIND SVP	DIALOG (File 766) LEXIS-NEXIS (MKTRES) XLS
Hoover's Company Profiles	www.hoovers.com
Toolbox	www.hoovers.com

Congress (US)

StateNet	www.statenet.com
Thomas	http://thomas.loc.gov

Consumer Research

Marketing & Advertising Reference Service (MARS)	DIALOG (File 570) InSite Pro LEXIS-NEXIS

Consumer Spending

Communications Industry Forecast	XLS

Consumer Trends

IAC: Newsletter Database	DIALOG (File 636)
Predicasts Overview of Markets & Technology (PROMT)	DataStar (PTSP) DIALOG (File 16) InSite Pro LEXIS-NEXIS

Consumption Figures

Beverage Marketing	DIALOG (File 770) www.investext.com Profound
Globalbase	DataStar (EBUS) DIALOG (File 583)

Contract Awards

Jane's Information Group   DIALOG (File 587)
DOW JONES (PUB LIBRARY)
LEXIS-NEXIS (JANDEF)

Contract Bids

BidAlert   www.bidnet.com

Contribution Agreements

Corporate Family   DIALOG (File 513)
FT Profile

LIVEDGAR   www.gsionline.com

Corporate Governance

Securities Data Company (SDC)   LEXIS-NEXIS (MSTAT)
XLS

Corporate Name Change

LIVEDGAR   www.gsionline.com

Corporate Strategy

Beverage Marketing   DIALOG (File 770)
www.investext.com
Profound

Predicasts Overview of Markets &   DataStar (PTSP)
Technology (PROMT)   DIALOG (File 16)
InSite Pro
LEXIS-NEXIS

Corporate Structure

Inter-Corporate Ownership (CICO)   Infomart Online
Securities Data Company (SDC)   LEXIS-NEXIS (MSTAT)
XLS

Cost Analysis

Business Trend Analysts (BTA)   www.investext.com

Country Profiles

EIU: Country Analysis   LEXIS-NEXIS
Profound
DIALOG (File 627)
FT Profile
Investext: Research Bank Web
(MarkIntel)

Country Risk

EIU: Country Risk & Forecasts

LEXIS-NEXIS
Profound
DIALOG (File 627)
FT Profile
Investext: Research Bank Web
(MarkIntel)

Credit Reports

Creditel Commercial Law Record (CCRE) Infomart Online

Debt Issuing Companies

Indepth Data

XLS

Decrease Authorized Shares

LIVEDGAR

www.gsionline.com

Demographics

FIND SVP

DIALOG (File 766)
XLS

Direct Mail

Business & Industry

DIALOG (File 9)
XLS

Directories

Contact Canada

http://contactcanada.com

Disclosure

Global Access

Disclosure

Distribution Channels

Asian Business Intelligence

DIALOG (File 568)
LEXIS-NEXIS (MKTRES)

Beverage Marketing

DIALOG (File 770)
www.investext.com
Profound

Business Trend Analysts (BTA)

www.investext.com

Corporate & Marketing Intelligence (CAMI) Profound

Marketing & Advertising
Reference Service (MARS)

DIALOG (File 570)
InSite Pro
LEXIS-NEXIS

Marketline International Market
Research Reports

LEXIS-NEXIS (MKTLIN)
DataStar (MKTL)

Distribution Methods

ABI/INFORM	DIALOG (File 15) LEXIS-NEXIS (ABISEL)
IAC Trade & Industry Database	DIALOG (File 148) InSite Pro LEXIS-NEXIS
Investext Analyst Reports	Dow Jones Interactive DIALOG (File 545) Investext: Research Bank Web
Predicasts Overview of Markets & Technology (PROMT)	DataStar (PTSP) DIALOG (File 16) InSite Pro LEXIS-NEXIS

Distribution Networks

Business Communications Company	Investext: Research Bank Web

Dutch Auction

LIVEDGAR	www.gsionline.com

Earnings & Dividends

IAC Trade & Industry Database	DIALOG (File 148) InSite Pro LEXIS-NEXIS

Earnings Announcement (Time Stamped)

Dow Jones Wires	Dow Jones Interactive

Earnings Projections

NELERN Nelson's Consensus Earnings Estimates	LEXIS-NEXIS XLS

Economic Climate

IAC Trade & Industry Database	DIALOG (File 148) InSite Pro LEXIS-NEXIS

Economic Indicators

Predicasts Overview of Markets & Technology (PROMT)	DataStar (PTSP) DIALOG (File 16) InSite Pro LEXIS-NEXIS

Efficiency Levels

Business & Industry	DIALOG (File 9) XLS

Emerging Markets

Emerging Markets	LEXIS-NEXIS (WLDSRC)
ISI Emerging Markets	www.securities.com

Emerging Technologies

Company Technologies	Knowledge Express
Globalbase	DataStar (EBUS) DIALOG (File 583)
Government Technologies	Knowledge Express
IAC: Newsletter Database	DIALOG (File 636)
International Business Opportunities	Knowledge Express
Jane's Information Group	DIALOG (File 587) DOW JONES (PUB LIBRARY) LEXIS-NEXIS (JANDEF)
University Technologies	Knowledge Express

Employee Benefits

Employee Benefits Infosource	DIALOG (File 22) Westlaw

Employees - Number Of

Corptech	Knowledge Express
Hoover's Company Profiles	www.hoovers.com

End-User Packaging

Corporate & Marketing Intelligence (CAMI)	Profound

Environment

IAC: Newsletter Database	DIALOG (File 636)

Environmental Impact Statements

Environmental Impact Statements (EIS) Collection	www.library.nwu.edu/transportatio n/tleis.html

Euro Currency Conversion

LIVEDGAR	www.gsionline.com

Executive Changes

IAC Trade & Industry Database	DIALOG (File 148) InSite Pro LEXIS-NEXIS

Executives By Job Function

Federal Employer Identification Number (FEIN)

CDB Infotek
LEXIS-NEXIS
www.hoovers.com0

Technimetrics Executive Directory (idEXEC)

www.xls.com
www.technimetrics.com

Financial Information

Communications Industry Report

XLS

Corptech

Knowledge Express

FP Corporate Survey (CFPS)

Infomart Online

Globalbase

DataStar (EBUS)
DIALOG (File 583)

IAC Trade & Industry Database

DIALOG (File 148)
InSite Pro
LEXIS-NEXIS

WorldScope

Dow Jones Interactive

Financial Information - In-Depth

Hoover's Company Profiles

www.hoovers.com

Financing Foreign Operations

EIU: Country Analysis

LEXIS-NEXIS
Profound
DIALOG (File 627)
FT Profile
Investext: Research Bank Web (MarkIntel)

Financings

Securities Data Company (SDC)

LEXIS-NEXIS (MSTAT)
XLS

Forecasts

Asian Business Intelligence

DIALOG (File 568)
LEXIS-NEXIS (MKTRES)

Beverage Marketing

DIALOG (File 770)
www.investext.com
Profound

Computer Industry Forecasts

XLS

Corporate & Marketing Intelligence (CAMI)

Profound

EIU Country Risk & Forecasts

LEXIS-NEXIS
Profound

	DIALOG (File 627)
	FT Profile
	Investext: Research Bank Web (MarkIntel)
FIND SVP	DIALOG (File 766)
	XLS
IAC Trade & Industry Database	DIALOG (File 148)
	InSite Pro
	LEXIS-NEXIS
Marketline International Market Research Reports	LEXIS-NEXIS (MKTLIN)
	DataStar (MKTL)
Predicasts Overview of Markets & Technology (PROMT)	DataStar (PTSP)
	DIALOG (File 16)
	InSite Pro
	LEXIS-NEXIS

Forecasts - Sales & Shipments

Computer Industry Forecasts	XLS

Foreign Military Sales (FMS)

Jane's Information Group	DIALOG (File 587)
	DOW JONES (PUB LIBRARY)
	LEXIS-NEXIS (JANDEF)

Going Concern Opinions

LIVEDGAR	www.gsionline.com

Government Policies & Regulations

Globalbase	DataStar (EBUS)
	DIALOG (File 583)
IAC: Newsletter Database	DIALOG (File 636)
Marketing & Advertising Reference Service (MARS)	DIALOG (File 570)
	InSite Pro
	LEXIS-NEXIS
Predicasts Overview of Markets & Technology (PROMT)	DataStar (PTSP)
	DIALOG (File 16)
	InSite Pro
	LEXIS-NEXIS

Grants

Grants	Knowledge Express

Holding Company Information

LIVEDGAR	www.gsionline.com

Hostile Tender

    LIVEDGAR   www.gsionline.com

Income Statements

    MG Financial/Stock Statistics   DIALOG (File 546)

    MGFS Common Stock Database   XLS

Increase Authorized Shares

    LIVEDGAR   www.gsionline.com

Increase Par Value

    LIVEDGAR   www.gsionline.com

Industrial Production

    Industrial Production & Capacity Utilization Data   http://bos.business.uab.edu/browse/frbg17.htm

    Predicasts Overview of Markets & Technology (PROMT)   DataStar (PTSP)
                                 DIALOG (File 16)
                                 InSite Pro
                                 LEXIS-NEXIS

Industry Comparative Data

    MG Financial/Stock Statistics   DIALOG (File 546)

    MGFS Common Stock Database   XLS

Industry Forecasts

    Current Industrial Reports   www.census.gov/pub/cir/www/index.html

    Globalbase   DataStar (EBUS)
                                 DIALOG (File 583)

    TableBase   DIALOG (File 93)
                                 XLS

Industry History

    IAC Trade & Industry Database   DIALOG (File 148)

    Industry Insider.   Investext: Research Bank Web

Industry Information

    Business & Industry   DIALOG (File 9)
                                 XLS

    Industry Insider.   www.insitepro.com

    Toolbox   www.hoovers.com

Industry Profiles

Asia Pulse

Bloomberg
Dow Jones
LEXIS-NEXIS
Profound

Business & Industry

DIALOG (File 9)
XLS

Investext: Research Bank Web

www.investext.com
DIALOG (File 545)

Industry Stucture

Business & Industry

DIALOG (File 9)
XLS

Business Communications Company
BCC

DIALOG (File 764);
MARKETFULL
Investext: Research Bank Web
LEXIS-NEXIS
Profound

Initial Public Offerings

EDGAR Online

www.edgar-online.com

IPO Data Systems

XLS

LIVEDGAR

www.gsionline.com

Securities Data Company (SDC)

DIALOG (File 550)
XLS
LEXIS-NEXIS (MSTAT)

Toolbox

www.hoovers.com

Insider Trading

CompanySleuth

www.companysleuth.com

EDGAR Online

www.edgar-online.com

Installed Base

Computer Industry Forecasts

XLS

Institutional Equity

Vickers Stock Research

www.xls.com

International Arms Acquisitions

Jane's Information Group

DIALOG (File 587)
DOW JONES (PUB LIBRARY)
LEXIS-NEXIS (JANDEF)

Internet Domains

    CompanySleuth   www.companysleuth.com

Inventions

    Federal Bio-Technology   Knowledge Express
    Transfer Directory

Investing

    EIU: Country Analysis   LEXIS-NEXIS
                                        Profound
                                        DIALOG (File 627)
                                        FT Profile
                                        Investext: Research Bank Web
                                        (MarkIntel)

Investment Research Reports

    Investext: Research Bank Web   www.investext.com
                                        DIALOG (File 545)

    Multex   Dow Jones Interactive
                                        www.multex.com

    NELSON (Group File)   LEXIS-NEXIS

    Nelson's Company Research Report   LEXIS-NEXIS (NELREP)
    Headlines

    Zacks Investment Research   www.ultra.zacks.com

Issuer Counsel

    LIVEDGAR   www.gsionline.com

Job Postings

    CompanySleuth   www.companysleuth.com

Joint Marketing partnerships

    Marketing & Advertising Reference   DIALOG (File 570)
    Service (MARS)   InSite Pro
                                          LEXIS-NEXIS

    Small Business Innovation Research   Knowledge Express
    Awards (SBIRs)

Joint Ventures

    Predicasts Overview of Markets &   DataStar (PTSP)
    Technology (PROMT)   DIALOG (File 16)
                                          InSite Pro
                                          LEXIS-NEXIS

    Securities Data Company (SDC)   DIALOG (File 554)

LEXIS-NEXIS (MSTAT)
XLS

Lawsuits - Federal

CompanySleuth   www.companysleuth.com

Lawsuits (Major)

IAC Trade & Industry Database   DIALOG (File 148)
                                                        InSite Pro
                                                        LEXIS-NEXIS

Predicasts Overview of Markets &   DataStar (PTSP)
Technology (PROMT)   DIALOG (File 16)
                                                        InSite Pro
                                                        LEXIS-NEXIS

Lead Finder

Hoover's Company Profiles   www.hoovers.com

Leading Players

Corporate & Marketing Intelligence CAMI Profound

Legislative Tracking (US States)

StateNet   www.statenet.com

License/Sales Agreements

BioScan   Knowledge Express

Federal Laboratory Technologies FLTDB Knowledge Express

Globalbase   DataStar (EBUS)
                                                        DIALOG (File 583)

Government Technologies   Knowledge Express

Marketing & Advertising Reference   DIALOG (File 570)
Service (MARS)   InSite Pro
                                                        LEXIS-NEXIS

Predicasts Overview of Markets &   DataStar (PTSP)
Technology (PROMT)   DIALOG (File 16)
                                                        InSite Pro
                                                        LEXIS-NEXIS

University Technologies   Knowledge Express

Licensing & Trading

EIU: Country Analysis

LEXIS-NEXIS
Profound
DIALOG (File 627)
FT Profile
Investext: Research Bank Web
(MarkIntel)

Licensing Opportunities

Federal Bio-Technology Transfer
Directory

Knowledge Express

List Generator

Hoover's Company Profiles

www.hoovers.com

Lock Up Agreements

LIVEDGAR

www.gsionline.com

Management Techniques

Business Management Practices TM
BAMP TM

DIALOG (File 13)
XLS

IAC Trade & Industry Database

DIALOG (File 148)
InSite Pro
LEXIS-NEXIS

Management Theory & Practice

Trade Industry Database

DIALOG (File 148)
InSite Pro

Manufacturing Capabilities

Company Needs/Capabilities

Knowledge Express

Manufacturing Industries

Business & Industry

DIALOG (File 9)
XLS

Manufacturing Processes (New)

Predicasts Overview of Markets &
Technology (PROMT)

DataStar (PTSP)
DIALOG (File 16)
InSite Pro
LEXIS-NEXIS

Market Analysis

Investext: Research Bank Web

www.investext.com

Marketing & Advertising Reference Service (MARS)

DIALOG (File 570)
InSite Pro
LEXIS-NEXIS

Market Conditions

Delphes European Business

DataStar (DELP)
DIALOG (File 481)
Questel (DELPHES)

IAC: Newsletter Database

DIALOG (File 636)

Market Contrasts

IAC Trade & Industry Database

DIALOG (File 148)
InSite Pro
LEXIS-NEXIS

Market Penetration

Business & Industry

DIALOG (File 9)
XLS

Business Communications Company BCC

DIALOG (File 764);
MARKETFULL
Investext: Research Bank Web
LEXIS-NEXIS
Profound

Globalbase

DataStar (EBUS)
DIALOG (File 583)

IAC Trade & Industry Database

DIALOG (File 148)
InSite Pro
LEXIS-NEXIS

TableBase

DIALOG (File 93)
XLS

Market Research

Investext: Research Bank Web

www.investext.com

Market Segmentation

Asian Business Intelligence

DIALOG (File 568)
LEXIS-NEXIS (MKTRES)

Business Communications Company (BCC)

DIALOG (File 764);
MARKETFULL
Investext: Research Bank Web
LEXIS-NEXIS
Profound

Datamonitor

DataStar (DMON)
DIALOG (File 761)
LEXIS-NEXIS (MKTRES)

Market Share

Beverage Marketing	DIALOG (File 770) www.investext.com Profound
Business Trend Analysts (BTA)	Investext: Research Bank Web
Computer Industry Forecasts	XLS
Computer Product Index	LEXIS-NEXIS (MKTRES)
Datamonitor Market Research	DIALOG (File 761)
Globalbase	DataStar (EBUS) DIALOG (File 583)
Marketing & Advertising Reference Service (MARS)	DIALOG (File 570) InSite Pro LEXIS-NEXIS
Marketline International Market Research Reports	LEXIS-NEXIS (MKTLIN) DataStar (MKTL)
Predicasts Overview of Markets & Technology (PROMT)	DataStar (PTSP) DIALOG (File 16) InSite Pro LEXIS-NEXIS
Register Meal	LEXIS-NEXIS (MKTRES)
ScanTrack	LEXIS-NEXIS (MKTRES)
TableBase	DIALOG (File 93) XLS
World Market Share Reporter	LEXIS-NEXIS (MKTSHR) Investext: Research Bank Web (MarkIntel)

Market Size

Asian Business Intelligence	DIALOG (File 568) LEXIS-NEXIS (MKTRES)
Beverage Marketing	DIALOG (File 770) www.investext.com Profound
Corporate & Marketing Intelligence (CAMI)	Profound
Corporate & Marketing Intelligence (CAMI)	Profound
FIND SVP	DIALOG (File 766) XLS
Globalbase	DataStar (EBUS) DIALOG (File 583)
Marketing & Advertising Reference Service (MARS)	DIALOG (File 570) InSite Pro

	LEXIS-NEXIS
Marketline International Market Research Reports	LEXIS-NEXIS (MKTLIN) DataStar (MKTL)
TableBase	DIALOG (File 93) XLS

Market Trends

| Asian Business Intelligence | DIALOG (File 568) LEXIS-NEXIS (MKTRES) |
| FIND SVP | DIALOG (File 766) XLS |

Marketing Campaigns

| Marketing & Advertising Reference Service (MARS) | DIALOG (File 570) InSite Pro LEXIS-NEXIS |
| Predicasts Overview of Markets & Technology (PROMT) | DataStar (PTSP) DIALOG (File 16) InSite Pro LEXIS-NEXIS |

Marketing Personnel

| Marketing & Advertising Reference Service (MARS) | DIALOG (File 570) InSite Pro LEXIS-NEXIS |

Marketing Strategy

| Business Communications Company BCC | DIALOG (File 764); MARKETFULL Investext: Research Bank Web LEXIS-NEXIS Profound |
| Marketing & Advertising Reference Service (MARS) | DIALOG (File 570) InSite Pro LEXIS-NEXIS |

Merger & Acquisition Data

Firstlist	Knowledge Express
Globalbase	DataStar (EBUS) DIALOG (File 583)
IAC Trade & Industry Database	DIALOG (File 148) InSite Pro LEXIS-NEXIS
Jane's Information Group	DIALOG (File 587) DOW JONES (PUB LIBRARY)

LEXIS-NEXIS (JANDEF)

Mergerstat

LEXIS-NEXIS (MSTAT)
XLS

Predicasts Overview of Markets &
Technology (PROMT)

DataStar (PTSP)
DIALOG (File 16)
InSite Pro
LEXIS-NEXIS

Securities Data Company (SDC)

DIALOG (File 551)
LEXIS-NEXIS (MSTAT)
XLS

New Technologies

Business Communications Company
BCC

DIALOG (File 764);
MARKETFULL
Investext: Research Bank Web
LEXIS-NEXIS
Profound

Business Management Practices TM
BAMP TM

DIALOG (File 13)
XLS

Cambridge Market Intelligence

Profound

Non-SEC Offering Circulars (144a & Reg S)

Non-SEC Offering Circulars (144a & Reg S)   www.gsionline.com

Officers & Directors

Directory of Directors (DDOD)

Infomart Online

Hoover's Company Profiles

www.hoovers.com

IAC Trade & Industry Database

DIALOG (File 148)
InSite Pro
LEXIS-NEXIS

Technimetrics Executive Directory
(FINEX)

www.xls.com

Marquis Who's Who

DIALOG (File 234)
LEXIS-NEXIS (BUSREF,
PEOPLE)

Operating Ratios

MG Financial/Stock Statistics

DIALOG (File 546)

Orders & Contracts (Major)

Predicasts Overview of Markets &
Technology (PROMT)

DataStar (PTSP)
DIALOG (File 16)
InSite Pro
LEXIS-NEXIS

Ownership Data - 5% Equity

The Disclosure/Spectrum Ownership Database	DIALOG (File 540)
Vickers Stock Research	www.xls.com

Ownership Data - Fixed Income

Vickers Stock Research	www.xls.com

Ownership Data - Insider Equity

Vickers Stock Research	www.xls.com

Packaging

Beverage Marketing	DIALOG (File 770) www.investext.com Profound
Marketing & Advertising Reference Service (MARS)	DIALOG (File 570) InSite Pro LEXIS-NEXIS

Patents

CompanySleuth	www.companysleuth.com
Federal Bio-Technology Transfer Directory	Knowledge Express
Government Technologies	Knowledge Express
MicroPatent Alert MPA	Knowledge Express
University Technologies	Knowledge Express

Patents & Copyrights

Predicasts Overview of Markets & Technology (PROMT)	DataStar (PTSP) DIALOG (File 16) InSite Pro LEXIS-NEXIS

People

BioScan	Knowledge Express
CorpTech	Internet
Directory of Directors (DDOD)	Infomart Online
EDGAR Online	www.edgar-online.com
IAC Trade & Industry Database	DIALOG (File 148) InSite Pro LEXIS-NEXIS
IAC: Newsletter Database	DIALOG (File 636)

Magazine Database	DIALOG (File 47)
	InSite Pro
	LEXIS-NEXIS
Marquis Who's Who	DIALOG (File 234)
	NEXIS File=MARQUIS
Standard & Poor's Register - Biographical	DIALOG (File 526)
Technimetrics Executive Directory (FINEX)	www.xls.com

Planned Purchases

Computer Industry Forecasts	XLS

Plants & Facilities (New)

Globalbase	DataStar (EBUS)
	DIALOG (File 583)
Predicasts Overview of Markets & Technology (PROMT)	DataStar (PTSP)
	DIALOG (File 16)
	InSite Pro
	LEXIS-NEXIS

Poison Pills

LIVEDGAR	www.gsionline.com

Pooling of Interests

LIVEDGAR	www.gsionline.com

Price Histories

MG Financial/Stock Statistics	DIALOG (File 546)

Pricing

Datamonitor Market Research	DataStar (DMON)
	DIALOG (File 761)
	LEXIS-NEXIS (MKTRES)

Private Company Information

Company Intelligence Database	DIALOG (File 479)
	InSite Pro
	LEXIS-NEXIS (COMPNY)
Hoover's Company Profiles	www.hoovers.com
Standard & Poor's Register - Corporate	DIALOG (File 527)
TableBase	DIALOG (File 93)
	XLS

Processes

International Business Opportunities — Knowledge Express

Product Brands

Delphes European Business — DataStar (DELP)
DIALOG (File 481)
Questel (DELPHES)

Product Differentiation

IAC Trade & Industry Database — DIALOG (File 148)
InSite Pro
LEXIS-NEXIS

IAC: Newsletter Database — DIALOG (File 636)

Investext: Research Bank Web — www.investext.com

Predicasts Overview of Markets & Technology (PROMT) — DataStar (PTSP)
DIALOG (File 16)
InSite Pro
LEXIS-NEXIS

Product Evaluations

IAC Trade & Industry Database — DIALOG (File 148)
InSite Pro
LEXIS-NEXIS

Product Features & Analysis

Cambridge Market Intelligence — Profound

International Business Opportunities — Knowledge Express

Product Forecasts

TableBase — DIALOG (File 93)
XLS

Product Introductions

ABI/INFORM — DIALOG (File 15)
LEXIS-NEXIS (ABISEL)

Globalbase — DataStar (EBUS)
DIALOG (File 583)

IAC Trade & Industry Database — DIALOG (File 148)
InSite Pro
LEXIS-NEXIS

IAC: New Product Announcements/Plus® — DIALOG (File 621)

IAC: Newsletter Database — DIALOG (File 636)

Marketing & Advertising Reference — DIALOG (File 570)

    Service (MARS)   InSite Pro
                                                   LEXIS-NEXIS

Product Positioning

    Business & Industry   DIALOG (File 9)
                                                   XLS

Product Pricing

    Corporate & Marketing Intelligence   Profound
    (CAMI)

Product Reviews

    IAC Trade & Industry Database   DIALOG (File 148)
                                                     InSite Pro
                                                     LEXIS-NEXIS

Product Search

    CorpTech   Internet

Products

    Datamonitor Market Research   DIALOG (File 761)

Products - End Uses

    Predicasts Overview of Markets &   DataStar (PTSP)
    Technology (PROMT)   DIALOG (File 16)
                                                     InSite Pro
                                                     LEXIS-NEXIS

Products & Services

    Business & Industry   DIALOG (File 9)
                                                   XLS

    Predicasts Overview of Markets &   DataStar (PTSP)
    Technology (PROMT)   DIALOG (File 16)
                                                     InSite Pro
                                                     LEXIS-NEXIS

Profitability Analysis

    Business Trend Analysts (BTA)   www.investext.com

Prospectuses

    EDGARPLus - Prospectuses   Dialog (File 774)

Public Offering to Affiliates

    LIVEDGAR   www.gsionline.com

Rabbi Trusts

LIVEDGAR   www.gsionline.com

Rankings

TableBase   DIALOG (File 93)
                                            XLS

Raw Materials (Availability)

IAC Trade & Industry Database   DIALOG (File 148)
                                            InSite Pro
                                            LEXIS-NEXIS

Predicasts Overview of Markets &   DataStar (PTSP)
Technology (PROMT)   DIALOG (File 16)
                                            InSite Pro
                                            LEXIS-NEXIS

Reduce Par Value

LIVEDGAR   www.gsionline.com

Registration Statements

EDGARPlus - Registration/Statements   DIALOG (File 775)

Reincorporation - (Change of State of Incorporation)

LIVEDGAR   www.gsionline.com

Reorganizations

Predicasts Overview of Markets &   DataStar (PTSP)
Technology (PROMT)   DIALOG (File 16)
                                            InSite Pro
                                            LEXIS-NEXIS

Report on Option Repricing

LIVEDGAR   www.gsionline.com

Requests for Proposals (RFPs)

Jane's Information Group   DIALOG (File 587)
                                            DOW JONES (PUB LIBRARY)
                                            LEXIS-NEXIS (JANDEF)

Research & Development

BioScan   Knowledge Express

Company Needs/Capabilities   Knowledge Express

CORDIS   www.cordis.lu

Government Technologies .... Knowledge Express

Predicasts Overview of Markets & .... DataStar (PTSP)
Technology (PROMT) .... DIALOG (File 16)
InSite Pro
LEXIS-NEXIS

TEKTRAN USDA .... Knowledge Express

University Technologies .... Knowledge Express

Research (Federally Funded)

Federal Research In Progress (FEDRIP) ... Knowledge Express
National Technical Information
Services (NTIS)

Research firm

NELRF Nelson's Research Firm Profiles ... LEXIS-NEXIS

Reverse Stock Split

LIVEDGAR .... www.gsionline.com

Risk Analysis

BARRA Global & Single Country .... www.xls.com
Equity Models

Risk Assessments

EIU Country Risk & Forecasts .... LEXIS-NEXIS
Profound
DIALOG (File 627)
FT Profile
Investext: Research Bank Web
(MarkIntel)

Sales

Predicasts Overview of Markets & .... DataStar (PTSP)
Technology (PROMT) .... DIALOG (File 16)
InSite Pro
LEXIS-NEXIS

Sales By Product

Computer Product Index .... LEXIS-NEXIS (MKTRES)

MarketTrack .... LEXIS-NEXIS (MKTRES)

Register Meal .... LEXIS-NEXIS (MKTRES)

ScanTrack .... LEXIS-NEXIS (MKTRES)

Sales Volume

Beverage Marketing	DIALOG (File 770)
	www.investext.com
	Profound
Globalbase	DataStar (EBUS)
	DIALOG (File 583)
Marketing & Advertising Reference Service (MARS)	DIALOG (File 570)
	InSite Pro
	LEXIS-NEXIS
TableBase	DIALOG (File 93)
	XLS

SEC Filings

CompanySleuth	www.companysleuth.com
EDGAR Online	www.edgar-online.com
Hoover's Company Profiles	www.hoovers.com
Trade Industry Database	DIALOG (File 148)
	InSite Pro

Secondary Offering

LIVEDGAR	www.gsionline.com

Section 16 Non-compliance

LIVEDGAR	www.gsionline.com

Service Industries

Business & Industry	DIALOG (File 9)
	XLS

Service Introductions

Marketing & Advertising Reference Service (MARS)	DIALOG (File 570)
	InSite Pro
	LEXIS-NEXIS

Shareholders - Institutional

Share/World	www.xls.com

Shelf Prospectuses

LIVEDGAR	www.gsionline.com

Shipments

Predicasts Overview of Markets & Technology (PROMT)

DataStar (PTSP)
DIALOG (File 16)
InSite Pro
LEXIS-NEXIS

Short Interest

CompanySleuth

www.companysleuth.com

Spin-off

LIVEDGAR

www.gsionline.com

Stock Performance

Trade Industry Database

DIALOG (File 148)
InSite Pro

Stock Screener

Toolbox

www.hoovers.com

Summary Compensation Tables

LIVEDGAR

www.gsionline.com

Suppliers

Corporate & Marketing Intelligence (CAMI)

Profound

Technologies (New)

Predicasts Overview of Markets & Technology (PROMT)

DataStar (PTSP)
DIALOG (File 16)
InSite Pro
LEXIS-NEXIS

Technology Analysis

Business Trend Analysts (BTA)

www.investext.com

Technology Needs

Company Needs/Capabilities

Knowledge Express

Technology Transfer

Acquisition, Technology Transfer, Licensing & Source of Capital Directory (ATTLAS)

Knowledge Express

Federal Bio-Tech. Transfer Directory

Knowledge Express

Ten Year Option Repricing Charts

    LIVEDGAR   www.gsionline.com

Tenders - Odd Lot

    LIVEDGAR   www.gsionline.com

Tenders - Self

    LIVEDGAR   www.gsionline.com

Trademarks

    CompanySleuth   www.companysleuth.com

Trends

    EIU Country Risk & Forecasts   LEXIS-NEXIS
                                              Profound
                                              DIALOG (File 627)
                                              FT Profile
                                              Investext: Research Bank Web
                                              (MarkIntel)

    Marketline International Market   LEXIS-NEXIS (MKTLIN)
    Research Reports   DataStar (MKTL)

Trends, Consumer

    Beverage Marketing   DIALOG (File 770)
                                                  www.investext.com
                                              Profound

Trends, Demographic

    Business & Industry   DIALOG (File 9)
                                                   XLS

    Marketing & Advertising Reference   DIALOG (File 570)
    Service (MARS)   InSite Pro
                                                  LEXIS-NEXIS

    Predicasts Overview of Markets &   DataStar (PTSP)
    Technology (PROMT)   DIALOG (File 16)
                                                  InSite Pro
                                                LEXIS-NEXIS

    TableBase   DIALOG (File 93)
                                                   XLS

Trends, Industry

    Business & Industry   DIALOG (File 9)
                                                   XLS

    Globalbase   DataStar (EBUS)

	DIALOG (File 583)
IAC Trade & Industry Database	DIALOG (File 148) InSite Pro LEXIS-NEXIS
IAC: Newsletter Database	DIALOG (File 636)
Predicasts Overview of Markets & Technology (PROMT)	DataStar (PTSP) DIALOG (File 16) InSite Pro LEXIS-NEXIS
TableBase	DIALOG (File 93 XLS

Trends, Market

Beverage Marketing	DIALOG (File 770) www.investext.com Profound
Business & Industry	DIALOG (File 9) XLS
Corporate & Marketing Intelligence (CAMI)	Profound
Globalbase	DataStar (EBUS) DIALOG (File 583)
IAC Trade & Industry Database	DIALOG (File 148) InSite Pro LEXIS-NEXIS
TableBase	DIALOG (File 93) XLS

Trends, Pricing

Business Communications Company BCC	DIALOG (File 764); MARKETFULL Investext: Research Bank Web LEXIS-NEXIS Profound
Globalbase	DataStar (EBUS) DIALOG (File 583)
TableBase	DIALOG (File 93) XLS

Underwriter Counsel

LIVEDGAR	www.gsionline.com

Venture Capital

Acquisition, Technology Transfer,	Knowledge Express

Licensing & Source of Capital Directory
(ATTLAS)

Whisper Number

CompanySleuth   www.companysleuth.com

Williams Act Filings

EDGARPlus - Williams Act Filings   DIALOG (File 773)

Year 2000 Compliance Costs

LIVEDGAR   www.gsionline.com

Year 2000 Compliance Statements

LIVEDGAR   www.gsionline.com

Year 2000 Impact Statements

LIVEDGAR   www.gsionline.com

Database Files List

ABI/INFORM
Dialog (File 15)
FT Profile (ABI)
DataStar (INFO)

Includes details on virtually every aspect of business, including company histories, competitive intelligence, and new product development. Database contains bibliographic citations and 25-150 word summaries of articles appearing in professional publications, academic journals, and trade magazines published worldwide. ABI/INFORM indexes and abstracts significant articles from more that 800 business and management periodicals. Full text is included for many of the articles added from January 1991 forward. Twenty-five percent of the journals are published outside the United States.

Acquisition, Technology Transfer, Licensing   Knowledge Express
& Source of Capital Directory (ATTLAS)

Contains information on over 2300 international companies, 5200 US companies and 22,000 healthcare executives. Good for identifying sources, acquiring new products, locating financing, expanding distribution and license technologies.

Advertiser & Agency Red Books
Dialog (File 177, 178)

Records include company name and address, business description, SIC codes, product types, trade names, sales figures, and phone and fax numbers. Additional details include: types of advertising media used, advertising agencies employed by the company, approximate dollars spent in each type of advertising medium, a breakdown of the products handled by each agency employed by the company, and e-mail addresses for key personnel.

AKTRIN Research
Profound

Databases cover the secondary wood products industry, including all aspects of the furniture industry.

Asian Business Intelligence
Dialog (File 568)
LEXIS-NEXIS (MKTRES)

Contains the complete text of detailed local reports focusing on the developing markets, industry and products of Asia.

Asia Pulse
Bloomberg
Dow Jones
LEXIS-NEXIS

Asia Pulse is a real-time business information service geared for business researchers, rather than for use in newsrooms.

Bankstat
XLS

Database of financial information on 10,000 banks in 190 countries.

Bankruptcy DataSource   LEXIS-NEXIS (BDS)
Contains information on US companies with more than $50 million in assets that are in bankruptcy. The file contains company profiles, reorganization plans, and other news. Coverage begins in 1989.

Bankruptcy File (CBKF)   Infomart Dialog
Database contains summary, estate, and status information on approximately 280,000 individual and corporate bankruptcies. It consists of all open files of Canadian bankruptcy records as well as on those files that have been closed since May 1990.

BARRA Global & Single Country Equity Models www.xls.com
The BARRA United States Equity Model Beta Book provides key risk analysis statistics on over 8000 US publicly traded companies in 55 industries. Beta calculations are based on the S&P 500 index.

Beverage Marketing   Dialog (File 770)
                                          www.investext.com
                                          Profound
Contains comprehensive beverage statistics, plus analysis of leading companies in the industry.

Bio/Pharma Surveys   Knowledge Express
European Biopharmaceutical Companies Survey - profiles of emerging European pharmaceutical and biotechnology companies; and National European pharmaceutical Companies Survey - profiles of established, small-to-medium size, pharmaceutical companies.

BioScan   Knowledge Express
Lists US and foreign companies actively involved in biotech research and development. Produced by American Health Consultants.

Business & Industry   Dialog (File 9)
                                          DataStar (BIDB)
                                          XLS
Database contains information with facts, figures, and key events dealing with public and private companies, industries, markets products for all manufacturing and service industries at an international level. B&I coverage concentrates on leading trade magazines/newsletters, general business press, regional newspapers and international business dailies.

Business & Management Practices (BAMP)   Dialog (File 13)
Contains information dealing with the processes, methods, and strategies of managing a business. Coverage focuses on those source publications that deal with management issues or business methodology from a practical approach.

Business Communications Company (BCC)   DIALOG (File 764);
                                          MARKETFULL
                                          Investext: Research Bank Web
Contains market analysis and technical assessments in areas of

advanced materials, high technology, and new technologies.

Business Trend Analysts
Investext: Research Bank Web
Profound

Contains macroeconomic data, competitors, market share, distribution channels, demand, as well as descriptions of technologies and the dynamics of technological change.

Cambridge Market Intelligence
Profound

Covers the information technology industry. For individual technologies, provides product information and analysis.

Canadian Corporate Names (CCCN)
Infomart Dialog

This database provides summary information on over 3 million federal and provincial incorporations and business names from all provinces except British Columbia and Quebec.

Canadian Corporate Profiles (DCCP)
Infomart Dialog

Database provides marketing intelligence on a wide range of Canadian companies and organizations. Records are updated on a regular basis through telephone verification, with ongoing monitoring of press notices for personnel and organizational changes. Data is supplied by Micromedia, the Canadian Corporate Profiles.

Canadian Federal Corporations & Directors (DCFC)
Infomart Dialog

Database contains over 225,000 federally incorporated companies. Records include name, location, details of incorporation, reported revenues, assets and earnings, names and addresses of all directors. The information is supplied by Consumer and Corporate Affairs Canada.

China Business Resources
Investext: Research Bank Web
Profound

Provides market share, forecasts and related data for China, Hong Kong, and Taiwan, covering a number of industries.

ChinaOnline
www.chinaonline.com

Provides business intelligence pertinent to China, including frequently updated industry information, reference materials, government organizational charts, economic news, biographies, and statistics.

Communications Industry Forecast
XLS

Contains quantitative data on end-user and advertising expenditures within each segment of the Communications/Media industry.

Communications Industry Report
XLS

Provides yearly and five-year financial data of the Communications Industry as a whole; performance of each of the 11 segments of the industry; individual performance of a total of 440+ companies in the 11 Communications segments.

Company Needs/Capabilities   Knowledge Express
Contains statements of technology needs, research and development activities from high tech companies in all industries.

Company Technologies   Knowledge Express
Contains abstracts of technologies available for license, collected from emerging high tech companies.

Computer Industry Forecasts   XLS
Contains sales, shipment market size and growth rate data excerpted from high-technology publications. Hundreds of hi-tech products are covered.

Conference Papers Index (CPI)   Dialog (File 77)
Provides access to records of the more than 100,000 scientific and technical papers presented at over 1,000 major regional, national, and international meetings each year. CPI provides a centralized source of information on reports of current research and development from papers presented at conferences and meetings; it provides titles of papers as well as the names and addresses (if available) of the authors of these papers.

Contact Canada   http://contactcanada.com
Database offers Canadian Biotechnology Directory, Pharma & BioPharma & Nutraceuticals Directory, and the Diagnostics & Biotech Directory.

CORDIS   www.cordis.lu
CORDIS databases provide information about Research and Development sponsored and supported by the European Union.

Corporate & Marketing Intelligence (CAMI)   Profound
So. African business research in food & packaging industries. Database includes market trends, forecasts, pricing, more.

CorpTech   Knowledge Express
                                                  www.corptech.com
                                                  Investext: Research Bank
                                                  Web
Contains company address, telephone number, employment data, key contact and title, primary Standard Industrial Classification (SIC) code, a detailed business description, and annual sales data for over 48,000 US technology companies. When a US technology company has a parent company located outside the US, a brief record is provided for the non-US parent. These brief, non-US records do not contain product, history, or performance data.

Creditel Commercial Law Record (CCRE)   Infomart Dialog
Database includes information on commercial legal suits and judgements from courts across Canada. Most of the items are writs and judgements,

but for Newfoundland, Nova Scotia, and New Brunswick, records include liens, mortgages, section 178 of the Bank Act, conditional sales contracts, conveyances, and discharges of liens. Covers legal actions that have been commenced in Canada in the last few years, many of which have become judgments, either defended or undisputed. The court file number almost always appears. Includes over 600,000 records. For most provinces records go back to spring of 1989. Records for Quebec are available from July of 1990 to September 1992 only.

Datamonitor
DataStar (DMON)
DIALOG (File 761)
MARKETFULL)
Contains market research reports that discuss products, the competitive environment, pricing, market share, and other key issues affecting industries. Most records have tables containing valuable facts and figures on companies and products.

Datapro
www.datapro.com
Database including details on over 97,000 products worldwide, including all the leading vendors in the information technology industry.

Delphes European Business
DataStar (DELP)
Dialog (File 481)
Questel (DELPHES)
This is considered the leading French database on markets, products, and companies. It contains bibliographic citations and informative abstracts on virtually every aspect of European business.

Directory of Directors (DDOD)
Infomart Dialog
Database provides information on approximately 15,500 Canadian business men and women; directors and executives of Canadian companies who reside in Canada. Information is provided by the individuals themselves or by their companies.

Disclosure
Dow Jones Interactive
Provides company financial and management information using a large collection of real-time and historical company filings; updates and analysis of insider trading; research reports, and business news from over 2,500 publications and newswires.

Dow Jones Wires
Dow Jones Interactive
Provides timely access to newswires covering the US, Canada, and the rest of the world.

Dun's Market Identifiers
Dialog (File 516)
Contains basic company data, executive names and titles, corporate linkages, D-U-N-S Numbers, organization status, and other marketing information on over ten million US business establishment locations, including public, private, and government organizations.

EDGAR-Online
www.edgar-online.com
Provides SEC electronic corporate filings and related business

intelligence tools. Premium subscription offers as real time SEC filings, 144 Insider Transaction filings, the ability to view presentation-quality SEC filings in popular word processor format, and drill-down tools like EDGAR Online People and EDGAR Online Glimpse.

EIU: Country Analysis   LEXIS-NEXIS
                                                              Profound
                                                              Dialog (File 627)

Database provides useful background for operating in 180 countries.

EIU: Country Risk & Forecasts   LEXIS-NEXIS
                                                              Profound
                                                              Dialog (File 627)

Database contains full text of the EIU's premium Country Risk Service and Country Forecasts. The Country Risk Service provides analysis of the short- and medium-term economic creditworthiness of over 90 countries. Country Forecasts gives a medium-term outlook into economic, political and business trends in 58 countries.

Encyclopedia of Associations   Dialog (File 114)
                                                              LEXIS-NEXIS (BUSREF)

Comprehensive source of detailed information on over 81,000 nonprofit membership organizations worldwide. The database provides addresses and descriptions of professional societies, trade associations, labor unions, cultural/religious organizations, fan clubs, groups of all types.

Environmental Impact Statements (EIS)   www.library.nwu.edu/
Collection   transportation/tleis.html

The Transportation Library, at holds nearly all the EIS's issued by federal agencies since 1969, often in draft as well as final form, and such related documents as environmental assessments, findings of no significant impact, records of decisions, etc.

Federal Bio-Technology Transfer Directory   Knowledge Express

Contains records about biotechnology and pharmaceutical licensing opportunities as well as technology transfer information on inventions, Collaborative Research and Development Agreements, patent licenses. Describes all federal biomedical basic biotechnology related inventions and technology transfers since 1980.

Federal Laboratory Technologies (FLTDB)   Knowledge Express

Contains descriptions of technologies available for licensing from various government agencies. Also contains historical data on past opportunities.

Federal Research In Progress (FEDRIP)   Knowledge Express
                                                 National Technical Information
                                                 Services (NTIS)

Abstracts describe the basis of the research and recent results. Compiled from input by Federal agencies. Includes title, investigator, contact information, funding agency, award amount, award number, description of research, and project status.

FIND/SVP Dialog (File 766)

Contains the full text of market studies from FIND/SVP and Packaged Facts. Reports cover the current and historical size and growth of the market, forecasts of the future market size and growth, assessments of market trends and opportunities, global market trends, profiles of influential competitors, and other pertinent market-related information.

Firstlist Knowledge Express

Merger and acquisition opportunities abound here, with profiles of both buyers and businesses available for sale, lists of companies seeking financing, and more.

FP Corporate Survey (CFPS) Infomart Dialog

Database combines the contents of The Financial Post Survey of Mines and Energy Resources and Survey of Industrials. The database publicly provides detailed corporate and investment information on all companies publicly traded in Canada, as well as information on close to 8,000 subsidiaries and affiliates.

FreeEDGAR www.FreeEDGAR.com

Provides convenient searching and navigation features to access SEC filings filed through the SEC's EDGAR system. FreeEDGAR's Watchlist offers e-mail notification of filings. FreeEDGAR generates an Excel spreadsheet from any table in a filing.

Frost & Sullivan Market Intelligence Dialog (File 765)
XLS

Contains in-depth analyses and forecasts of technical market trends. Reports contain five-year forecasts of market size by product category and end-user application. Discusses marketing and distribution strategies, as well as assessments of the competitive and legislative environment. European, US, and worldwide coverage. Studies are organized by geographic region and include an Executive Summary, Introduction, Scope and Methodology, Technical Review, Current Product Characteristics, End-user/Application Analysis, Competitor Market Shares and Profiles, Five-Year and Interim Forecast by Major National Market, Product Group and End-user/Application, Trends and Opportunities, and company names and addresses.

Global Access Disclosure

Provides data from the Disclosure database, combined with information from several other sources to help identify investment opportunities, perform competitive analysis, qualify M&A prospects, assess corporate finances, manage investment risk, track insider trading activity, monitor corporate activity, or perform case studies.

Globalbase Dialog (File 583)
DataStar (EBUS)
FT Profile (GLB)

Contains abstracts with summary of facts and figures from original article. Non-English titles have English language abstracts.

Government Technologies   Knowledge Express
Contains abstracts describing technologies collected from various US federal laboratories.

Grants   Knowledge Express
Contains data on grants from programs supporting disciplines in the sciences, arts, and community development.

Hoover's Company Profiles   www.hoovers.com
Members-only service contains company profiles, lead finder, in-depth financials, full lists of officers, real-time SEC documents, and Power Tool for list creation.

IAC: Company Intelligence   Dialog (File 479)
DataStar (INCO)
LEXIS-NEXIS - (CIUS)
Contains current address, financial, and marketing information on more than 140,000 private and public US companies and 30,000 international companies. Good for privately held companies not easily researched elsewhere.

IAC Marketing & Advertising   Dialog (File 570)
Reference Service (MARS)   InSite Pro
LEXIS-NEXIS
Contains abstracts and full-text records on advertising and marketing issues for a wide variety of consumer products and services. Includes market size and market share information. Also used to locate new product or service introductions, evaluate markets for existing products or services, and research the marketing and advertising strategies of competitors.

IAC New Product   Dialog (File 621)
Announcements/Plus   DataStar (PTNP)
FT Profile (PRP)
Contains the full text of press releases from all industries covering announcements elated to products, with a focus on new products and services.

IAC Newsletter Database   Dialog (File 636)
Contains the full text of specialized industry newsletters providing information on companies, products, markets, and technologies; trade and geopolitical regions of the world. Also covers government funding, rulings, and regulation and other legislative activities which impact the industries and regions covered.

IAC PROMT   Dialog (File 16)
DataStar (PTSP)
FT Profile (PRP)
Covers business and industry events, trends, issues, and relationships. Trends subject matter includes market, production, shipment, and sales information; major orders and contracts; and imports/exports.

Inter-Corporate Ownership (CICO)   Infomart Dialog

Database provides information on Canadian corporate structures. It is compiled from documents filed by companies under the Corporations and Labour Unions Returns Act (CALURA). The database includes every corporation that is carrying on business in Canada or incorporated under a federal or provincial law, whose gross revenues exceed $15 million or whose assets exceed $10 million.

International Business Opportunities   Knowledge Express

Records describe products and processes available for licensing from 2000 universities, government agencies, research institutes and companies worldwide.

INternational PAtent DOcumentation   Dialog (File 345)
Center - INPADOC   STN

Brings together information on priority application numbers, countries and dates, and equivalent patents (i.e., patent families) for patents issued by 66 countries and organizations. Legal status information is provided for 22 countries.

Investext Analyst   Dow Jones Interactive
Reports   Dialog (File 545)
        LEXIS-NEXIS (COMPNY)

Contains the full text of 700,000 company, industry, and geographic research reports written by analysts at more than 300 leading investment banks, brokerage houses and consulting firms worldwide. Provides in-depth analysis and data on approximately 50,000 publicly traded companies, including sales and earnings forecasts, market share projections and research and development expenditures. Other Investext reports analyze specific industries/products and businesses in geographic regions. The reports are useful for market research, strategic planning, competitive analysis, and financial forecasting.

Investext: Research Bank Web   www.investext.com

The Investext Group provides company, industry and market analysis, with nearly two million research reports direct from over 500 investment banks, 70 market research firms and 180 trade associations worldwide.

IPO Data Systems   XLS

Provides deal information on over 2000 public offerings and S&L conversions.

ISI Emerging Markets   www.securities.com

Database contains news, company and financial data direct from emerging markets.

Jack O'Dwyer's Newsletter   LEXIS-NEXIS

Covers the general news and trends of the PR industry; also provides editorial comment. Special sections of the newsletter cover job changes and promotions of PR professionals; new accounts added by PR firms; news of PR service firms; news of PR counseling firms; honors received by PR people; changes of address of PR firms and PR service firms.

Jack O'Dwyer's PR Services Report   LEXIS-NEXIS

Provides general news features about the public relations industry. Current trends in PR practice by professionals at PR firms and corporate PR departments are highlighted. News of new PR firms, executive appointments and new products are regular features.

Jane's Defense & Aerospace News/Analysis   Dialog (File 587)
DOW JONES (PUB LIBRARY)

Offers business intelligence involving the defense industry.

JICST-E Plus   DataStar
Dialog
STN

Database contains English language citations and abstracts covering literature published in Japan in all fields of science, technology and medicine. Also contains "preview" section of non-indexed records that will subsequently be indexed.

LIVEDGAR   www.gsionline.com

Databases provide for search and retrieval of real-time SEC filings, watch service for anticipated filings, and retrieval of exhibits.

Marketline International Market   DataStar (MKTL)
Research Reports

Database provides up-to-date, concise analysis and forecasts for numerous market sectors around the world.

MarketTrack   LEXIS/NEXIS
Investext:Research Bank Web

Provides tracking service for Canadian grocery markets.

Marquis Who's Who   Dialog (File 234)
LEXIS-NEXIS (BUSREF, PEOPLE)

Records can include vital statistics; education; family background; religious and political affiliation; home and office address; career history; creative works; civic and political activities; professional and club memberships.

Media General Financial Services   XLS

Contains financial performance data on 7000+ public companies.

MG Financial/Stock Statistics   Dialog (File 546)
XLS

Database contains annual and quarterly Balance Sheets, Income Statements and Statement of Cash Flows for over 9000 publicly traded companies on the NYSE, AMEX and NASDAQ (includes National Market & Small Cap Stocks; does not include OTC Bulletin Board or Pink Sheets).

MicroPatent Alert (MPA)   Knowledge Express
Contains summary information from all granted US patents since 1975.

Multex   Dow Jones Interactive
                                                www.multex.com
Multex offers online access to over 850,000 research reports and other
investment information from more than 400 leading investment banks,
brokerage firms and third-party research providers worldwide. Real-time
or delayed delivery are available for multimedia and rich-text research
reports, with print, fax, or e-mail options.

NELCOM Nelson's Public Company Profiles   LEXIS-NEXIS (NELCOM)
Nelson's Public Company Profiles contain brief descriptions of 22,000
publicly traded corporations worldwide and include contact information,
key executives and business descriptions. US companies include those
traded on the NYSE, and NASDAQ, plus any OTC and NASDAQ small
cap stocks with analyst coverage. Non-US companies include ADRs
(American Depository Receipts) as well.

NELSON   LEXIS-NEXIS
Nelson's Investment Research gives you a research edge on over
22,000 stocks worldwide. Complete analyst coverage assignments of
over 7500 research firms -representing 1,000 offices and over 9000
security analysts. Profiles of over 9000 US and 13,000 non-US public
companies including business description, 5-year operating summary,
complete address, phone and fax numbers, plus over 100,000 key
corporate executives.

Nelson's Analyst Company Coverage   LEXIS-NEXIS (NELANC)
Details over 10,000 different equity and fixed income securities analysts
who follow more than 22,000 publicly traded corporations worldwide;
includes contact information and company and industry coverage.

Nelson's Consensus Earnings Estimates   LEXIS-NEXIS (NELER)
                                                XLS
Nelson's Consensus Earnings Estimates Nelson provides consensus
earnings estimates and related statistics for over 6000 US and 7,000
non-US corporations. The information is compiled from the individual
estimates of hundreds of research firms.   Estimates older than 90 days
are NOT included in the consensus.

NELSON (Group File)   LEXIS-NEXIS
Nelson's Company Research Report Headlines is the "Master Index" of
nearly every research report published worldwide by more than 700
investment banks, brokers and independent research firms. More than
200,000 reports are catalogued each year - covering more than 14,000
different public companies, 97 different industries and specialties in nine
global regions. A description (headline/title) is provided for each report.

Nelson's Research Firm Profiles LEXIS-NEXIS (NELRF)

Research Firm Profiles comprise descriptions of over 750 investment banks, brokerage firms and independent research firms worldwide. Information includes contact information, key executives and analysts (research, sales and trading - both equity and fixed income) as well as research service offered.

Nelson's Company Research Report Headlines LEXIS-NEXIS (NELREP)

Nelson's Company Research Report Headlines is the "Master Index" of nearly every research report published worldwide by more than 700 investment banks, brokers and independent research firms. More than 200,000 reports are catalogued each year - covering more than 14,000 different public companies, 97 different industries and specialties in nine global geographic regions. A brief description (headline/title) is provided for each report.

Nelson's Specialty/ Regional Analyst Coverage LEXIS-NEXIS (NELSPE)

Nelson's Company Research Report Headlines is the "Master Index" of nearly every research report published worldwide by more than 700 investment banks, brokers and independent research firms. More than 200,000 reports are catalogued each year - covering more than 14,000 different public companies, 97 different industries and specialties in nine global geographic regions. A brief description (headline/title) is provided for each report.

ScanTrack LEXIS/NEXIS
Investext:Research Bank Web

Provides tracking service for US

Small Business Innovation Knowledge Express
Research Awards (SBIRs)

Contains information on current SBIR award recipients.

Standard & Poor's Register - Biographical Dialog (File 526)
LEXIS-NEXIS (SPBIO)

Provides personal and professional data on approximately 70,000 key business executives. Most officers and directors included in the file are affiliated with public or private, US or non-US companies with sales of $1 million dollars or more.

Standard & Poor's Register - Corporate Dialog (File 527)
LEXIS-NEXIS (SPCORP)

Covers all public companies and private companies with annual sales greater than $1 million or more than 50 employees. Provides important business facts on over 56,000 leading public and private corporations, including current address, financial and marketing information, and a listing of officers and directors with positions and departments.

StateNet www.statenet.com

State Net monitors 100% of all pending bills and regulations in the 50 states and Congress. Government affairs managers can track activity on their issues in the 50 states.

TableBase   Dialog (File 93)

Contains tabular information dealing with companies, products, industries, brands, markets, demographics, and countries from around the world. All records contain a table and the originating textual article when available.

Technimetrics Executive Directory (FINEX)   www.xls.com

This database identifies over 300,000 executive decision-makers from the top 55,000 public and private organizations in 152 countries. Executives are identified by specific job functions rather than titles alone.

Teikoku Databank: Dialog (File 502)
Japanese Companies   DataStar (TOKU)
                                                 Investext: Research Bank
                                                 Web

This directory of Japanese Companies provides information for approximately 220,000 Japanese companies. Information for these companies includes current address, telephone number, financial and employment data, and executive officer information. Full and condensed Balance Sheets and Income Statements are available for about 120,000 companies.

TEKTRAN/USDA   Knowledge Express

Contains summaries of the latest research results and pre-publication abstracts from USDA's Agricultural Research Service.

The Disclosure/Spectrum Ownership   Dialog (File 540)

Contains public corporate ownership information generated from the Disclosure (File 100) database and from three publications containing data produced by CDA/Spectrum: Spectrum 3 (institutional holdings), Spectrum 5 (5% ownership holdings), and Spectrum 6 (ownership by insiders). This database details the common stock holdings of major institutions, corporate insiders, and 5% beneficial owners for over 6,000 companies. The data indicate specific institutions and individuals, their relationship to the company, their holdings, and their most recent trades.

The Toolbox   www.hoovers.com

Free version of the Hoover's database. Contains company name and address, company type, key numbers, employees, key personnel, IPO Central, Stockscreener, List of Lists, Industry Zone, Career Center, and more.

Trade & Industry   Dialog (File 148)
Database   InSite Pro
                                                 LEXIS-NEXIS

Provides strong international coverage of over 65 major industries, including companies, products, and markets.

University Technologies   Knowledge Express

Contains abstracts of collaborative research and license opportunities from 150+ US and foreign universities and non-profit research institutes.

Vickers Stock Research   XLS

Includes Institutional Equity and Fixed Income Ownership data, 5% Equity Ownership data, and Insider Equity Ownership data, delivers single security report with information from a variety of sources, including 13F Filings, voluntary filings, share registers, 13D&G, forms 3, 4 and 144.

World Market Share Reporter   Investext: Research Bank Web

Contains market share data for industries or services, arranged by SIC code with indexes to products, companies, and brands.

Worldscope   Dow Jones Interactive

Contains financials on 11,000 non-US companies, offering either profiles or snapshots of these companies.

▬▬ Database File Coverage of Industries

Accounting

ABI/INFORM   DIALOG (File 15)

Advanced Materials

Business Communications Company   DIALOG (File 764);
(BCC)   MARKETFULL

FIND/SVP   DIALOG (File 766)

Aerospace & Defense

Frost & Sullivan Market Intelligence   DIALOG (File 765)

Agriculture / Agribusiness

Business & Industry   DIALOG (File 9)

TEKTRAN/USDA   Knowledge Express

Agriculture Products

Asian Business Intelligence   DIALOG (File 568)

Apparel

IAC Marketing & Advertising Reference   DIALOG (File 570)
Service (MARS)

Automotive

ChinaOnline   www.chinaonline.com

Aviation

China Business Resources   Investext: Research Bank Web

Banking

Bankstat   XLS

Beverages

Beverage Marketing   DIALOG (File 770)

Biotechnology

BioScan   Knowledge Express

Contact Canada   http://contactcanada.com

Federal Bio-Technology Transfer Directory Knowledge Express

Globalbase DIALOG (File 583)

Chemicals

Corporate & Marketing Intelligence (CAMI) Profound

Chemistry

Conference Papers Index (CPI) DIALOG (File 77)

Communications

Communications Industry Forecast XLS

Computer Hardware

Computer Industry Forecasts XLS

Consumer Products & Services

Business Trend Analysts Investext: Research Bank Web

Datamonitor DataStar (DMON)

Data Communications

Cambridge Market Intelligence Profound

Defense

Jane's Defense & Aerospace DIALOG (File 587)
News/Analysis

Trade & Industry Database DIALOG (File 148)

Energy

FP Corporate Survey (CFPS) Infomart DIALOG

Engineering

Federal Research In Progress (FEDRIP) Knowledge Express

Financial

Disclosure Dow Jones Interactive

Dow Jones Wires Dow Jones Interactive

Dun's Market Identifiers DIALOG (File 516)

Global Access Disclosure

Food & Beverage

Marketline International Market Research Reports	DataStar (MKTL)

Furniture Industry

AKTRIN Research	Profound

Grocery/Supermarket Products

MarketTrack	LEXIS-NEXIS
ScanTrack	LEXIS-NEXIS

Healthcare

Acquisition, Technology Transfer, Licensing & Source of Capital Directory	Knowledge Express

High Technology

Company Needs/Capabilities	Knowledge Express
Company Technologies	Knowledge Express
CorpTech	Knowledge Express

Information Technology

Datapro	www.datapro.com

Law

StateNet	www.statenet.com

Medicine

JICST-E Plus	DataStar

Multi-Industry

Advertiser & Agency Red BooksTM	DIALOG (File 177, 178)
Asia Pulse	Bloomberg
Bankruptcy DataSource	LEXIS-NEXIS (BDS)
Bankruptcy File (CBKF)	Infomart DIALOG
BARRA Global & Single Country Equity Models	www.xls.com
Business &Management Practices (TM) (BAMP)(TM)	DIALOG (File 13)
Canadian Corporate Names (CCCN)	Infomart DIALOG
Canadian Corporate Profiles (DCCP)	Infomart DIALOG

Canadian Federal Corporations & Directors (DCFC)	Infomart DIALOG
CORDIS	www.cordis.lu
Creditel Commercial Law Record (CCRE)	Infomart DIALOG
Delphes European Business	DataStar (DELP)
Directory of Directors (DDOD)	Infomart DIALOG
EDGAR-Online	www.edgar-online.com
EIU: Country Analysis	LEXIS-NEXIS
EIU: Country Risk And Forecasts	LEXIS-NEXIS
Encyclopedia of Associations	DIALOG (File 114)
Environmental Impact Statements (EIS) Collection	
Federal Laboratory Technologies (FLTDB)	Knowledge Express
Firstlist	Knowledge Express
FreeEDGAR	www.FreeEDGAR.com
Government Technologies	Knowledge Express
Grants	Knowledge Express
Hoover's Company Profiles	www.hoovers.com
IAC New Product Announcements/Plus	DIALOG (File 621)
IAC Newsletter Database	DIALOG (File 636)
IAC PROMT	DIALOG (File 16)
IAC: Company Intelligence	DIALOG (File 479)
Inter-Corporate Ownership (CICO)	Infomart DIALOG
International Business Opportunities	Knowledge Express
INternational PAtent DOcumentation Center - INPADOC	DIALOG (File 345)
Investext Analyst Reports	Dow Jones Interactive
Investext: Research Bank Web	www.investext.com
IPO Data Systems	XLS
ISI Emerging Markets	www.securities.com
LIVEDGAR	www.gsionline.com
Marquis Who's Who	DIALOG (File 234)
Media General Financial Services	XLS
MG Financial/Stock Statistics	DIALOG (File 546)
MicroPatent Alert (MPA)	Knowledge Express
Multex	Dow Jones Interactive

NELCOM Nelson's Public Company Profiles	LEXIS-NEXIS (NELCOM)
NELSON	LEXIS-NEXIS
NELSON (Group File)	LEXIS-NEXIS
Nelson's Analyst Company Coverage	LEXIS-NEXIS (NELANC)
Nelson's Company Research Report Headlines	LEXIS-NEXIS (NELREP)
Nelson's Consensus Earnings Estimates	LEXIS-NEXIS (NELERN)
Nelson's Research Firm Profiles	LEXIS-NEXIS (NELRF)
Nelson's Specialty/ Regional Analyst Coverage	LEXIS-NEXIS (NELSPE)
Small Business Innovation Research Awards (SBIRs)	Knowledge Express
Standard & Poor's Register - Biographical	DIALOG (File 526)
Standard & Poor's Register - Corporate	DIALOG (File 527)
TableBase	DIALOG (File 93)
Technimetrics Exec. Directory (FINEX)	www.xls.com
Teikoku Databank: Japanese Companies	DIALOG (File 502)
The Disclosure/Spectrum Ownership	DIALOG (File 540)
The Toolbox	www.hoovers.com
University Technologies	Knowledge Express
Vickers Stock Research	XLS
World Market Share Reporter	Investext: Research Bank Web

Pharmaceutical

Bio/Pharma Surveys	Knowledge Express

Public Relations

Jack O'Dwyer's Newsletter	LEXIS-NEXIS
O'Dwyer's PR Services Report	LEXIS-NEXIS

Publishing

Communications Industry Forecast	XLS
Communications Industry Report	XLS
Globalbase	DIALOG (File 583)
	DataStar (EBUS)
	FT Profile (GLB)
IAC Marketing & Advertising Reference Service (MARS)	DIALOG (File 570)
	InSite Pro
	LEXIS-NEXIS

Pulp & Paper

Business & Industry	DIALOG (File 9)
	DataStar (BIDB) XLS

Real Estate

ABI/INFORM	DIALOG (File 15)
	FT Profile (ABI)
	DataStar (INFO)
ChinaOnline	www.chinaonline.com

Recorded Music

Communications Industry Forecast	XLS
Communications Industry Report	XLS

Restaurants

IAC Marketing & Advertising Reference	DIALOG (File 570)
Service (MARS)	InSite Pro
	LEXIS-NEXIS

Retailing

Business & Industry	DIALOG (File 9)
	DataStar (BIDB) XLS
FIND/SVP	DIALOG (File 766)
Marketline International Market Research	DataStar (MKTL)
Reports	
Trade & Industry Database	DIALOG (File 148)
	InSite Pro LEXIS-NEXIS

Science & Technology

JICST-E Plus	DataStar
	DIALOG STN

Security & Access Controls

Frost & Sullivan Market Intelligence	DIALOG (File 765) XLS

Software Development

Cambridge Market Intelligence	Profound

Subassemblies & Components

CorpTech	Knowledge Express
	www.corptech.com
	Investext: Research Bank Web

Subscription Video Services

Communications Industry Forecast	XLS
Communications Industry Report	XLS

Taxation

ABI/INFORM	DIALOG (File 15) FT Profile (ABI) DataStar (INFO)

Telecommunications

ABI/INFORM	DIALOG (File 15) FT Profile (ABI) DataStar (INFO)
Asian Business Intelligence	DIALOG (File 568) LEXIS-NEXIS (MKTRES)
Business & Industry	DIALOG (File 9) DataStar (BIDB) XLS
Cambridge Market Intelligence	Profound
China Business Resources	Investext: Research Bank Web Profound
ChinaOnline	www.chinaonline.com
Frost & Sullivan Market Intelligence	DIALOG (File 765) XLS
Globalbase	DIALOG (File 583) DataStar (EBUS) FT Profile (GLB)
Marketline International Market Research Reports	DataStar (MKTL)
Trade & Industry Database	DIALOG (File 148) InSite Pro LEXIS-NEXIS

Telecommunications & Internet

CorpTech	Knowledge Express www.corptech.com Investext: Research Bank Web

Television & Radio Broadcasting

Communications Industry Forecast	XLS
Communications Industry Report	XLS

Test & Measurement

CorpTech	Knowledge Express www.corptech.com Investext: Research Bank Web

Textiles

Frost & Sullivan Market Intelligence	DIALOG (File 765) XLS

Tobacco & Cigarettes

Corporate & Marketing Intelligence (CAMI)	Profound

Toiletries & Cosmetics

Corporate & Marketing Intelligence (CAMI)	Profound

Transportation

ABI/INFORM	DIALOG (File 15)
	FT Profile (ABI)
	DataStar (INFO)
Asian Business Intelligence	DIALOG (File 568)
	LEXIS-NEXIS (MKTRES)
Business & Industry	DIALOG (File 9)
	DataStar (BIDB) XLS
China Business Resources	Investext: Research Bank Web
	Profound
ChinaOnline	www.chinaonline.com
CorpTech	Knowledge Express
	www.corptech.com Investext: Research Bank Web

Veterinary Medicine

Frost & Sullivan Market Intelligence	DIALOG (File 765) XLS
TEKTRAN/USDA	Knowledge Express

Waste Management

FIND/SVP	DIALOG (File 766)

Water Treatment

FIND/SVP	DIALOG (File 766)

Wood Products

AKTRIN Research	Profound

Online Vendors & Publishers

Database Producers

A.C. Nielsen Corporation

177 Broad St.
Stamford CT 06901
(203) 961-3000
Fax: (203) 961-3340
www.acnielsen.com

AKTRIN Research Institute

151 Randall St.
Oakville ON
(905) 845-3474
Fax: (905) 845-7459
www.aktrin.com

Beverage Marketing Corporation

850 Third Ave.
New York NY 10022
(212) 688-7640
Fax: (212) 826-1255
www.beveragemarketing.com

Business Communications Company (BCC)

25 Van Zant St.
Norwalk CT 06855
(203) 853-4266
Fax: (203) 853-0348
www.buscom.com

Business Trend Analysts

2171 Jerico Turnpike
Commack NY 11725
(516) 462-1842
Fax: (516) 462-1842
www.businesstrendanalysts.com

Cambridge Market Intelligence

Letts of London House
Parkgate Road
London England SW11 4NQ
44 171-924-7117
Fax: 44 171-403-6729
www.cmi.co.uk

Cambridge Scientific Abstracts

7200 Wisconsin Avenue
Bethesda MD 20814
301-961-6727
800-843-7751
Fax: 301-961-6720

China Business Resources Co. Ltd.

Room 3103, Hong Kong Plaza
188 Connaught Road West
852 2559-1399
Fax: 852 2540-8379
www.hk.super.net/~cbr

Collector Trends Analysis, Inc.

PO Box 361
Dayton OH 45409
937-885-9649
Fax: 937-885-9541

Corporate Technology Information Services, Inc (CorpTech)

12 Alfred St., Suite 200
Woburn MA 01801
800-333-8036 or 781-932-3100
Fax: 781-932-6335
www.corptech.com

Databank SpA

Via dei Piatti 11
I-20123 Milano
39 2-809556
Fax: 39 2-8056495

Datamonitor

1 Park Avenue, 14th Floor
New York NY 10016-5802
212-686-7400
Fax: 212-686-2626
www.datamonitor.com

Decision Resources

Bay Colony Corporate Center
1100 Winter Street
Waltham MA 02151-1238
781-487-3700
Fax: 781-487-5750
www.dresources.com

Disclosure

5161 River Road
Bethesda MD 20816
800-754-9690
Fax: 301-951-1753
www.disclosure.com

Drewery Shipping Consultants Ltd.

11 Heron Quay
London E14 9YP
44 171-538-0191
Fax: 44 171-987-9396

Economist Intelligence Unit

The Economist Building
111 West 57th Street
New York NY 10019
212-554-0600
Fax: 212-586-1181
www.eiu.com

Electric Power Research Institute (EPRI)

3412 Hillview Avenue
Palo Alto CA 94304-1395
650 855-2000
www.epri.com

Elsevier Science USA

655 Avenue of the Americas
New York NY 10010
888-437-4636
www.elsevier.com

Engineering Information Inc (Ei Village)

1 Castle Point Terrace
Hoboken NJ 07030-5996
800 221-1044 US & Canada
Fax: 201 216-8532
www.ei.org

Euromonitor Plc.

122 South Michigan Avenue, Suite 1200
Chicago IL 60603
312-922-1115
Fax: 312-922-1157
www.euromonitor.com

Federal Filings, Inc.

1250 H Street N.W., 11th Floor
Washington DC 20005
(202)393-7400
www.fedfil.com

Federal Laboratory Consortium

950 N. Kings Highway, Suite 208
Cherry Hill NJ 08034
609-667-7727
Fax: 609- 667-8009
www.federallabs.org/flc/flcrd2.htm

FIND/SVP Research Publications

625 Avenue of the Americas
New York NY 10011-2002
212-645-4500
Fax: 212-807-2676
www.findsvp.com

Frost & Sullivan
2525 East Charleston Road
Mountain View CA 94043
650-961-9000
Fax: 650-961-5042
www.frost.com

Gale Group
27500 Drak Rd
Farmington Hills MI 48331
248-699-4253
www.galegroup.com

Gartner Group
56 Top Gallant Road
Stamford CT 06904
203-316-1111
www.datapro.com

Groupe DAFSA
11, rue Robert de Flers
Paris France
33 1-44-37-2600
Fax: 33 1-33-37-2635
www.dafsa.fr

Houlihan Lokey Howard & Zukin
1930 Century Park West
Los Angeles CA 90099-5098
800-455-8871

IDC Greater China
Suite 3004 30/F
Universal Trade Center
3 Arbuthnot Road
852 845-6588

IDC Greater China
Four Crinan Street
London England N1 9UE
44 171-278-9517
Fax: 44 171-833-2124

Information Access Company (IAC)

362 Lakeside Drive
Foster City CA 94404
800-321-6388
415-378-5271
www.iacnet.com

infoUSA, Inc.

5711 South 86th Circle
Omaha NE 68127
800-321-0869

International Foundation of Employee Benefit Plans INFOSOURCE (Employee Benefits Database)

18700 W. Bluemound Rd.
Brookfield WI 53008-0069
414- 786-6700
Fax: 414-786-8670
www.ifebp.org

J.R. O'Dwyer Company

271 Madison Avenue
New York NY 10016
212-679-2471
Fax: 212-683-2750
www.odwyerpr.com

Japan Science and Technology Corporation, Information Center for Science and Technology (JICST)

2000 L Street. NW, Ste. 508
Washington DC 20036
202-872-4707
Fax: 202-872-4053

Jupiter Communications

10/11 St. Martin's Court
London WC2N 4AL UK
44 171-497-1020
Fax: 44 171-497-1021
www.jup.com

Key Note Ltd.

Field House
72 Oldfield Road
Hampton Middlesex TW12 2HQ
44 181-481-8750
Fax: 44 181-763-0049
www.keynote.co.uk

Killen & Associates

1212 Parkinson Avenue
Palo Alto CA 94301
650-617-6130
Fax: 650-617-6140
www.killen.com

Lafferty Group

The Graybar Building
420 Lexington Avenue, Suite 2531
New York NY 10170
212-557-6726
Fax: 212-557-7266
www.lafferty.co.uk

Leatherhead Food Research Association

Randalls Road
Leatherhead Surrey, England KT22 7RY
44 1372-376-761
Fax: 44 1372-386-228
www.lfra.co.uk

Market & Business Development (MBD)

Premier House
22 Deangate
Manchester England M3 1PH
44 161-839-2739
Fax: 44 161-839-9320

Market Vision

326 Pacheco Avenue, Suite 200
Santa Cruz CA 95062
408-426-4400
Fax: 408-426-4411
www.webcom.com/newmedia

Marketdata Enterprises, Inc.

2807 West Busch Blvd., Suite 110
Tampa FL 33618
813-931-3900
Fax: 813-931-3802
www.mkt-data-ent.com

Marketing Intelligence Service

6473 D Route 64
Naples NY 14512
716-374-6326
Fax: 716-374-5217
www.productscan.com

MarketLine International

16 Connaught Street
London England W2 2AF
44 171-624-2200
Fax: 44 171-372-0130
www.datamonitor.com

MDIS Publications

MDIS House
City Fields Business Park
City Fields Way
Chichester England PO20 6FS
44 1-243-533-322
Fax: 44 1-243-533-418

Mintel Marketing Intelligence

18-19 Long Lane
London EC1A 9HE
44 171-606-6000
Fax: 44 171-606-5932
www.mintel.co.uk

Moody's Investors Service

99 Church Street
New York NY 10007
www.moodys.com

MSI Marketing Research for Industry

Viscount House
River Lane
Saltney Chester CH4 8QY
44 1244-681-186
Fax: 44 1244-681-457

Multex Systems Inc.

33 Maiden Lane, 5th Floor
New York NY 10038
888-2MULTEX
Fax: 212-859-9810
www.multex.com

Nelson Information Inc.

1 Gateway Plaza
Port Chester NY 10573-4674
914-937-8400
Fax: 914-937-8908
www.nelsons.com

PIRA International

Randalls Road
Leatherhead Surrey KT22 7RU
44 1372-802-000
Fax: 44 1372-802-238
www.pira.co.uk

PJB Publications Ltd.

18-20 Hill Rise
Richmond Surrey TW10 6UA
44 181-948-3262
Fax: 44 181-948-6866
www.pjbpubs.co.uk

Political and Economic Risk Consultancy, Ltd.

233 Hollywood Road, Rms. 1603-1604
Hollywood Centre
Hong Kong
852 2541-4088
Fax: 852- 2815-5032
www.asiarisk.com

POV Incorporated

29 Park Street
Montclair NJ 07042
973-509-7740
Fax: 973-509-7480

PR Newswire

1375 East 9th Street
Cleveland OH 44114-1724
800-826-3133

Public Affairs Information Service (PAIS)

521 West 43rd Street, New York
New York NY 10036
800 288 7247 (Toll-Free in US and Canada)
Fax: 212 643 2848
www.pais.inter.net

Responsive Database Services (RDS)

23611 Chagrin Blvd., Suite 320
Beachwood OH
800-313-2212
Fax: 216-292-9621
www.rdsinc.com

Standard & Poor's Corporation

25 Broadway
New York NY 10004
212-770-4000
Fax: 212-770-0275
www.netadvantage.standardpoor.com/com

Strategic Directions International, Inc.

6242 Westchester Parkway, Suite 100
Los Angeles CA 90045
310-641-4982
Fax: 310-641-8851
www.strategic-directions.com

Taylor Nelson AGB Publications

14-17 St. John's Square
London England EC1M 4HE
44 171-608-0072
Fax: 44 171-608-2166
ww.tnagb.com

Technimetrics, Inc.

75 Wall Street, 18th Floor
New York NY 10005-2837
212-509-5100

Teikoku Databank Ltd.

747 Third Avenue, 25th Fl.
New York NY 10017
212-421-9805
Fax: 212-421-9806
www.teikoku.com

The Freedonia Group, Inc.

767 Beta Drive
Cleveland OH 44143-2326
440-684-9600
Fax: 440-646-0484
www.freedoniagroup.com

The Investext Group

40 West 57th Street, Suite 1000
New York NY 10019
212-484-4700
Fax: 212-484-4720
www.investext.com

Transportation Library, Northwestern University

1935 Sheridan Road
Evanston IL 60208-2300
847-491-5273
Fax: 847- 491-8601
www.library.nwu.edu/transportation/tleis.html

VerdictSearch/The New York Jury Reporter

128 Carlton Avenue
East Islip NY 17730
516-581-1930
www.verdictsearch.com

Veronis, Suhler & Associates

350 Park Avenue
New York NY 10022
212-935-4990
Fax: 212-486-3091
www.vsacomm.com

VISTA Information Solutions, Inc.

5060 Shoreham Drive
San Diego CA 92122
800-733-7606
www.vistacheck.com

WEFA, Ltd.

800 Baldwin Tower
Eddystone PA 19022
610-490-4000
Fax: 610-490-2770
www.wefa.com

Database Vendors - Internet

Acxiom DataQuick

9171 Towne Centre Dr., Suite 600
San Diego CA 92122
800-863-INFO
619-455-6900
http://products.dataquick.com

American Information Network

6470 Freetown Road, Suite 200-39
Columbia MD 21044
800-779-6938
410-715-6809
www.ameri.com/sherlock.htm

Asia Pulse Pte Ltd.

Level 7, 9 Lang Street
Locked Bag 21, Grosvenor Place
Sydney NSW 02000
61-2 9322 8634
Fax: 61-2 9322 8639

Asian Business Intelligence, Ltd.

POBox 52-118
Taipei, Taiwan
886-2-8754355
Fax: 886-2-8736602

Avert, Inc.

301 Remington Street
Fort Collins, CA   80524
800-367-5933
www.avert.com

CARL Corporation

3801 East Florida Avenue #200
Denver CO 80210
888-439-2275
303-758-3030
Fax: 303-758-5946
www.carl.org

CDB Infotek

6 Hutton Centre
Santa Ana CA 92707
800-427-3747
714-708 -2000
www.cdb.com

CenterWatch, Inc.

581 Boylston St., Suite 200
Boston MA 02116
617-247-2327
Fax: 617-247-2535
www.centerwatch.com

Corporate Intelligence
Trademarks.com

10 Caledonia Summit
Browns Point WA 98422
253-925-1000
Fax: 253-925-2000
www.1790.com

Data Downlink Corp.
XLS

101 Hudson St., 24th Floor
Jersey City NJ 07302
201-557-5850

DataStar Web
The Dialog Corporation

11000 Regency Parkway, Suite 400
Cary NC 27511
919-462-8600
Fax: 919-468-9890
www.dialog.com

Dow Jones Interactive Publishing

PO Box 300
Princeton NJ 08543
800-369-7466
www.djnr.com

Dun & Bradstreet

One Diamond Hill Road
Murray Hill NJ 07974
800-234-3867
www.dnb.com

EDGAR Online

50 Washington Street, 9th Floor
Norwalk, CT 06854
203-852-5666
Fax: 203-852-5667
www.edgar-online.com

Experian

505 City Parkway West   714-385-7000
Orange CA 92868-2912
www.experian.com

Global Securities Information (GSI)

419 Seventh St. NW
Suite 202
Washington DC 20004
800-669-1154
Fax: 202-628-1133
www.gsionline.com

IBM Patent Server

Attn: Blaine Sollazzi
650 Harry Road
San Jose CA 95120
www.patents.ibm.com

Infomart Dialog

1450 Don Mills Road
Toronto ON M3B 2X7
416-442-2198
800- 668-9215

Infonautics Corporation (Online Reference Services)
Electric Library

900 West Valley Road
Suite 1000
Wayne PA 19087
610-971-8840
Fax: 610-971-8859
www.infonautics.com

Informus Corporation
2001 Airport Road, Suite 201
Jackson MS 39208
601-664-1900

IPO Data Systems
74-16 Roosevelt Avenue, Suite 141
Jackson Heights NY 11372
www.ipodata.com

ISI Emerging Markets
Internet Securities, Inc.
695 Atlantic Avenue
Boston MA 02111
617 204-3100
http://securities.com

Jane's Information Group
1340 Braddock Pl., Ste. 300
Alexandria VA 22314
800-243-3852
www.janes.com

Knowledge Express Data Systems (KEDS)
3000 Valley Forge Circle, Suite 3800
King of Prussia PA 19407
800-529-5337
www.KnowledgeExpress.com

Lexis Public Records
PO Box 933
Dayton OH 45401
800-227-4908
www.lexis-nexis.com/ln.universe

Lexis-Nexis
PO Box 933
Dayton OH 45401
800-227-4908
www.lexis-nexis.com/ln.universe

Manning & Napier Information Services

1100 Chase Square
Rochester NY 14604
800-278-5356
Fax: 716- 454-2516
www.mnis.net

MicroPatent

250 Dodge Avenue
East Haven CT 06512
800-648-6787
www.micropat.com

National Library of Medicine

8600 Rockville Pike
Bethesda MD 20894
(888) FIND-NLM
(301) 594-5983 301-594-5983 (local and international calls)
http://igm.nlm.nih.gov

Northern Light Search

222 Third Street, Suite 1320
Cambridge MA 02142
617-577-2846
Fax: 617-621-3459
www.nlsearch.com

Partes Corporation

10635-B NE 38th Place
Kirkland WA 98033
425-803-5737
Fax: 425 822-3034

Powerize.com

1761 Business Center Drive
Reston VA 20190-5337
703-438-3500
www.k-link.com

Profound
US Headquarters

11000 Regency Parkway, Suite 400
Cary NC 27511

888 809-6193

Quote.Com (Financial Market Data)

10 G Street, NE, Suite 500
Washington DC 20002
800-733-1131
Fax: 202-898-3030
www.quote.com

State Net

2101 K Street
Sacramento CA 95816
916 447-1886
www.statenet.com

STN International
Chemical Abstracts Services

2540 Olentangy River Road
Columbus OH 43210
800-753-4227
www.cas.org

Stock Smart

PO Box 191408
Dallas TX 75219
www.stocksmart.com

Teltech Resource Network Corporation

2850 Metro Drive
Minneapolis MN 55425-1566
612-851-7500
Fax: 612-851-7744
www.teltech.com

The Online Sleuth (Inc Online)

38 Commercial Wharf
Boston MA 02110
617-248-8000
Fax: 617-248-8090
www.inc.com

The Uncover Company

3801 E. Florida Avenue, Suite 300
Denver CO 80210
303 758-3030

Thomson & Thomson (Trademark & Copyright w. Domain Name Search)

500 Victory Road
North Quincy MA 02171-1545
800-692-8833
www.thomson-thomson.com

Westlaw / West Group

620 Opperman Dr.
PO Box 64526
St. Paul MN 55164
800-328-9352
www.westpub.com

WinStar Telebase, Inc.

435 Devon Park Drive, Suite 600
Wayne PA 19087
610 254-2420

Database Vendors

AccuSearch Inc.

2727 Allen Parkway, Suite 1200
Houston TX 77019
800-833-5778
713-864-7639
www.accusearchinc.com

Aristotle Online

205 Pennsylvania Ave. SE
Washington DC 20003
800-243-4401
202-543-8345
http://products.aristotle.org/pages/online.htm

Asia Pulse Pte Ltd.

Level 7, 9 Lang Street
Locked Bag 21, Grosvenor Place
Sydney NSW 02000
61-2 9322 8634
Fax: 61-2 9322 8639

Avert, Inc.

301 Remington Street
Fort Collins, CA   80524
800-367-5933
www.avert.com

Burrelle's Information Services

75 E. Northfield Road
Livingston NJ 07039
800-631-1160
www.burrelles.com

CARL Corporation

3801 East Florida Avenue #200
Denver CO 80210
888-439-2275
303-758-3030
Fax: 303-758-5946
www.carl.org

CDB Infotek

Six Hutton Centre
Santa Ana CA 92707
800-427-3747
714-708 -2000
www.cdb.com

DAC Services

4110 S. 100th East Ave.
Tulsa OK 74146
800-331-9175
www.dacservices.com

DataStar Web
The Dialog Corporation

11000 Regency Parkway, Suite 400
Cary NC 27511
919-462-8600
Fax: 919-468-9890
www.dialog.com

DBT Online

4530 Blue Lake Drive, Bldg. 14
Boca Raton FL 33431
800-279-7710
www.dbt.net

DCS Information Systems

500 North Central Expressway
Ste. 280
Plano TX 75074
800-394-3274
www.dnis.com

Derwent North America

1725 Duke Street, Suite 250
Alexandria VA 22314
800-451-3451
Fax: 703-838-0450
www.derwent.co.uk

Disclosure

5161 River Road
Bethesda MD 20816
800-754-9690
Fax: 301-951-1753
www.disclosure.com

Dow Jones Interactive Publishing

PO Box 300
Princeton NJ 08543
800-369-7466
www.djnr.com

Dun & Bradstreet

One Diamond Hill Road
Murray Hill NJ 07974
800-234-3867
www.dnb.com

Economist Intelligence Unit

The Economist Building
111 West 57th Street
New York NY 10019
212-554-0600
Fax: 212-586-1181
www.eiu.com

Equifax (Consumer Credit Reports, Geo-Demographic & Econometric Information)

PO Box 740241
Atlanta GA 30374-0241
800-997-2493
www.equifax.com

Experian

505 City Parkway West
Orange CA 92868-2912

714-385-7000
www.experian.com

H.W. Wilson (Abstract & Full Text Databases, Indexes)

950 University Avenue
Bronx NY 10452-4224
800-367-6770
www.hwwilson.com

Infomart Dialog

1450 Don Mills Road
Toronto ON M3B 2X7
416-442-2198
800- 668-9215

Information America

245 Peachtree Center Avenue
Suite 1400

Atlanta GA 30303
800-235-4008
www.infoam.com

Institute for Scientific Information (ISI)

3501 Market Street
Philadelphia PA 19104
800-336-4474
Fax: 215-386-2911
www.isinet.com

IRSC Information Resource Service Corporation

3777 N. Harbor Blvd.
Fullerton CA 92835
800-640-4772
www.irsc.com/home.htm

Lexis Public Records

PO Box 933
Dayton OH 45401
800-227-4908
www.lexis-nexis.com/ln.universe

LEXIS-NEXIS

PO Box 933
Dayton OH 45401
800-227-4908
www.lexis-nexis.com/ln.universe

Manning & Napier Information Services

1100 Chase Square
Rochester NY 14604
800-278-5356
Fax: 716- 454-2516
www.mnis.net

OPEN Ohio Professional Electronic Network

1650 Lake Shore Drive, Suite 180
Columbus OH 43204
800-366-0106
614-481-6999
www.openohio.com

Ovid Technologies

333 Seventh Avenue
New York NY 10001
(800) 950-2035, Ext. 249 (toll-free)
212-563-3006
Fax: 212-563-3784
www.ovid.com

PACER

PO Box 780549
San Antonio TX 78278
800-676-6856

Profound
US Headquarters

11000 Regency Parkway, Suite 400
Cary NC 27511
888 809-6193

Proquest
UMI

300 N. Zeeb Road
PO Box 1346
Ann Arbor MI 48106-1346
800-521-0600
www.umi.com/proquest

QUESTEL-ORBIT, Inc.

Westpark Dr., Ste. 130
McClean VA 22102
800-456-7248
703 442-0900
www.questel.orbit.com

Securities Data Company

2 Gateway Center
Newark NJ 07102
973.622.3100

SilverPlatter World (Databases on CD-ROMs & Online)

100 River Ridge Rd.
Norwood MA 02062-0064
800-343-0064
www.silverplatter.com

STN International
Chemical Abstracts Services

2540 Olentangy River Road
Columbus OH 43210
800-848-653
8800-753-4227
www.cas.org

Superior Information Services

300 Phillips Blvd.
Trenton NJ 08650
800-848-0489
609-883-7000

The Conference Board

845 Third Avenue
New York NY 10022
(212) 339-0216
Fax: (212) 980-7014
www.conference-board.org

The Dialog Corporation

11000 Regency Parkway, Suite 400
Cary NC 27511
919-462-8600
Fax: 919-468-9890
www.dialog.com

The Uncover Company

3801 E. Florida Avenue, Suite 300
Denver CO 80210
303 758-3030

Trans Union Corporation (Credit & Fraud-Prevention Data)

555 W. Adams St.
Chicago IL 60661-3601

800-899-7132
www.transunion.com

Westlaw
West Group

620 Opperman Dr.
PO Box 64526
St. Paul MN 55164
800-328-9352
www.westpub.com

Document Delivery Services

Canada Institute for Scientific & Technical Information (CISTI)|National Research Council of Canada

Montreal Road, Jac, E. Brown Building
Ottawa ON K1A 0S2
800-668-1222
www.cisti.nrc.ca/cisti

CSC Networks (Prentice Hall Legal & Financial Services - Public Records)|CSC The United States Corporation Company

1013 Centre Road
Wilmington DE
800-927-9800
Fax: 302-636-5454
www.cscinfo.com

Derwent North America

1725 Duke Street, Suite 250
Alexandria VA 22314
800-451-3451
Fax: 703-838-0450
www.derwent.co.uk

Publishers

ChinaOnline, LLC

900 North Michigan Avenue, Suite 2180
Chicago IL 60601
312-335-8881
Fax: 312-335-9299
www.chinaonline.com

Hermograph Press

Box 69
Woodstock GA 30188
678-445-4189
Fax: 678-445-4136
www.hermograph.com

Information Today, Inc.

143 Old Marlton Pike
Medford NJ 07055-8570
609-654-6266
Fax: 609-654-4309
www.infotoday.com

Learned Information

Woodside
Hinksey Hill Oxford OX1 5BE   UK
+44 (0)1865 388100
Fax: +44 (0)1865 388056
www.learned.co.uk

Online Inc.

213 Danbury Road
Wilton CT 06897-4007
800/248-8466
www.onlineinc.com

Appendix A

SEC Filings, Defined

Part of the challenge in business intelligence lies in understanding the implications as well as the content of what you read. This is definitely true when dealing with the myriad filings made by public companies with the Securities & Exchange Commission.

Although terms like 10K, 10Q, etc. are commonly understood, many other SEC forms may be much less familiar. Companies don't always wish to broadcast the news that is contained in certain mandatory filings. Knowing what to watch for, and understanding the content of certain filings, therefore, can provide you with some interesting insights into the goings-on over at Company X.

Various commercial vendors of EDGAR SEC filings have been mentioned elsewhere in this book. The list of form definitions below is reprinted, with permission, from EDGAR ONLINE, at www.edgar-online.com/formdef.htm.

▬▬ Registration Statements:

S-1: This filing is a pre-effective registration statement submitted when a company decides to go public. Commonly referred to as an "IPO" (Initial **Public Offering) filing.**

S-1/A: This filing is a *pre-effective* amendment to an S-1 IPO filing.

S-1MEF: Registration of up to an additional 20% of securities for any offering registered on an S-1.

POS AM: This filing is a *post-effective* amendment to an S-Type filing.

S-2: This filing is an optional registration form that may be used by companies which have reported under the '34 Act for a minimum of three years and have timely filed all required reports during the 12 calendar months and any portion of the month immediately preceding the filing of the registration statement.

S-2/A: This filing is a *pre-effective* amendment to an S-2 filing.

S-2MEF: Registration of up to an additional 20% of securities for any offering registered on an S-2.

S-3: This filing is the most simplified registration form and it may only be used by companies which have reported under the '34 Act for a minimum of three years and meet the timely filing requirements set forth under Form S-2. The filing company must also meet the stringent qualitative tests prescribed by the form.

S-3/A: This filing is a *pre-effective* amendment to an S-3 filing.

S-3MEF: Registration of up to an additional 20% of securities for any offering registered on a S-3.

S-3D: Registration statement of securities pursuant to dividend or interest reinvestment plans which become effective automatically upon filing.

S-3D/A: Amendment to a previously filed S-3D.

S-3DPOS: This filing is a *post-effective* amendment to an S-3D filing.

S-4: This filing is for the registration of securities issued in business combination transactions.

S-4/A: This filing is a *pre-effective* amendment to an S-4 filing.

S-4EF: Filed when securities are issued in connection with the formation of a bank, savings and loan, or holding company.

S-4EF/A: This filing is a *pre-effective* amendment to an S-4EF filing.

S-4 POS: This filing is a *post-effective* amendment to an S-4EF filing.

S-6: Initial registration statement for unit investment trusts.

S-6/A: This filing is a *pre-effective* amendment to an S-6 filing.

S-8: This filing is required when securities are to be offered to employees pursuant to employee benefit plans.

S-8/A: Amendment to a previously filed S-8.

S-8 POS: This filing is a *post-effective* amendment to an S-8 filing.

S-11: Filing for the registration of securities of certain real estate companies.

S-11/A: This filing is a *pre-effective* amendment to an S-11 filing.

S-11MEF: Registration of up to an additional 20% of securities for any offering registered on a S-11.

S-20: Initial registration statement for standardized options.

S-20/A: Amendment to a previously filed S-20.

SB-1: An optional filing for small business issuers for the registration of securities to be sold to the public.

SB-1/A: This filing is a *pre-effective* amendment to an SB-1 filing.

SB-1MEF: Registration of up to an additional 20% of securities for any offering registered on a SB-1.

SB-2: Also an optional filing for small business issuers for the registration of securities to be sold to the public.

SB-2/A: This filing is a *pre-effective* amendment to an SB-2 filing.

SB-2MEF: Registration of up to an additional 20% of securities for any offering registered on a SB-2.

POS AM: Post-effective amendments.

POS AMI: Post-effective amendments.

424A: Contains substantive changes from or additions to a prospectus previously filed with the SEC as part of the registration statement.

424B1: A form of prospectus that discloses information previously omitted from the prospectus filed as part of a registration statement.

424B2: A form of prospectus filed in connection with a primary offering of securities on a delayed basis which includes the public offering price, description of securities and specific method of distribution.

424B3: A form of prospectus that reflects facts or events that constitute a substantive change from or addition to the information set forth in the last form of prospectus filed with the SEC.

424B4: A form of prospectus that discloses information, facts or events covered in both form 424B1 and form 424B3.

424B5: A form of prospectus that discloses information, facts or events covered in both form 424B2 and form 424B3.

DEL AM: Delaying amendment.

497: Definitive materials filed by investment companies.

497J: Certification of no change in definitive materials.

487: Pre-effective pricing amendment.

10-12B: A general registration filing of securities pursuant to section 12(b) of the Securities Exchange Act.

10-12B/A: Amendment to a previously filed 10-12B.

10-12G: A general registration filing of securities pursuant to section 12(g) of the Securities Exchange Act.

10-12G/A: Amendment to a previously filed 10-12G.

10SB12B: Filed for the registration of securities for small business issuers pursuant to section 12(b) of the Securities Exchange Act.

10SB12B/A: Amendment to a previously filed 10SB12B.

10SB12G: Filed for the registration of securities for small business issuers pursuant to section 12(g) of the Securities Exchange Act.

10SB12G/A: Amendment to a previously filed 10SB12G.

18-12B: Registration of securities filed pursuant to section 12(b) of the Securities Exchange Act.

18-12B/A: Amendment to a previously filed 18-12B.

18-12G: Registration of securities filed pursuant to section 12(g) of the Securities Exchange Act.

18-12G/A: Amendment to a previously filed 18-12G.

N-8B-2: Registration statement for unit investment trusts.

N-8B-2/A: Amendments to a previously filed N-8B-2.

N-1: Registration statement for open-end management investment companies.

N-1/A: Amendments to a previously filed N-1.

N-1A: Registration statement for Mutual Funds.

N-2: Registration statement for closed-end investment companies.

N-2/A: This filing is a *pre-effective* amendment to an N-2 filing.

N-3: Registration statement for separate accounts (management investment companies).

N-3/A: This filing is a *pre-effective* amendment to an N-3 filing.

N-4: Registration statement for separate accounts (unit investment trusts).

N-4/A: This filing is a *pre-effective* amendment to an N-4 filing.

N-5: Registration statement for small business investment companies.

N-5/A: This filing is a *pre-effective* amendment to an N-5 filing.

N-14: Registration statement for investment companies business combination.

N-14/A: Pre-effective amendment to a previously filed N-14.

F-1: Registration statement for certain foreign private issuers.

F-1/A: This filing is a pre-effective amendment to an F-1 filing.

F-1MEF: Registration of up to an additional 20% of securities for an offering filed on an F-1.

F-2: Registration statement for certain foreign private issuers.

F-2/A: Amendment to a previously filed F-2.

F-2D: Registration of securities pursuant to dividend or interest reinvestment plans (foreign).

F-2DPOS: Post-effective amendments to a previously filed F-2D.

F-3: Registration statement for certain foreign private issuers offered pursuant to certain types of transactions.

F-3/A: Amendment to a previously filed F-3.

F-3D: Registration statement for certain foreign private issuers offered pursuant to dividend or pursuant to dividend or interest reinvestment plans.

F-3DPOS: Amendment to a previously filed F-3D.

F-4: Registration statement for foreign private issuers issued in certain business transactions.

F-4/A: Amendment to a previously filed F-4.

F-6: Registration of depository shares evidenced by American Depository Receipts. Filing to become effective other than immediately upon filing.

F-6/A: Amendment to a previously filed F-6.

F-6 POS: Post-effective amendment to a previously filed F-6.

F-6EF: Registration of depositary shares evidenced by American Depository Receipts. Filing to become effective immediately upon filing.

F-6EF/A: Amendment to a previously filed F-6EF.

20FR12B: Registration of securities of foreign private issuers pursuant to section 12 (b) of the Securities Exchange Act.

20FR12B/A: Amendment to a previously filed 20FR12B.

20FR12G: Registration of securities of foreign private issuers pursuant to section 12 (g) of the Securities Exchange Act.

20FR12G/A: Amendment to a previously filed 20FR12G.

24F-1: Registration of securities by certain investment companies pursuant to rule 24f-1. Notification of election.

24F-2EL: Registration of securities by certain investment companies pursuant to rule 24f-2. Declaration of election.

24F-2EL/A: Amendment to a previously filed 24F-2EL.

24F-2NT: Registration of securities by certain investment companies pursuant to rule 24f-2. Rule 24f-2 notice.

24F-2NT/A: Amendment to a previously filed 24F-2NT.

POS462B: Post effective amendment to proposed Securities Act Rule 462(b) registration statement.

POS462C: Post effective amendment to proposed Securities Act Rule 462(c) registration statement.

8-A12B: Registration of certain classes of securities pursuant to section 12(b) of the Securities Exchange Act.

8-A12B/A: Amendment to a previously filed 8-A12B.

8-A12G: Registration of certain classes of securities pursuant to section 12(g) of the Securities Exchange Act.

8-A12G/A: Amendment to a previously filed 8-A12G.

8-B12B: Registration of securities of certain successor issuers pursuant to section 12(b) of the Securities Exchange Act.

8-B12B/A: Amendment to a previously filed 8-B12B.

8-B12G: Registration of securities of certain successor issuers pursuant to section 12(g) of the Securities Exchange Act.

8-B12G/A: Amendment to a previously filed 8-B12G.

8A12BEF: Registration of listed debt securities pursuant to section 12(b) - filing to become effective automatically upon filing.

8A12BT: Registration of listed debt securities pursuant to section 12(b) - filing to become effective simultaneously with the effective of a concurrent Securities Act registration statement.

8A12BT/A: Amendment to a previously filed 8A12BT.

485A24E: Registration statement for separate accounts (management investment companies). Post-Effective amendment filed pursuant to Rule 485(b) with additional shares under 24e-2.

485A24F: Registration statement for separate accounts (management investment companies). Post-Effective amendment filed pursuant to Rule 485(b) with additional shares under 24f-2.

485APOS: Registration statement for separate accounts (management investment companies). Post-Effective amendment filed pursuant to Rule 485(a).

485B24E: Registration statement for separate accounts (management investment companies). Post-Effective amendment filed pursuant to Rule 485(a) with additional shares under 24e-2.

485B24F: Registration statement for separate accounts (management investment companies). Post-Effective amendment filed pursuant to Rule 485(b) with additional shares under 24f-2.

485BPOS: Registration statement for separate accounts (management investment companies). Post-Effective amendment filed pursuant to Rule 485(b).

Registration, Withdrawal & Termination Statements

RW: Request for a withdrawal of a previously filed registration statement.

AW: Amendment to a previously filed RW.

15-12G: Certification of termination of registration of a class of security under Section 12(g) or notice of suspension of duty to file reports pursuant to Section 13 and 15(d) of the Securities Exchange Act. Section 12 (g) initial filing.

15-12G/A: Amendment to a previously filed 15-12G.

15-15D: Certification of termination of registration of a class of security under Section 12(g) or notice of suspension of duty to file reports pursuant to Section 13 and 15(d) of the Securities Exchange Act. Section 13 and 15 (d) initial filing.

15-15D/A: Amendment to a previously filed 15-15D.

15-12B: Certification of termination of registration of a class of security under Section 12(g) or notice of suspension of duty to file reports pursuant to Section 13 and 15(d) of the Securities Exchange Act. Section 12 (b) initial filing.

15-12B/A: Amendment to a previously filed 15-12B.

24F-2TM: Registration of securities by certain investment companies pursuant to rule 24f-2. Termination of declaration of election.

Proxies & Information Statements:

PRE 14A: A preliminary proxy statement providing official notification to designated classes of shareholders of matters to be brought to a vote at a shareholders meeting.

PREC14A: Preliminary proxy statement containing contested solicitations.

PREC14C: Preliminary information statement containing contested solicitations.

PREN14A: Non-management preliminary proxy statements not involving contested solicitations.

PREM14A: A preliminary proxy statement relating to a merger or acquisition.

PREM14C: A preliminary information statement relating to a merger or acquisition.

PRES14A: A preliminary proxy statement giving notice regarding a special meeting.

PRES14C: A preliminary information statement relating to a special meeting.

PRE 14C: A preliminary proxy statement containing all other information.

PRER14A: Proxy soliciting materials. Revised preliminary material.

PRER14C: Information statements. Revised preliminary material.

PRE13E3: Initial statement - preliminary form.

PRE13E3/A: Amendment to a previously filed PRE13E3.

PRRN14A: Non-management revised preliminary proxy soliciting materials for both contested solicitations and other situations. Revised preliminary material.

PX14A6G: Notice of exempt solicitation. Definitive material.

DEF 14A: Provides official notification to designated classes of shareholders of matters to be brought to a vote at a shareholders meeting. This form is commonly refered to as a "Proxy."

DEFM14A: Provides official notification to designated classes of shareholders of matters relating to a merger or acquisition.

DEFM14C: A definitive information statement relating to a merger or an acquisition.

DEFS14A: A definitive proxy statement giving notice regarding a special meeting.

DEFS14C: A definitive information statement regarding a special meeting.

DEFC14A: Definitive proxy statement in connection with contested solicitations.

DEFC14C: Definitive information statement indicating contested solicitations.

DEFA14A: Additional proxy soliciting materials - definitive.

DEFN14A: Definitive proxy statement filed by non-management not in connection with contested solicitations.

DFRN14A: Revised definitive proxy statement filed by non-management.

DFAN14A: Additional proxy soliciting materials filed by non-management.

DEF13E3: Schedule filed as definitive materials.

DEF13E3/A: Amendment to a previously filed DEF 13E3.

DEFA14C: Additional information statement materials - definitive.

DEFR14C: Revised information statement materials - definitive.

Quarterly Reports:

10-Q: A quarterly report that provides a continuing view of a company's financial position during the year. The filing is due 45 days after each of the first three fiscal quarters. No filing is due for the fourth quarter.

10-Q/A: Amendment to a previously filed 10-Q.

10QSB: A quarterly report that provides a continuing view of a company's financial position during the year. The 10QSB form is filed by small businesses.

10QSB/A: An amendment to a previously filed 10QSB.

NT 10-Q: Notification that form type 10-Q will be submitted late.

NT 10-Q/A: Amendment to a previously filed NT 10-Q.

10-QT: Quarterly transition reports filed pursuant to rule 13a-10 or 15d-10 of the Securities Exchange Act.

10-QT/A: Amendment to a previously filed 10-QT.

13F-E: Quarterly reports filed by institutional managers.

13F-E/A: Amendment to a previously filed 13F-E.

Annual Reports:

ARS: An annual report to security holders. This is a voluntary filing on EDGAR.

10-K: An annual report which provides a comprehensive overview of the company for the past year. The filing is due 90 days after the close of the company's fiscal year, and contains such information as company history, organization, nature of business, equity, holdings, earnings per share, subsidiaries, and other pertinent financial information.

10-K/A: Amendment to a previously filed 10-K.

10-K405: An annual report that provides a comprehensive overview of the company for the past year. The Regulation S-K Item 405 box on the cover page is checked.

10-K405/A: This filing is an amendment to a previously filed 10-K405.

NT 10-K: Notification that form 10-K will be submitted late.

NT 10-K/A: Amendment to a previously filed NT 10-K.

10KSB: An annual report that provides a comprehensive overview of the company for the past year. The filing is due 90 days after the close of the company's fiscal year, and contains such information as company history, organization, nature of business, equity, holdings, earnings per share, subsidiaries, and other pertinent financial information. The 10KSB is filed by small businesses.

10KSB/A: Amendment to a previously filed 10KSB.

10-C: This filing is required of an issuer of securities quoted on the NASDAQ Interdealer Quotation System, and contains information regarding a change in the number of shares outstanding or a change in the name of the issuer.

10-C/A: Amendment to a previously filed 10-C.

10-KT: Annual transition reports filed pursuant to rule 13a-10 or 15d-10 of the Securities Exchange Act.

10-KT/A: Amendment to a previously filed 10-KT.

10KSB40: An optional form for annual and transition reports of small business issuers under Section 13 or 15 (d) of the Securities Exchange Act where the Regulation S-B Item 405 box on the cover page (relating to section 16 (a) reports) is checked.

10KSB40/A: Amendment to a previously filed 10KSB40.

10KT405: Annual transition report filed pursuant to Rule 13a-10 or15d-10 of the Securities Exchange Act.

10KT405/A: Amendment to a previously filed 10KT405.

11-KT: Annual report of employee stock purchase, savings and similar plans. Filed pursuant to rule 13a-10 or 15d-10 of the Securities Exchange Act.

11-KT/A: Amendment to a previously filed 11-KT.

18-K: Annual report for foreign governments and political subdivisions.

18-K/A: Amendment to a previously filed 18-K.

11-K: An annual report of employee stock purchase, savings and similar plans.

11-K/A: Amendment to a previously filed 11-K.

NT 11-K: Notification that form 11-K will be submitted late.

NT 11-K/A: Amendment to a previously filed NT 11-K.

NSAR-A: Semi-Annual report for management companies.

NSAR-A/A: Amendments to a previously filed NSAR-A.

NSAR-AT: Transitional semi-annual report for registered investment companies (Management).

NSAR-AT/A: Amendments to a previously filed NSAR-AT.

NSAR-B: Annual report for management companies.

NSAR-B/A: Amendments to a previously filed NSAR-B.

NSAR-BT: Transitional annual report for management companies.

NSAR-BT/A: Amendments to a previously filed NSAR-BT.

NSAR-U: Annual report for unit investment trusts.

NSAR-U/A: Amendments to a previously filed NSAR-U.

NT-NSAR: Request for an extension of time for filing form NSAR-A, NSAR-B or NSAR-U.

NT-NSAR/A: Amendments to a previously filed NT-NSAR.

N-30D: An annual and semi-annual report mailed to shareholders. Filed by registered investment companies.

N-30D/A: Amendments to a previously filed N-30D.

20-F: Annual and transition report of foreign private issuers filed pursuant to sections 13 or 15 (d) of the Securities Exchange Act.

20-F/A: Amendment to a previously filed 20-F.

ARS: Annual report to Security Holders.

Statements of Ownership:

SC 13D: This filing is made by person(s) reporting beneficially owned shares of common stock in a public company.

SC 13D/A: An amendment to a SC 13D filing.

SC 13G: A statement of beneficial ownership of common stock by certain persons.

SC 13G/A: An amendment to the SC 13G filing.

SC 13E1: Statement of issuer required by Rule 13e-1 of the Securities Exchange Act.

SC 13E1/A: Amendment to a previously filed SC 13E1.

SC 13E3: Going private transaction by certain issuers.

SC 13E3/A: Amendment to a previously filed SC 13E3.

SC 13E4: Issuer tender offer statement.

SC 13E4/A: Amendment to a previously filed SC 13E4.

SC 14D1: Tender offer statement.

SC 14D1/A: Amendment to a previously filed SC 14D1.

SC 14D9: Solicitation/recommendation statements.

SC 14D9/A: Amendment to a previously filed SC 14D9.

SC 14F1: Statement regarding change in majority of directors pursuant to Rule 14f-1.

SC 14F1/A: Amendment to a previously filed SC 14F1.

Insider Trading:

3: An initial filing of equity securities filed by every director, officer, or owner of more than ten percent of a class of equity securities. Contains information on the reporting person's relationship to the company and on purchases and sales of equity securities. This form type is not required to be filed with the EDGAR system.

3/A: An amendment to a 3 filing. This form is not required to be filed with the EDGAR system.

4: Any changes to a previously filed form 3 are reported in this filing. This form type is not required to be filed with the EDGAR system.

4/A: Amendment to a previously filed 4.

5: An annual statement of ownership of securities filed by every director, officer, or owner of more than ten percent of a class of equity securities. Contains information on the reporting person's relationship to the company and on purchases and sales of equity securities. This form type is not required to be filed with the EDGAR system.

5/A: Amendment to a previously filed 5.

144: This form must be filed by "insiders" prior to their intended sale of restricted stock (issued stock currently unregistered with the SEC). Filing this form results in each seller receiving an automatic exemption from SEC registration requirements for this one transaction. A Form 144 is NOT an EDGAR electronic filing; each 144 is filed by the seller in paper during the day at the SEC. *EDGAR Online* cumulates and adds all of the current day's 144 paper filings to our electronic database at the END of each business day.

The value of the *EDGAR Online* end-of-day listing of 144's is that the first notification of a 144 filing sometimes is the precursor of other 144 filings. 144 sales frequently come in clusters caused by events such as the end of a "lock-up" period or stock options being exercised and can be used to successfully project the onset of increased "sell side" activity in the stock of the target company.

Other uses of 144's include targeting individuals who will be coming into money and may wish to deploy such funds. Thus this timely information is the source of myriad business intelligence uses.

144/A: Amendment to a previously filed 144.

Filings pursuant to the Trust Indenture Act:

305B2: Initial statement filed pursuant to the Trust Indenture Act.

305B2/A: Amendment to a previously filed 305B2.

T-3: Application for qualification of trust indentures. Filed pursuant to the Trust Indenture Act.

T-3/A: Amendment to a previously filed T-3.

Filings Pursuant to the Public Utility Holding Company Act:

U-1: Application of declaration under the Public Utility Holding Company Act.

U-1/A: Amendment to a previously filed U-1.

U-13-1: Application for approval for mutual service company filed pursuant to Rule 88 of the Public Utility Holding Company Act.

U-13-1/A: Amendment to a previously filed U-13-1.

U-12-IB: Annual statement pursuant to section 12(i) of the Public Utility Company Act or by a registered holding company or a subsidiary thereof.

U-13-60: Annual report for mutual and subsidiary service companies filed pursuant to Rule 94 of the Public Utility Holding Company Act.

U-13-60/A: Amendment to a previously filed U-13-60.

U-33-S: Annual report concerning Foreign Utility Companies pursuant to section 33(e) of the Public Utility Holding Company Act.

U-3A-2: Statement by holding company claiming exemption from provisions of the act pursuant to Rule 2.

U-3A-2/A: Amendment to a previously filed U-3A-2.

U-3A3-1: Twelve-month statement by bank claiming exemption from provisions of the act pursuant to Rule 3 of the Public Utility Holding Company Act.

U-3A3-1/A: Amendment to a previously filed U-3A3-1.

U-57: Notification of Foreign Utility Company Status under section 33(a)(2) of the Public Utility Holding Company Act.

U-57/A: Amendment to a previously filed U-57.

U-6B-2: Certificate of notification of security issue, renewal or guaranty filed pursuant to Rule 20(d) of the Public Utility Holding Company Act.

U-7D: Certificate concerning lease of a utility facility filed pursuant to Rule 7(d) of the Public Utility Holding Company Act.

U-7D/A: Amendment to a previously filed U-7D.

U-R-1: Declaration as to solicitations filed pursuant to Rule 62 of the Public Utility Holding Company Act.

U5A: Notification of registration filed under section 5(a) of the Public Utility Holding Company Act.

U5B: Registration statement filed under section 5 of the Public Utility Holding Company Act.

U5B/A: Amendment to a previously filed U5B.

U5S: Annual report for holding companies registered pursuant to section 5 of the Public Utility Holding Company Act.

U5S/A: Amendment to a previously filed U5S.

35-APP: Statement concerning proposed transaction for which no form of application is prescribed filed pursuant to Rule 20(e) of the Public Utility Holding Company Act.

35-APP/A: Amendment to a previously filed 35-APP.

35-CERT: Certificate concerning terms and conditions filed pursuant to Rule 24 of the Public Utility Holding Company Act.

35-CERT/A: Amendment to a previously filed 35-CERT.

Miscellaneous Filings:

8-K: A report of *unscheduled* material events or corporate changes which could be of importance to the shareholders or to the SEC. Examples include acquisition, bankruptcy, resignation of directors, or a change in the fiscal year.

8-K/A: Amendment to a previously filed 8-K.

N-14AE: Initial statement with automatic effectiveness for investment companies business combination.

N-14AE/A: Pre-effective amendment to a previously filed N-14AE.

N-30B-2: Periodic and interim reports mailed to shareholders. Filed by registered investment companies.

2-E: Reports of sales of securities pursuant to Regulation E. Filed by investment companies.

2-E/A: Amendment to a previously filed 2-E.

SP 15D2: Special financial report pursuant to Rule 15d-2 of the Securities Exchange Act.

SP 15D2/A: Amendments to a previously filed SP 15D2.

NT 15D2: Notification of late filing Special report pursuant to section 15d-2.

NT 15D2/A: Amendment to a previously filed NT 15D2.

6-K: Report of foreign issuer pursuant to Rules 13a-16 and 15d-16 of the Securities Exchange Act.

6-K/A: Amendment to a previously filed 6-K.

8-K12G3: Notification of securities of successor issuers deemed to be registered pursuant to section 12(g) of the Securities Exchange Act.

8-K12G3/A: Amendment to a previously filed 8-K12G3.

8-K15D5: Notification of assumption of duty to report by successor issuer.

8-K15D5/A: Amendment to a previously filed 8-K15D5.

Appendix B

Current Industrial Reports

The Bureau of the Census makes available statistical data on the industries listed below. This data can be downloaded in various formats for manipulation using spreadsheets or other software. The Internet address for this material is: www.census.gov/pub/cir/www/index.html.

M20A, Flour Milling

MA20D, Confectionery

M2OJ, Fats and Oils: Oilseed Crushings

M20K, Fats and Oils: Production, Consumption, and Stocks

MQ22D, Consumption on the Woolen System

MA22F, Yarn Production

MA22K, Knit Fabric Production

M22P, Consumption on the Cotton System

MA22Q, Carpets and Rugs

MQ22T, Broadwoven Fabrics

MQ23A, Apparel

MA23D, Gloves and Mittens

MQ23X, Bed and Bath Furnishings

MA24T, Lumber Production and Mill Stocks

MA28A, Inorganic Chemicals (Annual)

M28AT, Titanium Dioxide (Monthly)

MQ28A, Inorganic Chemicals (Quarterly)

MA28B, Fertilizer Materials (Annual)

MQ28B, Fertilizer Materials (Quarterly)

MA28C, Industrial Gases (Annual)

MQ28C, Industrial Gases (Quarterly)

MA28F, Paint and Allied Products

MQ28F, Paint, Varnish, and Lacquer

MA28G, Pharmaceutical Preparations

MA31A, Footwear (Annual)

MQ31A, Footwear (Quarterly)

MQ32A, Flat Glass

MA32C, Refractories

MQ32D, Clay Construction Products

MA32E, Glassware

M32G, Glass Containers

MA33A, Iron and Steel Castings

MA33B, Steel Mill Products

M33D, Aluminum Ingot and Mill Products

MA33E, Nonferrous Castings

M33J, Inventories of Steel Producing Mills

MA33L, Insulated Wire and Cable

MQ34E, Plumbing Fixtures

MA34K, Steel Shipping Drums and Pails

MA35A, Farm Machinery and Garden Equipment

MA35D, Construction Machinery

MA35F, Mining Machinery

MA35J, Industrial Air Pollution Control Equipment

MA35L, Internal Combustion Engines

MA35M, Refrigeration and Heating Equipment

MA35N, Fluid Power Products

MA35P, Pumps and Compressors

MA35Q, Antifriction Bearings

MA35R, Computers and Office

MA35U, Vending Machines

MQ35W, Metalworking Machinery

MA36A, Switchgear and Industrial Controls

MQ36C, Fluorescent Lamp Ballasts

MA36E, Electric Housewares and Fans

MA36F, Major Household Appliances

MA36H, Motors and Generators

MA36K, Wiring Devices and Supplies

MA36L, Electric Lighting Fixtures

MA36M, Consumer Electronics

MA36P, Communication and Other Electronic Equipment

MA36Q, Semiconductors and Electronic Components

M37G, Civil Aircraft and Aircraft Engines

MA37D, Aerospace Industry

M37L, Truck Trailers

MA38B, Measurement Instruments and Related Products

MA38R, Electromedical and Irradiation Equipment

Appendix C

Periodicals' Special Issues

Economic Overviews, Previews, & Forecasts

Many journals and magazines include, in their **December** or **January** issues, feature articles covering economic information. This often takes the form of forecasts, outlooks, reviews/previous of the past/present year, state-of-the industry reports, etc. The list below, dated 1998, is reprinted with permission, from *Directory of Business Periodical Special Issues*, edited by Trip Wyckoff, and published by The Reference Press. See the "For Further Enrichment" section of this book for additional details.

Economic Outlooks - Business Services

ABA Journal

Ad Age's Creativity

Advertising Age

Association Management

Bank News

Barron's

Business Facilities

Business Geographics

Cablevision

Canadian Printer

Canadian Underwriter

California Real Estate

Card Marketing

CCM - The American Lawyer's Corporate Counsel Magazine

Chicago Daily Law Bulletin

Collections & Credit Risk

Commercial Investment Real Estate Journal

Communications Industries Report

Contingency Planning & Management

Counselor, The

Credit Card Management

Direct

Editor & Publisher

Expo

Financial Service Online

Financial World

Flexo

Government Product News

Graphic Arts Monthly

Incentive Magazine

Industry Week

Insurance Journal: The Property Insurance Magazine of the West

Health Insurance Underwriter

Journal of Business Strategy

Marketing News

MC

Mediaweek

Meetings In the West

Mortgage Banking

Nation's Business

National Mortgage News

National Real Estate Investor

Pensions & Investments

Print & Graphics

Printing Impressions

Printing News East

Printing Views

Promo

Publishers Weekly

Public Relations Tactics

R&D Magazine

Real Estate Forum

Real Estate New York

Real Estate News

Real Estate Weekly

Registered Representative

Report on Business Magazine

Research

Resource

ResponseTV

Risk Management

Rough Notes

Russian Magazine

School Planning & Administration

Security

Security Distribution & Marketing

Security Sales

Site Selection

Skylines

Southern Graphics

T H E Journal

Teleprofessional

Television Broadcast

Today's Realtor

Tradeshow Week

Trusts & Estates

Tuned In

US News & World Report

Variety's On Production

Economic Outlooks - Business Journals

Alaska Business Monthly

Arizona Business Magazine

Bellingham Business Journal

Birmingham Business Journal

Business Examiner

Business Journal Serving Charlotte & the Metro′Areas

Business Journal Serving Phoenix & the Valley of the Sun

Business Journal Serving San Jose & the Silicon Valley

Business Journal Serving Sonoma & Marin County

Business News Serving the Dayton-Miami Valley Region

Business Life Magazine

Business News New Jersey

Business NH Magazine

Business Times (CT)

BusinessWest

Capital District Business Journal

Caribbean Business

Cecil Business Ledger

Central Penn Business Journal

Colorado Business Magazine

Colorado Springs Business Journal

Corporate Report Minnesota

Crain's Chicago Business

Crain's Cleveland Business

Crain's Detroit Business

Crain¹s New York Business

Daily Business Review

Daily Record, The

Detroiter

Eastern Pennsylvania Business Journal

Everett Business Journal

Florida Trend

Georgia Trend Grand Rapids Business Journal

Greenville Business & Living

Hartford Business Journal

Houston Business Journal

Illinois Business

Ingram's For Successful Kansas Citizens

Inland Empire Business Journal

Inside Tucson Business

Island Business

Journal of Business

Journal Record

Long Beach Business Journal

Long Island

Los Angeles Business Journal

Memphis Business Journal

Metro Journal

Minneapolis/St. Paul CityBusiness

Nashville Business Journal

Nevada Business Journal

New Castle Business Ledger

North Carolina Magazine

Pacific Business News

Providence Business News

Puget Sound Business Journal

Sacramento Business Journal

San Francisco Business Times

San Gabriel Valley Business Journal

Seattle Daily Journal of Commerce

State Journal

Tampa Bay's The Maddux Report

Triangle Business Journal

Washington CEO

Wenatchee Business Journal

Appendix D

About SCIP - The Society of Information Professionals

▬▬ The Need for a CI Community

We all know that information is not enough anymore. Managers need skilled professionals to turn a sea of data into actionable intelligence that will provide the company with a competitive edge. Just as satellites and radar allow ships to reexamine their course at any moment, so too does CI employ the latest tools and techniques coupled with cutting-edge technology and resources to carefully sketch out the constantly changing competitive terrain. In a world where one right decision can make millions of dollars or one wrong choice can destroy you, wouldn't you want to have the most sophisticated tools at your disposal?

As an organization of individual CI professionals from countries across the globe, the Society is dedicated to providing the training and knowledge to pilot companies towards competitive success while maintaining the highest ethical standards. From educational seminars to networking opportunities, the Society emphasizes the need for CI professionals to learn from each other and stay abreast of the latest developments in information gathering, analysis, and dissemination. Through their special events and publications, members are made aware of the changes in the business environment and know before anyone else what lies ahead.

Benefits & Dues

The fee to join the Society of Competitive Intelligence Professionals is $155 per year, in return for which you receive the following key benefits:

Contacts

The SCIP Membership Directory (members receive one per year, published in mid-July) is the primary tool for reaching other CI practitioners, consultants, vendors, and academics to share professional experiences.

The Society also has an active program of chapters around the country and overseas where members meet and exchange valuable techniques with counterparts in other companies and with service firms that specialize in CI.

Skills

Through educational programs , CI products, and professional contacts, members have the opportunity to increase skills in every aspect of CI — from data gathering and database management to analysis and strategy development. Members receive advance notification of all CI programs and products, and, of course, enjoy reduced rates at conferences and meetings.

News & Views

Members receive the quarterly publications *Competitive Intelligence Review* and *Competitive Intelligence Magazine*. These excellent journals not only contain full-length articles and timely tips, but also regular columns, book and product reviews, and much more. Members also receive the monthly newsletter, *Actionable Intelligence*, which keeps members informed of CI happenings and programs scheduled throughout the regions and chapters.

How to Join

An electronic membership application is available at the web site - www.scip.org. Also, you can call or write SCIP at:

Society of Competitive Intelligence Professionals
1700 Diagonal Road, Suite 600
Alexandria, VA 22314

(703) 739-0696, fax (703) 739-2524

Frequently Asked Questions

The following information is taken from SCIP's web site and reprinted with permission.

Is CI espionage?

No. Espionage is the use of illegal means to gather information. In fact, economic espionage represents a failure of CI. Almost all the information a CI professional needs can be collected by examining published information sources, conducting interviews, and using other legal, ethical methods. Using a variety of analytical tools, a skilled CI professional can fill by deduction any gaps in information already gathered. Promoting CI as a discipline bound by a strict code of ethics and practiced by trained professionals is the paramount goal of the Society.

Are CI and counterintelligence the same thing?

No. The term counterintelligence describes the steps an organization takes to protect information sought by "hostile" intelligence gatherers. One of the most effective counterintelligence measures is to define "trade secret" information relevant to the company and control its dissemination.

Why is CI important?

The pace of technological development and the growth of global trade mean that today's business environment changes more quickly than ever before. Executives can no longer afford to rely on instinct or intuition when making strategic business decisions. In many industries, the consequence of making one wrong decision may be to see the company go out of business.

Does CI really make a difference to the bottom line?

Yes. Research shows that companies with well-established CI programs enjoy greater earnings per share than companies in the same industry without CI programs.

Isn't it true that CI is only important for big businesses?

No. Executives at many global companies, like Xerox, IBM, and Motorola, have already realized the importance of CI and have developed their own operations. But small businesses, like large corporations, must compete in the marketplace. It's just as important for decision-makers in small businesses to know what lies ahead as for CEOs at Fortune 500 companies.

Is it possible for a company to practice some form of CI without realizing it?

Yes. Any employee that visits a trade show, reads a newspaper, or talks to friends in the same industry is doing research (one of the components of CI). But other components of CI are often missing in businesses today. CI adds value to information gathering and strategic planning by introducing a disciplined system not only to gather information, but also to perform analysis and disseminate findings tailored to the needs of decision-makers.

How does the Society of Competitive Intelligence Professionals enter the picture?

The Society (SCIP) is a global, non-profit organization providing education and networking opportunities for business professionals working in the rapidly growing field of CI.

Does SCIP have an impressive membership?

Yes. SCIP is rapidly becoming the association of choice for CI professionals. Currently, its membership is more than 6000 (and has been increasing at a rate of 40% annually). Many SCIP members have backgrounds in market research, government intelligence, or science and technology. They work in a broad variety of industries. There are more than 40 SCIP chapters around the world, with more than 1500 members from 44 countries outside the USA. The growth in the Society's membership reflects the growing awareness of the value of CI in the global business community.

Is CI truly valued in the business community?

Yes. In companies all over the world, SCIP members are enabling executives to make the informed decisions that keep companies responsive, well positioned, and profitable. Robert Flynn, the former CEO and chairman of NutraSweet, said in a keynote address to the Society's ninth annual conference that CI was worth up to $50 million each year to his company. The demand for CI professionals suggests that other CEOs agree: A recent study by SCIP finds that salaries for CI professionals have increased 21% in the last two years, from an average of $57,000 in 1995 to an average of $69,000 in 1997.

What is SCIP's standpoint on the "spy" perception that stigmatizes CI?

CI is not spying. It isn't necessary to use illegal or unethical methods in CI. In fact, doing so is a failure of CI, because almost everything decision-makers need to know about the competitive environment can be discovered using legal, ethical means. The information that can't be found with research can be deduced with good analysis, which is just one of the ways CI adds value to an organization. By joining SCIP, a member agrees to abide by the Society's code of ethics. The code of ethics forbids breaching an employer's guidelines, breaking the law, or misrepresenting oneself.

Appendix E

For Further Enrichment . . .

Important Reading
for the Online Searcher

Magazines/Newspapers

BiblioData's PriceWatcher. BiblioData, PO Box 61, Needham Heights, MA 02494. 781-444-1154.

Business Information Alert. Alert Publications, 401 W Fullerton Pkwy, Ste. 1403E, Chicago, IL 60614-2857, 312-525-7594.

Database. Online Inc, 213 Danbury Road, Wilton, CT 06897-4007. 800-248-8466, www.onlineinc.com.

Information Advisor, The. FIND/SVP, 625 Avenue of the Americas, New York, NY 10011-2002.

Information Today. Information Today Inc., 143 Old Marlton Pike, Medford, NJ 07055-8570. 609-654-6266, Fax 609-654-4309, www.infotoday.com.

Online. Online Inc, 213 Danbury Road, Wilton, CT 06897-4007. 800-248-8466, www.onlineinc.com.

Searcher. Information Today Inc., 143 Old Marlton Pike, Medford, NJ 07055-8570. 609-654-6266, Fax 609-654-4309, www.infotoday.com.

The Cyberskeptic's Guide to Internet Research. BiblioData, PO Box 61, Needham Heights, MA 02494 781-444-1154.

Books

Berinstein, Paula. *Finding Statistics Online.* Information Today Inc, 143 Old - Marlton Pike, Medford, NJ 07055-8570, 609-654-6266, Fax 609-654-4309, www.infotoday.com.

Berkman, Robert Irving. *Finding Business Research on the Web.* Research Publications Group, 625 Avenue of the Americas, New York, NY 10011-2002. 800-346-3787, (outside the US 212-807-2657), Fax 212-645-7681.

Fulltext Sources Online. Information Today Inc., 143 Old Marlton Pike, Medford, NJ 07055-8570. 609-654-6266, Fax 609-654-4309, www.infotoday.com.

Net.Journal Directory. Hermograph Press, Box 69, Woodstock, GA 30188. 678-445-4189, Fax 678-445-4136, www.hermograph.com.

Sankey, Michael; Flowers Jr., James R. *Public Records Online.* Facts on Demand Press, 1999. ISBN 1-889150-10-X

Schlein, Alan M. *Find It Online.* Facts on Demand Press, 1999. ISBN 1-889150-06-1

The Online Manual. Learned Information (Europe) Ltd., Woodside, Hinskey Hill Oxford, UK.

Wyckoff, Trip. *Directory of Business Periodical Special Issues.* Reference Press, 6448 Highway 290 East, Austin, TX 78723.

A Selected CI Reading List

Articles

Aaron, Robert D. *KnowledgeX: Finding hidden relationships for CI analysis.* Competitive Intelligence Review v8n3 PP: 92-94 Fall 1997

Aaron, Robert D. *Internet search engines: A false sense of security.* Competitive Intelligence Review v7n3 PP: 83-85 Fall 1996

Achard, Pierre. *The annual report: A legal document that you should read at regular intervals.* Competitive Intelligence Review v7n1 PP: 78-82 Spring 1996

Anonymous. *Leveraging the business intelligence quotient.* Chief Executive n119 PP: 68-71 Dec 1996

Anonymous. *Using a company's behaviors to predict its future (part II)* American Society for Information Science. Bulletin v23n1 PP: 16-18 Oct/Nov 1996

Anonymous. *New Internet service provides competitive intelligence for insurance direct marketers.* LIMRA's MarketFacts v15n5 PP: 10 Sep/Oct 1996

Anonymous. *Competitive Intelligence Guide.* Information Today v13n8 PP: 1, 61 Sep 1996

Anonymous. *Intelligence pitfalls.* Management Review v85n10 PP: 51 Oct 1996

Anonymous. *Business intelligence: A step beyond due diligence.* Asian Business v32n8 PP: 36 Aug 1996

Anonymous. *Patent information essential for global market success.* Adhesives Age v39n6 PP: 10 May 31, 1996

Anonymous. *Search & employ.* Forbes ASAP Supplement PP: 88 Jun 3, 1996

Anthes, Gary H. *Competitive intelligence.* Computerworld v32n27 PP: 62-63 Jul 6, 1998

Attaway, Morris C Sr. *A review of issues related to gathering & assessing competitive intelligence.* American Business Review v16n1 PP: 25-35 Jan 1998

Barnes, David R. *Why business intelligence is never an oxymoron.* Global Finance v10n6 PP: 6 Jun 1996

Bensoussan, Babette. *Why spy?* Management-Auckland v45n7 PP: 56-58 Aug 1998

Boucher, Jim. *Using information services to sneak a peek at the competition.* Bank Marketing v28n3 PP: 32-35 Mar 1996

Briceno, Carlos. *Little brother is watching your commercials.* Beverage World v115n1625 PP: 250-251 Oct 1996

Call, Melissa Peery. *Using open sources for competitive intelligence: Myths & realities.* Competitive Intelligence Review v8n3 PP: 81-84 Fall 1997

Calof, Jonathan L. *For king & country...and company.* Business Quarterly v61n3 PP: 32-39 Spring 1997

Cleaver, Joanne. *Corporate sleuths dig data, not dirt • Private why: Business' need to gather competitive intelligence fuels growing industry.* Crains Chicago Business (Chicago, IL, US), v21 n10 p15 980309

Darbonne, Nissa. *Industry professionals using Internet for spying on competition.* Oil & Gas Investor v18n10 PP: 26 Oct 1998

Dellecave, Tom Jr. *Gaining a Net advantage.* Sales & Marketing Management v148n10 PP: 104-106 Oct 1996

Ettorre, Barbara. *I won't tell if you won't.* Management Review v87n9 PP: 9 Oct 1998

Fiora, Bill. *Ethical business intelligence is NOT mission impossible.* Strategy & Leadership v26n1 PP: 40-41 Jan/Feb 1998

Fraumann, Edwin. *Economic espionage: Security missions redefined.* Public Administration Review v57n4 PP: 303-308 Jul/Aug 1997

Fuld, Leonard. *Beginner's guide to world-class snooping.* Forbes ASAP Supplement PP: 90 Jun 3, 1996 CODEN: FORBA5

Fuld, Leonard M. *Spyer beware.* CIO v11n20 (Section 2) PP: 26-28 Aug 1, 1998

Fuld, Leonard M; Bilus, Frann. *Why bad intelligence happens to good people.* Marketing News v31n15 PP: 6, 9 Jul 21, 1997

Gilad, Gen; Smith, Rose. *Why pharmaceutical companies lack real competitive intelligence.* Pharmaceutical Executive v18n5 PP: 94-104 May 1998

Golub, Igor. *Snipers in the boardroom.* Director v50n8 PP: 44-47 Mar 1997

Greco, Susan. *The on-line sleuth.* Inc v18n14 PP: 88-89 Oct 1996

Green, William. *I spy.* Forbes v161n8 PP: 90-100 Apr 20, 1998

Gulliford, James. *The challenge of competitor intelligence.* Management Services v42n1 PP: 20-22 Jan 1998

Hadley, Mark. *Pace of change fuels focus on competitive info.* Publication Central New York Business Journal (DeWitt, NY, US), v10 n25 p1 961209

Hannon, John M. *The nexus between human resource management & competitive intelligence: An international perspective.* Management International Review v37n1 (Special Issue) PP: 65-84 1997

Harris, Roy. *Getting the goods on your rivals.* CFO: The Magazine for Senior Financial Executives v12n6 PP: 51 Jun 1996

Harrison, Ann. *Why IS must go spying.* Software Magazine v18n7 PP: 30-44 May 1998

Hays, Daniel. *Insurers serve up an Online feast• for competitors.* Best's Review (Life/Health) v98n2 PP: 86 Jun 1997

Heath, Rebecca Piirto. *The competitive edge.* American Demographics Marketing Tools Supplement PP: 66-73 Sep 1996

Heath, Rebecca Piirto. *What good is the government?* American Demographics Marketing Tools Supplement PP: 55 Jul/Aug 1996

Heath, Rebecca Piirto. *Competitiveintelligence.* American Demographics Marketing Tools Supplement PP: 52-54+ Jul/Aug 1996

Hendrick, Lyle G Jr. *Is competitive intelligence getting the proper attention?* Security Management v40n7 PP: 150, 149 Jul 1996

Hewitt-Dundas, Nola; McFerran, Brendan; Roper, Stephen. *Competitor knowledge among small firms: A pilot examination of fast growing Northern Ireland companies.* International Small Business Journal v15n2 PP: 76-82 Jan/Mar 1997

Hise, Phaedra. *Getting smart on-line.* Inc v18n4 (Inc Technology Supplement) PP: 59-65 1996

Kaltenheuser, Skip. *Where to find security intelligence information.* World Trade v12n2 PP: 51 Feb 1999

Kaltenheuser, Skip. *Computers in trench coats.* World Trade v10n12 PP: 80-82 Dec 1997

Kight, Leila K. *How to predict companies' future actions• a three-part series.* American Society for Information Science. Bulletin v23n1 PP: 14-16 Oct/Nov 1996

McBride, Hugh. *They snoop to conquer.* Canadian Business v70n8 PP: 45-47 Jul 1997

McCafferty, Joseph. *Online intelligence.* CFO: The Magazine for Senior Financial Executives v12n10 PP: 21 Oct 1996

McCune, Jenny C. *Snooping on the Net.* Management Review v86n7 PP: 58-59 Jul/Aug 1997

Mendell, Ronald L. *Using intelligence wisely.* Security Management v41n9 PP: 115-120 Sep 1997

Monroe, Ann; Harris, Roy. *Tuning in to competitive intelligence.* CFO: The Magazine for Senior Financial Executives v12n6 PP: 46-52 Jun 1996

Montgomery, David B; Weinberg, Charles B. *Toward strategic intelligence systems.* Marketing Management v6n4 PP: 44-52 Winter 1998

Montgomery, Glenn E; Spiers, James P. *Competitive intelligence: An antidote to downsizing.* Public Utilities Fortnightly v134n6 PP: 22-25 Mar 15, 1996

Ojala, Marydee. *Trademarks for the business searcher.* Online v20n2 PP: 52-57 Mar/Apr 1996

Ojala, Marydee; Laursen, Jesper Vissing. *Head to head for competitive intelligence.* Online v22n6 PP: 62-63 Nov/Dec 1998

Pagell, Ruth. *Economic espionage.* Database v21n4 PP: 23-30 Aug/Sep 1998

Pawar, Badrinarayan Shankar; Sharda, Ramesh. *Obtaining business intelligence on the Internet.* Long Range Planning v30n1 PP: 110-121 Feb 1997

Prior, Vernon. *Trade shows & exhibitions: The intelligence gatherer's cornucopia.* Competitive Intelligence Review v7n4 PP: 77-78 Winter 1996

Richards, Amanda. *Unite & conquer.* Marketing PP: 24-25 Sep 18, 1997

Rook, Frederick W. *More than just executive tool.* Computing Canada v22n4 PP: 38 Feb 15, 1996

Rose, Rob. *Web changing BI landscape.* Computing Canada v23n4 PP: 40 Feb 17, 1997

Ruotolo, Frank. *Burning down the data warehouse.* Chief Executive n118 PP: 14 Nov 1996

Saccomano, Ann. *Knowledge is power.* Traffic World v256n5 PP: 47-48 Nov 2, 1998

Sandman, Michael A. *Confidentiality, CI, & the IBM Patent Server.* Competitive Intelligence Review v8n4 PP: 85-86 Winter 1997

Schwarzwalder, Robert. *Competitive intelligence primer.* Database v19n4 PP: 89-91 Aug/Sep 1996

Vezmar, Judith M. *Competitive intelligence at Xerox.* Competitive Intelligence Review v7n3 PP: 15-19 Fall 1996

Yovovich, B G. *Browsers get peek at rivals' secrets.* Marketing News v31n23 PP: 1, 6 Nov 10, 1997

Zanasi, Alessandro. *Competitive intelligence through data mining public sources.* Competitive Intelligence Review v9n1 PP: 44-54 Jan-Mar 1998

Books

Advances in Applied Business Strategy: Business Intelligence Theory, Principles, Practices & Uses. Jai Press, 1996. ISBN: 0-7623-0181-3

Cooper, H. H. *Business Intelligence: A Primer.* Exec Protect Inst, 1996. ISBN: 0-9628411-2-9

Dewitt, Michelle. *Competitive Intelligence, Competitive Advantage: Real Internet Tactics.* Abacus MI, 1997. ISBN: 1-55755-324-6

Dutka, Alan. *Competitive Intelligence for the Competitive Edge.* NTC Contemp Pub Co, 1999. ISBN: 0-8442-0293-2

Fialka, John. *War by Other Means: Economic Espionage in America.* Norton, 1997. ISBN: 0-393-04014-3

Friedman, G.; Friedman, Meredith. *The Intelligence Edge: How to Profit in the Information Age.* Random House Value, 1997. ISBN: 0-609-60075-3

Fuld, Leonard M. *The New Competitor Intelligence: The Complete Resource for Finding, Analyzing, & Using Information about Your Competitors.* Wiley, 1994. ISBN: 0-471-58508-4 EDITION: 2nd ed.

Hansen, James H. *Japanese Intelligence: The Competitive Edge.* Natl Intel Bk Ctr, 1996. ISBN: 1-878292-16-1

Herring, Jan P. *Measuring the Effectiveness of Competitive Intelligence: Assessing & Communicating CI's Value to Your Organization.* Society of Competitor Intelligence Professionals, 1996. ISBN: 0-9621241-2-5

How to Find Business Intelligence in Washington. Washington Researchers, 1997. ISBN: 1-56365-053-3 EDITION: 12th ed.

Kahaner, Larry. *Competitive Intelligence.* Simon & Schuster, 1998. ISBN: 0-684-84404-4

Kahaner, Larry. *Competitive Intelligence: From Black Ops to Boardrooms - How Businesses Gather, Analyze, & Use Information to Succeed in the Global Marketplace.* Simon & Schuster, 1996. ISBN: 0-684-81074-3

Keeping Abreast of Science & Technology: Technical Intelligence in Business. Battelle, 1997. ISBN: 1-57477-018-7

McGonagle, John J.; Vella, Carolyn M. *Protecting Your Company Against Competitive Intelligence.* Greenwood, 1998. ISBN: 1-56720-117-2

McGonagle, John J.; Vella, Carolyn M. *The Internet Age of Competitive Intelligence.* Greenwood, 1999. ISBN: 1-56720-204-7

McGonagle, John J.; Vella, Carolyn M. *A New Archetype for Competitive Intelligence.* Greenwood, 1996. ISBN: 0-89930-973-9

Park, Mary W. *InfoThink: Practical Strategies for Using Information in Business.* Scarecrow, 1998. ISBN: 0-8108-3424-3

Sankey, Michael; Flowers Jr., James R. *Public Records Online.* Facts on Demand Press, 1999. ISBN 1-889150-10-X

Shaker, Steven M.; Gembicki, Mark P. *The WarRoom Guide to Competitive Intelligence.* McGraw, 1998. ISBN: 0-07-058057-X

Schlein, Alan M. *Find It Online.* Facts on Demand Press, 1999. ISBN 1-889150-06-1

Tyson, Kirk W.M. *The Complete Guide to Competitive Intelligence.* K Tyson Intl, 1998. ISBN: 0-9663219-0-1

Glossary of Terms

Used in Online Competitive Intelligence

The following are explanations of some of the terms used in this book. Some terms pertain to the vocabulary of the Internet, while others are related to business intelligence. Terms defined within the text of the book are not included here.

Adverse items - Issues, or filings with government offices, which could be considered to have a negative impact on the individual or company in question. These items often involve financial obligations or possible violations of laws or regulations.

Alert services - Services offered by information vendors whereby requestor is informed when particular subject matter is published in specified sources such as news media, trade publications, government materials, etc. (Sometimes called Current Awareness Services).

Analyst reports - In-depth studies of companies or industries, created and published by financial institutions such as brokerage houses. Reports help determine the status and to make forecasts regarding the financial performance of a company or industry.

ASCII - (American Standard Code for Information Interchange) an encoding scheme used by PC's for the exchange (or interchange) of information between programs. ASCII files can be read by machines or humans, without any special handling.

Background checks - The system of investigating the credentials of an individual such as a job applicant, to verify information on topics such as education, previous employment, criminal record (or lack thereof), etc.

Bias factor - The knowledge that information found on an Internet web site expresses the views of those who created the site, and that although these views may be one-sided, the site may contain useful information.

Bookmark - The process of saving to a computer file (and possibly organizing) the web addresses of sites to which you plan to return. Bookmarks may be managed by your browser or by specialized products available from software producers. The Internet Explorer browser calls these *Favorites*.

Chat rooms - Places on the Internet where people conduct synchronous line-by-line communication in real time, as opposed to email.

Current awareness services - Services offered by information vendors whereby requestor is informed when particular subject matter is published in specified sources such as news media, trade publications, government materials, etc. (Synonym for Alert Services)

Cyberspace - A popular term used to describe the range of information resources available through computer networks.

Database - A computer file consisting of fielded information, arranged consistently in the form of individual records. Some fields in a database record may contain brief amounts of information or data, while others could include the full text of a document.

Defendant-Plaintiff tables - Listings of cases filed in a given jurisdiction. These listings indicate pending cases as well as those that have been heard or settled. They are a useful source of information that may not appear in LEXIS or Westlaw or in other case law databases.

Document retrieval service - A commercial service that obtains copies of specified documents from government or other sources, by request. Such services usually pay copyright and other costs as applicable, and bill these back to their clients.

Download - The process by which files or data is saved or pulled down from a remote computer.

EDGAR - (Electronic Data Gathering, Analysis, and Retrieval system) An automated system used for the collection, validation, indexing, acceptance, and forwarding of submissions by companies and others who are required by law to file forms with the U.S. Securities and Exchange Commission (SEC).

E-mail - (Electronic mail) Messages, usually in the form of text, that are sent from one individual to another individual or group of individuals on a network or over the Internet.

FTP - (File transfer protocol) A means for transferring files from one computer to another. Anonymous FTP is used to transfer public files from a computer where you don't have a password or account. With the increased popularity of the World Wide Web, FTP is used less frequently than in the past.

Insider trading - Every director, officer, or owner of more than ten percent of a class of equity Securities is considered an "insider". Prior to their intended sale of restricted stock (issued stock currently unregistered with the SEC), insiders must make certain filings with the SEC. These filings contain information on the reporting person's relationship to the company and on purchases and sales of equity securities. Filing this form gives the seller an automatic exemption from SEC registration requirements for this one transaction.

Lag time - The time between when information is published in hardcopy and the date when it appears in electronic databases. Lag time varies from a day or so to several weeks, depending upon the publication involved. It is usually included as part of a licensing agreement between print publishers and database vendors, and is sometimes used to help retain circulation levels for print subscriptions.

Mailing list - A way of having a group discussion or distribution of announcements by electronic mail. You join the list and then receive other people's postings by email. You may respond to the list, where all can read your comments, or you may simply read what is posted by others. This process is handled automatically by programs called mailing list managers or mail servers.

Meta-search engines - Hybrids of search engines and subject directories that allow you to search several sites at once. Popular examples of meta-sites include Dogpile, MammaMetaSearch, or ProFusion.

Push technology - A popular distribution method for providing information over the World Wide Web. Periodic updates are scheduled and automatically sent to the user's PC screen or window.

Real time - A method used online for providing information is being broadcast at the present time, live, not delayed or recorded.

Search tools - The tools used to search the Internet. They include search engines, which are a type of software that creates indexes of databases of Internet sites and allows you to type in what you are looking for and it then gives you a list of results of your search. Other tools include subject directories, which are catalogs of resources, collected and ranked by human beings, and meta-tools, which allow you to search several search tools at once.

URL - (Uniform Resource Locator) The address for a resource or web site.

Usenet - A collection of newsgroups and a set of agreed-upon rules for distributing and maintaining them.

Web browser - Software that provides a (usually) graphical interface for searching the Internet's World Wide Web. The browser searches for and displays documents specified in a search request.

Web page - A document created with HTML (HyperText Markup Language) that is part of a group of hypertext documents or resources available on the World Wide Web. It usually contains hyptertext links to other documents on the Web. Collectively, these documents and resources form what is known as a web site.

Page Index